BEYOND
LIBERALISM AND
COMMUNITARIANISM

BEYOND LIBERALISM AND COMMUNITARIANISM

Studies in Hegel's *Philosophy of Right*

edited by

ROBERT R. WILLIAMS

State University
of New York
Press

Published by
State University of New York Press, Albany

© 2001 State University of New York

Production by Susan Geraghty
Marketing by Patrick Durocher

Printed in the United States of America

For information, address State University of New York Press,
90 State Street, Suite 700, Albany, NY 12207

Library of Congress Cataloging-in-Publication Data

Beyond liberalism and communitarianism : studies in Hegel's Philosophy of right /
edited by Robert R. Williams.
    p. cm.
  Includes bibliographical references and index.
  ISBN 0-7914-4933-5 (hc : alk. paper) — ISBN 0-7914-4934-3 (pbk. : alk. paper)
    1. Hegel, Georg Wilhelm Friedrich, 1770–1831—Contributions in political science. 2.
Hegel, Georg Wilhelm Friedrich, 1770–1831. Grundlinien der Philosophie des Rechts. I.
Williams, Robert R., 1939–

JC233.H46 B496 2001
320.1′1—dc21

                                                                    00-041057

10 9 8 7 6 5 4 3 2 1

CONTENTS

Introduction

Robert R. Williams

It has been more than fifteen years since the last volume of essays on Hegel's social and political philosophy appeared,[1] but interest in Hegel's political philosophy continues strong and unabated as attested by the recent appearance of several books on Hegel's ethics and practical philosophy.[2] The studies in this volume continue the reassessment of Hegel's thought in English-speaking scholarship that began with J. N. Findlay's *Hegel: A Re-Examination*, and continued in Avineri's *Hegel's Theory of the Modern State*.[3] Many essays in this volume reflect recent themes and issues identified in this reevaluation: Hegel's concept of freedom, its relation to and criticism of the Enlightenment (Kant); the mediation of freedom through the recognition as the existential genesis of the concept of right.

The mediation of freedom through recognition implies that for Hegel freedom is not adequately conceived by either liberal individualism or communitarianism. While he upholds autonomy against collectivist views that do not recognize individual subjective freedom, Hegel attacks individualism as a spiritless abstraction that is symptomatic of social disintegration. The individual per se is insufficient to serve as a basis for rationality, freedom, or rights. For Hegel, individual freedom, rationality, and rights are intersubjectively mediated; autonomy is a mediated autonomy that is actual in relationship. This seems to be a nod in the direction of communitarianism. Yet although Hegel believes freedom is intersubjectively mediated through recognition and thus requires and presupposes community, this does not mean that individual subjective freedom is nullified by or subordinate to community. On the contrary, Hegel's concept of community is not only ontological but ethical. This means that Hegel's idea of community is one that recognizes and protects individual freedoms and rights. Hegel remains close to the

1

Enlightenment in that he refuses to reduce normative issues of right to merely historically and culturally relative social practices and traditions. Hegel's position seeks to be a third alternative, in which the universal end and interest of the community "does not attain validity or fulfillment without the interest, knowledge and volition of the particular. . . . The universality of the [social] end cannot make further progress without personal knowledge and volition of the particular individuals who must retain their rights."[4] Only when both individual rights and community "are present in full measure can the state be regarded as articulated and truly organized."[5]

Hegel is a modern thinker who is at the same time a critic of modernity and its liberal versus communitarian alternatives. He pursues the development of a social and historical conception of reason and freedom that raises issues concerning the normativity and positivity of right. Following Rousseau, Hegel believes that freedom is the fundamental principle of the state. Self-determining freedom is the critical norm from which Enlightenment thinkers criticize traditional societies, laws, and constitutions as heteronomous (Kant). Autonomous self-determination implies a break with nature and natural law as the organizing principle of the state and political theory. This break with natural law requires major philosophical and sociopolitical reconstruction. However, while Kant's account of freedom has important social and political implications, as a transcendental conception it remains formal, abstract, unable to be concretely normative, and apparently individualistic. Kant's transcendental consciousness is not yet an intersubjectivity or spirit. As a corrective to Kant, Hegel raises the problem of the other and brings it into relation to freedom. The consciousness of freedom, which for Kant remains problematic, is mediated by recognition by others. Hegel deepens and enlarges the concept of freedom by showing that autonomy is mediated through recognition. This makes possible an important transition from an apparently individualistic reason to a social reason that is actual in and as a community and its institutions.

While Hegel sides with modernity on the right of subjectivity and subjective freedom, he is also critical of modernity's main alternative to traditional natural law theory, namely, liberal utilitarianism and social contract theory. He believes that these views make the social realm and the state dependent on antecedent wills of independent individuals and tend toward an atomistic individualism. Hegel's project is to work out an alternative to the classical natural law theory of the state and to the individualistic interpretation of modernity's assertion of the rights of subjectivity and subjective freedom.[6] Elsewhere I have tried to show that Hegel's concept of recognition (*Anerkennung*) provides the mediating basis that allows Hegel to side with modernity's assertion of the rights of individual freedom, while at the same time appropriating and reformulating the ethical substance of classical natural law theories.[7] The latter is transformed into a theory of social institutions that establish, mediate, and preserve individual freedom.

While agreeing that freedom is the fundamental principle of the state, Hegel is critical of the atomistic individualism of political liberalism in part because atomism is a condition of social alienation, and in part because liberalism tends to confuse the state with civil society. In civil society, human beings may and do recognize their freedom, but only in an impoverished sense as property owners, producers, and consumers.[8] Hegel by no means rejects civil society; indeed he is the first philosopher to incorporate it in his social theory as a necessary modern development alongside the traditional institutions of family and state. However, while civil society is an important dimension of freedom and ethical life, it is inadequate when taken as an exhaustive account of ethical life. One of its central categories is contract, and contract is borrowed from the sphere of property and property relations. Liberalism's confusion of the state with civil society is evident, Hegel believes, in its view that the state is a social contract. In this theory the state is conceived on the model of a commercial contract. This view has two implications that Hegel rejects. The first is that state is derivative from the antecedent wills of independent individuals and appears to be optional. The second is that the state appears to be an instrument that subserves and protects private rights, including property rights.

The external character of this state is evident in the machine metaphors that accompany and express it. In a machine, the whole is external to the parts so that even in the whole the parts remain what they are independent of the whole. As the external state, the state as the understanding (mis)construes it, civil society is ethical life in its disintegration. It is based on and reflects deficient modes of recognition, in which human beings relate to each other primarily in economic categories as producers, consumers, property owners, and tax payers, rather than in political categories as members of the body politic. Civil society is a universal system of interdependence and mutual exploitation. From this perspective, universal social, political, and religious life are regarded merely instrumentally and exploited as means to private interests. Since civil society makes the pursuit of individual private interests its universal end, it is not surprising that it disintegrates into the extremes of wealth and poverty, and thus creates not only a penurious rabble, but also a rabble mentality that threatens to undermine its legitimacy.[9]

From the beginning of his career, Hegel criticized the instrumental view of the state as a machine. This criticism was not a simple rejection, however. Hegel acknowledged the importance of civil society, but only when situated within the larger context of the ethical state based on the idea of freedom. The ethical state is supposed to bring the individualistic, disintegrating forces of civil society back to the universal life as an end in itself or ethical substance. This requires a transformation (*Aufhebung*) of self-seeking individuals and the merely instrumental universality constitutive of civil society. It also involves a transformation of mutual recognition from the formal external reciprocity of contract, which leaves individuals unaffected, into a mutually enhancing union in which the I becomes a We.[10] In this way, acquisitive self-seeking individualism undergoes transformation into a universal ethical altruism and patriotism. This theme of the political community as a liberation and enhancement of individual life and freedom runs throughout Hegel's writings, from the earliest to the latest. It also runs throughout the various subthemes and discussions of the *Philosophy of Right*, as well as several of the essays selected for this volume.

I want to outline for the reader the various themes and issues presented in the essays selected for this volume, which raise important issues and offer provocative interpretations and criticisms of Hegel. In this way I hope not only to convey what the volume is about, but also to outline some of the main issues and controversies. The final judgment on these is left to the reader.

The first two essays by Ardis B. Collins and Kevin Thompson deal in different ways with the issues of positivity and normativity in Hegel's political philosophy. Hegel's treatment of positivity is connected with Kant's analysis of heteronomy, a situation of determination by or bondage to alien drives, ideas, values, and laws.[11] From this perspective, traditional values, laws, and institutions are subject to the criticism that they are merely positive givens, and as such they may be without rational justification because they have not yet been derived from or shown to be requirements of autonomous freedom.

Hegel was concerned with positivity as a social-historical issue from the beginning of his career.[12] In *Early Theological Writings* he focuses on positivity as a problem in the historical development of traditional Christianity; for Hegel positivity is a process of decline that can happen to any institution. Hence the problem of positivity plays a role in Hegel's analysis of historical change. Institutions become positive when they no longer reflect or address vital human needs and interests; under such conditions traditional institutions can be maintained only by external supports, such as authorities. The appeal to authority indicates a deeper alienation or cultural breakdown for which authority is invoked as the solution. In his *Difference Essay*, Hegel connects positivity with dichotomy and alienation.[13] Positivity describes a cultural situation in which "the might of union vanishes."[14] The ensuing alienation between human beings and their social institutions points to a need for a philosophy that is supposed to suspend dichotomies and oppositions.

Although Hegel agrees with the Enlightenment that rational criticism of positive traditions, laws, and institutions is necessary, he is also critical of Enlightenment rationalism. He believes that such rationalism considers as normative only what is abstractly universal, and regards sociocultural particularity and determinacy as nonessential. Hegel believes that Kant's ethics illustrates a problem in such rationalism, which Hegel identifies as formalism. Kant's ethics is unable to be concretely normative, unable to generate any positive duties, and thus paradoxically falls back into the very dependence on positivity that Kant sought to avoid and overcome.

Hegel believes it is necessary to find a third alternative to merely positive historical traditions and to formal rationalism. Hegel's claim is that dialectical reason itself is positive, that is, it suspends and mediates the opposition of universal and particular. The claim that reason itself is positive is related to and expressed by Hegel's famous remark from the preface of the *Philosophy of Right*, that the rational is (or becomes) actual.[15] Hegel's practical philosophy will be neither merely historical and traditional, nor ahistorically formal, but rather historical and communal, embedded in social institutions and practices.

The first two essays deal with the issue of Kantian formalism (Collins), and explore Hegel's alternative concerning the positivity of reason, namely, the rationality of the actual or reason in the determinate shape of social institutions (Thompson). The first essay by Ardis B. Collins examines Hegel's treatment of Kantian morality. Hegel's treatment is by no means an outright rejection of Kant, but rather a critical appropriation and transformation. Collins refers to current debates between Kant's defenders and Hegel's defenders. The latter maintain that for Hegel Kant's theory has no right to a moral law with any determinate content.

Collins addresses this issue by examining Hegel's philosophical method and the necessity for transforming the morality position into ethical life. Collins argues that the issue between Hegel and Kant is not simply formalism, or the emptiness charge. Even if Kant's position has determinate ethical content (as it clearly does in the practical imperative of respect for humanity), Kant's concept of the highest good cannot accept or receive determinations from the contingent particularities of human life. Thus the morality of pure practical reason remains independent, not only of any particular empirical content, but also of anyone's particular ends, and independent of social-historical context and community. The highest good remains abstract.

In contrast, Collins shows that for Hegel the will must be motivated both by the universal principle of right to make its actions good, and by its own particularity in order to render the good actual. In ethical life, the good does not exist except through and by means of the particular subjective will, and the particular is no longer a 'raw' particular opposed to the universal, but rather must be identified with and brought into conformity with the universal good. Hence ethical life is a social-communal life, the spirit of a people. Mediated by mutual recognition, reason becomes actual, that is, positive.

Kevin Thompson addresses the issue of the positivity of right by means of a historical investigation of Hegel's thought as a third alternative to the codification controversy between Thibaut and Savigny. The codification controversy presented two alternatives concerning the foundation and authority of right. According to Thibaut, right resides in the natural moral order, a position that requires and presupposes human reason's ability to discern that order. According to Savigny, right resides in the historical traditions of a people and the ability of legal scholars to interpret the legal foundations of its traditions. The upshot of this controversy is that political institutions are either superfluous because they mirror natural structures (the Thibaut position) or coercive social constructions that express and reflect merely the interests of the dominant social classes (Savigny).

According to Thompson, Hegel rejects both alternatives in favor of the positivity of reason and right. The normativity of right is located in autonomous freedom, but this autonomy is conceived as requiring and finding expression in certain social institutions. The positivity of reason is found in an account of social institutions necessary for the realization and preservation of autonomy, namely, the institutions of family and civil society. Civil society is a system of interdependence, a system of needs and the resources for their satisfaction. Civil society is the locus of the existence of right as it is universally known, recognized, and willed.

The positivity of right thus articulates a mutual interdependence between the form and the content of right. Without the universal rational authority of right, institutions would be without basis or justification. But without institutions, universal right would be formal and vacuous. The positivity of reason and freedom are the middle that joins the form and the content of right to one another.

Mark Tunick and Richard Dien Winfield address the question of the normativity of right from different angles, and come to different assessments of Hegel's position. In "Hegel on Political Identity and the Ties That Bind," Tunick notes that Hegel regards the modern state as ethical substance, which is so important that humans should be prepared and willing to sacrifice their lives for it. This suggests, claims Tunick, that Hegel thinks of the state as a close-knit, culturally, ethnically, and religiously homogeneous community. However, as Tunick demonstrates, Hegel's state does not require racial or ethnic identity, does not require a monolingual culture, and does not require that everyone practice the same religion. For example, Hegel advocates toleration for Quakers and Jews, which shows that his state is pluralistic and committed to diversity. But these commitments to pluralism may undermine any substantive unity. Thus, Tunick asks, given this pluralism and diversity, what is left of ethical substance? Specifically, do the citizens of Hegel's state share enough in common to form a substantial union that is worth dying for? What, he asks, are the ties that bind Hegel's modern state together?

While Tunick is correct in noting that Hegel's state is religiously pluralistic, it is also the case that in Hegel's view the state has a religious foundation that informs and underlies its ethical substance. Hegel explicitly declares that religion is the substance of ethical life. The state, he maintains, rests on the ethical disposition, and the ethical disposition rests on the religious. For this reason Hegel regards it as a modern folly to try to alter the political constitution of a state without also changing its religion, or, in Hegel's words, "to make a revolution without having made a reformation."[16] The religious critique of freedom and authority precedes and conditions the political critique of authority and tradition. The question is whether that critique of religious authority establishes a single religious disposition, or one that is pluralistic in principle. There may be a tension between Hegel's concept of the state as religiously pluralistic, and his claim that ethical life, including the state, rests on the religious disposition. However, Hegel's state is not so much secular as nonsectarian. If freedom is respected, the religious disposition that underlies the political must be plural, as Tunick points out.

Hegel believes that freedom is a criterion for distinguishing not only genuine political institutions but also genuine religious institutions: true religion and authentic religious practice both establish and flow out of free ethical life. Could it be, then, that freedom itself is the unifying basis, and the love of freedom the chief virtue, of Hegel's state? If so, could mutual recognition of freedom be the "tie that binds," the ethical substance that Tunick believes is missing from Hegel's account? Or is the idea of freedom too vacuous or "philosophical" to serve as an existential "tie that binds"?

Richard Dien Winfield's essay, "Postcolonialism and Right," examines issues concerning the normativity of modernity in a three-way debate among modernity, traditional, and postmodern views. Modernity distinguishes itself from prior traditional forms of civilization by calling tradition into question and asserting that practices and institutions are legitimate only if they are justifiable by reason and freedom. Modernity undertakes a critique of positivity. In Winfield's view, modern institutions that give reality to self-determination qualify as the real that is rational because freedom exhibits independence from foundations that reason must exhibit if it is to provide any justification that does not rely on dogmatically asserted criteria, rules, procedures, and the like. Free institutions do not draw their legitimacy from conformity to given tradition. Winfield agrees with William Maker that the universality of modernity's institutions of freedom implies their independence from all prior grounds or foundations. Modernity's institutions of freedom are rationally self-generating and self-justifying. This means that they do not depend on nature. The *idea* of modernity signifies for Winfield "a uniquely valid form of civilization" and as such must be distinguished from any particular cultural instantiation, including Western culture. Thus modernity's institutions of freedom do not depend on any particular culture for their legitimacy. Western cultures are neither unique nor exclusive forms of realization of the idea of modernity. Moreover, if any empirical culture is a hybrid presenting both modern and premodern traditional elements, Western cultures may be no less "hybrids" of modernity and tradition than non-Western cultures.

Winfield exposes a thorny problem: once modern institutions of freedom arise in a particular geographic sphere, a new situation is created. When the modern emerges based on self-initiating and self-determining freedom, all other cultures are placed in the awkward position of being premodern. Viewed from the perspective of modernity, this emergence renders other cultures traditional, "obsolete." This is modernity's globalizing tendency. However, viewed from the perspective of premodern cultures, the issue becomes one of colonialism and Westernization. Premodern cultures are confronted with the necessity of change, and the options they face are either internal modernization or external modernization. In the latter case, modernization and Westernization may coincide.

Winfield's essay is provocative for several reasons. First, he points out that the apparent domination of modernity over premodernity is not necessarily malicious or malevolent; on the other hand, neither is it benign, since any posture of domination expressly contradicts modernity's own fundamental values and norms of freedom. Second, Winfield argues that modernity, although it has emerged in history, is nevertheless unique—its anti-foundationalism, or freedom from privileged foundations, renders its validity timeless. Such a bold claim may involve some version of an end of history thesis, which is surprising in view of Winfield's view of the historicity of freedom. Nevertheless, some such notion lies behind his contention that there are only three fundamental options: (1) the traditional privileging of a particular set of practices and institutions; (2) modernity, or embracing institutions of freedom; (3)

postmodernity, which Winfield characterizes as a dogmatic assertion of a particular form of life with brazen admission of its own arbitrary, perspectival character. Traditional views, regarded from the perspective of modernity, are oppressive regimes. Postmodernity also faces a serious problem, namely, if reason is incapable of self-determination without prior foundations, the truth of this situation cannot be established or justified. This leaves Winfield arguing for modernity—interpreted along Hegelian lines—as the only viable alternative because only here is self-determining, self-justifying rational freedom taken seriously. This is a very strong normative claim, far stronger apparently than Tunick is willing to credit to Hegel's position. Winfield's essay is audacious, but it is not blind or insensitive to the problem of modernity's relation to traditional cultures.

The next group of essays all treat specific themes in the *Philosophy of Right*: punishment, embodiment, social contract theory, and Hegel's "implicit" solution to the problem of poverty. Angelica Nuzzo examines Hegel's treatment of the body. She demonstrates his divergence from typically modern (Cartesian) views concerning the body as external to the subject, as its property and instrument. Hegel's subject is an embodied subject. Thus the body shifts from the "object" to the "subject" side of the so-called subject/object dichotomy. The body subject is for Hegel the condition of intersubjective recognition, as well as the condition of legal personality, of ownership. As such, the body subject is constitutive of the legal person, the bearer of property right. Nuzzo focuses on the latter dimensions rather than the intersubjective.

Nuzzo shows that possession becomes property by an extension of the act of embodiment. In Hegel's analysis property is a subcategory of philosophical anthropology. The right to property is grounded in a prior right to one's body, that is, a right to be free in one's body. This calls for the transformation of the natural body into a "soul-inspired instrument" and spirit's willing organ. Nuzzo shows the distinction and the intertwining of natural and juridical considerations in Hegel's account. She points to an important distinction between the free acquisition of life and body, whereby these become the extension of freedom into the world, and the free renunciation of life and body. Although Hegel acknowledges that abstract freedom is the capacity of the subject to abstract from every determinacy, including its own life, this capacity is not unrestricted from the juridical point of view. Since life and the body are necessary conditions of legal personality, the right to one's life and the free use of one's body are imprescriptible, that is, they cannot be alienated as the object of contract or market relations. From this imprescriptibility Hegel derives a limited right of the person to dispose of his/her body, and an unlimited right for each to be respected by others as a person. The limited right to dispose of oneself leads Hegel to argue against a right to suicide and against a right to self-mutilation.

Dudley Knowles criticizes Hegel's theory of punishment as a "confused near miss." He believes that Hegel's view could be improved by a hypothetical social contract argument for punishment. Since Knowles's essay criticizes and proposes improvements on Hegel's view by drawing on social contract theory—a theory that Hegel explicitly rejected—some discussion of the issues he raises is called for. Knowles identifies three theses that he believes are central to Hegel's account: (1) punishment is the reconciliation of right; (2) this reconciliation has an objective dimension, namely, the restoration of right against a challenge to it; and (3) reconciliation also has a subjective dimension, namely, punishment is applied to the criminal on the grounds that he endorses its application. Knowles maintains that all three have to be taken together, but that even so, Hegel's defense and justification of punishment remain flawed.

Knowles objects that retributive theory does little but dress up the idea that the criminal cannot complain if he is treated in the same fashion as he has treated his victim. This may be psychologically satisfying, but Knowles questions whether it can be acceptable to the punishing agency, because then the latter must accept and do the very thing it condemns in the criminal. The punishing agency coerces, and thereby it adopts coercion as its own principle. This is not only the dubious doctrine that two wrongs make a right; it implicates the punishing agency in the very offense and violation of right that it punishes.

This criticism appears to discredit the retributive theory of punishment by making it appear both barbarous and hypocritical. Knowles distinguishes between the principle and the measure of punishment. He points out that the punishing authority must not adopt the principle of the criminal (for then it would commit the very crime it punishes) but may take the crime into account in determining the measure of punishment. Something like this is suggested by Hegel's distinction between retribution (an act of the impartial general will) and revenge (which is a self-seeking act of the particular will).[17]

Hegel believes that in punishing wrong, the punishing agency should neither do wrong itself nor endorse the criminal's transgression and its principle. But it would do precisely this if it failed to punish him. For then it would allow the transgression to stand as right, and thereby undermine right.[18] Hegel's retributive theory of punishment does not imply that the punishing agency accepts coercion per se as valid; rather the coercive activity of punishment is carefully restricted to allowing the criminal act to recoil upon itself and manifest its own self-contradiction and nullity. Just punishment makes coercion cancel itself. Punishment is not coercion for coercion's sake, but a coercion directed against coercion.

Knowles believes that Hegel's justification of punishment can best be formulated by a version of social contract argument. This is a polemical point. Knowles is aware that Hegel rejects the social contract theory of the state. For Knowles, this rejection was unwise. Knowles believes that punishment is legitimate and serves its purpose only when it is reconciled with freedom, and reconciliation involves or implies the consent of the criminal to his punishment. Knowles does not mean that an explicit act of consent by the criminal is necessary. An implicit consent, or a *hypothetical* social contract argument, will do.

Something like a hypothetical social contract position was argued by Beccaria. Like Knowles, Beccaria maintains that the subjective justification of punishment is bound up with the criminal's own consent. Beccaria does not mean that an empirical consent to punishment is necessary; rather Beccaria locates the consent of the criminal to punishment in his presumed acceptance of the social contract. By accepting the contract, the criminal has consented in principle to his own punishment if he should violate the contract.

Hegel does not follow Beccaria in part because Hegel rejects the social contract theory of the state. Nevertheless, he accepts the principle that the subjective justification of punishment requires and resides in the criminal's consent. However, Hegel locates this consent, not in the acceptance of a social contract, but rather in the criminal's own transgression and violation of the order of right.[19] By his act of coercing someone else, the criminal has actually consented to coercion. But only he has consented to it. So the punishing agency, in retributively punishing the criminal, applies his own principle (to which he and no one else consents) to him. The reader will have to decide whether Knowles is correct in charging that Hegel's argument concerning punishment is a "near miss," or whether the differences between Hegel's view and Knowles's hypothetical contract argument for punishment are vanishingly small.

Lawrence S. Stepelevich analyzes not only the American Civil War, but also recent scholarship on that war, drawing on some of Hegel's central concepts such as recognition, nationality, tragic conflict, mastery and slavery, contradiction, irony and ironic reversals. He situates the Civil War in the context of Hegel's philosophy of history, which is a tragic vision of the historical realization of freedom and liberation. Stepelevich notes the emergence of Northern and Southern sectionalism, each of which presented different accounts of what freedom and popular sovereignty are supposed to mean. The Civil War was the "irrepressible conflict" that grew out of the clash of these visions of freedom and nationhood. For this reason it was not a conflict between right and wrong, but between two visions of freedom, two views of right, and so counts, Stepelevich contends, as tragic in Hegel's sense.

Slavery and continued racial inequality count as perhaps the major unresolved contradictions in American culture and ideology of freedom. To illustrate these contradictions, Stepelevich points to Thomas Jefferson (whose republicanism was strangely compatible with pre-Revolutionary French aristocracy and with Jefferson's ownership of slaves) and to Abraham Lincoln, who emancipated the slaves while reluctantly believing in racial inequality.

Stepelevich relates these contradictions to Hegel's analyses of master and slave, and his dialectical analysis of history and historical change. Taking his departure from the conflict between abolitionists and pro-slavery forces, he shows that Hegel's account of the historical progress of the idea of freedom aids in the analysis of the conflict and Lincoln's search for a middle ground. Although Hegel agrees with the abolitionists that slavery is an outrage on human nature, nevertheless he observes that men are not by nature equal or free. The concept of nature is ambiguous. On the one hand, it means what is raw and uncultivated; on the other, it means what is rationally cultivated and developed. Taking nature in the first sense, humans are not free or equal, but unequal. Political equality and equal rights are not natural givens, but socio-historical accomplishments, dependent on and mediated by certain types of communities, and ultimately by a social-historical rationality. Given an historicist account of rationality, Hegel can assert that slavery is relatively justified, namely, it belongs to a transitional period between the so-called state of nature and modern recognition of freedom, a period in which wrong was still taken to be right. Perhaps Jefferson and Lincoln, who lived on both sides of this tragic conflict, would have agreed with Hegel's analysis.

Finally, Stepelevich notes certain ironies and ironic reversals in the pursuit of freedom: the Union troops who liberated the slaves from their owners, but nevertheless refused to protect them from being attacked by pursuing Southern troops; the abolitionists who preached abstract equality, but when the South was militarily defeated, abandoned the former slaves who were without property, place, or education and both unprepared and forbidden to participate in established civil society. The abolitionists thus recapitulate in their own way Hegel's dialectic of the beautiful soul, and like the latter, show themselves to be hypocritical.

Alan Patten believes that Hegel accepts the standpoint of social contract theory with its commitment to individual freedom, but only as a starting point. Hegel parts company with social contract theory as an account of the state because, like a commercial contract, this would imply that the state is derivative from the antecedent wills of independent individuals. Such individuals would remain independent in spite of their membership in the state, and this would also suggest that they could regard the state as instrumental to their private interests, for example, an instrument for the protection of property. The fact that Hegel starts with the contractarian position but does not end with that position raises the following question: How is it possible to move from an apparently individualist premise (social contract) to an apparently "communitarian" position?

According to Patten, the answer lies in Hegel's concept of recognition. For Hegel, recognition names that intersubjective process wherein freedom comes to actual expression in the world. Recognition by others is the public dimension and mediation of freedom. It is in recognition that Hegel, following Fichte, locates the existential conditions of the concept of right. Through mutual recognition the individual "I" is not only acknowledged, but becomes a "We," a member of a larger whole.

Patten next considers recognition in relation to the state. Granted that the state is constitutive of community, why is a *state* a necessary feature of community? The answer is that mutual recognition is not merely a single act or just an open-ended process; it is supposed to culminate in a "We." This "We" in turn both requires and creates institutionalization, which Hegel terms ethical life. Recognition is the general structure and pattern of ethical life, and the determinate structures of ethical life constitute what Hegel calls objective spirit. The central institutions of ethical life—family, civil society, and state—are determinate shapes and embodiments of mutual recognition, and at the same time are necessary conditions for the realization of freedom in the world. Recognition, then, as the existential origin of right, grounds and secures traditional rights. The recognitive institutions of ethical life are necessary conditions for the realization of subjective, individual freedom in the world. Patten claims that these institutions are objective and necessary conditions of freedom, whether or not particular individuals have consented to them. They belong to Hegel's substantive concept of ethical freedom.

Patten believes that recognition provides Hegel's reply to social contract theory. Put simply, the point is that recognition is the prior condition of social contract.[20] Consequently, while Hegel may begin with the individualistic standpoint of contract, he shows that the very institutions that contract theory may regard as contingent and optional, are objective, necessary, and legitimate independent of any particular individual act of consent, and are in fact conditions of such consent. It is truer to say that individual freedoms depend on such institutional mediations of freedom than that institutions are contingent, merely optional creations of individuals.[21]

In his influential study, *Hegel's Theory of the Modern State*, Shlomo Avineri maintains that Hegel was among the first to understand that poverty is not an aberration, but an inevitable accompaniment of capitalism when it functions the way it is supposed to. Further, Avineri believes that poverty is one of the few problems for which Hegel failed to provide any solution. Hegel's failure to offer any solution to the problem of poverty signals an important limitation of his philosophical program. Many scholars have followed Avineri's reading, making it a "standard interpretation."

Recently Stephen Houlgate has challenged this standard interpretation, and Joel Anderson's essay seeks to develop this challenge still further.[22] Anderson does not maintain that Hegel actually presents an explicit solution to the problem of poverty, but rather argues that there are resources within Hegel's thought for a more positive engagement with the problem that Avineri overlooked. Hegel can do far more than merely describe what the problem is. Anderson's thesis is: (1) poverty as a structural problem can be overcome only through structural changes in the patterns and practices of production and consumption; (2) these changes include more self-consciously ethical practices of consumption; and (3) there is a need for an institution that mediates between individuals and state, that develops small-scale but significant changes in both production and consumption, namely, what Hegel calls the corporation (*Korporation*).

Focusing on the issues of societal resources (*Vermögen*), Anderson notes that civil society effects a revolution in the concept of resources. Resources are no longer natural givens, but are both socially created and distributed. The general resources are the capacity of civil society to provide individuals with opportunities to earn a living and to satisfy their needs. However, when people are deprived of resources, this is not a natural, but a political problem, and social disintegration is a likely result. This disintegration manifests itself in the extremes of extravagant wealth and misery of poverty, and in the physical and ethical corruption common to both. The disintegration of society into the extremes of wealth and poverty, means, according to Anderson, that production and consumption have come out of balance. Civil society exposes its members to contingency and imbalance, and provides no guarantee that their needs will actually be met.

However, rather than simply follow Adam Smith's optimistic view that the market is self-correcting (guided as it were by an invisible hand), Hegel doubts that the free market automatically corrects its imbalances in a politically acceptable way. He pours scorn on this naive belief: "The plague also comes to an end and thus rights itself. But hundreds of thousands have perished of it. They are all dead, and so everything has been finally straightened out."[23] Hegel's sarcasm suggests that he regards certain free market 'autocorrections' as socially and ethically unacceptable. The possibilities for satisfaction of needs that civil society offers must not remain mere possibilities; if they do, then needs will go unsatisfied, and this will undermine the legitimacy of free market political economy. Hegel holds that to prevent the emergence of a penurious rabble, there is need for an ethical-social-political intervention in the economy that seeks to guarantee that needs are actually met.

Hegel outlines three possible solutions to the imbalances of production and consumption: public authority, colonization, and the corporation. As Anderson observes, public authority's intervention is similar to a command economy. Although it may be well intentioned, public authority does not succeed because it is perceived as external to the self-seeking individuals who comprise the market. Moreover, while it might redistribute the wealth, public authority's intervention does not necessarily transform patterns of consumption. Further, any redistribution/transfers of wealth that occur without the mediation of work contradicts civil society's ethos of self-supporting self-sufficiency. The second alternative, colonization, is at best a temporary stopgap measure that only postpones the crisis of overproduction and ends up perpetuating social-economic inequalities on a global scale. As Anderson points out, colonization embodies Hegel's idea of a false infinite.

The third alternative is the corporation. The corporation is a mediating institution that is historically related to medieval trades and guilds, and to the modern labor unions and cooperatives in that it is constructed around a trade, industry, or profession. The corporation is an extension of subjective freedom that is less external to individuals than public authority. Anderson argues that the corporation represents a reflective ethical transformation of individuals, namely, in place of mutual exploitation between atomized individuals, members work for the common good of the trade or industry. This provides the possibility of an increased rationality in the economy by affecting and altering attitudes of production and consumption. The crux of the matter is that both production and consumption can become ethically and socially motivating issues within the context of the corporation. Rather than an external command economy imposed by public authority, the members of the corporation have as their self-interest management of an appropriate, sustainable level of production. It is in their self-interest to promote responsible consumption that contributes positively to the general social resources. The corporation thus represents the development of an ethical institution within civil society that, by extending recognition and honor to its members and by transforming their consumption and production, can curb civil society's excesses and its disintegration into the extremes of wealth and poverty. Although Anderson may be more accurate in his interpretation of Hegel's argument than Avineri, it remains to be seen whether his interpretation constitutes a plausible solution to the problem of poverty.

The final three essays bring Hegel's thought into dialogue and relation to Habermas (Buchwalter), Foucault (Durst), and Rawls (Houlgate). Andrew Buchwalter's thesis is that constitutional law with respect to its meaning and validity presupposes and reflects Hegel's concept of ethical life (*Sittlichkeit*). Hegel follows Montesquieu in conceiving law and constitution as not merely positive legal documents, but as expressions of spirit, the objective spirit of a people. Following Hegel, Buchwalter contends that the constitution is not something made, because 'making' presupposes an explicit act of creation on the part of individuals who are isolated atoms prior to and independent of the act of constitution-making. Since a people is always already constituted, the constitution is not so much an act of making, but an act of interpretation (*Auslegung*). Buchwalter goes on to argue that, contrary to Habermas, Hegel's sociohistorical approach to law entails neither a subordination of law to ordinary politics nor an undermining of its normativity.

David C. Durst presents an interpretation of Hegel opposed to Buchwalter's. He reads Hegel through Foucauldian lenses, and not surprisingly emphasizes a potentially sinister ambiguity in Hegel's account of the state. Although Hegel unequivocally asserts that the end of the state is the happiness of its citizens, when read through the lenses of Foucault's hermeneutics of suspicion, this turns out to mean that Hegel's state targets the happiness of individuals as a means to promote its own stability. While Hegel regards the patriotic union with the state as the liberation of freedom, Durst suggests that liberation here is illusory, the result of a productivistic reason and coercive politics of ethical life. Consequently, where Hegel describes the relation of rights and duties in ethical life as a liberation from moralizing reflection, Durst believes that ethical life has a dark side that promotes a normalized, regimented form of life and that augments the coercive mechanisms of abstract right and morality. Although Hegel may achieve a liberation from externally coercive, repressive power, this "liberation" may merely mark a new stage in the sophistication of societal mechanisms of disciplinary control that hides itself by rendering the welfare and happiness of individuals instrumental to the reinforcement of disciplinary power and control. Thus Durst's reading of Hegel produces a view that resembles Fichte's police-state, which Hegel described as a nation of galley slaves where everyone spies on everyone else; more important, such a state is based not on mutual recognition and freedom, but on coercion.[24]

Durst thus manages to effect a collision between two discourses—Hegel's and Foucault's—which both criticize power, hegemony, and domination. But of these two, only Hegel presents an account of reconciliation, liberation, and free public life. For Foucault these are always promised yet always deferred. From Foucault's perspective, any reconciliation, including Hegel's, falls under suspicion. We might draw the ironic conclusion that, far from being a bulwark against totalitarianism, Durst's Hegel is its most insidious representative, because he disguises the hegemony of productivist reason and power in the discourses of freedom, liberation, and happiness. This reading might please Karl Popper, but whether it accurately captures Hegel's thought is another matter. From a Hegelian perspective, the continued deferral of liberation and overcoming of oppression flirts with the very nihilism that it opposes.

Stephen Houlgate brings Hegel and Rawls into dialogue. He shows that despite initial appearances of radical differences, such as Rawls's putative individualistic liberalism versus Hegelian communitarianism, the two have some surprising convergences. Both present versions of the modern liberal state but reach their conclusions through different philosophical methodologies. Rawls works out a practical procedural rationality that presupposes individuals who are methodologically purified, co-equal rational choosers, while Hegel develops the speculative dialectical logic of the idea of freedom. These different methodologies result in different conceptions of the modern state. Rawls insists on procedural rationality, that is, what free and equal persons would choose in the original position, namely, freedom of choice, equality, and justice as fairness. In contrast, Hegel seeks to determine the modern state through an analysis of the idea of freedom. In Hegel's state, choice, equality, and fairness, while important, are nevertheless not the principal values, but subordinate to the logical-metaphysical analysis of the idea of freedom and what it requires. Specifically, Hegel's analysis requires that certain freedoms to which Rawls gives the highest priority are to be restricted by the requirements of freedom itself. Hegel's analysis of the requirements of freedom leads him to defend what Rawls would consider as unfair inequalities—notably in political representation—as nevertheless in accordance with the deeper interests of freedom.

Houlgate concedes that Hegel's modern state is less democratic than Rawls's well-ordered society. But he defends Hegel by arguing that his state is less democratic because of what Hegel believes to be necessitated by the very idea of substantive freedom, and not because of any desire to preserve premodern traditional privileges. Houlgate offers a quasi-immanent critique of Rawls from a Hegelian point of view that presents an argument for the preferability of speculative theory over Rawlsian practical consensus. If Hegel's concept of freedom as requiring certain undemocratic inequalities turns out to be true, then, Houlgate believes, Rawls would be placed in the uncomfortable dilemma of having to work (unfairly) against truth in the name of justice as fairness, or he must allow the truth of the idea of freedom to undermine the possibility of an overlapping consensus of plural points of view. If Houlgate is correct, then the so-called deeper interests of freedom (speculatively conceived) work against the ideal of justice as fairness and equality.

Houlgate acknowledges that such a criticism of Rawls hinges on whether Hegel's conception of freedom is true. Surely there is some political danger in a theoretical truth that asserts that the *idea* of freedom *requires* unfair inequalities. It is one thing to argue, as do both Hegel and Rawls, that it may be necessary to restrict certain freedoms for the sake of the development and actualization of freedom. This is clear in Hegel's account of the 'transition' from the state of nature to the civilized condition, and in his account of marriage. What from one perspective is a restriction of freedom (arbitrariness) is from another, higher perspective a liberation of freedom (as intersubjective, social, and communal). However, it is another matter to claim that freedom requires inequalities. It is not clear how far Houlgate is prepared to go in defending such a Neo-Aristotelian teleology of freedom that requires and justifies certain inequalities. After all, it was such a teleological conception of freedom that misled Aristotle into a defense of slavery.

So two questions seem to be in order. First, what is the relation between theoretical-speculative truth and politics? Assuming that the speculative idea of freedom as requiring certain inequalities is true, how is such a truth related to the political sphere? As Hannah Arendt has observed, the public-political sphere is inherently pluralistic, and such pluralism is not merely a recent concern of modern democracies, but rather the human condition.[25] To override this pluralism in the name of truth is the ever-present tendency and danger of totalitarianism.

Second, the dilemma Houlgate constructs for Rawls may also be present in his account of Hegelian freedom—specifically, there may be a tension between the substantive Idea of freedom, which in Houlgate's account involves hierarchy and inequalities, and subjective individual freedom.[26] It is notable that Hegel's elaboration of freedom does not include a defense of popular sovereignty because of its proximity to the social contract view of the state. Yet mutual recognition implies coequality, and such coequality seems to undermine hierarchy or inequality. Does Hegel's concept of substantive freedom contain or imply some sort of hierarchy and inequality? Houlgate suggests that it does. If so, how can the hierarchical principle inherent in the idea of substantive freedom be reconciled with the egalitarian principle inherent in popular sovereignty and subjective freedom? Does the hierarchy inherent in substantive freedom undermine mutual recognition? If it were to undermine recognition, then the speculative idea of freedom would undermine its own condition of actualization in the world.

If Houlgate is correct that Hegel's idea of freedom may undermine Rawlsian consensus and is preferable to consensus because it is true, then Houlgate's claim that the speculative idea of freedom requires undemocratic inequalities may appear to confirm Durst's Foucaultian suspicions concerning the potentially dark side of Hegel's state and ethical life. This irony leads to another, namely, Houlgate's Hegel, in upholding the truth of substantive freedom as requiring inequalities, appears to resemble Plato and the Platonic philosopher king so roundly criticized by Hegel for being unable to come to terms with the modern principle of subjective freedom.[27]

NOTES

These essays were first presented under the title "Hegel's Philosophy of Right" at the fifteenth biennial meeting of the Hegel Society of America, which was held at the University of Georgia, Athens, Georgia, from October 2 to October 4, 1998. I would like to thank Richard Dien Winfield for helping organize that conference, and the authors, not only for their essays, but also for their helpful and lively discussions at the meeting. Thanks are also due to Hiram College for supporting the publication of this volume, and to Adrienne Cvektovic, Julia Levin, and Kristen Myers for assisting in its preparation.

1. Z. A. Pelczynski, *The State and Civil Society: Studies in Hegel's Political Philosophy* (Cambridge University Press, 1984).

2. Harry Brod, *Hegel's Philosophy of Politics: Idealism, Identity, and Modernity* (Boulder: Westview Press, 1992); David Kolb, *The Critique of Pure Modernity: Hegel, Heidegger and After* (University of Chicago Press, 1986); Stephen Houlgate, *Freedom Truth and History* (London: Routledge, 1991); Michael Hardimon, *Hegel's Social Philosophy: The Project of Reconciliation* (Cambridge University Press, 1994); David Macgregor, *Hegel, Marx, and the English State* (University of Toronto Press, 1996); Robert Pippin, *Idealism as Modernism: Hegelian Variations* (Cambridge University Press, 1997); Terry Pinkard, *Hegel's Phenomenology: The Sociality of Reason* (Cambridge University Press, 1994); Robert R. Williams, *Hegel's Ethics of Recognition* (Berkeley: University of California Press, 1998); Allen W. Wood, *Hegel's Ethical Thought* (Cambridge University Press, 1991).

3. J. N. Findlay, *Hegel: A Re-Examination*, 1951; Shlomo Avineri, *Hegel's Theory of the Modern State* (Cambridge University Press, 1976).

4. Hegel, *Philosophy of Right*, ed. A. Wood, tr. H. Nisbet (Cambridge: Cambridge University Press, 1991), §260 and Addition.

5. Ibid.

6. The project has been described as one of reconciling and synthesizing Kant and Aristotle. But this way of stating the issue merely recasts it as a quarrel between the ancients and moderns, and an invitation to take sides with one or the other. Hegel does not come down on one side or the other, but formulates a third alternative, a concept of a social reason and autonomy, in which recognition plays an important, pivotal role.

7. Williams, *Hegel's Ethics of Recognition*, op. cit., ch. 6.

8. A notable exception to this is found in Hegel's account of the corporations. See Joel Anderson's essay in this volume.

9. Cf. Williams, *Hegel's Ethics of Recognition*, ch. 11, and A. Wood, *Hegelian Ethical Theory* pp. 246–55.

10. See Williams, Hegel's *Ethics of Recognition*, ch. 10.

11. Kant sought to purify reason from the merely positive and given. He insisted that pure reason is itself practical, that is, capable of determining its own ends. For Kant pure reason is self-initiating, autonomous, and therefore capable of guiding conduct and action.

12. Lukacs, *The Young Hegel*, tr. R. Livingstone (Cambridge, Mass.: MIT Press, 1975), pp. 74–89.

13. Hegel, *Difference Essay*, tr. W. Cerf and H. S. Harris (Albany: SUNY Press, 1977).

14. Ibid., p. 91.

15. See Hegel, *Lectures on Natural Right and Political Science* (1817), tr. J. Michael Stewart and Peter C. Hodgson (Berkeley: University of California Press, 1995). Here Hegel writes, instead of the rational is actual, that the rational must come about. §134, p. 242.

16. Hegel, *Philosophy of Mind*, tr. W. Wallace (Oxford University Press, 1971), §552.

17. Hegel's theory of punishment is not driven by revenge, but by the demands of justice, understood as a form of reconciliation of the criminal with the established order of recognition.

18. The transgressor asserts his own principle (e.g., the coercion of freedom) as superior to right, and tries to make this principle prevail over right, at least in his particular action. If transgression succeeds, that is, is not canceled by punishment, then the very order and idea of right would be altered. Wrong would have appeared as right. Punishment is required to cancel this appearance.

19. Igor Primoratz, *Justifying Legal Punishment* (Atlantic Highlands, N.J.: Humanities Press, 1989). See also idem, *Banquo's Geist: Hegels Theorie der Strafe*, *Hegel-Studien* Beiheft 29 (Bonn: Bouvier Verlag, 1986).

20. For a fuller analysis, cf. Williams, *Hegel's Ethics of Recognition*, ch. 12.

21. Hegel, *Philosophy of Right*, §268 Zusatz.

22. Houlgate, *Freedom Truth and History*.

23. Hegel, *Vorlesungen uber Rechtsphilosophie*, 1818–1831, Hrsg. Karl-Heinz Ilting (Stuttgart: Frommann-Holzboog, 1973), vol. IV, p. 625. I am indebted to Joel Anderson for pointing out this passage.

24. Hegel, *Lectures on Natural Right and Political Science* (1817) op. cit., p. 212; see also Williams, *Hegel's Ethics of Recognition*, ch. 12, p. 288f.

25. Hannah Arendt, *The Human Condition* (University of Chicago Press, 1958).

26. Allen Wood notes this tension between substantive freedom and subjective freedom in his *Hegelian Ethical Thought*, op. cit., pp. 241–46.

27. Hegel, *Philosophy of Right*, op. cit., §185.

CHAPTER 1

Hegel's Critical Appropriation of Kantian Morality

Ardis B. Collins

In recent years, a significant debate has developed between contemporary defenders of Kant's moral philosophy and those who interpret and defend Hegel's critique of Kantian morality. The participants in this debate discuss the disagreement between Kant and Hegel as a confrontation between two different philosophical positions. In the *Philosophy of Right*, however, Hegel's critique of a morality point of view belongs to the philosophical development of a concept, the concept of right; and Hegel himself associates this account of morality with Kant's moral philosophy.[1] Since Hegel's philosophical procedure both justifies and criticizes, cancels and preserves, the positions it passes through, morality becomes integrated into Hegel's own position. We can ask, therefore, how Hegel's philosophical procedure affects the position on morality he develops in the *Philosophy of Right* and what difference this makes to the issues raised by the Kant–Hegel debate. This essay addresses that question.

1. THE KANT–HEGEL DEBATE

The defenders of Kant have focused on Hegel's charge that Kant's moral philosophy is an empty formalism. Patrick Riley defends Kant against this charge by distinguishing between subjective and objective ends. Although Kant's moral law remains detached from the empirical content of subjective ends, like happiness or pleasure, the moral law itself commands all rational beings to treat persons as ends-in-themselves. This command gives moral action a definite end to be pursued, and hence it has content. But since the end is derived from what practical reason requires of every rational being, it has the legitimacy of an objective end.[2]

Sally Sedgwick makes a similar point. Pure moral philosophy has the task of proving the possibility of morality in general; and it does this by deriving the moral law from the nonempirical "fact" that we have practical reason. This project has content in the form of a priori requirements that any empirical content must meet in order to qualify as moral. Sedgwick, however, also calls attention to other projects that Kant acknowledges as essential to moral philosophy. The metaphysics of morals brings in the empirical concept of human nature and uses this to determine what morality requires of human beings. Applied ethics determines the particular duties of a particular person; and for this task, it needs a posteriori knowledge of the agent's particular situation and character together with judgment refined by experience.[3]

Allen Wood and Robert Pippin deflect this defense of Kant by shifting the force of Hegel's critique to a different issue. According to Wood, Hegel's position implicitly claims that Kant has no right to a moral law with content. The law has its ground in an empty notion of the moral will. If, therefore, the law has content, this content is not derived from the principle that gives the law its legitimacy and moral authority.[4]

According to Pippin, Hegel's disagreement with Kantian morality arises from the concern for what a "free, self-determining life" requires. Kantian rationality remains independent of my particular ends and preferences, my social and historical context, the real community to which I belong. It uses these for its own purposes, directs them to its own communal ideal, applies its rule to them. Hegel denies that a life determined by what any rational person ought to will can really be a life determined by me; and this applies even to what any rational person ought to will in these particular circumstances.[5]

With these issues in mind, we examine the treatment of morality developed in the *Philosophy of Right*. Since, however, I interpret Hegel's position according to the demands of Hegelian philosophical procedure, we look first at the way Hegel describes this procedure in the *Science of Logic* and the *Philosophy of Right*.

2. HEGEL'S PHILOSOPHICAL PROCEDURE

According to these texts, philosophy undertakes to prove the legitimacy of its beginning concepts, instead of taking these for granted or picking them up from the culture; and it derives its method from the concept of the subject matter itself, instead of using a method brought to the subject matter from the outside.[6] The examination of the concept shows that it implies a necessary connection to what contradicts or negates it.

This proves that the contradictory opposite belongs to the concept itself, since it follows necessarily from what the concept requires. From this result, Hegel derives a new concept in which the necessary connection between opposites is acknowledged.[7] The *Logic* describes this procedure as a retreat into a ground. By showing that the concept is necessarily connected to its opposite, the demonstration proves that the opposites presuppose a common principle or ground that holds them together as different factors in the same relational whole.[8]

It is important to note, however, the limited claims made by Hegel's procedure. The demonstration proves that the concept is necessarily connected to its opposite. This allows us to assert nothing more than the opposition itself. We may not assume that contradiction is untrue, that the opposites must be unified without contradiction, and then go looking for a concept that will hold the opposites together without opposition. The demonstration proves the necessity of rethinking the original concept as involved in an opposition connection. It does not prove that the opposites must be rethought as not really opposed. When Hegel retreats into a ground, he thinks the sameness of the ground as a law or necessity that drives the connection between opposites and reduces them to differences within the same opposition relation.

We should note, too, that Hegel does not assume the legitimacy of this inferential structure and then impose it on the subject matter he is examining. His introductory essays only give us a preview of what we will find developing as we follow the implications of the concept itself.[9] Thus, he says:

> To consider something rationally means not to bring reason to bear on the object from outside in order to work upon it, for the object is itself rational for itself . . . ; the sole business of science is <to bring> this work which is accomplished by the <rationality> of the <subject-matter> itself <to consciousness>.[10]

I take this to mean that even the structures of Hegel's logic cannot be used as a set of categories and logical movements imposed on the subject matter from the outside. If the categories and structures of Hegelian logic constitute the essence of right, Hegelian philosophical procedure requires that this be demonstrated by developing them from what the concept of right itself necessarily implies. We may not settle for a procedure that imposes on questions of right an interpretive framework appropriated from the logic and used as an external method for investigating what right is.

Hegel tells us explicitly in the Introduction to the *Philosophy of Right* that the concept of right is proved by what has preceded it in philosophical science, and hence its justification does not belong to the science of right itself.[11] Since, however, the issues in the Kant–Hegel debate are significantly affected by presuppositions taken for granted in the concept of right, I will at least identify these presuppositions and give a sketchy indication of why Hegel considers them legitimate.

3. THE BEGINNING CONCEPT OF RIGHT

The *Philosophy of Right* begins with a concept that conceives human beings as independent persons. This is justified by developments in the philosophy of subjective spirit. Phenomenology takes over from the feeling soul the singularity and isolation of self-feeling. But in phenomenology, the self feels itself related to an object, an other that it is conscious of; and consciousness lets all its own specific characteristics go into this object dimension. Thus, phenomenology begins with an empty ego conscious of every definite "what," including its own, as something else that it is conscious of.[12] In the transition from consciousness to self-consciousness, the relation between self and world shifts from an object-dominated relation to a subject-dominated relation. The self separates itself from a relation in which the conscious subject is dependent on the object and posits the self's own independence as the essential element in the relation between self and world. But in order to bring this dominance to reality in the way the world actually exists, the independence of the self must be joined to the discipline and work of another self, who refrains from the immediate satisfaction of desire and gives to nature the enduring condition of being "for" the self. By remaining immersed in the resistance of natural reality, the working self makes the world exist explicitly and persistently as the dominant self's own world.[13]

The independence of the ego is preserved within the structure of reason. Rational thought, which belongs to the inner conscious life of this single self, remains an empty ego determined only as pure thought detached from and independent of all the givens of nature and self. But reason incorporates into its presuppositions what becomes explicit in self-consciousness: (1) that the independent subjectivity of this self is necessarily connected to the self-consciousness of another person; (2) that the independence of the self is necessarily connected to an independent objective world, which exists in a form that corresponds to what the independent self essentially is. Reason is convinced that the laws and principles governing the independent thought of this single self also constitute the true essence of objective reality and the true self of other rational beings. Hegel's Psychology defines the rational will as independent thought deriving the differentiated content of self and world from thought's own self-determination.[14]

These different factors give us the beginning concept of right. The independent thought of this single self takes the form of a rational will. This will is a detached subjectivity, set off from everything that it wills and characterized by nothing but its own independence in willing. Yet this detached subjectivity has the status of reason, which means that its inner principle or law is one with the principle that governs both the world and other rational wills. The rational will, therefore, has the right to be determined by nothing other than its own independent willing and yet to make itself existent as the ruling principle of what confronts it as other. Moreover, this empty will wills itself as an end. All particulars get their status as rational from being that in which this will wills its own freedom.[15] Hegel explicitly refers to this freedom as a "universal content" (*allgemeinen Inhalt*); and he explicitly distinguishes this universal content from "subjective or selfish interests."[16] Thus, Hegel acknowledges from the very beginning points made by Patrick Riley and Sally Sedgwick, namely, that an empty will, detached from material concerns, has content, and that this content provides the will with a definite direction or end.

4. THE SELF-CONTRADICTION OF ABSTRACT RIGHT

Let us consider, then, what this concept of embodied free will implies. The will gives itself reality first in its own living body. Life belongs to the very essence of the rational will and cannot be separated from its right, because life is a necessary condition for the existence of reason as an objective reality. The objective existence of the self's life, however, must be transformed into something rational by becoming the organ and instrument of the rational will. Thus, the will moves from the isolation of its own willing into the reality of its physical life, which belongs to a context shared with other natural things.[17] From its presence in this context, the will moves beyond its own singular existence to a thing existent outside itself. It claims some external thing as its own.[18] From its existence as property, the will returns to its existence within the singularity of its own life by using property to satisfy its own particular needs and interests.[19] Because this whole property dynamic is governed by the independent choosing of this single will, property necessarily takes the form of private property.[20]

The will's existence in property alone, however, does not give objective existence to the will's special status. Things can manifest the self's power over them; but only another person can acknowledge the self as one who has authority over things, one who rules them by right. Therefore, the will of this single self embodies itself in property contracts.

Contracts involve linguistic commitments that represent each party's recognition of the other as having authority over the things involved in the property transfer. Only in this form does a person's abstract right exist as right in the objective world outside the self.[21]

According to Hegel, the concept of abstract right necessarily implies a conflict of wills that takes the form of wrong and its punishment.[22] The necessity arises from two factors in the beginning concept of right. First, abstract right belongs to the arbitrary, singular will of an individual person. Nothing other than the will's own independent choosing determines how it makes itself existent in the particulars of property relations. Hegel explicitly refers to this embodiment as "for myself and excluding the will of another."[23] But the substantial element in the embodiment of right, the element in which the will's right primarily exists, is the element that expresses the will of other persons.[24] Since the other person's will, no less than my own, is singular and exclusive, his willingness to acknowledge my right depends on his singular, arbitrary, contingent will. This contingency becomes explicit and real in wrong.[25] Wrong manifests the singularity and independence of persons when confronted by another person's property claims. They decide for themselves, according to their own arbitrary resolution or choice, whether to acknowledge this person's right or to deny it.

Since abstract right carries with it the presuppositions of reason, a rational subject who wrongs another wills coercion and the negation of right as a universal law governing the embodiment of freedom in property relations. This produces a condition in which the person wronged cannot embody her freedom and thereby reestablish the rule of right unless she opposes her will to the will embodied in wrong. She embodies her freedom in the punishment of wrong, which negates the other person's right to deny her right. Thus, she asserts her right not as a particular right, the right to this or that property, but as the infinite right of a rational will to rule the world and the will of other persons. Within the framework of abstract right, however, the punishment of wrong is also wrong, since the one who punishes must assert the right of this person's independent, exclusive will. Punishment takes the form of revenge. As a result, the person punished is also wronged, and the law implicit in revenge demands that he oppose the wrong by taking revenge on the one who punished him. Thus, abstract right dissolves into an endless conflict in which each person maintains his or her right by forcing other persons to abide by a will that is not their own; and hence every assertion of right becomes a denial of the same right in other persons.[26] Abstract right is necessarily connected to its opposite.

5. THE TRANSITION TO MORALITY

The conceptual development of abstract right changes the structure of right in four significant ways. First, a will asserting its right to property becomes engaged in two kinds of self-determination. It determines itself objectively by claiming as its own some particular thing useful for satisfying a particular set of needs. But it also determines itself subjectively by asserting its will and right as "mine and not yours."[27] Second, the objective side of right gets its essential determination, its determination as right, from the subjective determination. The appropriation and surrender of property exists as right in honest contracts, as wrong in fraud and crime, as both right and wrong in revenge. It all depends on how each will determines its own willing in relation to the will of other persons. Thus, right exists primarily not in the appropriation and surrender of property but in what a person means by it, what kind of willing it represents to others.[28] Third, the independent, arbitrary will of individual persons turns out to be only contingently related to the rationality that establishes a person's right to make claims on the world and other persons. Rationality becomes existent in relations between persons if and only if each person independently decides to give it reality in the determination of this person's singular will.[29]

Finally, of course, the development of abstract right reveals that abstract right is necessarily connected to its own opposite. This proves the necessity of asserting as a new definition of right the original definition together with its opposite, abstract right together with its negation. Individual freedom and right persist. But they exist within a fluid system of relations that negates every member of the system as not the determining principle of the whole. Something else, therefore, defines and determines the whole. This something else is the law that necessitates the connection between the right of each person's singular will and the negation of this right by the will of other persons. Right requires, therefore, that each person will this law as the true ground of this person's own right. Each will must negate its own exclusivity and identify itself with the law that connects it to the rights of others.[30]

What form, then, does right take when these structural shifts are acknowledged in the morality position? First, the relation between the will and its embodiment shifts from the static form of property to the fluid form of action and thereby acknowledges the complex relational structure that connects each person's will to the will of others. Second, morality acknowledges that freedom-embodied is accomplished primarily in the way individual persons determine their own subjectivity. Hence, a moral agent has the right of subjectivity—the right (1) to disclaim responsibility for any consequences of the agent's action that do not correspond to the agent's knowledge and will; (2) to feel the satisfaction of particular needs or inclinations as a way of knowing the action's necessary relation to the person embodied in this particular life; (3) to know every aspect of the action as essentially determined by what the agent intends.[31]

Finally, morality acknowledges that this subjective self-determination may or may not embody the rational principle that gives persons the right to make claims on the world. This principle functions as a requirement, an ought-to-be. It becomes existent as an actual determination of the will only if individual persons freely decide to act on it. Thus, individual persons transform themselves into rational beings by making the universal principle of right the ruling principle of their projects, by willing it as what they have decided to make of themselves and their world. For morality, therefore, the "absolute and ultimate end of the world" is a world of free persons who independently decide to act on principles derived from the rationality common to them all. Hegel calls this ultimate end "the good."[32]

6. HEGEL'S CRITIQUE OF MORALITY

We come now to the point where Hegel sets out to prove that morality is necessarily connected to its own opposite. The Kant–Hegel debate calls this the emptiness argument, which refers to Hegel's claim that the good is "indeterminate."[33] It is important, therefore, to explain explicitly and precisely what Hegel means by the indeterminacy of the good and why he insists on it. To do this, we must look again at the demands of Hegel's philosophical procedure.

The argument developed in abstract right retreats into a ground. It moves from the conditioned to its condition, from a free will asserting its right in the real world to what it must presuppose in order to have this right. Thus, the argument demonstrates that the right to impose one's independent decisions on the external world and to demand recognition from other persons depends on the necessity or law that connects the right of each person to the rights of others.[34] This result demands an inversion of argument strategy. The development of abstract right demonstrates that abstract right is not the ultimate condition or ground of right, that it depends on a prior condition. In abstract right, therefore, we have been thinking backwards, beginning with what turns out to be dependent on a prior principle and using this to demonstrate that there is a prior principle. Now that this has been demonstrated, we must shift into a way of thinking that thinks the prior condition first, and derives abstract right from it. This means that the concept of a rational will must be thought as prior to the determinations of right and welfare and as the ground or principle from which they are derived.

Hegel analyzes the good into two essential factors: the concept of the will, and the realization of this concept in the various facets of free action.[35] Abstract right's retreat into a ground gives the concept of the will dominance and independence in its relation to the reality factor. If, however, we conceive the universal good as prior to and independent of all the singular and particular determinations of active life, then we think nothing more than the demand that the rational will remain the same will, the same rationality, throughout all its various realizations. In this form, the good cannot explain why the rational will ought to have any determinations at all, since determinations divide the unity of the rational will into different wills pursuing different purposes focused on the exclusive subjectivity of each person's private intentions.[36]

But the good must be conceived as existent in the actions of free persons. The only evidence we have for its legitimacy as the ruling principle of freedom and right comes from its actual appearance in the dynamic of abstract right and its derivation from the way abstract right negates its own claims.[37] If, therefore, the good as a principle detached from the subjectivity of persons and their actions cannot account for its existence in these determinate forms, then moral principle cannot by itself determine what is good. It must get the determinations required for becoming a real force in the field of action not from itself but from its existence in the moral subjectivity of individual persons. Thus, the universality of rational principle loses its dominant position, and moral subjectivity becomes an equally important factor in the structure of the good. Moral rationality takes the form of conscience. A conscientious agent feels convinced that a specific project is good and acts with the intention of doing what the universality of the good requires of him or her. In this form, the universality of the good becomes identified with the subjectivity of each person and hence is willed as each one's personal freedom.[38]

The subjectivity of moral agents, however, has its own kind of indeterminacy, which carries over from abstract right. In order to be self-determining, a person must remain independent of all given particulars in the self or in the world; and this independence factor must take charge of how such particulars become incorporated into this person's life. In morality as conscientiousness, a person claims the right to make his own independent judgments about what is good. Since these judgments must be independent of all given particulars, moral subjectivity gets its strategy for moral judgment from its own arbitrary devising. An action is good if I can find one good reason, or one moral authority, supporting a course of action; or if my intentions are good, whatever the particular action may be; or if I feel convinced that a particular interest is good.

Thus, each person determines her or his own moral character and wills this as good. Moreover, each person determines independently whether to develop a moral character that is truly universal or to impose on others this person's arbitrary, exclusive will. Thus, the conscientious agent is always on the verge of becoming evil.[39]

Hegel articulates this result as the development of two opposed totalities. The good requires that moral subjectivity become subject to the demands of universality and sameness; all right and welfare ought to be willed according to a principle that identifies the freedom of each with the freedom of all. Conscience requires that the universality and sameness of the good become subject to the demands of moral subjectivity; the good must be willed as my personal, exclusive free will. The examination of morality demonstrates that each totality is necessarily connected to the other. The subjectivity of conscience can demand recognition from others only if it is objectively good, that is, if it asserts a principle that others can acknowledge as a principle of their own freedom. The objectivity of the good can become real in the subjectivity of moral agents only if each moral agent can acknowledge it as a principle endorsed by the agent's own personal conviction or conscience. Although both laws require some kind of existence in the particulars of individual decisions and subjective interests, neither determines exactly and specifically what these particulars must be.[40]

7. THE KANT–HEGEL DEBATE REVISITED

Let us look now at the way the critique of morality, interpreted according to the demands of Hegel's philosophical procedure, affects the issues raised by the Kant–Hegel debate. First, we must ask whether the structure of morality is close enough to Kant's own position for Hegel's critique of it to count as a critique of Kant.[41] To answer this question, we must look in the right place. Hegel's idea of the good corresponds not to Kant's moral law but to Kant's notion of the highest good.

Kant's notion of the highest good has three components: the moral law, a virtuous will, and welfare in the form of happiness. The moral law presupposes the idea of freedom, which Kant defines both negatively and positively. According to its negative definition, freedom is a will not determined by what is other than itself. For Kant, this means being free from the inclinations and dispositions given in the self's empirical constitution. But Kant also distinguishes the rational will from the unstable human will, which chooses between duty and inclination, rational autonomy and natural heteronomy. Choice is a symptom of a divided self, one that belongs to nature and necessity as well as to reason and freedom. For Kant as well as for Hegel's beginning account of morality, the universal law of practical reason is independent of both the human self's given empirical determinations and the arbitrariness of free choice.

But Kant, like Hegel, turns this negative into a positive. Kant conceives pure practical reason as reason giving itself the law that determines action. A human will participates in rational autonomy by making the universal law of practical reason the determining principle of its action.[42] This is virtue, which belongs to the highest good as its supreme condition. Virtue alone, however, is not the perfect or complete good. In a person who needs the complete satisfaction of desire, which is happiness, action occurs in the pursuit of this desire satisfaction. This aspect of action can be rational, therefore, only if virtue actually operates in it and determines it. Hence, when Kant solves the practical antinomy, he conceives the highest good as virtue causing happiness, causing it not according to the law of physical forces, but according to the law of a possible intelligible world conceived as the rational ground of the sensible world and its laws.[43]

Thus, Kant's notion of the highest good has the same kind of indeterminacy and the same kind of self-determining relation to the particulars of human life as that found in Hegel's initial idea of the moral good. This changes the framework for dealing with the issues raised by Patrick Riley and Sally Sedgwick. Hegel begins morality by accepting all the claims they make in defense of Kant. The good has a definite content of its own. It functions as an end. It defines certain definite requirements. It has a necessary relation to the specifics of human existence and to the particulars of each person's life. According to Allen Wood, however, Kant's moral law cannot accept determination from the particulars of human life, since Kant's way of defining the rational will requires its complete independence of all empirical content.[44] Does the same objection apply to Hegel's account of morality?

When Kant conceives practical reason and its laws as the ground of sensible reality, he conceives it only as a possibility, as a way in which it is possible to think about sensible reality. This possibility depends on the possibility of liberating thought from the requirements of the sensible world as it appears, so that there will be no contradiction between free causality and natural causality.[45] Hegel's philosophy of right begins with a different concept of reason. It conceives reason and its laws as the true essence of an actual world formed by human work, which was established in the philosophy of subjective spirit.[46] Thus, the beginning concept of right includes both the independence of thought and its actual embodiment in the realities of personal life. Moreover, Hegel proves the legitimacy of the good as the ruling principle of freedom and right by demonstrating that the opposition dynamic played out in thought's embodiment implies such a principle as its ground.[47] If, therefore, the concept of a rational will cannot by itself account for its appearance in the particulars of right and welfare, then it cannot by itself meet either the requirements of reason in general or the specific requirements determined by the dynamic of abstract right. Hence, Hegel can legitimately shift to a definition of the good in which the other factor in the good, its realization in the subjectivity of individual persons, gives the good its particulars.

The real bone of contention between Kant and Hegel, therefore, is whether the universal concept of a rational will is a sufficient condition for the rationality of real action. According to Hegel, it is not, since this concept does not determine the conditions required for reason's existence in the real world. What, then, are the conditions required for reason's existence in the real world? Here, too, we find a fundamental disagreement between Kant and Hegel. In Hegel's account of morality, the realization of the good involves certain motivating factors. It stays close to Kant in the way it treats two of these, the satisfaction of desire and doing one's duty. A person who acts simply to satisfy desire surrenders to determinations not derived from this person's own will, determinations imposed by nature or by the system of relations established in the field of action. Hence, this kind of action is not free. A person who acts in order to do what duty requires derives the action from the universal concept of practical reason. In this case, the satisfaction of particular interests belongs to a larger intention, the intention of living a morally good life; and it satisfies a person's moral aspirations, which aim at a world governed by the rational freedom common to all persons. A person whose life is dominated by such motives is free, because the laws that give this life its character and orientation belong to the rationality of this person's own will.

Hegel's account of morality, however, adds a third motivating factor, the assertion of one's individual freedom. Kant treats desire and duty as alternative commitments for human choice. Humans can choose between duty and inclination, between rational autonomy and natural heteronomy. But this is only because they are not completely rational and hence are not completely free.[48] Thus, Kant's account of the highest good gives the universal principle of practical reason the dominant role in determining what counts as the moral agent's own will.[49] In Hegel's account of morality, a person motivated by duty must will it as the embodiment of this person's singular, exclusive will. According to Hegel, a will must be motivated by the assertion of its own individual subjectivity in order to give the good reality as its own personal freedom. Hence, duty is inseparable from a person's right to know and will the good in a form that is personal and individual to him or her.

Pippin, therefore, identifies one of the most important issues in the disagreement between Hegel and Kant. Hegel insists that freedom requires a kind of self-determination derived from who I am as me and no one else. Kant is satisfied with the kind of self-determination derived from who I am as a rational being and not just a natural being. Within the moral context, however, the personal characteristics described by Pippin—the specifics of my desires, preferences, historical situation, and communal relations—continue as something other than the will; and they continue to play a subordinate role in the will's self-determination. But the "universal content" of this will has now been distinguished into two elements: the freedom to assert one's own individual self-determination, and the obligation to will the good.

8. THE TRANSITION TO ETHICAL LIFE

Morality demonstrates the necessity of uniting two sets of opposites: the opposition developed within morality between the objectivity of the good and the subjectivity of conscience; the opposition between the abstract, indeterminate necessity of these two laws and the contingent particulars in which these laws work out their relations. According to the demands of Hegel's philosophical procedure, ethical life must acknowledge a common ground that establishes the necessary connections between these various factors.

Hegel calls this principle the spirit of the nation or folk, which defines the way this society knows the good. The detachment and independence of the good is acknowledged in the rule of law. An objective system of laws imposes on the special interests and arbitrary decisions of individual citizens the requirement that these be willed according to the law. This transforms the independent decisions and self-interested projects of different persons into rights derived from the same set of principles. These principles also exist as the personal convictions of individual citizens, who feel society's fundamental values as identical with their own sense of self. Thus, ethical life preserves the opposites developed in morality as different ways of knowing the same good.[50]

Ethical life also establishes a necessary connection between the indeterminacy of universal law and the random diversity of independently determined life-plans. Individuals look after their welfare and develop their personalities in a relational system. This system preserves the dynamic of action derived from the conflicts of abstract right and carried over as the reality dimension of the moral good. Ethical life preserves this relational system as the place where the universality of the nation's life becomes identified with and realized in the diversity of its citizens. In this system, each person's work contributes to society's resources for satisfying the needs of its citizens; and this earns them the right to draw on these resources for the satisfaction of their own needs. The whole system operates according to the principle of self-interest. Within the limits set by law, but also in virtue of rights guaranteed by law, individuals use the system of needs and work as a resource for their own well-being and self-development. Thus, ethical life explicitly acknowledges that the principle of singularity and exclusivity, which morality condemns as wicked, plays an essential and legitimate role in determining the particulars of the nation's life. But ethical life also develops from this pursuit of self-interest a necessary connection to the universality of social life.

In the workplace, where families look after their welfare, the particulars of need and work fall into certain groupings. Similar needs addressed by certain kinds of work become the basis for particular associations. In these associations, individual persons become conscious of the interests, skills, and moral principles they share by being involved in the same kind of work. Participation in work associations gives individuals status in the need-work system. They are acknowledged as committed to the norms of competence and service espoused by these associations, and as providing the system of needs with an important resource. Thus, the random collection of individual decisions and interests becomes an organized system of particulars. Individuals must create their personality and life within this system. Moreover, the notion of the good shared by society as a whole becomes determinate in the professional standards and moral principles of work associations. In these professional codes of conduct, each association represents itself as carrying out a duty to society as a whole by providing a particular resource needed by the whole system.

Individuals participating in these associations become identified with this commitment to society as a whole. As a result, they develop a particularized conscience, a sense of the individual's personal duties; and this conscience does not depend on some arbitrarily chosen principle or strategy for making moral judgments. Thus, the inverted world governed by the principle of singularity and exclusivity develops a necessary connection to social life as a shared life governed by shared principles. Moreover, representatives of the particular areas of interest and of their particularized moral codes participate in the lawmaking process. This brings the diversification of the nation's life back to the nation's shared knowledge of the good, which is articulated in its legal system.[51]

According to Hegel, therefore, the good cannot become an accomplished reality without a social dynamic that organizes the particulars of life into a system in which different sets of particulars become mutually supportive. As a member of society, I form my personality and life-plan from the particular possibilities presented to me by this organized system. What I make of these possibilities, therefore, fits into a world that integrates my chosen particulars with the particulars available to the other members of my society. This makes it possible for me to embody my freedom as a life determined by me and still be committed to the same freedom in others.

LIST OF ABBREVIATIONS FOR THE
WORKS OF G. W. F. HEGEL

Enzyklopädie der Philosophischen Wissenschaften im Grundrisse (1830) in *Werke* (Frankfurt: Suhrkamp, 1986).
> The parts of the *Enzyklopädie* are cited as follows: the first part, "die Wissenschaft der Logik" as *EL*; the third part, "die Philosophie des Geistes" as *EG*. Citations refer to section numbers (§) common to all editions and English translations; Remarks are indicated by R, Addenda by A following the section number.

The Encyclopaedia Logic, trans. T. F. Geraets, W. A. Suchting, H. S. Harris (Indianapolis/Cambridge: Hackett, 1991).

Grundlinien der Philosophie des Rechts, ed. Johannes Hoffmeister (Hamburg: Felix Meiner, 1955).
> Cited as *PhR*. Citations refer to section numbers (§) common to all editions and English translations; Remarks are indicated by R, Addenda by A following the section number. If page numbers are needed they refer to *Grundlinien der Philosophie des Rechts*, ed. J. Hoffmeister (Hamburg: Felix Meiner, 1955) preceded by H/.

Elements of the Philosophy of Right, ed. Allen W. Wood, trans. H. B. Nisbet (Cambridge/New York: Cambridge University Press, 1991.
> Adjustments to this translation will be indicated thus: < >. If page numbers are needed they are indicated by N/.

Phänomenologie des Geistes, eds. Hans-Friedrich Wessels & Heinrich Clairmont, according to the text of *Gesammelte Werke* Band 9, eds. Wolfgang Bonsiepen & Reinhard Heede (1980).
> Cited as *PhG*. Citations refer first to the numerical ordering carried over from *Gesammelte Werke* Band 9 followed by the page numbers of the Wessels & Clairmont edition, thus: *PhG* 53/57.

Hegel's Phenomenology of Spirit, trans. A. V. Miller (Oxford/New York: Oxford University Press, 1977).
> Included within citations of the *Phänomenologie des Geistes*, indicated as M followed by the section number, e.g. (M §73).

Wissenschaft der Logik: Die Lehre vom Sein (1832), ed. Hans-Jürgen Gawoll (Hamburg: Felix Meiner, 1990) according to the text of *Gesammelte Werke* Band 21, eds. F. Hogemann & W. Jaeschke (1985).

Cited as *WL* (1832). Citations refer first to the numerical ordering carried over from *Gesammelte Werke* Band 21 followed by the page numbers of the Gawoll edition, thus: *WL* (1832) 27/25–26.

Hegel's Science of Logic, trans. A. V. Miller (London:Allen & Unwin/New York: Humanities Press, 1969).

Included within citations of the *Wissenschaft der Logik*, indicated as M followed by the page number, e.g. (M/43).

NOTES

1. *PhR* §135R.

2. Patrick Riley, "On Kant as the Most Adequate of the Social Contract Theorists," *Political Theory*, vol. 1, no. 4 (November 1973), 460–71. See also Riley, "The 'Elements' of Kant's Practical Philosophy: The *Groundwork* After 200 years (1785–1985)," *Political Theory*, vol 14, no. 4 (November 1986), especially pp. 564–67.

3. Sally S. Sedgwick, "On the Relation of Pure Reason to Content: A Reply to Hegel's Critique of Formalism in Kant's Ethics," *Philosophy and Phenomenological Research*, vol. 49, no. 1 (September 1988), 59–80.

4. Allen W. Wood, *Hegel's Ethical Thought* (Cambridge and New York: Cambridge University Press, 1990), 161–72. When Sedgwick acknowledges that empirical content cannot determine the moral worth of a maxim, she implicitly grants Wood this point. Whatever the role played by empirical content in determining the conditions for applying the moral law, this content does not determine what is essential to being moral.

5. Robert B. Pippin, "Hegel, Ethical Reasons, Kantian Rejoinders," *Philosophical Topics*, vol. 19, no. 2 (Fall 1991), 99–132. Also published in *Idealism as Modernism: Hegelian Variations* (Cambridge: Cambridge University Press, 1997), 92–128.

6. *WL* 1–2/27 (M/43); 16–19/37–38 (M/53–55); 43–44/57–58 (M/71); *EL* §1; *PhR*, Preface H/4–6 (N/10–11), §§2, 3 Remark.

7. "All that is necessary to achieve scientific progress . . . is the recognition of the logical principle that the negative is just as much positive, that what is self-contradictory does not resolve itself into a nullity, into an abstract nothingness, but essentially only into the negation of its particular content . . . and therefore the result essentially contains that from which it results; . . . It is a fresh <concept> but higher and richer than its predecessor; for it is richer by the negation or opposite of the latter, therefore contains it, but also something more, and is the unity of itself and its opposite" (*WL* [1832] [M/54] 18/38). See also *PhR* §31, including the Remark; *WL* (1832) 29–31/28–30 (M/46–47).

8. *WL* (1832) 44–45/57–58 (M/71–72). See also *PhR* §§31 R, 141 R; *WL* (1832) 7–9/6–7 (M/27–28); 39–41/40–41 (M/55–56).

9. *PL* §19R; *WL* (1832) 27–28/25–26 (M/43); 38–39/39 (M/54–55); 44/45 (M/59).

10. *PhR* §31R.

11. *PhR* §2.

12. *EG* §§411–413.

13. *EG* §§424–425, 429–435. See also *PhG* 107/125 (M §§172–173); 110–117/129–138 (M §§186–197).

14. *EG* §§436–439, 465–469.

15. *PhR* §§4–5, 14–15, 20–21, 27, 34–39, 44–45; *EG* §§476–485, 488–490.

16. *EG* §469. See also *PhR* §21.

17. *PhR* §§47–48, 70.

18. *PhR* §§41–45.

19. *PhR* §59.

20. *PhR* §46.

21. Hegel insists that reason itself lies hidden behind the need to make contracts. Contracts do not just happen when persons own property. The concept of right itself, at least in the form of abstract right, requires the embodiment of right in contracts (*PhR* §§45, 51, 71, including Remark, 73, 78–79).

22. *PhR* §81R.

23. Hegel introduces the exclusiveness of the will's embodiment when he argues for the necessity of private property (*PhR* §46). When he has developed the concept of right into the contract structure, he refers to being an owner of property as "having being for myself and excluding the will of another" (§72).

24. *PhR* §79.

25. *PhR* §§73, 75, 81, 82.

26. *PhR* §§81–83, 87, 89–90, 92–95, 97, 99, 100, 102, 104.

27. *PhR* §§104, including Remark, 105.

28. Both together constitute what Hegel refers to as the "particular" will. This will has a formal aspect, which is the subjectivity of willing, and a content aspect, which is the set of particular things and interests that manifest this willing in the natural world (*PhR* §§81, 109, 111, 114, 121, 123, 128).

29. *PhR* §104 Remark. See also §102.

30. *PhR* §§103, 112.

31. *PhR* §§113–115, 117–124. See also *EG* §505.

32. *PhR* §§106–111, 128–129, 131–133.

33. *PhR* §135.

34. *PhR* §§112–113, 129–131.

35. "The *good* is the *Idea*, as the unity of the *concept* of the will and the *particular* will, in which abstract right, welfare, the subjectivity of knowing, and the contingency of external existence [*Dasein*], as *self-sufficient for themselves*, are superseded; but they are at the same time *essentially contained* and *preserved* within it.—[The good is] *realized freedom, the absolute and ultimate end of the world*" (*PhR* §129).

36. *PhR* §§133–135.

37. *PhR* §§129, 135. See also §114 (c).

38. *PhR* §§114 (c), 128, 132, 136, 137 Remark.

39. *PhR* §§137–139, 140, including Remark.

40. *PhR* §141, including Remark.

41. Allen Wood distinguishes between Kant's position, which Hegel criticizes, and the morality position "as Hegel accepts it" (*Hegel's Ethical Thought*, 172). There is some reason for this, since some of the presuppositions in Hegel's account of the morality position do not belong to Kant's own position. Nevertheless, the similarity to Kant's position is striking. Moreover, Hegel himself inserts in the morality account a Remark that explicitly refers to Kant, which suggests that Hegel associates the morality position with Kant's moral philosophy (*PhR* §135R).

42. Immanuel Kant, *Grundlegung zur Metaphysik der Sitten*, Akademie ed., vol. 4, pp. 446–63; *Grounding for the Metaphysics of Morals*, tr. James W. Ellington (Indianapolis and Cambridge: Hackett, 1981), 49–62. Hereafter cited thus: *Gr.* 446–63 (49–62). *Kritik der praktischen Vernunft*, Akademie ed., vol. 5, 42–50, 86–87; *Critique of Practical Reason*, tr. Lewis White Beck, 3rd ed. (New York: Macmillan/Library of Liberal Arts, 1993), 43–52 (pt. I, bk. I, ch. I, "Of the Deduction of the Principles of Pure Practical Reason"), 90. The *Critique of Practical Reason* will be hereafter cited thus: *KpV/CPR* 42–50 (43–52), 86–87 (90). See also Kant, *Kritik der reinen Vernunft*, Akademie ed., vol. 3, vol. 4 (*Critique of Pure Reason*), A547/B575–A558/B586; *Kritik der Urteilskraft*, 403–4; *Critique of Judgment*, tr. Werner S. Pluhar (Indianapolis: Hackett, 1987), 286–87.

43. *KpV/CPR* 108–15 (114–21). Kant explicitly argues this point by appealing to the idea of perfect rationality in action. He asks us to conceive "the perfect volition of an omnipotent rational being." In other words, conceive a will-act that is completely and unqualifiedly rational with unlimited power to produce as the consequence of its willing exactly what it wills, without the distortions or qualifications caused by irrational or random forces. Now conceive of a rational being such as human beings are, beings whose actions occur as the pursuit of happiness; and conceive this being as virtuous. Here we have a rational being in whom particular principles of action express the will to be morally good, which is the will to act rationally. If this person's inclinations are not satisfied, then the overall intention carried out in them, the intention of being rational and morally good, will have failed. But this is not in accordance with the idea of perfect rationality in action, since according to this idea everything is the result of a will that is perfectly rational and has the power to achieve perfectly everything that it wills (110–11 [116–17]). For an analysis of the practical antinomy and its resolution, see Victoria S. Wike, *Kant's Antinomies of Reason: Their Origin and Their Resolution* (Washington, D.C.: University Press of America, 1982), 139–49. For an excellent study of the happiness issue in Kant's moral philosophy, see her *Kant on Happiness in Ethics* (Albany: SUNY Press, 1994).

44. For Kant's own articulation of this, see *Gr.* 457–59 (57–59); *KpV/CPR* 109 (115).

45. *KpV/CPR* 114–15 (120–21).

46. *EG* §§436–439, 465–469.

47. *PhR* §129. See also §114 (c).

48. Kant, *Gr.* 446–63 (49–62).

49. "Consequently, though the highest good may be the entire *object* of pure practical reason, i.e., of a pure will, it is still not to be taken as the *motive* of the pure will; the moral law alone must be seen as the ground for making the highest good and its realization or promotion the object of the pure will" (*KpV/CPR* 109 [115]).

50. *PhR* §§137, 142–149, 151–156, 209–211, 217, 219, 258 Remark, 261, 272, 274.

51. *PhR* §§150, 154, 157, 182–183, 187, 189, 192, 197–201, 206–207, 209, 251–256, 258, 260–265, 300–303.

CHAPTER 2

Institutional Normativity: The Positivity of Right

Kevin Thompson

In §3 of the *Grundlinien der Philosophie des Rechts* Hegel claims that "right is in general *positive* ("das Recht ist *positiv* überhaupt")."[1] Although it articulates one of the core doctrines that, along with the account of freedom, form the conceptual framework within which Hegel constructed his distinctive theory of right, this paragraph has typically been neglected by commentators. Insight into it is thus of vital importance for gaining a clearer understanding of the normative theory that the *Grundlinien* attempts to establish. In fact, lack of attention to this text has led to a general failure to discern the central problematic of the *Grundlinien* and has contributed to a basic misunderstanding of the unique character of Hegel's approach to political thought.[2] Thus, in what follows, I argue that developing a proper understanding of this paragraph provides an important key to a comprehensive explication of Hegel's contribution to political philosophy. It presents us, however, with a twofold obstacle to its interpretation: the first, exegetical, the second, historical. Let us briefly examine each in turn.

The exegetical problem lies in an ambiguity in the central term of art Hegel employs. To designate something *positiv* can indicate either the mere existence of something insofar as it is without a rational foundation or justification, or it can express the positedness of something as being the necessary rational embodiment of an essence or principle. Now if the former sense is taken to be the meaning Hegel intends, then the text would seem to indicate that the primary concern of the *Grundlinien* is with the mere existence of right in its various manifestations, for example, in the laws, customs, and practices of a specific state or society. Hegel does draw a distinction in the paragraph at issue between what he calls the form and the content of the positivity of right. The content, he maintains, refers to right's historical appearance in terms of the specific character of a nation, its application through a legal code to particular kinds of objects and actions, and its employment in a court system with regard to judgments concerning individual cases. The form refers, he says, to the recognition of right as a valid authority governing public affairs and human conduct and that, as such, it forms the principle enabling a scientific comprehension of right itself (PR §3).

Following this distinction, it has been tempting to read Hegel's discussion of *Sittlichkeit*, in particular, as an elaboration of the historically embedded character of political life. As such, it appears to be a work of *positive Recht*, concerned solely with the *content* of right. But Hegel clearly rejects accounts that appeal to the historical emergence of legal practices, that is, "as they appear in time" (PR §3A), arguing that such accounts are insufficient for addressing the properly philosophical concern with the justification of the validity (*Gültigkeit*) and authority (*Autorität*) of right (PR §3A). It seems then we ought to conclude that the real issue with which the Grundlinien is concerned is not the content but the *form* of right and so see Hegel's work as a continuation, albeit to be sure not an uncritical member, of the tradition of modern natural law; a work of *Naturrecht*.[3]

But this, too, fails to recognize the uniqueness of Hegel's approach. In the *Enzyklopädie* he takes note of what he believes is a deep ambiguity in the term *Naturrecht*. It can be understood, he tells us, as it has traditionally—to refer to right as it exists in an "immediately natural manner" such that legal codes and state authority are understood to constitute a "restriction" (*Beschränkung*) on natural freedom (E §502A). But the term may also refer, Hegel argues, to right insofar as it is determined by the "nature of the matter" (*die Natur der Sache*), "the Concept" (*Begriff*) (E §502A). Now Hegel, of course, identifies his own project with this latter signification of the term and it is in this sense that he endorses it, including it even as part of the alternate title of the *Grundlinien: Naturrecht und Staatswissenschaft im Grundrisse*.[4] But what precisely does it mean to comprehend right as it is determined by the "nature of the matter, the Concept"? Moreover, if the concern that organizes the *Grundlinien* is neither simply the form nor the content of right, then just what is it?

A proper answer to these questions is further obscured by the fact that the historical context from which Hegel's categories and theorems emerged has largely been forgotten. The remark to §3 clearly indicates this context through its careful separation of a genuinely philosophical approach to the question of right from concern with the historical development of practices and institutions of right, a concern that had been characteristic of the work of Gustav Ritter von Hugo and his influential student Friedrich Carl von Savigny, and of the so-called Historical School of Right to which they gave birth. But Hegel's discussion fails to reveal the full contours of the problematic within which he seeks to set out his own distinctive position. This problematic was not in any sense particularly new, but it took on a special urgency in what came to be known as the *Kodifikationsstreit*; specifically, in the debate between Anton Friedrich Justus Thibaut and Savigny that began in 1814 around the question of drafting a new legal code for the German states of the post-Napoleonic order. The significance of this intellectual dispute, however, transcends mere philological interest. At the core of the debate between Thibaut and Savigny lay the question of the source of the authority of right, the locus of normativity, and its relationship to political institutions. A proper understanding of Hegel's discussion of the positivity of right thus requires us to recover this neglected point within the conceptual space from which his political philosophy emerged. Only after having done so, can one truly begin to understand the distinctive character of Hegel's work and, more specifically, his theory of normativity and its relationship to the institutions of the political sphere.

In what follows then, I argue that the answer, for Hegel, to the question concerning the comprehension of right lies in demonstrating the necessity of the interrelation between right's form and its content, between its recognition as a validly binding authority and its historical development, application, and actual employment. In short, comprehending right as it is determined by the Concept requires showing its necessary positedness, or, as Hegel says, why "right must become positive" (PR §3A). In order to do this, one must establish how the authority of right is valid only insofar as such authority becomes actual, that is, takes on a definite form. The *Grundlinien* fulfills both of these tasks. In so doing, it provides us with what I will call an account of institutional normativity.[6] This phrase designates the set of binding requirements laid on public conduct and interaction in and through the various institutional structures of the family, civil society, and the state, the "circle of necessity whose moments are the *ethical powers* (*sittlichen Mächte*) which govern the lives of individuals" (PR §145). The positivity of right is an expression of Hegel's thesis that the normative force of such requirements, their claim that it is right that they be obeyed, is dependent on their being embodied in certain sorts of institutional arrangements. The legitimacy of these claims requires, then, that they possess a specific type of concrete existence. This means that the form of right and its content are, for Hegel, necessarily dependent on one another to be what they most truly are. This doctrine, in turn, is rooted in Hegel's conception of genuine autonomy and, in particular, in his demonstration that the normative appeal of political institutions arises solely from their being embodiments of true freedom. I believe that Hegel's account of institutional normativity and its foundation in his view of autonomy together mark the true distinctiveness of his work in political philosophy and that it is the question of their union that ultimately proves to be the organizing problematic of the *Grundlinien*.[7]

The essay is divided into three parts. I begin with a précis of the debate between Thibaut and Savigny, focusing particularly on the deeply philosophical problematic that was ultimately at issue in this conflict (I). I then turn to more directly exegetical matters and examine Hegel's account of the relation between right and autonomy, his theory of institutional normativity, as a response to this historical debate. I also discuss the institutional formations genuine autonomy requires by investigating Hegel's account of civil society, where right is shown to become necessarily positive in specific and concrete forms (II). I conclude by returning to the relationship between the form and content of right and examine how Hegel's response to the problems at issue in the debate over codification reveals the organizing problematic of the *Grundlinien* (III).

I. THE *KODIFIKATIONSSTREIT*

The controversy surrounding the attempts to draft a unified German legal code began primarily as a dispute over the appropriateness of such an undertaking. However, the conflict quite quickly became multilayered and its external appearance subsequently hid the deeper philosophical dimension that was of such importance to its original participants. To borrow a metaphor, the controversy had what can be called an *outer shell*—the question of whether a single German legal code should be drafted, an *inner layer*—a dispute over the role of the professoriate in the practice of creating legal statutes, and, finally, an *inner core*—the question of the locus of the normativity of right itself.[8] To understand the significance of the controversy and especially the way in which it set a specific context for Hegel's thought, we must briefly examine the intertwining of these various layers as they emerged in the pamphlets Thibaut and Savigny published in 1814.[9]

Before doing so, however, a word of caution is in order. Most discussions of the debate present Thibaut and Savigny as strictly opposed combatants in a kind of intellectual duel: Thibaut on the side of democracy, cosmopolitanism, and the authority of Reason, and Savigny fighting in defense of aristocracy, nationalism, and the authority of History.[10] This rather simplistic account, however, fails to capture the substantial degree of consensus within which the controversy actually emerged. The debate grew out of the widespread rejection of the so-called *Code Napoléon* (or *Code Civil*, as it was officially designated) in the formerly French-held territories.[11] August Wilhelm Rehberg articulated this sentiment particularly well in a work published early in 1814 arguing that the imposition of such a code was illicit and an attempt, through its appeal to the freedom and equality of all, to eradicate the recognition of historically significant social differences among the various Germanic peoples.[12] It was in this climate that many influential jurists, among them Gustav Hugo and Karl Ernst Schmid, began to advocate two basic ideas: that Roman law, specifically the *Corpus Iuris Civilis*, be accepted as the common law of the German lands, and that legal scholars be entrusted with the task of creating further legal statutes.[13]

Thibaut found himself, on the one hand, generally sympathetic to Rehberg's rejection of the *Code Napoléon*, although he was severely critical of both the style and reasoning that lay behind it. On the other hand, he also clearly believed that endorsing Roman law was an inappropriate course since there was an important historical gap between the experiences of the Romans of the Justinian period and the German peoples of the nineteenth century. The impetus for Thibaut's entry into this developing controversy was thus twofold: (1) to set forth what he believed was the foundation for a genuinely native legal code, and (2) to argue against turning the process of codification over to the professoriate. In seeking to fulfill these aims, however, he deepened the conflict such that the very nature of the authority of right itself came to be at issue.

Thibaut's contribution, *Über die Notwendigkeit eines allgemeinen bürgerlichen Rechts für Deutschland* (1814),[14] shared a Romantic concern, already evident in Rehberg, Schmid, and Hugo, with the renewal of Germany. They all believed this could be accomplished through the unification of its various states. The work also shared a kind of nostalgia for the superiority of things that predated the Enlightenment, and Thibaut even adamantly employed the Romantic appeal to the *Volk* and *Volks-ideen* in making his case. He argued that adopting Roman law would constitute nothing other than another imposition of foreign principles on German soil. What was required instead, he maintained, was a revival of the native legal forms that had been present before the revolution of the sixteenth century. Such a renewal could take place only if the people (*Volk*), what he also called "the civil community" (*das bürgerliche Wesen*), were allowed, through the process of codification, to create their own comprehensive system of rule that would govern the entirety of the German lands. Thibaut believed this would keep the welfare of the German people out of the hands of the professoriate, with its concern for philological rigor, and return it to its proper home in the educated citizenry. In this way, Thibaut argued, a vital and sustainable union could be created between the people and its legal system.[15]

What lay behind this appeal to the people, and more specifically to its educated members, was Thibaut's belief that the ultimate principles of right were accessible to all rational beings.[16] The power of reason alone, he maintained, could discern the appropriate standards of public conduct because a comprehensive system of morality already existed within the practices that had been most recently overrun during the period of Napoleonic rule. These ultimate standards could, through codification, be expressed in a set of positive legal statutes and corresponding institutions. This process could thus allow an at once authentically native and universal body of law to emerge that, in its general applicability, would unite the various German states. The foundation for such a code, and the ultimate basis for Thibaut's endorsement of this Enlightenment ideal, was, he argued, the moral order that thrived in these native legal forms, together with the ability of reason, if properly educated, to ascertain the principles of this system. This meant then that, in Thibaut's judgment, the very possibility of codification lay in a set of discernable moral verities, a set of laws of reason, that could provide a foundation for the civil positive law, the proposed legal code. Hence, the basis for the authority of such an instrument, and the key to its universality, was the natural moral order already embedded in the native practices of the Germanic peoples. Thibaut's stand on the question that was to be at the core of the debate with Savigny was thus clear: the locus of normativity is a transcendent moral order, the natural law, from whence all legal codes and institutions derive their authority.

Savigny's contribution, the more famous *Vom Beruf unsrer Zeit für Gesetzgebung und Rechtswissenschaft* (1814),[17] was a direct and, in many ways, polemical response to Thibaut and, at the same time, a wide-ranging systematic program for historical investigation into legal structures and practices. Savigny shared the goal of reviving Germany through unification with the debate's other participants. He went so far in fact as to affirm the desire to accomplish this aim through the eventual production of a stable system of law. The conceptual foundations on which he drew to construct his response were, as they had been for Thibaut, largely those of Herder and the early Romantics. There was thus a substantial degree of continuity between the disputants. What vehemently divided them, of course, was, at least on the surface, the issue of codification. But underneath this lay a different conception of the proper role for the professoriate and, at its core, a very different view of the source of the binding authority of legal codes.

Savigny rejected Thibaut's proposal because he believed that the ideal Thibaut endorsed grew out of a loss of sensitivity, emergent especially in the Enlightenment, to the limited and historical character of reason. For Savigny, genuine attention to the historical traditions and practices of the German peoples in all their varied peculiarity required, foremost, recognition of the finite character of reason and its impotence before the task of constructing explicit legal prescriptions. Hence, even the idea of proposing a truly universal code in and of itself neglected the very particularity of the societies for which such an instrument was supposed to provide guidance, order, and structure. Accordingly, such a code could be, he argued, nothing other than a sterile set of rules that would fail to fit the diverse peoples it was to govern.

Savigny countered Thibaut's charge that Roman law was a system alien to the German states by showing that careful examination of the various traditions of these societies revealed that Roman law had already been virtually incorporated into the practices of these societies. In doing so, Roman law had become in effect German. And yet, Savigny maintained, because the German peoples were separated from one another, both physically and spiritually, and thus without a fixed and unifying locality, their traditions lacked any sense of deep coherence with one another; they did not form an integrated line of development. Savigny concluded that in order to form a system of law sensitive to the radical diversity of these traditions it would be necessary to have jurists who not only possessed the ability to relate legal concepts to one another in a systematic fashion, but ones that also had an understanding of the mass of historical detail about the societies that they served. The joining of these concerns, what Savigny famously called the "systematic" and the "historical," defined for him the proper vocation of the modern jurist.

But Savigny believed that such scholars were lacking in his own time. And thus the people were not yet adequately prepared for the process of codification. Hence, he believed this task had to fall to the scholars most familiar with the legal principles and tradition that had effectively become common law, the Romanists. They alone, he claimed, were equipped to act on behalf of the people. Through the protection afforded them by the academy—a freedom Savigny was especially fervent in upholding—these jurists could publish treatises, without threat of state sanction, that judges could in turn employ in crafting their decisions, thereby setting the precedents which would in effect become the system of law for the various states. Savigny thus concluded that, paradoxically, it was only under the "rule of the jurists" that the spontaneous living order between the people and their legal forms that Thibaut had so desired could be created.

The basic thesis underlying Savigny's case for this conservative reform, then, was his appeal to the centrality of historical tradition for the creation of legal statutes. This insistence could be read as merely a call for historical reflection in a discipline, namely jurisprudence, where such insight was normally lacking. But Savigny claims that not only must the systematic concerns of legal scholarship be joined with knowledge of the historical circumstances from which the legal concepts in question arose, but that it is in fact only in light of these circumstances that legal principles are able to be placed in their proper relationship with one another and so form a truly systematic and organic whole. Savigny thus moved beyond a simple demand for including history as a matter of concern for legal research. He instead appealed to history as the ultimate standard, the ultimate authority, for legal science itself. Hence, insofar as he believed judges must ultimately have recourse to this science in rendering their decisions, and thus in the act of lawmaking itself, it is history for Savigny that created the binding authority of legal statutes. The various kinds of institutions needed to embody these principles were thus themselves justified by their historical emergence rather than through their inherent rationality. In short, then, the locus of normativity for Savigny was history itself, the historicality of right.

The dispute between Thibaut and Savigny was thus not simply confined to the question of codification, nor merely to the duty of the professoriate. Although it was sustained, as we have noted, by a substantial degree of consensus, the issue contested at its core—the locus of normativity—was a deeply philosophical matter. The legacy of the debate can be summarized in the form of a familiar dilemma: either the foundation of the authority of right lies in a natural moral order and the ability of human reason to discern its principles, or it is to be found in the historical development of a specific society and the sensitivity of its scholars in uncovering the intrinsic legal forms of its traditions. This dilemma set the parameters for subsequent discussions throughout the German states of the nature of right and its relationship to political institutions, and it was thus of crucial importance in subsequent attempts to develop an understanding of the normative foundations of the institutions of political life. If, on the one hand, the bindingness of such institutions was thought to be grounded in some transcendent moral order, then these institutions would be structures merely mirroring natural forms, and thereby possess no intrinsic normative significance. On the other hand, if their validity was grounded in a society's historical development, then their authority would be nothing other than an expression of the power obtained by those dominant within the culture. In more general terms, then, given the space opened by the *Kodifikationsstreit*, political institutions were, it seemed, doomed to be either wholly superfluous or wholly coercive.

Hegel sought to rethink precisely this space, and he did so by calling the dilemma itself into question.[18] His aim was to produce an account of the normativity of institutions that avoided the types of reductionism he believed stood on either side of the debate, whether a reduction of the normative to nature or to history. Neither one, he thought, captured the distinctive status and purpose of institutions within society. In the main, however, his remarks were directed against Savigny, his intellectual rival in Berlin, and the Historical School he founded. Eduard Gans, Hegel's influential student and editor, famously continued this polemic and, unfortunately, left the impression that Hegel simply sided with Thibaut, his friend from his days at Heidelberg, and the so-called Philosophical School in the debate.[19]

But Hegel proposed something much more radical, a rethinking of both the source of right itself and its relation to societal institutions. What this required, he believed, was an account that did justice to both the objectivity and normativity of these sorts of institutions. In order to achieve this goal, he argued, the locus of normativity itself, the source of right, had to be reconceived in terms of human autonomy. In doing so, of course, Hegel was following in the tradition of Kant, Fichte, and the early Schelling. But what he believed was fundamentally lacking in this legacy was an adequate understanding of the intrinsic relationship between autonomy and the concrete institutions of society. Achieving this, he argued, required a rethinking of the nature of autonomy itself. If autonomy could be shown to be the ultimate source of normativity, and specific institutional forms could be demonstrated to be necessary to autonomy's fulfillment, then the claims placed on us by these institutions would be justified and their function established as both integral and necessary. In other words, because they were necessary for the fulfillment of autonomy, their existence would be intrinsic to right itself. Such institutions would be then at once objective and normative. This is precisely the project Hegel set for himself in the *Grundlinien* and it is, as our examination of the historical context has suggested and as we can now explore in more detail, the impetus behind his claim that "right must become positive" (PR §3A).

II. AUTONOMY AND RIGHT

The connection among the concepts of freedom, institutions, and positivity is clear in the introduction to the *Grundlinien*, but it is made most concrete in the account of civil society. Hegel's argument in essence is that the distinctive activities of this sphere bear within them a set of normative standards and that these activities can only be genuinely autonomous if these standards are given institutional form. Hence, the normative criteria inherent within the activities of civil society must become positive if these activities are to be genuinely free. In this sense, then, autonomy serves as the foundation for Hegel's claim that right must become positive. With this general sketch now before us, let us turn to an examination of the salient details of Hegel's analysis of freedom.

In the introduction to the *Grundlinien*, Hegel argues that right is grounded in autonomy and that the system of right is a system of institutions of freedom. It is well known that his examination of the structure of a genuinely free will shows that true autonomy lies neither in the will's ability to abstract itself from any limitation, its ability to engage in "pure reflection into itself" (PR §5), nor in its capacity to will something definite, its "*positing* of a determinacy as a content and object" (PR §6), but rather in the joining of these opposed moments in an act whereby the will wills something definite while at the same time remaining related to itself, with itself (*bei sich*), in and through the object of its willing (cf. PR §7; E §§481, 484). This immanent progression, from abstract universality through particularity to concrete individuality, "*particularity* reflected into itself and thereby restored to *universality*," is, for Hegel, the basic structure of the will's "*self-determination*" (PR §7), its autonomy.[20] The link between the concept of right and this theory of freedom is established through the notion of actualization (*Verwirklichung*) (PR §1).[21] To become actual, for Hegel, is for something to come *necessarily* into existence. Hence, right is defined as "any existence (*Dasein*) in general which is the *existence* of the *free will*" (PR §29, cf. E §486). Since to fulfill this condition requires the existence in question to be such that the will can be with itself in this otherness, the science of right can be said to be the progressive actualization of freedom and the institutional system of right to be this progression's concrete embodiment.

Although this theory is familiar to most readers of the *Grundlinien*, two aspects of it are often overlooked: (1) the way in which the conceptual progression in the structure of autonomy lays the foundation for Hegel's claim concerning the positivity of right, and (2) how this conceptual foundation is employed in his actual demonstration of this claim in the account of civil society. The key to the former lies, to employ the language of the *Enzyklopädie*, in the union of theoretical and practical spirit (E §481).[22] That is, in the role thought (*Denken*) plays in the passage from the will's willing something definite to its being with itself in and through the object of its willing (PR §§4A, 1A). The key to the latter lies in the relationship between the activities of formation Hegel sets out in his account of civil society and the institutions that are necessary for these activities to be genuinely self-determining. Together these moments serve to show why what Hegel takes to be the fundamental concepts of right, the normative standards of personhood and subjectivity, must become institutionally embodied. This demonstration thus constitutes the core of his theory of institutional normativity. Let us examine each of these matters in turn.

A. *Thought and Autonomy*

Hegel argues that when the will engages in its distinctive activity, when it wills something definite, it is confronted by a variety of different sorts of objects: needs, inclinations, external things, and relations with other individuals (PR §§9–12; E §§471–472, 483). The will can, of course, abstract itself from any of these, and so in this sense it can be unrestricted. But the will's activity is, for Hegel, fundamentally a "positing" (*setzen*) (PR §6) in which it takes up and appropriates these various objects in view of a set of ends. In this sense, the will is engaged in a process of positing over, what Hegel calls "translating" (*übersetzen*), the realizing of these ends in an objective realm (PR §§8, 9). This means that the activity of positing is bound to the objects it confronts because it is only in and through them that the will can express itself. However, since these objects possess no inherent structure, no ordering of them into some type of rational hierarchy, the judgment whether to realize one end over another, whatever its basis, must be a purely contingent, arbitrary act. A definite criterion to serve as a guide for the will is missing. The result is that the will is in contradiction with itself. It is unrestricted and at the same moment tied to its own objects; at once, free and bound.

The resolution of this contradiction, and the progression out of the concept of the will as a mere positing, requires that the immediate and natural character of these objects be abolished so that they can be appropriated by the will, as Hegel says, taken possession of by it, as truly its own. Only in this way can they become a "rational system of the will's determination" (PR §19). Insofar as the objects that confront the will remain mired in the immediacy and contingency of their natural givenness, they appear simply as empirical givens and thus without any discernable ranking whereby the will could be guided to select one object over another. The unique function of thought here, then, is to grasp a hierarchy that lies underneath this immediacy, and in so doing thereby take possession of them. Thought does this by categorizing, distinguishing, and comprehending the given objects in accordance with the forms that subjectivity brings to this encounter (cf. E §§465–468).[23] Hence, the determinations of the objects of the will are the same as the determinations of thought itself. Their rational ordering is nothing other than the ordering necessary for them to be objects of thought at all. Thus, insofar as thought guides the will, its self-determining can be said to be, at the same time, a raising of these objects out of their immediacy and natural determinacy into their own proper categories, grasping them then as the rational system they implicitly already are.

Hegel lays out this process in terms of the union of practical spirit, the will, with theoretical spirit, thought, a union he calls the "will as free *intelligence*" (E §481; cf. PR §21A). This is a process of discriminating among the objects confronting the will and evaluating them in terms of the ends one seeks. It is an activity of formation (*Bildung*) (PR §20) in which the objects of the will are freed from their natural immediacy, a process Hegel terms a "*purification (Reinigung) of the drives*" (PR §19). Fundamentally, the "will as free *intelligence*" estimates, compares, and evaluates the diverse objects with which it is confronted with regard to the following aspects: (1) each object's relation with the others; (2) the means needed to obtain or fulfill them; (3) the consequences of obtaining or fulfilling them; and, finally, (4) their contribution to the general satisfaction of the will as a whole, what Hegel calls "*happiness*" (*Glück-seligkeit*) (PR §20; E §479), and later "welfare" or "well-being" (*Wohl*) (PR §§114, 123, 183, 230; E §§505, 533). This evaluation classifies and ranks the objects and, insofar as this operation is ultimately guided by a concern with the will's general satisfaction, the resultant categorization is determined by the ends set by subjectivity itself. Happiness or well-being thus functions as the criterion needed to choose among the various objects of the will. In that this criterion is set by the activity of thought, the will is rationally determined and thus is genuinely autonomous. In organizing the objects of the will in this way, thought is a "*taking possession*" (*Besitznahme*) (E §468) of these objects and they are thereby moved out of their natural immediacy into a rational ordering that, by categorizing them, confers on them "*formal universality*" (PR §20). Consequently, thought enables the will to be with itself in its object in that it is the process of thinking that determines the hierarchical relations of the will's objects. However, since this ordering is for Hegel a determination that is immanent within the objects themselves, this process also restores these objects to their own proper relations. Each is thereby brought back to what Hegel calls their "substantial essence" (PR §19). In this way, the true object of the will is itself, the "will as free intelligence." And in this self-relation all mere dependence has been eliminated and the will is thus truly free, with itself (*bei sich*), in and through its determinations.

The union of thought and will in free intelligence, then, is the key to understanding true autonomy. But it is also the key to understanding the necessary positedness of right. Specifically, the progression from the pursuit of satisfaction, construed as happiness or well-being, to genuine self-determination outlined above is, for Hegel, the conceptual structure that underlies his claim that "right must become positive" (PR §3A) and it is the role of thought that establishes this necessity. The full demonstration of this lies in the account of civil society.

B. *The Activities of Formation*

In the account of civil society Hegel is concerned with two basic determinations of the will. Its ability to abstract itself from any definite context and to its capacity to act in pursuance of its needs and aims. These are the moments whose rights are elaborated in the discussions of abstract right and morality, respectively: personhood and subjectivity. What the analyses of these sections show is that each concept, as a concept of right, lacks adequate justification when considered purely in terms of itself. Both find their foundation, Hegel shows, only in *Sittlichkeit*. They do so, most particularly, in the institutions of civil society. Specifically, Hegel here demonstrates how each of these concepts arises within the activities whereby families attempt to secure their own well-being and how these activities in turn establish the necessity of the institutionalization of each of these concepts, the positing of right. At the center of this account lies the function of thought in its guidance of the will's pursuit of satisfaction. Accordingly, a closer examination of the activities of this sphere is in order.

Hegel claims that individuals, and more specifically families, are incapable of self-sufficiency. To satisfy their needs they require access to and the usage of things that are external to them and consequently beyond their control. But these necessities cannot be freely acquired as purely natural objects. They are always already the "*property* and product of the needs and *wills* of others" (PR §189; cf. E §524). This means that as each head of a family in civil society seeks to fulfill their family's needs, the means at their disposal are always relationally dependent; the object required for their satisfaction possesses what Hegel calls "*being for others*" (*Sein für andere*) (PR §192).[24] However, the needs at issue here are not wholly peculiar. A set of commonly held but distinctly social needs develops through a process Hegel terms "*refinement*" (*Verfeinerung*) (PR §191).

The function of this process is to distinguish among needs as they are naturally given, what can be called natural necessities (e.g., food, clothing, shelter, etc.), and among the means required to fulfill them. To accomplish this, natural needs must be compared and contrasted with one another according to type. This requires that their most basic traits be abstracted from their concrete immediacy. And this is precisely the work of *"purification"* (*Reinigung*) (PR §19) Hegel attributed to thought in his account of the structure of autonomy. Here that process of formation (*Bildung*) raises the defining characteristics of natural needs to a level of formal universality by categorizing and arranging them in a rational hierarchical order based on the aims set by each family's ultimate well-being. With this basic ranking established, Hegel shows that a proliferation of genuinely conventional needs, what he calls "spiritual needs" (PR §194), is able to arise through collaboration among the various participants in civil society. However, insofar as the means needed to satisfy these spiritual needs as well as each family's natural necessities must be abstract, that is, that these means must be able to fulfill the needs of a variety of different sorts of families, and insofar as their fulfillment is dependent on others, a system of exchange of common goods is required, an intersubjective system of dependence, a "system of needs."[25] The activity of refinement requires such institutional interdependence as its foundation. But this entails that the system of needs will be governed by the intrinsic relations inherent within this activity. The one most important for our understanding of the necessary positedness of right is a repetition of the contradiction Hegel showed to be intrinsic to the structure of freedom itself.

Recall that when the will wills something definite it is said to be at once unlimited in that it can choose to realize any of its aims, and yet still bound, insofar as it is tied to external objects as the means to posit or achieve its ends. This inherent contradiction arises for the will confronted by both its natural and social needs. It is at once bound to them, to the extent that they are the sole means of engaging in action at all, and free from them in its ability to consider them abstractly in terms of their various types. The process of refinement produces a rational ordering of such needs, but it cannot in and of itself fulfill them. As such, each family is forced into dependence on others and thus is not genuinely self-determining. Hence, Hegel maintains that the contradiction between abstractness and determinacy uncovered in the structure of autonomy remains and becomes incorporated into the social activities whereby families interact productively with one another in the system of interdependence, the activities he terms *"liberation"* (*Befreiung*) (PR §194) and *"labor"* (*Arbeit*) (PR §196).

Liberation, for Hegel, is the process whereby each family head conforms to a basic set of conventions as demanded by the system of social relations. The social needs that arise out of the process of refinement establish a basic similarity among the heads of families. There is thus in the system of interdependence what Hegel calls a "demand for *sameness*" (*die Forderung der Gleichheit*) (PR §193).[26] Sharing similar needs is the fundamental criterion, Hegel argues, for *"being recognized"*

(*Anerkanntsein*) (PR §192) as a member of the social relation. Satisfaction of a family's basic needs thus requires the head of that family to conform to this criterion. This includes not only sharing the basic natural needs for food, clothing, and the like, but also adopting social customs and practices such as styles of dress and work routines. Hence, participants in civil society must purify their own immediate drives and inclinations in accordance with social convention. However, since, as we have seen, these conventions arise out of the process of refinement, the family heads, for Hegel, are acting in accordance with their own intersubjective expansion of their most immediate needs. Hence, Hegel is able to reach a rather paradoxical conclusion: the necessity of conforming is a distinctly "self-made necessity" (PR §194). It is only by acting in accordance with these intersubjectively created constraints that each family's well-being, in terms of both its natural and spiritual needs, can be genuinely satisfied.

However, mere compliance with these conventions is not enough. In order to obtain the means for satisfying the needs of his own family, each family head must also produce goods that can satisfy the distinctly social needs of other families. This is what Hegel calls labor and he defines it as the acquisition, preparation, and production of means for the satisfaction of the natural and spiritual needs of the society. Such needs must become, Hegel argues, labor's "end-determination" (*Zweckbestimmung*) (PR §193). Labor, too, is an activity in which the producer limits and constrains their capacities, purifying their drives, in accordance with the will of others. Hegel therefore describes it as a "habit of *objective* activity and *universally* applicable skills" (PR §197).

And yet, in each of these activities of formation, the structural contradiction remains. Liberation and labor both serve as means for translating (*übersetzen*) the subjective ends of families, principally their concern with their own welfare, into an objective realm. The participants in civil society are thus at once unrestricted and yet still dependent. In the compliance of both activities to the standards set by society, there is a moment of abstract universality and freedom from externality. But in that same compliance, the dependency of each family, its needs both natural and conventional, is made evident as well. Hegel therefore concludes that by engaging in these practices and thereby conforming one's desires and inclinations to the standards implicitly set therein, each individual family head is recognized and conceived by the other members of society in terms of the most universal traits of societal membership. Hegel says that in these activities one is "apprehended as a *universal* person" (PR §209A; cf. E §529). At the same time, these activities reveal the specificity and uniqueness of human need, what Hegel calls the *"particular welfare"* (PR §230; cf. E §533) of each family. Thus, in these activities each member of civil society is recognized as being essentially the same as all other members, and as such as what Hegel calls a *person*, and, at the same time, as a distinct and particular member with specific needs, wants, and desires, that is, as what he calls a *subject*. As abstract universality and determinate particularity, personhood and subjectivity thus stand opposed in the carrying out of the activities of formation. How, then, is this decisive contradiction to be resolved? The answer, according to Hegel, lies in the nature of the institutions in which the activities of civil society have their ultimate fulfillment and foundation.

C. The Institutions of Freedom

Hegel has shown thus far that both liberation and labor are necessary for sustaining oneself and one's family. The critical point we must now consider is his claim that for these activities to be genuinely self-determining practices, the rights and duties attendant to the concepts they bring into recognition, namely, personhood and subjectivity, must be secured and provided for in a manner that possesses stability and objective permanence; that is to say, they must become actual and that means being embodied in concrete social institutions. These concepts function as standards both for being recognized as a legitimate participant in the system of interdependence, and as dependent on this same system. Their institutionalization, Hegel argues, derives from the necessity of ensuring the rights of both producers and consumers in the system of needs and this in turn is grounded in the requirement that both sorts of pursuits be genuinely autonomous.

What drives Hegel to conclude that certain specific institutions are necessary for the freedom of those in civil society is precisely the considerations concerning autonomy that were discussed above. The pursuit of satisfaction, for Hegel, must be accomplished not only in a way that simply provides for the needs pursued. That could be brought about through a myriad of systems without concern for the autonomy of its participants. What Hegel's theory of freedom and right requires is that such pursuits be fulfilled in a manner that enables the various participants in civil society to be self-related and thereby self-determining in and through these pursuits. The issue then is how to enable people to be genuinely free precisely in their striving for the fulfillment of their own and their families' welfare.

The account of autonomy has demonstrated that in general what makes this possible is the formative role thought plays in the positing of the will. The operation of the "will as free *intelligence*" has already been shown to be a key element in the process of refinement, establishing in particular that such a process could be self-governing since the ordering of both natural and spiritual needs on which it depends is an arrangement produced in and through intersubjective reflection, abstraction, and interaction. The function of thought in the activities of liberation and labor goes even further in that in order for each of these activities to fulfill the ends of providing for a family's well-being, they must take the needs of society as a whole as their guiding interests. This means that the needs as defined by all the families of civil society are to be the ends pursued in and through the system of interdependence. As we have seen, complying with this self-made constraint reveals those engaged in this pursuit as at once abstract persons and determinate subjects. These concepts, then, are the ultimate fruitions of the process of thought as it is operative in the various practices distinctive of civil society. As such, engaging in the activities of liberation and labor, under the guidance of thought, is to grasp these concepts, to know and recognize them, as appropriate norms governing this sphere of interaction (cf. PR §210). Since the process of thought reduces these concepts to their most basic forms, it presents these concepts to consciousness as universal binding standards of public conduct.

Hegel holds that this positing, as accomplished by thought, brings the concepts at issue into existence (*Dasein*) and that it thereby presents them as what they already were implicitly, the fundamental principles governing the system of needs (PR §212). In particular, by the very act of undertaking the activities of liberation and labor and thereby entering into compliance with the standards set by refinement, the participants in civil society are endorsing the concept of personhood as a legitimate norm for recognition as a member of the social relation. Hegel thus concludes that right is thereby given an *"existence"* (*Dasein*) such that it is *"universally recognized, known, and willed"* (PR §209; cf. E §529). In so doing, the members of civil society grasp one another as beings with the right to acquire and own property, to engage in binding contractual agreements, and as having a legitimate claim for redress when such rights are violated. Similarly, Hegel argues that in these same practices the participants in civil society are also recognized as subjects bearing a right to their own honor and to the attainment of their happiness and well-being (cf. PR §229; E §533). As such, the concept of subjectivity is likewise grasped as a legitimate norm for membership in the social relation. It, too, is recognized, known, and willed in and through these activities.

In this way, the contradiction between abstract universality and determinate particularity implicitly at issue in the activities of refinement, liberation, and labor becomes explicitly posited. But because both are presented as wholly formal aspects of each and every member of civil society, this positing is a placing of both in contradiction to one another in existence as universally valid standards. Hence, since this positing is necessary for the practices in question to be accomplished, both personhood and subjectivity must become actual. The bindingness of these norms, their "obligatoriness" (*Verbindlichkeit*) (PR §212) as Hegel says specifically of personhood, must take on institutional form. It is only in such an embodiment that the genuinely stable and objective permanence of these norms can be obtained. This means, then, that the rights accruing to each standard must be secured and provided for and this sets the purpose for each institution. For personhood, this is the function of the administration of justice (*Rechtspflege*); for subjectivity, it is the task of the public authority (*Polizei*) and the corporation (*Korporation*).[27]

But this positing merely transfers the contradiction inherent within the activities of civil society into the realm of institutional existence. The rights to property and welfare as determinations of the will's universality and its particularity respectively are, Hegel argues, in inherent conflict. For instance, taking the property of another for the sake of sustaining one's own life or that of one's family, out of the so-called "*right of need*" (*Notrecht*), is not the same as common theft and this, Hegel maintains, reveals the oppositional character of the relationship between the norms of personhood and subjectivity (cf. PR §§127–128). Hence, to be genuinely autonomous, the practices of civil society must not be torn between the competing claims of these norms, between the securing of property and the provision of welfare. Rather, these standards and the institutions that embody them must be joined together in a higher union that preserves the rightful claim of each. To put the problem explicitly in terms of the will, if the "will of all" in civil society is to become what Hegel calls a "substantial *will*" (PR §258), that is, a truly rational will in which all are self-determining, then these institutions must be bound together in an interdependent relation in the state, specifically in its legislative and executive powers (PR §§260–265, 287–297, 298–319).[28] Again, the role of thought is determinative here, for it is in thinking through their needs and interests, an activity afforded by the practices and institutions of civil society and the state together, that individuals and families are able to see that the particular ends they set for themselves are ultimately concretely universal ends they share with all others. Hence, the interests of the state, what Hegel calls the "interest of the universal" (PR §260), are just the interests of each and every individual, their "immanent end" (PR §261), and as such it is only in the unity of the institutional sphere of the state that the rights of personhood and subjectivity can be reconciled and the pursuit of familial satisfaction become genuinely self-determining.

The answer, therefore, to the question of how the contradiction inherent within the activities of civil society is resolved, as well as the answer to our more specific guiding question concerning the necessary positedness of right, is the same. True autonomy requires actualization. The will must take up its objects in such a way as to be fully with itself in and through them in order for it to be free. Hence, the activities of civil society—refinement, liberation, and labor—can be genuinely autonomous only if the standards they intrinsically develop are given concrete embodiment, that is, given an existence (*Dasein*) and thereby secured. The guidance of positing by thought requires such. To claim that right must become positive means, then, for Hegel, that what is right must not only be shown to be *implicitly* recognized and willed as legitimate by those under its governance, but that it must at the same moment become *explicitly* posited in the form of distinct institutions charged with the task of assuring the rights flowing from these standards. The administration of justice, the public authority, and the corporations, as institutions under the governance of the powers of the state, are thus all formations in and through which the wills of the families in civil society can be genuinely self-determining. In this sense, they are at once objective and normative. Their justification lies neither in their reflection of some transcendent moral order nor in their historical efficacy. Rather, their normative force arises from their foundation in the concept of autonomy and it is this conclusion announced in §3—that right must be posited—that comprises the nerve of Hegel's theory of institutional normativity. Hegel's account of civil society thus allowed him to obtain the goal he had set himself in response to the *Kodifikationsstreit*.

III. THE PROBLEMATIC OF THE *GRUNDLINIEN*

Let us conclude by returning to the set of issues raised by the *Kodifikationsstreit*. Hegel's discussion of each flows from his attempt to rethink the foundation of right itself. We can begin with the outer shell, codification. Hegel clearly affirms the right of a nation to create for itself a legal code (cf. PR §211A). The basis for this lies in his claim that the activities of civil society, as expressions of the "will as free intelligence," necessarily require that what they recognize, affirm, and will implicitly be made known explicitly and universally. This entails that a specific, simple, and public code laying down the regulations governing property and contracts and the punishments attendant on those who violate its statutes be created (cf. PR §§215–218). But he does argue that philosophy as a rational science can set forth only the most basic criteria for such a code; it cannot provide the kinds of details that would vary from society to society (cf. PR §216A). Such particulars must be left to the specific and intrinsic historical development of each state. Institutional normativity thus sets forth universal prescriptions concerning such matters as property and welfare. However, it cannot dictate the specific measures required for institutions of law and regulation to fulfill their necessary functions. The science of right, as a philosophical discipline, can provide only the foundation for such principles and set forth the necessity for certain specific institutions in order to embody these rights. It cannot prescribe the internal structures and procedures for such bodies. In this way, Hegel stakes out a path joining the Enlightenment goal of Thibaut with the historical insights of Savigny without sacrificing the philosophical problem of the normative justification of societal institutions.

As for the inner layer, the role of the professoriate in creating legal statutes, Hegel holds that the creation of a public code can be performed either by the nation as a whole or simply by its juristic estate (cf. PR §211A). This would seem to be a decidedly noncommittal position, but it, too, follows from the theory of institutional normativity. A system of law for Hegel is not a creation of something wholly new. As we have seen, codification is the recognition and positing of the universality already present within the activities of civil society, the rights of personhood and subjectivity in particular. What is right implicitly in the structure of autonomy is made explicit through the creation of specific legal statutes. Thus, it matters little whether the entire nation or merely its scholarly community draws up the document since both must affirm the principles already inherent in the practices of civil society. Hegel does argue that the dispensation of right in the court system must itself be a process that is public and presided over by a professional judge (PR §§224–226). But the ultimate legal decision concerning specific cases lies for him with a jury composed of those from one's own estate and not with a collection of judges or scholars (PR §228). The right to such a court system, Hegel argues, arises because it is only in and through such an arrangement that both the defendant and society in general can find the process to be genuinely self-determining rather than simply in the control of a few. Hegel thus again here preserves the ideals of Thibaut with the historical sensitivity of Savigny, albeit again on a wholly new foundation.

Finally, then, the inner core, the locus of normativity. Hegel formulated this issue in terms of the relationship between the form and content of the positivity of right. The difference between the two is the difference between the legitimate authority of right and its institutional embodiments. The exegetical problem we confronted was to understand how the concept of positivity articulated the relationship between these elements. Our examination of the historical context revealed that what lies behind Hegel's claims is a fundamental conflict over the locus of the authority of right itself. Although Thibaut and Savigny proved to be irreconcilably opposed over this issue, what their conflict made abundantly clear to Hegel was that neither an appeal to a transcendent moral order nor to a society's historical tradition was sufficient to capture the truly distinctive normative character of public institutions. On either account, such entities become positive precisely in the sense of mere existence, wholly superfluous or dangerously coercive. Normativity and institutions, on these accounts, bore no intrinsic relation. The form and content of right were ultimately, in Hegel's terms, left asunder.

Hegel's response to this conflict, as we have seen, was to rethink the options this debate took to be exhaustive. Starting from an investigation of autonomy, he was able to demonstrate an intrinsic relationship between right and specific institutions. His analyses of the activities inherent in the sphere of civil society and his understanding of the role of thought in such activities proved that the standards immanently developed within them, personhood and subjectivity, must necessarily take on institutional form. The authority of these standards, their normativity, arose then from their being recognized and affirmed by those engaged in these activities and their institutionalization and their union in the state emerged from the requirement that these activities be genuinely self-determining. On Hegel's account, then, the form and content of right are joined in and through the positing nature of an autonomous will as it is governed by thought. The concept of positivity, then, as the necessary positedness of right, articulates a mutual interdependence between right's form and its content. Without the authority of right, institutions are without ground. Without institutions, the authority of right is merely a vacuous chimera. The normative force of institutions flows, then, from the nature of autonomy. Thus, the claims placed on human conduct by these institutions are rooted in the nature of freedom itself. Positivity, as the expression of the will's distinctive activity, is thus the middle (*die Mitte*) that joins the form and content of right to one another in an articulated and indissolvable bond and this is the core of Hegel's theory of institutional normativity.

A general lesson, I believe, ought be drawn from our investigation. The *Grundlinien* should be viewed neither as a work of *positive Recht* nor of *Naturrecht*. It is something much more radical. It seeks to comprehend right as it is determined by the Concept. What this means, as I hope to have shown, is that its task is to understand the mutual interdependence of the form of right, its authority, and its content, its institutions. Hegel's uniqueness was to have set the theory of autonomy to work with the problem of institutions in a way that established their distinctly objective and normative status. This approach, of course, transformed not only the meaning of freedom, but the understanding of institutions as well. Hence, the organizing problematic of the science of right for Hegel is precisely the joining of right with the institutions of public life. This is what §3 teaches us and it behooves all those who would wrestle with the doctrines of this work to consider its centrality. It is only then that we may begin to gauge the truly revolutionary character of Hegel's work.

NOTES

1. All references to Hegel's writings are included in the text according to the following system of abbreviations. Paragraphs are cited by an '§' followed by the appropriate number, and the "Anmerkungen (Remarks)" are designated by the paragraph number followed by an 'A'.

PR   *Grundlinien der Philosophie der Rechts. Mit Hegels eigenhändigen Randbemerkungen in seinem Handexemplar der Rechtsphilosophie*, ed. Johannes Hoffmeister, 4th ed. (Hamburg: Felix Meiner, 1955); *Elements of the Philosophy of Right*, tr. H. B. Nisbet (Cambridge: Cambridge University Press, 1991)

E   *Enzyklopädie der philosophischen Wissenschaften (1830)*, ed. Udo Rameil, Wolfgang Bonsiepen, and Hans-Christian Lucas, *Gesammelte Werke*, vol. 20 (Hamburg: Felix Meiner, 1992)

2. This criticism does not apply to the work of Manfred Riedel and Armin von Bogdandy. See Riedel's "Dialektik in Institutionen," in his *Zwischen Tradition und Revolution. Studien zu Hegels Rechtsphilosophie* (Stuttgart: Klett-Cotta, 1982), 40–64, "Dialectic in Institutions," in *Between Tradition and Revolution: The Hegelian Transformation of Political Philosophy*, tr. Walter Wright (Cambridge: Cambridge University Press, 1984), 31–53, and Bogdandy's *Hegels Theorie des Gesetzes* (Munich: Karl Alber, 1989), esp. 81–92, 206–23. Bogdandy, however, focuses specifically on the concept of law as it is employed in civil society. My concern is to explicate Hegel's more basic doctrine on which that particular analysis is based.

3. Franz Wieacker draws a distinction between what he calls "natural law" (*Naturrecht*) and the "law of reason" (*Vernunftrecht*), arguing that the former properly designates the classical view of law, while the latter marks the transformation this view underwent in the seventeenth and eighteenth centuries. While I agree with the reasons underlying Wieacker's choice of this terminology, I here employ *Naturrecht* as a more general term covering the basic traits that remained constant throughout the changes he discusses, most principally, the foundation of law in a transcendent moral order. See Wieacker's *A History of Private Law in Europe*, tr. Tony Weir (Oxford: Clarendon Press, 1995), 199–275.

4. See Manfred Riedel, "Hegels Kritik der Naturrecht," in his *Zwischen Tradition und Revolution*, 84–115, "Criticism of Natural Law Theory," in his *Between Tradition and Revolution*, 76–104.

5. Some research has been done on this matter, but it mainly focuses on comparisons of Savigny and Hegel: see Hermann U. Kantorowiscz, "Volksgeist und historische Rechtsschule," *Historische Zeitschrift* 8 (1912): 295–325; and Wolfgang Schild, "Savigny und Hegel. Systematische Überlegungen zur Begründung einer Rechtswissenschaft zwischen Jurisprudenz und Philosophie," *Anales de la catedra Francisco Suarez* 18–19 (1978–79): 271–320.

6. For a survey of some of the recent work that has been done on the relationship between norms and institutions, see Hubert Rottleuthner, "Recht und Institution," in *Die Rationalität politischer Institutionen*, ed. Gerhard Göhler, Kurt Lenk, and Rainer Schmalz-Bruns (Baden: Nomos Verlagsgesellschaft, 1990), 337–55.

7. Among the few commentators to focus carefully on the role of institutions in Hegel's thought, see Manfred Riedel, "Dialektik in Institutionen," in his *Zwischen Tradition und Revolution*, 40–64, "Dialectic in Institutions," in *Between Tradition and Revolution*, 31–53, and Dieter Henrich, "Einleitung der Hersausgebers: Vernunft in Verwirklichung," in G. W. F. Hegel, *Philosophie des Rechts: Die Vorlesung von 1819/20 in einer Nachschrift*, ed. Dieter Henrich (Frankfurt am Main: Suhrkamp, 1983), 9–39, esp. 30–38.

8. I adopt this way of describing the *Kodifikationsstreit* from Frederick Beiser's discussion of the more widespread, but in many ways similar, Pantheism controversy of the late eighteenth century. See his *The Fate of Reason: German Philosophy from Kant to Fichte* (Cambridge, Mass.: Harvard University Press, 1987), chs. 2–4; the threefold layering of the debate is set forth on 47–48.

9. For useful studies of the debates and developments surrounding the introduction and eventual adoption of the Civil Code in Germany, see Elisabeth Fehrenbach, *Traditionale Gesellschaft und revolutionäres Recht. Die Einführung des Code Napoléon in den Rheinbundstaaten* (Göttingen: Vandenhoeck & Ruprecht, 1974), and Michael John, *Politics and the Law in Late Nineteenth-Century Germany: The Origins of the Civil Code* (Oxford: Clarendon Press, 1989).

10. Joachim Rückert presents a strident critique of this quite influential view in his *Idealismus, Juriprudenz und Politik bei Friedrich Carl von Savigny* (Ebelsbach: Rolf Gremer, 1984), 160–93.

11. On this point, see W. Schubert, "Das französische Recht in Deutschland zu Beginn der Restaurationszeit," *Zeitschrift der Savigny Stiftung für Rechtsgeschichte (Germanistische Abteilung)* 94 (1977): 129–84, and his *Das Französische Recht in Deutschland* (Cologne: Böhlau, 1977).

12. Anton Wilhelm Rehberg, *Über den Code Napoléon und dessen Einführung in Deutschland* (Hanover, 1814). For a discussion of the important role of Rehberg's work in the *Kodifikationsstreit*, see Hans Hattenhauer, "Einleitung," in *Thibaut und Savigny. Ihre Programmatischen Schriften*, ed. Jacques Stern (München: Franz Vahlen, 1973), 40–42.

13. Karl Ernst Schmid, *Deutschlands Wiedergeburt* (Jena, 1814).

14. Anton Friedrich Justus Thibaut, "Über die Notwendigkeit eines allgemeinen bürgerlichen Rechts für Deutschland," in *Thibaut und Savigny*, 61–94.

15. Most commentators generally miss this aspect of Thibaut's proposal. See, however, James Q. Whitman, *The Legacy of Roman Law in the German Romantic Era* (Princeton, N.J.: Princeton University Press, 1990), 104–5.

16. On this point, see Albert Kitzler, *Die Auslegungslehre des Anton Friedrich Justus Thibaut* (Berlin: Duncker & Humboldt, 1986), 13–22, 44–60.

17. Friedrich Carl von Savigny, "Vom Beruf unsrer Zeit für Gesetzgebung und Rechtswissenschaft," in *Thibaut und Savigny*, 95–192.

18. Jean-François Kervégan has taken up this issue, albeit in a direction different than that pursued here. See his "Le Droit entre Nature et Histoire: Hegel," in *Recht zwischen Natur und Geschichte/Le droit entre nature et histoire*, ed. Jean-François Kervégan and Heinz Mohnhaupt (Frankfurt am Main: Vittorio Klostermann, 1997), 223–56.

19. See Norbert Waszek, "L'histoire du droit selon Edouard Gans. Une critique hégélienne de F. C. von Savigny," in *Recht zwischen Natur und Geschichte/Le droit entre nature et histoire*, 257–80.

20. For useful studies of the introduction to the *Grundlinien*, see Robert Theis, "Volonté et liberté: Commentaire de l'Introduction à la Philosophie du Droit de Hegel," *Archiv für Rechts-und Sozialphilosophie* 65 (1979): 369–86, Donald J. Maletz, "An Introduction to Hegel's 'Introduction' to the *Philosophy of Right*," *Interpretation* 13 (1985): 67–90, "The Meaning of 'Will' in Hegel's Philosophy of Right," Interpretation 13 (1985): 195–212, Denis L. Rosenfield, *Politique et liberté: Une étude sur la structure logique de la Philosophie du droit de Hegel* (Paris: Aubier, 1984), 42–60, and Allen W. Wood, Hegel's *Ethical Thought* (Cambridge: Cambridge University Press, 1990), 36–52.

21. On this passage, see Robert Pippin, "Hegel's Political Argument and the Problem of *Verwirklichung*," *Political Theory* 9 (1981): 509–32, and "Hegel's Ethical Rationalism," in his *Idealism as Modernism* (New York: Cambridge University Press, 1997), 417–50.

22. On the unity of theoretical and practical spirit, see Stephen Houlgate, "The Unity of Theoretical and Practical Spirit in Hegel's Concept of Freedom," *Review of Metaphysics* 48 (1995): 859–81. Houlgate, however, focuses primarily on the significance of thought for the *awareness* of freedom itself rather than its import for the objects that confront the will.

23. For a more detailed discussion of the process of thought, see William deVries, *Hegel's Theory of Mental Activity* (Ithaca, N.Y.: Cornell University Press, 1988).

24. On the connection between needs and being-for-others, see Nathan Rotenstreich, "Needs and Interdependence," *Hegel-Studien* 19 (1984): 179–203.

25. On the normative and prescriptive character of Hegel's "system of needs," see Richard Dien Winfield, "Hegel's Challenge to the Modern Economy," in *Hegel on Economics and Freedom*, ed. William Maker (Macon, Ga.: Mercier University Press, 1987), 29–63, and his *The Just Economy* (New York: Routledge, 1990), esp. chs. 1 and 4.

26. The term *Gleichheit* can be translated several different ways: equality, similarity, likeness, even as identity. Given the context, I have chosen "sameness," since the qualitative rather than the quantitative connotations of the term seem most important here. See Hegel's discussion of the term, G. W. F. Hegel, *Wissenschaft der Logik. Erster Band. Die Objective Logik*, ed. Friedrich Hogemann and Walter Jaeschke, *Gesammelte Werke. Kritische Ausgabe*, Band 11

(Hamburg: Felix Meiner, 1992), 268–70, *Science of Logic*, tr. A. V. Miller (Atlantic Highlands, N.J.: Humanities Press, 1969), 419–21.

27. For a more thorough discussion of the administration of justice, see Armin von Bogandy, *Hegels Theorie des Gesetzes*, 76–117, and Roland Maspétiol, "Unité sociale et liberté de la 'Personne' dans la philosophie du droit de Hegel," in *Droit et liberté selon Hegel*, ed. Guy Planty-Bonjour (Paris: Presses Universitaires de France, 1986), 165–204.

On the public authority and the corporations, see Wolfgang Kersting, "Polizei und Korporation in Hegels Darstellung der bürgerlichen Gesellschaft," in *Hegel-Jahrbuch 1986*, ed. Heinz Kimmerle, Wolfgang LefÈvre, and Rudolf W. Meyer (Bochum: Germinal, 1988), 373–382, G. Heiman, "The Sources and Significance of Hegel's Corporate Doctrine," in Hegel's Political Philosophy: Problems and Perspectives, ed. Z. A. Pelczynski (Cambridge: Cambridge University Press, 1971), 111–135, and Friedrich Müller, Korporation und Assoziation. Eine Problemgeschichte der Vereiningungsfreiheit im deutschen Vormärz (Berlin: Duncker & Humboldt, 1965), 146–219.

28. On this problem, see Manfred Baum, "Gemeinwohl und allgemeiner Wille in Hegels Rechtsphilosophie," *Archiv für Geschichte der Philosophie 60* (1978): 175–98, esp. 188–91.

CHAPTER 3

Hegel on Political Identity and the Ties That Bind

Mark Tunick

Most of us feel we have ties, sometimes obligations or duties, to people we do not even know. I am in the High Sierras, hiking for days without having seen another human being. When I spot a hiker in the distance, I feel a tie, a connection, just because this is another human being. We will greet each other, and if we speak the same language, we will share our experiences. If she is low in provisions and I have extra, I will offer her some of mine. I feel I have an obligation, just because she is another human being.

I, an American, am in the Bavarian Alps, and for days have encountered only Europeans. When I come to a lake, I see an American couple. Not having had any contact with people from home, I walk over to them. We exchange news, and compare the Alps with the Sierras. We feel there is a bond between us, just because we are Americans.

I have just moved and am visiting my new primary care physician for a checkup. It turns out he is from my hometown in Florida, and attended my elementary school. We share some memories of our childhood, and compare where we grew up with where we are now. There is some sort of tie between us—not a very strong one, but still, there is some tie, just because we grew up in the same place.

We have all sorts of ties—to those with whom we work or go to school, to our friends, or those who live in our neighborhood; to those who practice our religion, or who share our interests. Class, race, age, interests, ethnicity, occupation, gender, religion, language, dialect, schooling, political judgments, shared experiences all can create ties among people, ties of varying strengths. Political theorists focus on one particular tie, which we single out from others as special: the tie among members of the same body politic.

"Body politic" is a concept the boundaries of which are difficult to draw. In ancient Greece it might have referred to a *polis*; in our day it usually refers to a state. It is easier to identify where there is a constitution that establishes membership and rights of citizens. The body politic is in part a juridical entity. But to belong to the body politic is not simply to be subject to the laws of the state. Resident aliens, subject to the laws of the United States but not sharing in all of the rights of citizenship—such as the right to vote, serve on juries, and qualify for some government jobs—and perhaps unfamiliar with the country's history and traditions, are connected in important ways to the body politic, but are not yet members, and may not fully identify with it. What makes a group of people a body politic? Why should they feel special commitments and ties to one another? What is it that they share?

This essay discusses G. W. F. Hegel's answer to these questions. Hegel refers to the modern state as our "ethical substance."[1] He alludes to the special sense "substance" has in philosophy. A substance is what exists independent of anything else. It is "original and underived."[2] If something is part of my substance, I could not exist without it. The sense of exist, here, is moral: to say the modern state is an ethical substance is to say that this state is essential to the *meaningful* existence of its members.[3] Hegel thinks the state is so important that we should be willing to give our lives for it. Of course some classical liberals, such as Locke, also thought one could be obliged to risk death in war; but where for Locke war is justified to protect life, limb, and property, for Hegel war is justified to preserve the common life of the community that makes each individual's life *worth living*.[4]

What is the basis of this common life that is supposed to engender such strong sentiments? It is easy to get the impression from his claim that the modern state is a substance that Hegel thinks its members form a tightly knit, culturally and ethnically homogeneous community. In the past Hegel's philosophy of the state has inspired nationalists and even racists.[5] My purpose in this chapter is to show just how little in fact Hegel thinks citizens of a modern state must share. A close reading of his texts suggests that he does not think they must be of the same race or ethnicity, or that they must speak the same language, practice the same religion, or even like each other. Indeed, once we see what he thinks they all must share, we may be puzzled by Hegel's claim that the state is our substance, something worth dying for.

In section I I show how Hegel, in contrast to other theorists, thinks there are substantial ties among members of a state, ties he thinks we should be willing to give our lives to preserve. Section II pinpoints what Hegel thinks citizens need *not* share. Having seen what does not bind citizens on Hegel's view, I offer some tentative remarks in section III on what Hegel thinks *is* essential to citizens' having an identity distinguishing them from people of other states.

I. THREE VIEWS

It will be helpful in situating Hegel's view of political identity to identify three competing accounts of the ties and special obligations we have to members of our state. On one view, there are no special ties. Thoreau suggests this when he reminds his countrymen "that they are men first, and Americans at a late and convenient hour," and that "the only obligation which I have a right to assume, is to do at any time what I think right."[6] Philosophical anarchists suggest this when they argue that "we are not *specially* bound to obey *our* laws or to support *our* government simply because they are ours."[7] Those who hold to what Joseph Tussman refers to as the 'power' conception suggest this as well. On this view, to be a member of a body politic is only to be "under the control of" a particular governing authority.[8] Members share nothing but a common master.

On a second view, a body politic "is a group of persons related by a system of agreements; to be a member of a body politic is to be a party to the system of agreements." A body politic, on this classical liberal account, is a "voluntary group" of members and agents, with rights and obligations based on consent.[9] Individuals create obligations by contracts and promises. They can do this with *anyone*, the argument goes, since all human beings of sound mind can promise or contract. What leads particular people to form bonds is contingent on with whom they happen to interact. Throughout history these have been people who live in the same territory and who encounter each other repeatedly. But in principle we can be bound to any other human being. For example, on Immanuel Kant's account, we enter a civil condition and form a common or general will through what Kant sometimes refers to as an "original contract" and agree to live under public laws that provide the conditions for putting into effect the moral laws that respect our innate rights and dignity as autonomous subjects.[10] But who is the "we" that enter into this contract? Why is it this "we" and not another? For Kant, what unites individuals in a general or common will is that they "can come into practical relations with one another" (MM 263). That there is a general will is a postulate derived a priori from reason (MM 338). The general will presupposes only that individuals come in contact with one another in ways that affect each other's rights, which they will do given the spherical shape of the earth (MM 311; cf. 263). A state consists of a group of people whose members "cannot avoid interacting" (MM 312). Eventually Kant thinks that "since the earth's surface is not unlimited but closed," we will come to interact with all human beings in a "community of all nations" (MM 352) and the right of nations will lead "inevitably" to a cosmopolitan Right (MM 311).[11] Liberal contractarians such as Kant implicitly rely on geographical proximity to account for who the we is. Not even an emotional tie to a place, just spatial proximity, connects fellow citizens.

Kant's cosmopolitan ideal has been echoed recently by Francis Fukuyama, who writes that "[a]s mankind approaches the end of the millennium, the twin crises of authoritarianism and socialist central planning have left only one competitor standing in the ring as an ideology of potentially universal validity: liberal democracy, the doctrine of individual freedom and popular sovereignty." This "global culture"—which presumably will replace Confucian, Japanese, Islamic, Hindu, Slavic, Latin American, and African cultures—is rational, right, and true; it is the only proper way of life for "adults." Fukuyama foresees the "political neutralization of nationalism" and a world devoid of "irrational" commitments to particular cultural, ethnic, or religious groups.[12]

What to Fukuyama are irrational commitments, to others are the bonds that make us who we are. There is a third view regarding the ties among members of the body politic. On this view, "habit and custom embodied in institutions are the unifying and stabilizing bases of social life."[13] If we had to place Hegel's position in one of these three categories it would fall here. Hegel, although a liberal in several respects, rejects the view that agreement of the sort that arises from a promise or contract establishes the bond between members of a body politic.[14] Hegel thinks fellow citizens have special ties, ties of such importance that we are willing to give up our lives to protect them,[15] but these ties are not contractual. Contractual ties are what he calls "abstract," to be distinguished from ethical ties. The practices constituting ethical life do not arise out of reciprocal agreements. Hegel also seems to oppose the implication Kant and others draw, that eventually there will be a single, liberal cosmopolitan community.[16] In characterizing the members of the modern state as sharing in an ethical substance, which is to say they share, among other things, practices, institutions, customs, laws, and a collective memory, none of which were explicitly consented to or chosen, and all of which help to foster a common political identity, Hegel implies that members of a state have an identity that is necessarily distinct from that held by members of other body politics with different forms of ethical life.

Hegel's view toward the power conception is more complicated. For Hegel, what identifies a group of people as a body politic is not simply that they are all under the control of the same power, but that they share in an ethical life. The practices of ethical life may have been at one point created by someone with power, by the mythical founder.[17] We learn their requirements through pedagogical coercion. At first, as children, we are "suckled at the breast of universal ethical life."[18] The practices and institutions of modern ethical life, which include private property, promising, contracting, legal punishment, marriage, raising children, and working at a job in civil society, are not chosen by us in some deliberative process. Rather, we are taught that we must respect property and keep our promises, and are pressured into getting married and working, without ever having a say about whether we should have these institutions. Hegel refers to this socialization process as *Bildung*. Hegel's idea of *Bildung* is of a culture that shapes and educates, through which we develop and mature.[19] Hegel emphasizes the etymological connection between *Bildung* and *Bild*, or picture. In his *Philosophy of History*, a compilation of lectures Hegel gave in Berlin, he says that prior to the Trojan War the Greeks lacked an ethical bond. But through his personal (as opposed to physical) strength Agamemnon assembled the Greeks and led them to victory, and the collectivity he created, while not resulting in a lasting political union, provided the foundation on which the Greek poets created an eternal picture of the youth and spirit of Greece; the poets created a *Bild* that became the basis of the *Bildung* (or *paideia*) which shaped Greek ethical life and expressed its "spirit."[20]

Hegel's account of political identity raises important questions and difficulties. Precisely what is it that Hegel thinks citizens of a modern state share that leads him to say they are an ethical substance, that they are part of something that is so important to their identity that they should be willing to risk their very lives for its protection? Are the ties among those who share in an ethical life (*Sittlichkeit*)—the ties forged by *Bildung*—political ties, or, rather, are they both less extensive, such as ties among family members, and more extensive, such as ties among those sharing a civilization, than the special ties unique to members of a body politic? Do the heterogeneous citizens of our modern states really have a common political identity, or, rather, in forging (by theorizing) a common identity among such a diversity is Hegel forced to tie the binds so loosely that they cannot resist the unlocking forces of cosmopolitanism, despite Hegel's apparent protests?

II. WHAT MUST BE SHARED BY MEMBERS OF AN ETHICAL SUBSTANCE?

Some may think it strange to claim that the state, often associated with bureaucracies, the military, and police, has the moral significance Hegel claims it does in saying it is our "substance." When we think of the ties that bind, we might think of friendship, love, family, religion, or even some of the other ties that are based on less deeply personal attributes we share with others, such as class, race, age, hobbies, sports, or schooling. Just what does Hegel think members of the state share that lets him say they share in one substance and have a common political identity?

One possibility, suggested in several passages, is that they share a connection to the same place, a natural tie to the land, or country. This is not the same argument we saw some classical liberals make, that what binds people is mere geographical proximity; rather, the suggestion is that a people may identify with the special character of the land they share, and it could become a unifying element, promoting shared activities, perceptions, and ideals. Daniel Kemmis, for example, offers an account of the importance of place to political community by arguing that the natural beauty of Montana provides a basis for a shared identity among the people there.[21] In his *Philosophy of Nature*, the second part of his three-part *Encyclopaedia*, also from his Berlin period, Hegel suggests, cryptically and briefly, that there is some connection between a people (*Volk*)—which, as I discuss shortly, is not necessarily coextensive with the members of a state—and the natural or geographical features of the land in which they reside:

> the Old World exhibits the perfect diremption into three parts, one of which, Africa, the compact metal, the lunar principle, is rigid through heat, a land where man's inner life is dull and torpid—the inarticulate spirit which has not awakened into consciousness; the second part is Asia, characterized by Bacchanalian extravagance and cometary eccentricity. . . . But the third part, Europe, forms the consciousness, the rational part, of the earth, the balance of rivers and valleys and mountains—whose centre is Germany.[22]

In his lectures on the philosophy of right, also of the Berlin period, Hegel says that "every people (*Volk*) has an immediate natural determination in itself, a particular character and geographical relation. The spirits of people do not differ by accident" (Rph I: 247, 466–71). In the *Philosophy of History*, Hegel devotes a lengthy section to the "geographic basis of world history" (PH, pp. 79–102), which he characterizes as "an essential and necessary basis" (PH, p. 79). Nature is important in that, for example, where a land is too frigid or torrid, world-historical peoples could not develop.

Hegel says nature's role "should not be rated too high nor too low" (PH, p. 80). He says that "the natural type of the locality" is "intimately connected with the character of the people which is the offspring of the soil" (PH, pp. 79–80), and he notes how land or climate affects the mode of production, or legal relations, and suggests that coastal lands are prone to empire, since "the sea gives us the idea of the infinite," stimulating man to "stretch beyond the limited" (PH, p. 90). Yet while he links the character of a people with land or soil, implying that a people may dress similarly in response to their land's climate, or eat similar foods because of the qualities of their land's soil, Hegel emphasizes other factors in accounting for ties among a people. In another passage from *Philosophy of History*, in which Hegel discusses the ties that bind Englishmen, no mention at all is made of ties to a place:

> Every Englishman will say: We are the men who navigate the ocean, and have the commerce of the world; to whom the East Indies belong and their riches; who have a parliament, juries, etc.—the relation of the individual to that Spirit is that he appropriates to himself this substantial existence, that it becomes his character and capability, enabling him to have a definite place in the world—to be something.[23]

The ties Hegel emphasizes here include not shared attitudes toward a place of common upbringing, but rather, shared accomplishments, memories, possessions, practices, and institutions.[24]

Natural geography or place plays some role for Hegel in shaping national identity. But even though he suggests that the character of *a people* (*Volk*) is linked to the soil from which they have sprung, it does not follow that Hegel thinks nature or geography plays a significant role in forging a common identity in *citizens of a state*. A *Volk* is not a state. Hegel casually acknowledges this in noting that all *citizens* of North America are of European descent (PH, p. 81).

In his major work on the modern state, *Philosophy of Right*, Hegel rarely points to the natural or geographical basis of shared identity among citizens, as opposed to among a *Volk*. He cites Montesquieu three times, but never echoes Montesquieu's well-known argument connecting the spirit of laws with geography.[25] In the *Philosophy of History*, Hegel does point, once, to the "natural features [of the state (*Staat*)], its mountains, air, and waters," as in part constituting the "existence" or "being" of its members.[26] But in the same passage he points to other features as well: "the history of this state (*Staat*) [are its members'] deeds; what their ancestors have produced belongs to them and lives in their memory. All is their possession, just as they are possessed by it; for it constitutes their existence, their being." Natural geography and place influence a people, helping to distinguish them from other peoples; they play a role in shaping what Hegel famously refers to as the spirit of a people (*Volksgeist*).[27] But it does not follow that Hegel thinks a shared spirit, or the tie to nature and place that plays some role in creating this spirit, are essential features of states, are what binds citizens.

In saying a *Volk* share a spirit Hegel suggests that they share an aesthetic sensibility, practice the same religion, have a similar philosophical outlook, speak the same language, and have similar dispositions and manners—something like what we mean in saying we possess a civilization or culture.[28] His Berlin period lectures on religion, on aesthetics, on philosophy, and on history all purport to show how history occurs in discrete stages, each stage typified by a *Volk* sharing a spirit reflected in its art, religion, and philosophy. But while a nation is inclined to form a state (PH, p. 498), a nation is not necessarily coextensive with the modern state. Although Hegel says that the state is the "spirit of the nation" and "the customs and consciousness" of its members (PR 274), and speaks of the "nation as state" (PR 331), in PR 344 he distinguishes states from nations. There are stateless nations,[29] and a nation may consist of several states—the Germanic people, for Hegel, include Franks, Normans, English, Scandinavians, and the peoples of France, Italy, Spain, and Portugal.[30] This suggests that the ties of a *Volksgeist* are not identical with the ties unique to members of a modern state.[31]

Hegel observes not only that a nation may consist of several states, but that people of different nations can be members of one state. In an important passage from the lecture notes of the philosophy of right, Hegel says:

> It can happen that a nation decays, becoming several states, but then the nation (*Nation*) loses its vigor (*Kraft*). But if different nations (*Nationen*) make up one state, the weakness of this state (*Staat*) can only be overcome through amalgamation (*Amalgamierung*), after centuries. This is what happened with the Jews, who have their own religion and politics . . . they hold fast to their religion and exclude all others on the basis of their religion, and do not even eat or drink with non-Jews. Insofar as the Jews have their principles in their religion, which makes impossible their being connected with (*Verbindung*) other citizens and hinders the unity of the state (*Staateinheit*), it might seem necessary to exclude the Jews from the state. But such exclusion is not necessary. . . . Ethical life (*Sitten*) and universal rationality overcomes this disharmony, and subdues the principle [of the Jews].[32]

A state can overcome the weakness of nationalist and religious diversity when it amalgamates. Unfortunately, Hegel does not make clear the distinction between amalgamation and assimilation. In this passage Hegel refers to ethical life "subduing the principle" of the Jews ("Die Sitten sind es, die das Prinzip ueberwaeltigen"—"the principle" must refer to *die Juden Prinzipien*, to which Hegel had just referred). Hegel isn't clear about what "subdue" implies here, to what extent it means assimilation. I believe his use of "amalgamation" is intended to imply that while the Jews have their own religion and culture, and eat and drink among themselves, they are still part of the diverse modern state—they are at once citizens and Jews. While Hegel says that amalgamation will take centuries and implies that it will be an arduous process, he does not seem to think that this process is the exception, and the perpetuation of homogeneous nation-states the rule. As the final line of the passage makes clear, "universal rationality" triumphs over cultural particularity. This does not mean that Jews, or members of other cultures, give up their ways; but it does mean that they become part of a rational ethical life incorporating other peoples. As is apparent in the very structure of the *Philosophy of Right*, in which the section on the modern state pre-supposes the discussion of civil society, which Hegel characterizes as a sphere of particularity and difference, for Hegel modernity consists in part in an arduous, long, but inexorable process of amalgamation—the creation of a new political identity that preserves previous cultural identities.

The passage just cited from the lectures not only points to the distinction between modern states and nations, but also makes clear that Hegel does not think members of the state must practice the same religion. He suggests that religion, on the contrary, tears a state apart—it "has made the greatest contribution to annulling the state."[33] In the *Philosophy of Religion*, also of the Berlin period, Hegel suggests members of a *nation* inherit their religion: "[the] national spirit constitutes the substantial foundation . . . it is the absolute ground of faith. By this standard it is determined what counts as truth . . . all individuals are born into the faith of their forefathers."[34] But in the *Philosophy of Right* Hegel argues that the *state* should tolerate different religions, even that of Quakers, whose religion makes demands that conflict with the demands of the state:

> a state which is strong because its organization is fully developed can adopt a more liberal attitude in this respect, and may completely overlook individual matters which might affect it, or even tolerate communities whose religion does not recognize even their direct duties towards the state (although this naturally depends on the numbers concerned).[35]

Hegel's parenthetical caveat that the toleration the state can extend to minority religious groups will depend on the size of these groups is not a recantation of his belief that a rational modern state incorporates multiple religions. Rather, it addresses the difficult issue of conflicts of duties. Even in the United States, which provides religious groups a significant degree of constitutional protection, accommodation to religious practices that clash with laws is limited by practical necessity.

Religion can be the basis of community, but is not a tie needed to bind members of a modern state.[36] That Hegel distinguishes the state from "communities" within the state such as the Quakers indicates the complexity of his views on political identity, a complexity largely unacknowledged by those who assume that for Hegel the modern state is an internally homogeneous paradigm of community.

Nor does Hegel seem to think citizens must speak the same language. For a theorist so closely linked to nationalist thought, it is surprising that Hegel rarely addresses this question. When he does discuss language, it is almost never with an eye to its political implications.[37] One exception is a passage in his early essay, *The German Constitution*:

> In our day the tie between members of a state in respect of manners [*Sitten*], education [*Bildung*], language may be rather loose or even non-existent. Identity in these matters, once the foundation of a people's union, is now to be reckoned amongst the accidents whose character does not hinder a mass from constituting a public authority. Rome or Athens, like any small modern state, could not have subsisted if the numerous languages current in the Russian Empire had been spoken within their borders, or if amongst their citizens manners [*Sitten*] had been as different as they are in Russia, or for that matter, as manners and education are now in every big city in a large country. Difference in language and dialect (the latter exacerbates separation even more than complete unintelligibility does), and difference in manners and education in the separate estates, which makes men known to one another in hardly anything but outward appearance—such heterogeneous and at the same time most powerful factors the preponderating weight of the Roman Empire's power (once it had become great) was able to hold together, just as in modern states the same result is produced by the spirit and art of political institutions. The dissimilarity in culture and manners is a necessary product as well as a necessary condition of the stability of modern states. . . . [I]n religion at least an identity might have been thought necessary, but this identity too is something which modern states have found that they can do without.[38]

The little evidence available suggests that for Hegel, in a modern state linguistic ties aren't coextensive with political ties, and incorporating people who speak different languages may even strengthen the state by stimulating the development of institutions that unite diverse peoples.

While Hegel says a people share a "spirit" that is reflected in their art, philosophy, and religion, members of an ethical substance need not all be, say, Catholic; and Hegel surely does not think they all must be surrealists, or Benthamite utilitarians. In the passage just quoted at length from *The German Constitution*, perhaps more revealing than any other of his views on political identity, Hegel emphasizes the diversity among members of a modern state. The passage reinforces the view that Hegel does not think religion and language must be shared by members of a body politic, and suggests further that members needn't share "manners and education" either.

That this passage occurs in an early essay may be important. Some scholars argue that the Hegel of the first decade of the 1800s does not give a "normative" meaning to *Staat*, and instead uses the word to mean merely the uniting of masses for collective defense of property claims— people are bound by something akin to Fichte's *Schutzvertrag*.[39] The later Hegel, it is suggested, meant something else—precisely the shared culture and manners that make up ethical life.[40] If this is so, we cannot use the above passage to prove the mature Hegel of the Berlin period thinks people in a modern state needn't share the same language, religion, education, or manners, the argument would go.

But we must not draw so sharp a dividing line between the early and late Hegel when trying to understand his political thought. Rather than referring in the passage above to a narrow sense of "state" which the later Hegel is said to disavow in favor of a "normative" sense, the early Hegel expresses what for both the early and later Hegel is a truth about political identity in the modern world, which, fragmented and heterogeneous, has as its central feature the rise of civil society and particularity. It is a truth coming to light already when the Greek poleis broke up, leaving in their place the Roman Empire, and later, feudal societies. The early Hegel did conflate the state with 'political institutions', while the later Hegel distinguishes state in a 'normative sense'—the state as an ethical substance, as the highest embodiment of ethical life (*Sittlichkeit*)— from mere political institutions.[41] But just as the early Hegel refuses to conflate state with nation, so too the later Hegel does not see ethical life as homogeneous and coextensive with a nation.[42]

Hegel's claim in the *German Constitution* essay—that members of a state needn't share manners and education—is consistent with his views in *Philosophy of Right*. In the later work Hegel notes that there are "inequalities of intellectual and moral education" among people of different classes (*Stände*) within the state.[43] For the agricultural class, family relations and trust are especially important, rather than the abstract relations among the class of trade and industry (*Stand des Gewerbes*) (PR 203). The agricultural class retains "the patriarchal way of life and the substantial disposition associated with it" (PR 203 Addition). Hegel notes in his lectures that religion, too, is a function of class—he suggests, for example, that farmers tend to be Catholic.[44] There is some sense in which education and manners (*Sitten*) must be shared by members of a state. Hegel writes in his early *Natural Law* essay, after all, that fellow citizens are "suckled at" the same breast of "universal ethical life"— what this sense is I address in section III. But in the modern state, both the early and late Hegel believe that the religion an individual practices, his specific moral education, or what he eats and drinks, is more likely a function of class, or, as the Berlin period passage on the Jews suggests, of what is commonly called race or ethnicity, than of citizenship.

What, then, must be shared by members of a modern state if not language, religion, manners, or education? Feelings of love and friendship? Hegel does think friendships are an important tie. He writes in a letter to his friend and patron F. I. Niethammer, "You and [your wife] together constitute the major portion, the substance of my existence."[45] But Hegel does not think we have to befriend or even like our fellow citizens. Hegel himself strongly disliked some of his fellow Germans, certain Bavarian Catholics whom he compares unfavorably to donkeys and oxen. "For all these animals retain a certain consistency and orderliness in their respective kinds of stupidity and rudeness. . . . These [Bavarians] are rather swines whose nature it is, piglike and devoid of all modesty, to produce a swinish mixture of understanding and stupidity, ignorance and insolence, meanness and cowardice, craftiness and banality."[46]

Not only needn't members of a state like each other, on Hegel's view; they do not have to interact face to face. There is one passage suggesting otherwise, from the *Encyclopaedia*, in which Hegel implies that members of an ethical substance "know each other":

> The social disposition of the individuals is their sense of the substance, and of the identity of all their interests with the total; and *that the other individuals mutually know [wissen] each other and are actual only in this identity, is confidence (trust) [Vertrauen]—the genuine ethical temper [Gesinnung, disposition]* (Enc 515, my emphasis, insertions).

But Hegel, here, is not saying that a condition of having a shared political identity is that members be acquainted; he says only that the condition of their knowing "each other . . . in this identity" is what we call trust, and is an ethical disposition. Even if it were a condition, the stipulation that members "know each other" does not imply they must have face-to-face familiarity; if Hegel meant that, he could have used the word *kennen* instead of *wissen*. Hegel refers, rather, to our having a certain understanding of our identity with our fellow citizens. To have this understanding we needn't personally know them. So, too, to define ourselves against others in war does not require we personally hate the enemy. Hegel says the virtue of gunpowder is that now one can direct oneself against not the person but the abstract enemy, and this facilitates consciousness of the whole (PH, p. 402). Consciousness of the whole, or the understanding of our identity with fellow citizens, comes not through acquaintances (*kennen*), but by theoretical knowledge (*wissen*) of an identity, but of an identity which Hegel does not think abstract in the sense of contractual.

If fellow citizens need not speak the same language, practice the same religion, eat the same foods, or be friends or even acquaintances to be all of one substance, must they at least share the same values?

Hegel thinks they must at least in some sense. Hegel's well-known and striking claim that punishing the criminal "is not only just *in itself*" but "is at the same time his will," is premised on the idea that the criminal's will is "split," that in violating the law he has acted contrary to his own implicit will.[47] Hegel's conception of punishment presumes that members of an ethical substance have the same implicit will to comply with the criminal laws of their state. This theory of punishment, developed in *Philosophy of Right*, draws on views Hegel espoused earlier. In his *Jenaer Realphilosophie* (1805–6) Hegel speaks of the power of the law as the common essence of the living people, of the "substance."[48] In lectures on the philosophy of right Hegel recounts how Napoleon was nearly killed by a German assassin in Vienna in 1809. The French, he says, could not reason with the assassin, who could not see the despicable nature of the action. "The French treated him as a wild animal and shot him." The phrasing is significant: the assassin was not punished, presumably because one cannot punish wild animals. Hegel then adds that the assassin was shot because he could not be brought to see his error; no common ground (*nichts Gemeinsames*) was shared between him and his victims.[49] Justified punishment presupposes shared values among members of the state under whose authority the criminal justice system operates.

But this does not imply that fellow citizens must have the same opinions about controversial ethical issues such as whether the state should allow abortions or execute murderers. I therefore disagree with A. S. Walton when he implies that Hegel's idea of a common good is defective for failing to acknowledge substantive disagreements.[50] Hegel recognizes that there are numerous practical controversies for which there is no philosophical resolution. Unfortunately, none of the examples he gives of such controversies have a significant moral point or are deeply divisive to us; for example, he scolds Plato for giving advice about whether nurses should stand still with children or rock them in their arms; he chides Fichte for stipulating in his theory of the state that passports of suspected persons should carry their painted likeness (PR, p. 21); and he says that whether to sentence a criminal to 364 or 365 days is best left to legislators, or perhaps to the capricious choice of the monarch.[51] These matters cannot be decided philosophically. Hegel does not say how extensive the range of these controversies is, but it may well include issues that do divide us, such as whether to execute certain criminals, when to suspend rights to person and property, or whether we regard a fetus as a person with rights. There is no reason to suppose Hegel thinks there is a philosophical resolution to these issues. Hegel suggests that some of the issues for which philosophy has no noncontroversial, undisputed resolution must be left to "custom," which might require that there be a consensus among a people.[52] Even if a consensus existed, it would be philosophically arbitrary, and it is unlikely Hegel would see such a consensus as an important tie, a tie with moral significance.

When we ask what, on Hegel's view, fellow citizens share that has the moral significance of making these citizens all one "substance" we are left, not with language, religion, friendships, or even manners and education, but primarily with shared memories, accomplishments, and practices and institutions.[53] Many of these can be shared by people of diverse backgrounds. For example, we needn't speak the same language, believe in the same God, have the same colored skin, or sing the same songs to come together, perhaps in response to a crisis like a natural disaster, acting together for a common goal that later becomes our deed, and later, a memory we share. This can be a quite powerful tie. Still, memories, deeds, and practices and institutions may seem a rather thin basis for uniting a group of citizens and distinguishing them from all others.

It is well acknowledged that Hegel's modern state is "inwardly differentiated," that while a sphere of universality and community, it incorporates the sphere of civil society and particular difference. This incorporation of difference is what distinguishes the modern state from the undifferentiated totalities Hegel understood the Greek city-states to be.[54] But surprisingly little has been said about what precisely the modern citizens with particular differences share as citizens, about the basis for their political identity. My point has been to show how little citizens of Hegel's modern state must share.

This leaves the problem of what Hegel's positive theory of citizenship is, what he thinks the basis of unity for citizens of modern states is in fact. What *do* citizens share?

III. HEGEL'S POSITIVE THEORY OF CITIZENSHIP

One of the things that a people, as well as members of a state, can share are memories and traditions. We've seen Hegel note how every Englishman can point to his country's past success at navigation and commerce, and that this is important to his identity. These are important in creating a historic community. But in *Philosophy of Right* Hegel emphasizes something else. The *Philosophy of Right* is primarily concerned, not with how historic communities are created, but with what it takes to be free. His argument is that to be free we require certain practices and institutions, and in this final section I want to suggest that it is the sharing of these practices and institutions that unites citizens of a modern state.[55]

Hegel argues that practices and institutions such as private property, contracts, marriage, and military service create bonds that preserve the system of ethical life and get each of its members to feel and be at home in it. In the *Philosophy of Right* he details how through the institutions of private property and contract individuals objectify their wills and are recognized by others in a common will; how through marriage an individual comes to be an ethical being; how in civil society, by working in corporations, we work for still a greater universal objective; and how all of these stages prepare us to be citizens in the state. Through these practices and institutions, citizens of a modern state become free—they recognize and are recognized by others as meaningful contributors to a shared ethical life in which we are at home, an experience that for Hegel constitutes freedom.[56]

In saying that citizens share in practices, I mean that they share not only in discrete rule-bound practices, but also in practices without determinate rules, and in *practice*, understood broadly as "way of doing things." This should not be understood too broadly, to refer to matters of fashion or taste or etiquette; for as we have seen, Hegel does not think "manners" must be shared by members of a state. Hegel does not draw a clear line between the broad sense of practice that he thinks citizens do share, and the manners he does not think they must share. He uses the word *Sitten* to refer to both the former and the latter. The German language lets him do this: *Sitte* can mean custom, habit, usage, mode, practice, fashion, manners, morals. *Sitte* can also refer to personal habits or to social customs.[57]

On Hegel's view, practice—discrete practices and the nondiscrete customary way of doing things—reflects a coherent set of principles and values, a moral background, shared by its participants. For Hegel, to share practices is not merely to share in artificially constructed and organized endeavors for the sake of convenience. To share even in a discrete practice such as promising is to share in an often unstated set of understandings that people in other societies may lack.[58]

Practices do not just presuppose shared understandings and preexisting ties. They also create them. On Hegel's view, practices themselves are ties that bind and a basis for a shared identity. One way practices play this role is by establishing common interests. People benefit from having certain practices, and consequently have a common interest in maintaining them.[59] In addition, through institutions and practices activity becomes habitualized, becomes "second nature" for members, what they are used to (*Gewohnheit*) (PR 268), and this provides a basis for a shared identity. Practices and institutions instill a shared disposition (*Gesinnung*) that binds members of an ethical substance.[60] Practices both engender and presuppose commonly held judgments about what is appropriate or right—the sharing of these judgments helps define and maintain a moral community.

Practices and institutions forge all sorts of ties. Marriage creates a tie that is different than the ties among members of a natal family, among co-workers in a corporation within civil society, or among citizens. While Hegel recognizes that family ties are distinct from ties we have at work and from ties among citizens of the state, he thinks they are connected. The former ties are a sort of training for citizenship. Hegel argues, for example, that in committing ourselves to one of the classes of civil society we develop an ethical disposition, a sense of honor and obligation—we acquire the disposition of "being a member" (PR 207), which helps make us good citizens. Consequently, Hegel thinks the state has an interest in the other spheres of ethical life—family and civil society. For example, he says the state has an interest in marriage, and points to the circumstances surrounding the Trojan War, and to the rape of Lucretia, both of which illustrate for him the great lengths to which states may go to preserve the ethical character of the marriage relation (Rph III: 141, 23–25). Certain members within a state will have special ties with each other that they lack with other members; but all are connected in that they participate in practices that engender these special ties.

Many Hegel commentators note the importance of *Sittlichkeit* in Hegel's political philosophy; but *Sittlichkeit* often becomes a catchall phrase to encompass nationalist, ethnic, racial, linguistic, religious, and other sorts of ties. My objective has been to ask precisely in what sense *Sittlichkeit* binds members and to suggest that what members of an ethical substance necessarily share, in Hegel's view, is practice: both discrete, rule-bound practices, and practice broadly understood as "what we do." I have argued that Hegel does not think that members of a body politic—an ethical substance—must be of one nation or ethnicity or religion, speak the same language, or even be a community. While people with ethnic or religious ties may make up communities, these communities Hegel distinguishes from the modern state, and are subordinate to the latter.

If we accept this account of political identity, we might think that in his effort to find a common identity in the fragmented modern world where the particularity of civil society holds sway, Hegel resorts to ties so pliant that they have little binding force. Hegel elevates the state to a level of such importance that he calls it our substance. Yet he writes off so many of the things that bind people, we might wonder how the state can be both so much yet so little. In saying our state is our ethical substance, Hegel claims the members of *this* state share in something that distinguishes them from people *not of this* state. Hegel opposes cosmopolitanism as an ideal. In a passage often cited because in it Hegel praises the idea that human beings count as universal persons insofar as they are human beings and not, say, Jews or Germans or Italians, he continues, "[t]his consciousness . . . is inadequate only if it adopts a fixed position— for example, as cosmopolitanism—in opposition to the concrete life of the state" (PR 209 Remark). Hegel criticizes those who suggest the state (Staat) should abandon its own independence to form a whole with another state; they "know little of the nature of a totality and of the self-awareness which an autonomous people (Volk) possesses" (PR 322 Remark). We have seen that Hegel thinks members should be willing to give up their lives for their state, and not just to protect life, limb, and property. Hegel defends war by pointing to how it prevents a hardening of particularity by shifting our focus to the universal. Through war we see that life and property are only finite, that the state exists not merely to protect life and property.[61] Hegel thinks our commitment to the state is a commitment worth dying for. But we might very well think that just because he insists on forging ties among so heterogeneous a group as those living in a modern state, Hegel's account of the basis of that commitment cannot say *why* we should die for our state.[62]

Hegel's positive theory of citizenship is ripe for further reflection, reflection Hegel does not always undertake in his texts. In particular, we should want to clarify what social background of knowledge, norms, and principles is entailed; why citizens of one state that share similar practices with citizens of other states (marriage, promising, property, legal punishment, contract are, after all, common to most modern states) should regard themselves as different from citizens of these other states; what are the implications for Hegel's account of our in fact having practices with conflicting principles; and how practice in the broad sense of "what we do," which Hegel thinks members of a state must share, is different from the "manners and education" Hegel thinks they need not share. The purpose of this essay was to argue that it need not entail many of the things we associate with nationalist, ethnic, and even community identity.

NOTES

Abbreviations used in citing Hegel's works: PR refers to Hegel, *Elements of the Philosophy of Right* (New York: Cambridge University Press, 1992)—I cite paragraph numbers and, where helpful, page numbers. Enc refers to *Encyclopaedia of the Philosophical Sciences (1830)*, tr. William Wallace (Oxford: Oxford University Press, 1971), vol. 3, and *Enzyklopädie der philosophischen Wissenschaften* (Frankfurt am Main: Suhrkamp, 1986)—I cite paragraph numbers. PH refers to *Philosophy of History*, tr. J. Sibree (New York: Dover, 1956), and *Werke in zwanzig Bänden*, ed. Eva Moldenhauer and Karl Michel (Frankfurt: Suhrkamp, 1986), vol. 12—I cite page numbers from the English edition. I also refer to lecture notes taken by students in Hegel's course on the philosophy of right. In doing so, I use the following abbreviations: Rph I: *Vorlesungen über Naturrecht und Staatswissenschaft*, ed. Claudia Becker et al. (Hamburg: Felix Meiner Verlag, 1983); Rph II: *Vorlesungen über Rechtsphilosophie (1818–1831)* in 4 vols., ed. Karl-Heinz Ilting (Stuttgart-Bad-Canstatt: Friedrich Fromann, 1973), vol. 1; Rph III: *Philosophie des Rechts: Die Vorlesung von 1819/20*, ed. Dieter Henrich (Frankfurt am Main: Suhrkamp, 1983); Rph V: Ilting, ed., vol. 3; Rph VI: Ilting, ed., vol. 4; Rph VII: Ilting, ed., vol. 4. When citing from the lecture notes, references are to volume, page, and line when needed—all translations are my own.

1. PR 260: The state is our own "substantial spirit." Cf. PH, pp. 66 (although Sibree translates *Substanz* as "existence" instead of "substance"), 67, 68; Enc 514–517.

2. See Hugh Reyburn's discussion in his *The Ethical Theory of Hegel* (London: Oxford University Press, 1921), pp. 27–28. See also Michael Hardimon, *Hegel's Social Philosophy: The Project of Reconciliation* (Cambridge: Cambridge University Press, 1994), p. 113.

3. See Rph V, 3:503, 11–13; PH, p. 74.

4. PR 324 Remark and Addition; see also Hardimon, pp. 234–35 and note.

5. On the appropriation of Hegel by nationalists and racists, see Hubert Kiesewetter, *Von Hegel zu Hitler* (Hamburg: Hoffmann und Campe, 1974); the account of Neuhegelians, many though not all of whom see Hegel as a precursor to the Third Reich, in Hubert R. Rottleuthner, "Die Substantialisierung des Formalrechts," in *Aktualität und Folgen dep Philosophie Hegels*, ed. Oscar Negt (Frankfurt: Suhrkamp, 1970), pp. 211–64; and Sidney Hook, "Hegel Rehabilitated," and "Hegel and His Apologists," in *Hegel's Political Philosophy*, ed. Walter Kaufmann (New York: Atherton Press, 1970), pp. 55–70, 87–105.

6. The latter quote is in "Resistance to Civil Government," in Henry Thoreau, *Reform Papers*, ed. Wendell Glick (Princeton, N.J.: Princeton University Press, 1973), p. 65.

7. A. J. Simmons, *Moral Principles and Political Obligation* (Princeton, N.J.: Princeton University Press, 1979), p. 194.

8. Joseph Tussman, *Obligation and the Body Politic* (New York: Oxford University Press, 1960), p. 4.

9. Ibid., pp. 7, 11.

10. Immanuel Kant, *The Metaphysics of Morals*, tr. Mary Gregor (Cambridge: Cambridge University Press, 1991), 315–16, 340. I refer to this work as MM, and cite page numbers from the Prussian Academy of Science edition, included in Gregor's edition.

11. Although not regarded as a classical liberal, another of Hegel's prede-cessors, Fichte, has a similarly contractualist view of what binds citizens. For Fichte, fellow citizens unite in a "protection contract" (*Schutzvertrag*). Why unite with some people and not others? Fichte considers the possibility that humans need only contract for protection with three or four of their nearest neighbors, but rejects this as inadequate, seeing as one has the right to encounter and interact with another "in any region of the state." Fichte's answer seems to be that we bind ourselves to all those for whom we can say that if they are harmed, we are harmed, and these are people with whom we can or have a right to interact. See Johann Gottlieb Fichte, *Foundations of Nat-ural Right According to the Principles of the Wissenschaftslehre*, sec. 17. A translation of this important work is being prepared for publication by Michael Baur, to whom I owe my thanks for sharing with me a draft of the section on the *Schutzvertrag*.

12. Francis Fukuyama, *The End of History and the Last Man* (New York: The Free Press, 1992), pp. 42, 126, 38, 275. Fukuyama says nationalism can be vanquished by liberalism and economic self-interest (270–71), or, if nationalism does not disappear, it will be relegated to the "realm of culture": "The French can continue to savor their wines and the Germans their sausages, but this will all be done within the sphere of private life alone" (271). For criticism of Fukuyama's appropriation of Hegel, see Mark Tunick, "Hegel Against Fukuyama's Hegel," *Clio* 22 (1993): 383–89.

13. Tussman, *Obligation and the Body Politic*, pp. 5–6. Tussman adds that a body politic, on this view, is analogous "to a language group." But, as we shall see, Hegel does not think that political ties will be coextensive with linguistic ties.

14. PR 75 Addition; cf. 75 Remark, 100 Remark, 258 Remark, 281 Remark. See Schwarzenbach, pp. 555–56.

15. Hegel notes that through war, in which the individual risks his life for the sake of the state, we see that the state does not exist merely to protect life and property, as the classical liberal suggests—Rph III: 276, 11–17 ("the Under-standing [here, classical liberals like Locke] errs in saying citizens must defend the state in order to defend their property and life—they fall to contradiction because they miss the point"); cf. PR 324 Remark; Rph II, 1:340, 25–27; Rph II, 1:338, 26–30; *Phenomenology of Spirit*, tr. A.V. Miller (Oxford: Oxford Uni-versity Press, 1977), pars. 455, 475, 476; Rph I, 248–50.

16. PR 209 Remark, 322 Remark.

17. Rph VII, 4:918.

18. *Natural Law: The Scientific Way of Treating Natural Law, Its Place in Moral Philosophy, and Its Relation to the Positive Sciences of Law*, tr. T. M. Knox (Philadelphia: University of Pennsylvania Press, 1975), p. 115.

19. George Armstrong Kelly notes the connection of *Bildung* with matura-tion, in *Idealism, Politics and History: Sources of Hegelian Thought* (Cam-bridge: Cambridge University Press, 1969), p. 342. Steven Smith has noted its relation to the ancient Greek notion of *paideia*, in *Hegel's Critique of Liberal-ism* (Chicago: University of Chicago Press, 1989), p. 175.

20. PH, p. 231; see pp. 225–39 in general.

21. *Community and the Politics of Place* (Norman: University of Oklahoma Press, 1990).

22. Hegel, *Philosophy of Nature*, pt. 2 of the *Encylopaedia*, tr. A. V. Miller (Oxford: Oxford University Press, 1970), p. 285. On the preceding page Hegel refers to the idea of a "universal man" as a "monster," and the product of an "empty imagination," implying that the living human being is shaped determinately by nature. I thank Jackie Stevens for pointing me to this work as a possible source for Hegel's views on identity.

23. PH, p. 74. For a strikingly similar passage, see Hegel, *Early Theological Writings*, tr. T. M. Knox (Chicago: University of Chicago Press, 1948), pp. 145–46, cited in Shlomo Avineri, *Hegel's Theory of the Modern State* (Cambridge: Cambridge University Press, 1972), p. 20.

24. Hegel notes elsewhere that one basis for identifying with the state is identification with great deeds of compatriots (Rph VI, 4:642, 7–13; cf. PR 268).

25. PR 3 Remark and PR 261 Remark both enthusiastically praise Montesquieu for realizing that the meaning and justification of particular practices can be appreciated fully only by seeing the practices as part of a coherent system of ethical life; PR 273 Remark discusses Montesquieu's views on the different forms of government.

26. PH, p. 52. Cf. PH, p. 46, where Hegel mentions "climate."

27. Cf. Rph I, 246–47: "Every people (*Volk*) has its own determinate anthropological principle and to this extent it is a nation"; Rph I: 247, 473–75: "Each is born according to nature so that he belongs to his nation (*Nation*) and has a determinate natural character more or less in common with his people (*Volk*)." Hegel usually uses the term *Volksgeist*, or spirit of a people or nation, as in PR 322 and PR 341. Occasionally he uses the term *Gemeingeist*, or "common spirit," as in Rph I: 180, 244–54. On Hegel's use of *Volksgeist*, see Shlomo Avineri, "Hegel and Nationalism," *Review of Politics* 24 (1961), pp. 474–79.

28. See Enc 556–577; PH, pp. 45–46: "the constitution adopted by a people (*Volk*) makes one substance—one spirit—with its religion, its art and philosophy, or, at least, with its conceptions (*Vorstellungen*) and thoughts—its culture generally (*Bildung überhaupt*)." Cf. Hegel, *Early Theological Writings*, p. 69: "each nation has an established national trait, its own mode of eating and drinking and its own customs in the rest of its way of living."

29. Hegel points to the Jews as an example, Rph I: 247–48.

30. PH, pp. 348–50; noted in PR, editor's note, p. 479.

31. It also seems that a single *Volksgeist* can consist of many nations: Hegel refers to Persia as a world-historical people, but also as a *Volkverein*, an empire extending over many nations, leaving to each its particular character (PH, p. 187).

32. Rph I, 247–48.

33. Hegel, *German Constitution*, in *Hegel's Political Writings*, tr. T. M. Knox (Oxford: Oxford University Press, 1964), pp. 190–91. He refers mainly to Catholicism and other religions that establish competing structures of authority to that of the state. Hegel does not think Protestantism is threatening to or disruptive of the state—see PR 270 Remark. In PR 331 Remark Hegel notes that some religious viewpoints (he mentions that of the Jewish and Mohammedan

nations) may subvert the "universal identity" that is required for states in modern times to be recognized as legitimate by other states.

34. Hegel, *Lectures on the Philosophy of Religion*, ed. Peter C. Hodgson (Berkeley: University of California Press, 1988), p. 195, n. 180 (from 1831 lectures).

35. PR 270 Remark, p. 295. See also PR 209; *The German Constitution*, pp. 158–59; Avineri, *Hegel's Theory of the Modern State*, p. 46; and Rph VI, 4:648, 10–15: members of sects who refuse to carry out their duties to the state can be tolerated only in larger states.

36. Harry Brod also notes how Hegel's modern state incorporates religious diversity: "Just as the universality of the state does not abolish economic differences in civil society, neither does it abolish doctrinal differences among various denominations. Hegel's theory in fact requires that there be multiple religious institutions." Harry Brod, *Hegel's Philosophy of Politics* (Boulder: Westview Press, 1992), pp. 125–26.

37. See *Phenomenology of Spirit*, pars. 508, 652–653; PR 2 Remark, 78, 164, 197; Enc 396 Z, 459; *Reason in History*, trans. Robert Hartman (Indianapolis: Bobbs-Merrill, 1953), 77–78.

38. Hegel, *German Constitution*; in *Political Writings*, p. 158. Avineri cites excerpts from this passage in his important discussion in *Hegel's Theory of the Modern State*, pp. 45–46.

39. See the discussion in note 11, *supra*.

40. Hans Maier, "Einige Historische Vorbemerkungen zu Hegels Politischer Philosophie," in *Hegel-Studien*, supplemental vol. 9 (1973), pp. 157–59; Z. A. Pelczynski, "The Hegelian Conception of the State," in *Hegel's Political Philosophy: Problems and Perspectives*, ed. Z. A. Pelczynski (Cambridge: Cambridge University Press, 1971), pp. 4–5. Shlomo Avineri, *Hegel's Theory of the Modern State*, suggests that the primary difference between the early and later writings in this respect is a difference not in substance, but in a "distinctive terminology" that the early Hegel had not yet articulated (p. 47). Avineri also notes that in his *Natural Law* essay, written around the same time as *German Constitution*, Hegel rejects the view that the state should be conceived "as an instrument for the preservation and defence of property" (Avineri, p. 85). Avineri says that Hegel's use of 'state' in *German Constitution* "hovers somewhat uncertainly between 'civil society' and 'state'" (p. 40).

41. Pelczynski, cited above, emphasizes how in *Philosophy of Right* Hegel distinguishes the state "proper" from the merely "political state." Cf. PR 269 Addition: the state produces and is maintained by the constitution.

42. Cf. Reyburn, *The Ethical Theory of Hegel*, p. 238: Hegel does not conflate state with nation, and Hegel is not a nationalist.

43. PR 200 Remark. Cf. PR 201: there are different *Stände*, each with different "theoretical and practical education."

44. Rph VI, 4:518, 12–31.

45. Hegel, *The Letters*, tr. Clark Butler and Christiane Seiler (Bloomington: Indiana University Press, 1984).

46. *Letters*, 207. Of course, Bavaria was (and some think it still is) a separate state; yet it was, and is, part of Germany. That it is hard to say whether

Hegel would regard Bavaria as its own ethical substance distinct from other German states is symptomatic of how Hegel's account is ambiguous in key respects.

47. PR 100; cf. PR 99 Remark; Rph VI, 4:283, 2–23. See Mark Tunick, *Hegel's Political Philosophy: Interpreting the Practice of Legal Punishment* (Princeton, N.J.: Princeton University Press, 1992).

48. Hegel, *Jenaer Realphilosophie*, ed. J. Hoffmeister (Hamburg: Felix Meiner, 1969), p. 235.

49. Rph VI, 4:388, 28–389, 6.

50. A. S. Walton, "Hegel, Utilitarianism, and the Common Good," *Ethics* 93, 4 (July 1983), p. 769; cf. pp. 767–69.

51. PR 214 Remark; cf. PR 101 Remark, PR 216, PR 234. See also Rph I, 23, 247–51: where several hunters wound an animal, and they have to divide it up, philosophy cannot help; PR 69 Remark: when borrowing from another's book becomes plagiarism cannot be determined as a matter of right; Rph VI, 4: 463, 11–16 (PR 177): reason cannot determine when one "comes of age"; Rph VI, 4:449, 21–27 (PR 168): reason cannot determine how close is too close regarding incest relations; PR 55 Addition: reason cannot determine to what extent I own the air rights above or coastal rights next to or mineral rights under my land; Rph V, 3:223 on this same point; Enc 529 Remark, and Rph VI, 4:86–87 on the limits of reason in determining the extent of punishment.

52. Hegel says that custom (*Sitte*) was more determinate in ancient Greece, where there was no moral conscience (Rph VI, 4:407, 7–13).

53. Recall PH, p. 74, and the discussion of that passage, *supra*.

54. See PR 185–187; Hardimon, pp. 209–12; Smith, pp. 140–45; Allen Wood, *Hegel's Ethical Thought* (Cambridge: Cambridge University Press, 1990), pp. 239–41.

55. I'd like to thank Stephen Houlgate for suggesting to me the distinction between creating a historic community and creating a community in which we are free.

56. For a detailed account of Hegel's conception of freedom that fills out what can only briefly be sketched here, see Tunick, *Hegel's Political Philosophy*, ch. 3.

57. *Das ist so seine Sitte* means "that is his way"; *das ist bei uns nicht Sitte* means "that is not the custom here."

58. See Mark Tunick, *Practices and Principles: Approaches to Ethical and Legal Judgment* (Princeton, N.J.: Princeton University Press, 1998), pp. 44–45, for a discussion of how promising presupposes a shared conception of the future, a conception that some societies seem to lack.

59. See Enc 515; PH, pp. 148, 436, 441.

60. Cf. Charles Taylor, *Hegel* (Cambridge: Cambridge University Press, 1975), p. 382. Hegel says dispositions themselves are too subjective a bond—we "require a mechanism, too" (Rph II, 1:326, 17–26; corresponding to PR 267). Dispositions and sentiments of patriotism themselves arise from institutions and practices (Rph VI, 4:641, 17–19). Hegel adds that while the state needs an ethical disposition on the part of its members, it cannot demand it as a duty, or punish those who lack it (Rph V, 3:735, 32–736, 13).

61. PR 324 Remark; cf. note 15, *supra*.

62. Avineri notes the "curious dichotomy in Hegel's view on war between the significance he attaches to the readiness of the citizen to go to war and the ultimate meaninglessness of the act of war itself and its results" (*Hegel's Theory of the Modern State*, p. 204).

CHAPTER 4

Postcolonialism and Right

Richard Dien Winfield

THE PROBLEM OF POSTCOLONIALISM

Amidst the euphoria greeting the end of the Cold War, the temptation has been great to welcome a new world order heralding the global triumph of democracy and free enterprise with a human face. Following fascism's defeat a half century before, the sudden collapse of superpower rivalry may relieve much of the totalitarian challenge to civil society and constitutional self-government. Yet celebrating the completed march of reason in history remains premature. Not only do daunting problems still plague the transition from communism to capitalism as well as capitalist democracy itself, but another unresolved opposition demands ever more attention. While the world stage has been commandeered by a century of interimperialist, fascist/anti-fascist, and communist/capitalist slaughter, the great majority of humanity has undergone a different ordeal. Traced by overlapping rubrics of colonialism, Westernization, modernization, and development, and culminating in the political liberations creating the postcolonial condition, this parallel history can no longer lie outside the limelight.

Both as an external opposition between North and South, the developed and the underdeveloped, or the West and its other, and as an internal opposition within postcolonial society, a chapter of history is unfolding, distinctly different from the birth of the modern that left and right Hegelians once viewed as the final combat. How is this development to be understood? Can the categories with which the master thinkers of modernity comprehended our age grasp the postcolonial predicament?

The problem at issue has key descriptive elements, most important of which concerns the contingent or noncontingent character of the contrast between how Western nations modernized themselves and how non-Western nations were generally subjected to a "Westernization" imposed through the yoke of colonial and imperial domination. Above all, however, what lies at stake is prescriptive inquiry addressing first the normativity of modernity and of the Western developments initially giving rise to modern institutions, but then extending to probe the separability of modernization and Westernization, the legitimacy of imposing modern institutions from without, and finally the normative tensions within postcolonial societies and between developed and underdeveloped nations.

All of these normative questions are decided as much by how modernity is understood as by how normativity is itself conceived. Defenders and detractors alike generally agree that modernity distinguishes itself from prior forms of civilization by calling into question given tradition and demanding that practices and institutions command legitimacy only to the degree that they are justified by reason. Hence, the institutions that modernity erects putatively in accord with reason lay claim to a universality reflecting their independence of the contingent particulars of given authority. Not surprisingly, the distinctively modern institutions that are understood to be universally valid are institutions of freedom, determined not by their conformity to particular cultural tradition, but by their realization of self-determination. The institutions giving reality to self-determination can qualify as the real that is rational precisely because freedom exhibits the independence from foundations that reason must exhibit if it is to provide any justification that does not rely on dogmatically accepted criteria, rules, procedures of construction, or any other privileged vocabularies. Precisely because free institutions do not draw their legitimacy from any conformity to given tradition, they can only be justified by a reasoning that rejects the traditional view that justification amounts to derivation from some foundation. Thus, when MacIntyre decries the failure of the Enlightenment to establish foundations for modern autonomy,[1] he is not exposing a crack in the façade of modernity, nor unmasking limits in reason; rather, as William Maker has so powerfully argued,[2] the very failure to locate foundations for modernity is indicative of how the universality of modernity's institutions of freedom involves their independence from all prior grounds.

It is the universality of modernity, enshrined in institutions of freedom, that allows the modern to represent not just a particular moment in history, inevitably overtaken by the postmodern of a later date, but a uniquely valid form of civilization, valid in the special sense of not falling prey to the problems of legitimacy that afflict any practices that claim authority on the basis of privileged foundations.

Traditionalist opponents of modernity can certainly cling to their fundamentalisms, especially when self-professed modern regimes fail to realize freedom in all its proprietary, moral, household, social, and political dimensions. So long, however, as the traditionalists' opposition to modernity rests on an appeal to given sacred or profane authority, they cannot overcome the arbitrariness of their own norms, norms that define premodernity to the degree that modern institutions emerge through the overthrow of foundational tradition.

Postmodernists, on the other hand, recognize the futility of absolutizing any particular foundations, but they assume that no values and no knowledge claims can be advanced without depending on some privileged vocabulary. On this assumption, modernity's claim to enjoy universal validity and freedom from the given is bogus, concealing some ground reflecting a particular culture or group whose advance of universal norms can only be a play for power, imposing its own values on all. This postmodern challenge to the legitimacy of modernity has one basic difficulty: if all normative claims are foundational, leaving reason and conduct incapable of self-determination, that is, free of determination by prior grounds, the truth of this very situation can never be authoritatively established. Postmodernists must either know with an autonomy they deny or admit that their claims are as ideological as any others. Hence, as much as postmodernism may give ideological support to the fascist challenge to modern institutions of freedom, it cannot refute the project of modernity.

Although modernity may enjoy special normativity, the traditional, modern, and postmodern alternatives represent the abiding, unmixed options that a civilization can take with regard to foundations: that is, it can remain traditional, privileging a particular set of given practices, it can be modern, embracing institutions of freedom, or it can be postmodern, advancing a particular form of life with brazen recognition of its own perspectival, arbitrary character. Accordingly, once all three forms of civilization have made their appearance, it is possible to speak of an "end" of history in the restricted sense that history may offer repetitions and hybrid combinations of these options, but no fundamentally novel forms of community.

Where postcolonial society fits in such a scheme results in large part from two consequences following from the universality of modernity.[3]

THE DUAL CHARACTER OF EMERGENT MODERNITY

First of all, because modernity's institutions of freedom do not depend on any particular culture for their legitimacy, they are inherently capable of global, not to mention, intergalactic, realization. By contrast, because premodern civilizations are distinguished by appealing to some particular heritage as their defining basis, they cannot consistently break with their parochial roots and achieve cosmopolitan hegemony.

Second, although the universality of modernity renders it capable of globalization, nothing in the structure of the institutions of freedom requires, guarantees, or even makes possible that they come into being universally at once. Rather, the supplanting of traditional forms of life by the different spheres of modern community is bound to occur origi- nally in some particular locality marked by some particular heritage. Moreover, wherever modernity originates, its distinct freedoms can only emerge in a series of developments fostering some of the institu- tions of freedom before other types come into being. The impossibil- ity of simultaneous birth is due to the structural relation of the differ- ent modes of freedom. Self-government may preside over all other forms of freedom, upholding and regulating their integration within the body politic. Yet no political act can freely create property rela- tions, moral autonomy, freedom in the family, or a civil society. This is precluded because citizens cannot engage in self-government unless they already count as property owners, moral agents, and equal part- ners in marriage, while enjoying equal economic opportunity and legal rights.[4] A deficit in any of these autonomies undercuts the equal polit- ical opportunity of citizens. This is why genuine political democracy need not be externally constrained to safeguard the pre-political rights of citizens. On the contrary, self-government cannot actualize itself unless citizens already enjoy their pre-political autonomy in family and society, whereas democracy cannot sustain itself unless the state continues to uphold these pre-political spheres of freedom. Accord- ingly, the genesis of political emancipation must be preceded by all the domestic, social, and cultural developments that make possible house- hold and social emancipation, developments whose own time and geo- graphical extension are prey to all the vagaries of historical accident that preclude either an instantaneous or uniform formation. Hence, even if the final release from feudalism may at one blow disengage kin- ship from commerce and rule, while separating social position from political power, the revolution that baptizes a free family, a civil soci- ety, and a republic will still present the universal rights of modernity in a regional debut.

Taken together, the universality of modernity and the regionality of the birth of the modern render the globalization of modernity something more complicated than merely a transformation of the premodern into the modern.

To begin with, the advent of modern institutions in a particular region creates a divide between two forms of premodernity. One premodernity stands distinguished as the womb of original revolution—that is, as that premodern civilization that transforms itself into the modern. The metamorphosis of this premodernity has a pathway defined by what must occur for the institutions of freedom to arise. The requirements of this original genesis of the modern are of course dictated by the structures of freedom and the reformations of culture that make it compatible with the exercise of rights. Accordingly, the conception of this genesis is posterior to the conception of the institutions of right, which is why Hegel in the *Philosophy of Right* is correct to analyze the history of the emergence of freedom[5] only after having conceived property right, morality, family, civil society, state, and international relations. Nonetheless, even if the genesis of the modern must include specific transformations, this requirement does not dictate that the historical emergence of modernity is itself necessary.

Hegel, of course, has often been alleged to treat the history of freedom, that is, the genesis of modernity, as a necessary process. Significantly, however, his lectures on the philosophy of history begin with the empirical hypothesis that institutions of freedom have in large part arisen in our day, a hypothesis that then enables us to interpret history up to the present as a history of the emergence of freedom.[6] Moreover, in analyzing that history, the different way stations do not comprise successive transformations of the same community. Rather, Hegel gives us more of a transmigration of soul, where the development of freedom leaps from one nation to another, albeit within the general orbit of the West, before a modernity arises that can spread its wings beyond a particular people and make itself a global civilization. If each successive form necessarily generated the next stage, one would expect a metamorphosis of one and the same people. That this is not the case suggests that although the original genesis of modernity may have a form dictated by its conclusion, the arrival at that destination rests on much that is contingent.

Even if this is so, once modern institutions first arise within a particular region, all other communities stand in a new situation. Some may manage, at least temporarily, to close themselves off from contact with the first modern society and then autonomously metamorphose into a modern society in their own right (as Japan may have done), or alternately linger in their own isolated premodernity. Wherever such seclusion is overcome, however, premodern societies become subject to a modernization from without. Since the original modern society has a regional identity, the modernization it may foist on other premodern societies will take on the appearance of a regional assimilation, even if it involves the establishment of universally valid institutions. In terrestrial terms, insofar as the original modern society has arisen in the

West, the external modernization will appear in some respect as a process of Westernization.

Whether "Westernization" and "modernization" completely converge depends on several factors. If the transformations in question simply entail establishing purely universal structures of freedom, "Westernization" will be identical with modernization from without. If, alternately, the transformations involve imposing practices specific to Western culture in its contingent particularity, "Westernization" becomes a particular form of modernization that may well diverge from the modernization that an isolated non-Western community may autonomously achieve. The latter option, assumes, of course, that what distinguishes Western civilization are not cultural features that uniquely enable a community to modernize itself autonomously. If non-Western culture did lack such features, as Hegel, Marx, and Weber all suggest, then the only way non-Western civilization could be modernized would be under the aegis of an external Westernization. In that case, a rigid divide would separate the premodernity that transformed itself into Western modernity and the premodernity of non-Western civilization.

THE GLOBALIZING TENDENCIES OF EMERGENT MODERNITY

Whether or not a premodern community is able to modernize itself, the whole question of an external modernization remains irrepressible due to the globalizing tendencies of any emergent modernity.[7] These globalizing tendencies have two parallel dimensions, one rooted in the structure of civil society, the other following from the exclusive normativity of self-determination.

Although civil society comprises an ethical community whose members interact in function of the pursuit of particular self-selected ends, their association is universal in scope, reaching as far as market interdependence, legal recognition, and economic welfare considerations extend. Political community may erect frontiers separating different states, but civil relations transcend all such borders. This is why economic, legal, and other civil rights warrant international guarantee under the rubric of "human rights," applying equally to noncitizens and citizens, in contrast to national rights to political participation.[8] It is also why states must take special measures to prevent transnational social developments, such as the growth of multinational enterprise and multinational financial and regulatory integration (e.g., the European Economic Community), from undermining national sovereignty. Moreover, as Hegel early observed,[9] and Marx and Rosa Luxemburg[10] would later stress, the commodity relations of civil society drive it beyond itself to penetrate premodern societies in search of an expanding market furnishing new consumers, new sources of raw materials and manufacture, and new pools of labor. With civil society endowing individuals with the freedom to determine their needs and occupation under the social condition of enabling others to do the same, the resulting market demand engenders a multiplication and refinement of needs and production, liberating the accumulation of wealth of any natural limits.[11] The resulting pressures of competition make an enterprise's survival depend on increasing sales and profits and the investment these make possible. To the degree that competitive success cannot always be achieved by increasing market share at the expense of other firms or by maintaining market share in a growing internal market, the expansion of civil society's market into other regions becomes an imperative of its own economic dynamic.

How this breakthrough occurs is colored by modernity's general normative tendencies to globalization. On its own self-understanding, the modern community must regard all premodern formations as oppressive regimes violating the rights that only institutions of freedom can actualize. Even though traditional communities must command sufficient consent to maintain their own authority and may well be enthusiastically supported by the overwhelming majority of their members, voluntary conformity to tradition is not equivalent to self-determination. This discrepancy between preference and freedom is most obvious in the case of popular dictators: they may have the consent of the majority, but they cannot provide the participation in self-government that political self-determination requires. The same deficit applies to the voluntary acceptance of family arrangements ruled by traditional hierarchies or of social orders organized by hereditary rank: without the institutions of free households and civil society, individuals cannot enjoy their family and social rights even if they experience domestic and social happiness. To the degree that modernity judges itself by the foundation-free standard of freedom, it must regard right as what alone has universal validity and not as a parochial heritage, in the manner of Rawlsian advocates of "reflective equilibrium" and communitarian particularists. But then modernity cannot consistently celebrate the diversity of premodern civilization; modernity must instead regard global modernization as a normative imperative.

This imperative would apply to premodern civilizations whether or not they have the capability for an internal, autonomous modernization. If a contemporaneous traditional community lacked the inner resources to revolutionize itself, then the modern community would face the burden of engineering that transformation from without. If, alternately, a traditional community had the ability to modernize itself, the coexisting modern community would still face the challenge of facilitating that metamorphosis with whatever external aid is possible.

These imperatives of global modernization assume that self-determination can be externally imposed, or, more specifically, that modernization can be forced on premodern civilization without corrupting the desired establishment of right. Yet can communities be compelled to be free? It is tempting to answer this question by drawing an analogy between the problem of making another individual autonomous and making another community self-determined. Kant formulates the general problem in his *Doctrine of Virtue* by arguing that individuals cannot make others autonomous (e.g., moral), but can only promote their happiness by helping secure the satisfaction of their desires.[12] Kant's argument might appear to apply uniquely to moral autonomy since moral self-determination revolves around choosing to act with the right purposes and intentions, an internal matter that external intervention can hardly control. By contrast, the other freedoms exercised in property, family, economic, legal, and political relations have an external dimension that could be affected from without. After all, if determining oneself as an owner, a spouse and parent, a market agent, a legal subject, and a citizen depends on recognition by others and common exercise of the freedoms comprising the different institutions of right, self-determination will depend on the contributions of other agents. Nevertheless, Kant argues that colonial or imperial domination of another people is unjust no matter what norms the latter obey and no matter what the liberating intentions of their new masters.[13] Since Kant models right after the self-legislation of moral autonomy, any external imposition of institutions will automatically lack that self-legislating character, even if the new order establishes the putative structures of freedom.

Yet might the absence of self-legislation in the establishment of the institutions of freedom be endemic to the process of modernization, whether that process be internal or external in origin? Self-legislation as an institutional engagement is specific to democratic self-government. Spouses and parents may codetermine household management, but the scope of the family is a particular right and welfare to which legislation cannot be restricted.[14] Although market activity may conform to economic law, economic agents do not consciously enact the rules of competition Only self-government involves a freedom with the universal reach requiring rule by law. Nevertheless, as a structure of ethical community, political democracy can itself only operate on the basis of an existing constitution, whose own establishment is not an act of self-government, but rather the result of a founding process involving a plurality of antecedent developments.

As Hegel has emphasized,[15] the emergence of self-government depends on the formation of pre-political institutions, including the universal recognition of property rights (and the abolition of slavery), the acceptance of moral autonomy (and the religious reformation it requires), the rise of civil society's market economy (and the overthrow of feudal bondage), the institution of civil courts and due process, and the formation of public welfare agencies to guarantee equal economic opportunity. Only with these pre-political transformations can any founding of a democratic constitution signify more than the charade that "people's democracies" once represented. Since these enabling pre-political developments are no more preordained than is political revolution, actual constitution-making is, as Hegel points out, a contingent affair of history, fundamentally different from self-legislation.[16] This is true whether the constitution-making be an internal affair or a product of external modernization.

Either way, the interconnection of pre-political and political freedom indicates that modernization requires a preponderant engagement of individuals in each of the practices in which right has its exercise. Moreover, because these practices are modes of self-determination, modern institutions cannot be imposed from without unless the recipients are willing to break with their interrupted tradition and interact in terms of their received rights. Although such willingness cannot be reduced to self-legislation, it has its own internal dimension.

Accordingly, it makes little sense to follow the Kantian/Rousseauian gambit of judging internal and external modernizations by whether they result from self-legislation. A more plausible strategy consists in first conceiving how the structure of the different institutions of freedom determines the possible interactions between an original modernity and the premodern communities it confronts. Once these possibilities are identified, a better judgment can be made of the ethical problems of external modernization and of the colonial and postcolonial predicaments it engenders.

MODERNITY AND THE LOGIC OF COLONIALISM

To understand colonialism and its postcolonial aftermath in relation to modernization, one must think through how the two globalizing tendencies of modernity work themselves out once a modern society has arisen in a particular locality. Since the modern norms that call into question premodern communities equally preside over how the emergent modern society interacts with its premodern counterparts, it makes sense to examine first how the globalizing dynamic of civil society impacts on premodernity and then to investigate how the principles of modern freedom apply to the resulting situation.

Although Hegel's analysis of the market is notoriously sketchy, he does identify the salient features that push civil society beyond itself, setting the stage for colonial and imperialist expansion. Enabling individuals to relate in terms of the pursuit of self-selected needs for commodities, the market not only multiplies and endlessly differentiates needs, means of satisfaction, and the forms of earning, creating demand for commodities that lie beyond its own borders, but equally engenders a predicament where demand may fall short of supply, leaving civil society too poor to sustain independently its ever-expanding pursuit of wealth.[17]

This confronts civil society with complementary alternatives to realize the economic freedom of its members. On the one hand, if civil society cannot adequately reduce unemployment through internal public interventions such as nonredundant public works or subsidized incentives for employers, it must export its own unemployable labor. On the other hand, if sufficient internal market growth cannot be sustained by credit expansion and deficit spending, civil society must draw on new supply and demand for which the only remaining source is the abiding premodern civilizations that have still escaped modernization.[18]

These parallel injunctions might seem achievable by means of the basic modality of civil association: commodity exchange. Although premodern society as such limits civil freedom by traditional divisions that organize household, economic, and legal relations by factors given independently of the self-determination of individuals, commodity exchange can still conceivably play a circumscribed role within the interstices of traditional community. Trade between premodern and modern societies is therefore possible, as the history of early European penetration of the non-Western world can testify. Unemployed settlers can find earning opportunities in the markets of premodern society, just as modern enterprises can obtain labor power, raw materials, and finished goods in exchange for whatever commodities (including money) traditional communities are willing to obtain in return. Yet can such possibilities satisfy the economic dynamic of civil society, or, for that matter, enable a traditional community to modernize through the purely economic expansion of market relations within its borders?

What frustrates either of these prospects is the fundamental disparity between the limits premodern tradition places on economic freedom and the unlimited pursuit of wealth that an unshackled market generates. Merchants and workshops in premodern society may earn through exchange with a fully developed civil society. Nevertheless, their own level of trade and production is inevitably constrained by the traditional arrangements that impose fixed limits on the needs and occupations of themselves and their compatriots, subordinating their own commerce within a wider scheme of social reproduction from which commodity relations are excluded. Because of such traditional limits on what can be freely bought and sold, market activity is not only constrained in ways that threaten the competitiveness of indigenous industry, but incapable of autonomously assimilating the economic relations that are regulated by nonmarket premodern relations.

The consequences of this limitation are prefigured in the genesis of the original civil society. Marx documents the key factor in his analysis of the "primitive accumulation of capital,"[19] expressly contradicting the base-superstructure economic determinism that would enfeeble Marxism. Namely, the only way that market relations can expand their reach in premodern society is through a political intervention that forcibly uproots future wage laborers from the conditions of their traditional sustenance and compels them to seek their living in the market. Otherwise whatever wealth has been already accumulated through trade and usury will be unable to find continually expanding opportunities for investment and fail to precipitate a transformation of the economy into a system producing goods for exchange and the realization of profit.

What applies to the genesis of the first civil society extends with a special twist to external modernization. Whereas primitive accumulation occurs through annihilation of the traditional livelihoods of people by political actions of their own rulers, lifting the barriers to market penetration in other premodern societies from without can only occur through an imperial domination, where the government of an emergent modern society uses its state power to force a premodern community to "open" itself to the globalization of the market. This "opening" cannot simply consist in allowing foreign goods to be imported for purchase; any such trade concessions still leave intact the premodern social formations that exclude commodity relations. Instead, those traditional arrangements must be uprooted by political means. The globalization of civil society through external modernization will thus require an external political intervention, enlisting intrigue and military force to overcome indigenous resistance. As the example of China indicates from the Opium Wars through the adventures of the Comintern, such intervention can retain local rulers but force them to adopt policies overturning traditional social relations or enlist revolutionary movements inspired by modern ideologies to replace traditional leaders with more accommodating native "progressives." Alternately, as the examples of the Americas, Africa, India, Southeast Asia, and Australia all testify, direct imperial rule can dispense with indigenous sovereignty in either of two basic ways: a civil society's own underemployed can be settled in conquered territory in colonies exporting the metropolitan society while banishing surviving traditional communities to unwanted enclaves still subject to metropolitan rule; or indigenous leadership can be replaced with a colonial administration directly governing the conquered society in accord with the conquerors' interests.

Any of these forms of imperial domination can serve the economic needs that push civil society beyond itself. Yet in so doing, each form gives rise to something distinctly different from the modern society that autonomously arises from within a premodern setting. And in each case, the new predicament challenges modernity's normative tendencies to globalization with all too familiar legitimation problems.

Settler colonies present two normative challenges. Although the settlers may reproduce a civil society in which property rights, moral accountability, family freedom, economic opportunity, and legal equality are all upheld, so long as they remain subject to the rule of the metropole, their right to self-government is violated. That right counts, of course, only so long as political freedom is regarded as an end in itself (as Hegel's *Philosophy of Right* maintains) rather than as a means to guaranteeing the pre-political civil rights of individuals (as social contract theory would have us believe). In the latter case, benevolent and appreciated colonial rule can satisfy the liberal criteria of protecting person and property with the consent of the governed. If, however, the settlers are to enjoy the full breadth of modernity's embrace of freedom, which liberalism, in contrast to the Hegelian alternative, is incapable of completely legitimating, either of two options must be followed: (1) the colony must be transformed into a province of the metropolitan nation, with the same political participation as any other, or (2) the colony must become an independent democracy. Any other halfway house, such as Puerto Rico's "commonwealth" status, violates modernity's norms for political right. Of course, because democracy is an ethical community that sustains itself only insofar as its members participate in self-government, the alternate options of integration into the metropole or independence can only provide a real solution if the settler population predominantly embraces one or the other.

A problem still remains even if national integration or independence gives a willing populace political freedom, at least so long as the indigenous population once banished to reservations has either chosen not or not been permitted to assimilate into the surrounding colonial society. If reservation life simply comprised an ethnic enclave in which the modern rights of property, morality, and family, civil, and political freedom were exercised as in any other neighborhood or district, independence or integration would already resolve all abiding normative tensions. If instead the indigenous community follows traditional arrangements at odds with right, and/or remains governed by an external authority (e.g., a Bureau of Indian Affairs), a consistent realization of modern principles of right becomes problematic. Any external authority that lords it over indigenous affairs deprives its subjects of the freedoms it usurps; yet that external rule may well reflect the unwillingness of the reservation population to give up their traditional community and assimilate themselves into the surrounding civil society and democracy that has been imposed on them. Of course, the encompassing modern society must, to be consistent with its own principles of right, eliminate any barriers to such assimilation. Can, however, the encompassing modern society consistently retain rule over reservations in which tradition trumps right or consistently give complete independence to traditional communities in which modern freedoms are ignored, albeit with the consent of the members?

The latter question dovetails with the central dilemma arising when an autonomously emergent modern regime forces commercial concessions from a premodern nation or advances beyond such intrusions to conquer the resisting nation and impose direct colonial rule. In both of these cases, the modern intruder might regard itself as the bearer of the principles of civil society if it moved beyond the rape and plunder of the indigenous society (of which Marx accuses the British in the early expansion of the East India Company)[20] to the introduction and enforcement of universal property relations (i.e., including outlawing slavery, serfdom, and other forms of bondage), the recognition of moral autonomy (i.e., enforcing a separation of religion and state and religious toleration), the transformation of family relations in accord with principles of equality and co-determination, the enactment of freedom of occupation and public welfare guarantees, and the institution of a legal code and court system in which due process is respected. If these measures are not undertaken, the colonial power can hardly justify its usurpations other than on grounds of a national interest that turns a blind eye to the rights of others. Yet, even if the colonial power moves beyond plunder to forced modernization, the very externality of its intervention raises problems.

These problems are twofold. First, even if it be granted that the rights of civil society (including property, moral, and household rights) are unconditionally valid, their very reality as modes of self-determination depends on a preponderance of voluntary conformity by entitled individuals. This prevailing rectitude need not involve ideological acceptance, personal happiness, or any other specific psychological attitude. It does, however, require that individuals interact more in recognition and respect than in disregard of the appropriate rights of one another. Consequently, if the external imposition of civil society is to succeed, it must somehow achieve that degree of internal recognition on which its freedoms depend. This, of course, presumes that the individuals involved are themselves acknowledged to be competent to exercise civil rights.

Can the latter acknowledgment be squared, however, with the deprivation of self-government that colonial rule incorporates? Admittedly, the premodern nation can hardly be said to afford its members self-rule if traditional governance is at odds with democracy. Yet colonialism's violation of the formal independence of the colonized equally fails to replace traditional tyranny with political autonomy. Arendt has observed that colonial regimes characteristically exercise an external bureaucratic management of their colonial subjects and succeed in doing so only by drawing a racial divide between the indigenous peoples and their metropolitan masters.[21] If the colonial rulers cannot ascribe racial inferiority to their subjects, how can they justify a domination that otherwise violates modern political right? Yet, as much as racism in colonial practice may pave the way for the introduction of racism into the internal political affairs of modern apartheid and fascist regimes, racism can hardly be consistently upheld by any regime that legitimates itself under the banner of modernization and development.

John Stuart Mill argued for a less inconsistent justification of colonialism: namely, that the subject peoples were not racially incapable of governing themselves but that they first had to undergo a tutelage weaning them from their oppressive cultural traditions before they would be able to participate in the institutions of freedom. Colonialism was therefore a temporary way station, superintending an external modernization that would culminate in independence once the formative process was over.[22] Hegel anticipates this view by arguing in paragraphs 350 and 351 of *Philosophy of Right* that the same unconditioned normativity of freedom that gives heroes the right to found states gives more civilized (e.g., more modern, free) states the right to regard the mores of traditional communities as inferior and to treat their independence as "merely formal,"[23] implicitly sanctioning an external modernization through imperialism. If Hegel's basic insight be granted that political freedom cannot operate without the prior formation of a civil society, including universal property rights, recognition of moral autonomy, the triumph of freedom and equality among spouses in the household, the achievement of equal economic opportunity, and the institution of civil law, Mill's and his converging arguments would have some merit, provided two conditions could be met. First, colonial rule would have to be capable of externally fostering these developments without succumbing to a self-serving exploitation of the colony's wealth, and second, colonialism would then have to eliminate itself as soon as possible in a transition to independent postcolonial regimes.

To object that such a transformation violates the political freedom of the colonial people has a certain formality if the only alternative were a process whereby a premodern regime exercises its own nondemocratic rule to modernize its society in preparation for metamorphizing into constitutional self-government. Without national independence, a subject community cannot possibly enjoy the political freedom that provides the capstone to modernity. Yet national independence alone may involve neither self-government nor a free society or household. Both external and indigenous rulers would have to eliminate their respective forms of political domination if political emancipation is to succeed. The modernizing initiatives of an indigenous ruler would have no automatic privilege unless only an internal modernization can engender the level of voluntary cooperation required for the operation of the institutions of freedom or that external modernization can never resist the temptations of colonial exploitations. Although the situations are somewhat distinct, the examples of postwar Japan and West Germany suggest that external rulers can expeditiously eliminate the remnants of pre- and postmodern tyranny and reconstruct modern family, social, and political institutions of freedom with widespread popular support.

Be this as it may, the genesis of the institutions of freedom can never conform to their actuality, because the volition founding constitutional democracy can never be an exercise of constitutional self-government. For this reason, neither route to independence can strictly accord with right any more than can the primitive accumulation helping form the first civil society. Since what is at stake in each case is realizing a good that is not yet at hand, the situation is one of moral accountability rather than of ethical responsibility, where one is bound by duties already realized in the institution to which one belongs. The prescribed task may consist clearly enough in contributing to the rise of universal property right, moral autonomy, household emancipation, civil society, and democratic self-government. Yet because the rights and duties contained in this result cannot be fully applicable until it is attained, their standard provides no unequivocal guidelines for what means to their implementation are genuinely necessary, let alone permissible.

Can the same predicament be said to apply to the postcolonial nation that a consistently modern colonizer must finally decolonize?

PRINCIPLES OF THE POSTCOLONIAL PREDICAMENT

In distinction from independent settler colonies, a postcolonial nation carries the burden of two decisive features. On the one hand, it contains the vestiges of premodern traditions, not isolated in reservations, but spread throughout society under the scaffold of a modern constitution mandating in varying degrees the institution of property, moral, family, social, and political self-determination. On the other hand, the postcolonial nation's emergent civil society bears the burdens of competing economically, culturally, and militarily with established modern states. These "developed" nations enjoy the benefit of both a longer, more matured formation of capital and escape from the internal handicaps posed by the persistence of premodern traditions as well as the deformations created by the exploitation of colonial masters.

The resulting discrepancy in economic, cultural, and military influence between developed and "underdeveloped" postcolonial nations has led some postcolonial theorists to regard the coming of independence to be a purely formal transition, where colonial rule is supplanted by a neocolonial domination changing the national identity of the local administrators but otherwise leaving the postcolonial masses in the same plight suffering with decimated traditions, chronic pauperization, and overwhelmed civil institutions struggling with corruption and bankruptcy. If Marx were right that capital dominates civil society and that civil society subordinates the state, independence would mean little more than this empty formality. The preponderant advantage of foreign capital would allow it to still control the decolonized society and utilize its newly independent government as no less a lackey for foreign exploitation as the defunct colonial administration.

The situation is very different, however, if Hegel is correct in (1) recognizing the ability of social interest groups, civil law, and public welfare agencies to uphold the economic opportunity of all, and (2) recognizing the state's preeminence over civil society, not only in legislating and enforcing the laws that uphold pre-political freedom, but in regulating civil society to prevent social inequality from translating itself into political privilege and in thwarting foreign economic interests from dominating domestic society and politics. If the state can protect itself from domestic and foreign social domination, while ensuring that social oppression is restricted and democratic freedom is maintained, postcolonial political independence can have a double significance. First, as a harbinger of political self-determination, it represents the culminating phase of modernization, adding the final structure of freedom that premodern community has lacked: constitutional democracy. Second, it offers the postcolonial nation all the opportunities that political intervention provides for restricting the influence of foreign and domestic interests on the development of its own society and political life.[24]

The history of colonial liberation reflects both of these gains.

Although independence movements have followed various ideologies, they have generally embraced modern ideals of social and political justice, diverging primarily by giving different interpretations of what institutions are required to realize freedom. Whether inspired by Jefferson or Marx, the makers of independence have made themselves vehicles of modernization, bringing modern political relations (and their deformities) to their nation, rather than resuscitating traditional rulers and their communities. Indeed, the very appeal to nationalism has involved the introduction of a very nontraditional community uniting individuals in terms not of premodern hierarchies, but the equality of citizenship in a nation of one's own.

Further, each independent nation has attempted to use its own political regulation over society and commerce to orient its development away from the self-serving policies of past colonial masters. This may not be an easy task, but that it can be entertained at all suggests that the supremacy of state over civil society is not just a Hegelian dream.

Nevertheless, the future of postcolonial development is no more predetermined than the fate of freedom in the nations that first autonomously modernized. Fundamentalist and tribal reaction may succeed in tearing down the incomplete constructions of civil society and political democracy, just as a resurgent fascism may threaten the "developed" nations that fail to fulfill the family, social, and political liberation that modernity has put before us. Whatever the future brings, the challenges of autonomous and external modernization will surface anew wherever the timeless normativity of freedom is rediscovered.

NOTES

1. See Alasdair MacIntyre, *After Virtue* (Notre Dame, Ind.: University of Notre Dame Press, 1981), 49ff.

2. William Maker, *Philosophy Without Foundations: Rethinking Hegel* (Albany: State University of New York Press, 1994), 21–45.

3. To the extent that Hegel's *Philosophy of Right* identifies normative validity with self-determination and employs a putatively self-determining conceptual development to specify the institutions of right, that work's anatomy of property right, moral autonomy, a free family, civil society, and constitutional self-government provides a recipe for modernity on its own distinctive anti-foundational terms.

4. This is why Hegel is correct to remark that a constitution cannot be produced through an act of making—as Napoleon learned in trying to impose a modern constitution on Spain. A constitution can become more than a piece of paper only if the nonpolitical prerequisites of political freedom are already at hand, and precisely because nonpolitical spheres are not directly administered by the state, they cannot be brought into being by political action alone.

5. G. W. F. Hegel, *Elements of the Philosophy of Right*, tr. H. B. Nisbet (Cambridge: Cambridge University Press, 1991), paragraphs 341–360, pp. 372–80.

6. G. W. F. Hegel, *The Philosophy of History*, tr. J. Sibree (New York: Dover, 1956), 9.

7. For if modern community inherently possesses a globalizing dynamic, any premodern community is liable to suffer that external impact, irrespective of its own internal metamorphic potential.

8. For this reason, recent U.S. legislation depriving resident aliens of welfare benefits is contrary to the rights of civil society.

9. Hegel, *Elements of the Philosophy of Right*, paragraphs 245, 246, 248, pp. 267–68, 269.

10. Rosa Luxemburg, *The Accumulation of Capital*, tr. Agnes Schwarzschild (New York: Monthly Review Press, 1968), 329ff.

11. Hegel spells out the basic logic of these developments in paragraphs 190–195 of his analysis of the "System of Needs" in the *Philosophy of Right*.

12. Immanuel Kant, *The Metaphysics of Morals*, tr. Mary Gregor (New York: Cambridge University Press, 1991), 191.

13. Kant, *The Metaphysics of Morals*, paragraphs 58 and 62, pp. 154–55 and 158–59.

14. Although Hegel undercuts the freedom of spouses by admitting a traditional hierarchy between husband and wife, he recognizes that the ethical community of the family is particular in scope. See Hegel, *The Philosophy of Right*, paragraphs 161–172.

15. See the remarks to paragraphs 273 and 274, and the addition to paragraph 274 of Hegel's *Elements of the Philosophy of Right*, pp. 311–13.

16. See the addition to paragraph 274 of Hegel's *Elements of the Philosophy of Right*, 313.

17. Hegel, *Elements of the Philosophy of Right*, paragraphs 190–192, 241–245, pp. 228–29, 265–67.

18. In arguing for the inevitable turn to premodern markets and the inevitable collapse of capitalism when they have all been assimilated within the relations of capital, Rosa Luxemburg ignores the internal resources that public works, credit expansion, and deficit spending provide for capital accumulation. This is due to her reliance on Marx's labor theory of value and the derivative reproduction schemes of capital developed by Marx in volume 2 of *Capital*, both of which preclude these and other facilitators of economic growth.

19. Karl Marx, *Capital*, vol. 1, tr. Samuel Moore and Edward Aveling (New York: International Publishers, 1967), 713ff.

20. Karl Marx, *Karl Marx on Colonialism and Modernization*, ed. Shlomo Avineri (New York: Anchor Books, 1968), 77–82, 84, 99.

21. Hannah Arendt, *The Origins of Totalitarianism* (New York: Harcourt Brace Jovanovich, 1973), 185ff.

22. See John Stuart Mill, *Considerations on Representative Government*, ch. XVIII, in John Stuart Mill, *Three Essays* (Oxford: Oxford University Press, 1987), 408–23.

23. Hegel, *Elements of the Philosophy of Right*, 376.

24. The richest and most competitive nations may promote a free trade ideology to roll back all such political intervention, but every independent state retains the option of regulating its own economy and its relation to foreign capital. Uncompensated nationalizations, tariff and import quotas, limits on foreign ownership of enterprises, flaunting patent and copyright agreements, and other subsidies for domestic commerce all have certain costs, but political independence alone makes it possible to wager these risks.

CHAPTER 5

Freedom in the Body: The Body as Subject of Rights and Object of Property in Hegel's "Abstract Right"

Angelica Nuzzo

The notion of "person" is central in the contemporary philosophical discussion because of its implications both for general ethics and for the theory of rights. In particular, the problem of the relation between the person and his/her own body deserves special attention. From that relation a series of questions arises that have a fundamental bearing in practical philosophy. We may ask: Are there any limits to the capacity of a person to dispose of his/her body? Can a person change or manipulate his/her own body, improve its physical capacities, sell either his/her body or parts or particular functions of it? Can/should the body become the object of a market exchange or of a contract among free persons? Does the regulation of all those practices belong to the sphere of rights or to the sphere of morality? Has the person duties and/or rights to his/her own body?

The answer to all these questions ultimately depends on the understanding of each of the terms of the relation. In the history of philosophy the connection of the person to his/her own body has been shaped in the most different ways. According to one model, the person is totally and essentially identical with his/her body. In the perspective of a "personalistic" metaphysics, the person is the substantial unity of body and soul, is the psycho-physical dimension in which the body manifests not simply the phenomenal exteriority of the human being, but rather his/her true ontological dimension. In this view, the body is neither an "object" nor, consequently, a "property" nor a "commodity"; it is rather the expression of the human dignity and worth and has a "value" that can never become, or be reduced to, a market value. According to the opposite model, on the other hand, the body is to be seen as the mortal and material "prison" or "grave" of an immortal and purely noumenal soul. In the tradition of modern philosophy, the attention has been drawn both to the body as a *material* principle of *individuation* and to its sheer *instrumental* function. The human being *is* not his/her body; he/she merely has a body that should be used like any other object of property.[1]

The notion of 'person' that Hegel develops first in the Logic and then along the whole exposition of the philosophy of spirit (from the anthropology of 'subjective spirit' to the philosophy of religion in 'absolute spirit') seems to offer a perfect example of the modern understanding of the concept. What defines personality is the capacity to make abstraction from all determinations and conditions that affect thinking as well as the will. The body is considered precisely as one of those external conditions—indeed the most immediate and constantly present one. Furthermore, the person can and must take possession of his/her body, thereby reducing it to the form of his/her phenomenal existence. The body is the person's own *Dasein*, is the mirror and the *instrument* of his/her free activity. The person is therefore master of his/her body although this cannot be claimed in a totally unconditional way. It is the systematic context in which Hegel places his discussion of the concept of personality and of its necessary relation to the body, that sets the limits of the possibility for subjectivity to subordinate its own physical nature.

It is important to stress the fact that a strong systematic project underlies Hegel's development of the idea of "person" as a particular figure or moment in his theory of modern subjectivity. At the level of subjective spirit, the idea of person is preceded by the "soul," by "consciousness" and "self-consciousness," and finally by the moment of "free will." In the sphere of objective spirit, the relation between the person and his/her body is placed by Hegel in a dialectical progression that shows how the person in his/her activity is constantly and necessarily bonded to nature as well as to the different forms of social and political life. In this context the relation to the body remains the objective basis out of which the person is going to develop the whole set of conditions that allow him/her to live a really universal "ethical life." However, if the structures of subjectivity vary along the development of spirit, the notion of "body" changes accordingly. Systematically, the "body" that relates to the soul *is not the same "body"* that relates to self-consciousness or to the free will.

In the sphere of right the body does not simply *naturally* belong to the person, as was still the case for the soul or for consciousness, but rather needs to be "artificially" appropriated by a particular act of the will that is placed in the context of a juridical recognition. At this level the person cannot be free just making abstraction from all natural and physical presuppositions. The body must now be recognized as a constitutive rather than accidental condition of free personality. The concept of person is the birthplace of subjective, abstract freedom viewed as the highest capacity of abstracting from all content—even from what is mostly "ours." Yet abstract freedom is not the highest form of freedom. According to Hegel, the "idea" of freedom needs to be "realized" in the objective world, engaging in a complete involvement with—rather than in a total abstraction from—all forms of worldly existence. The body is precisely the very first and immediate incarnation of subjective reason in the objective world, representing also, at the same time, the spirit's first rational transformation or cultivation of nature. On the other hand, the body, being the person's most immediate form of existence, constitutes the first given condition of *intersubjectivity*. The body is the immediate "being-for-other" (*Sein-für-Anderes*) of personality. Therefore, it represents one of the essential presuppositions of "recognition" (*Anerkennung*).[2]

In the following reflections, I am going to analyze the function of the body (as *Leib* and *Körper*)[3] in the first section (*Property*) of the first part of Hegel's *Philosophy of Right*. In "Abstract Right" the notion of the body is posited in a mutual interaction with that of personality. I argue that the relation between the person and his/her body is a highly *dialectical* one. According to it, despite the person's *logical priority* over the body, it is only a sort of necessary identification between the person and his/her own body that justifies the dialectical advancement of the first sphere of objective spirit. That identification ultimately puts the body on the same level as the person and thereby guarantees to it a particular *ontological status* over all other natural things (*Sachen* and *Dinge*). This ontological status, in turn, grounds the *juridical privilege* of the body over the other "external" things. The natural as well as juridical determination of the body is precisely what sets the limits of the person's free activity as subject of "rights," and what grounds the possibility of an intersubjective relation among persons. The result is a logical movement that goes from the representation of the body as an *object of property* to its *being person* and therefore the very *subject of rights*. Hegel expresses this dialectical relation in the transition between the two first sections of "Abstract Right"—the transition from "property" to "contract." The claim that the person "*has*" a body in his or her possession leads one to acknowledge that the body "*is*" person as subject of rights and consequently is the subject—and never the object—of the mutual relation juridically established by the contract.

The dialectical tension that relates the person to his/her body at the level of "Abstract Right" is inherited from the sphere of subjective spirit and more precisely from the development of the structures of self-consciousness in the *Phenomenology*.[4] Both the "struggle for recognition" and the "master/slave relationship" express a self-contradictory double relation between self-consciousness and the body. In those moments, self-consciousness experiences on the one hand its own superiority and independence from the body—viewed as its objective *Anderssein*—while on the other hand, it acquires the precise consciousness of the necessary and exclusive bond with it. Only at the level of right is personality eventually able to transform the acceptance of a necessary relation to the body in the free act of its voluntary appropriation. Yet the dialectical nature of the relation reveals itself in the possibility of a *separation* of the two sides—this possibility is *death*. However, in the sphere of "abstract right" a voluntarily chosen death is impossible. The living being that the embodied person as subject of rights is, is only a finite individual being whose true "reality," or really meaningful "life," can be reached only on a higher level of universality. The "transformation" that this move requires from subjectivity implies a metamorphosis of the individual body toward the collective whole of a "body politic"—the sphere of *Sittlichkeit*. Only life in this ethically expanded "body" eventually allows the individual "person" to live a really "universal" *ethical life*. Only at this level can death be the object of free choice.

1. THE WILL, THE BODY, AND THE PERSON

The notions of "person" and "personality" have a crucial meaning in the first part of Hegel's *Philosophy of Right*. The systematic as well as ontological "basis" (*Boden*) of right is the realm of spirit[5] that brought the transition from its subjectivity into objectivity to completion. This accomplished transition is precisely what constitutes the scientific "proof and deduction" of the concept of right[6] and thereby guarantees the necessary beginning of the new "science of right." This philosophical science is grounded as a 'part' of the system of speculative philosophy (R §2). The problem of this new systematic sphere is for Hegel to offer a concept of subjectivity that can develop into the different forms and figures (*Gestaltungen*) of spirit's own actuality (*Wirklichkeit*). The notion of the "will" presents itself as the most appropriate candidate for this function. The preceding realm of subjective spirit ended with the moment of the "free will."[7] But the will cannot be *really* free in its limited subjectivity because freedom is self-actualization and self-manifestation of the concept in the element of existence. Therefore, in order to exist in its *objective freedom*, the will must take up the successive figures of its *Dasein*. This is the logical program of Hegel's *Philosophy of Right*. The first moment of this process is represented by the notion of '*Person*'.

At the beginning of his treatise, Hegel gives us two methodological devices. (1) Since the philosophical science of right has the "Idea" of right as its object, the method has to follow the immanent development of two related sides: the determination of the "concept of right" on the one side, and its actual realization on the other.[8] (2) Furthermore, according to the specific nature of those two sides, the philosophical exposition must present the concrete figures that each time correspond to the different moments of the concept, that is, universality, particularity, and individuality. Hegel identifies the beginning of the science of right with the task of developing the structures of the "will" according to those three moments of the concept (R §7). Now, the concept of the will is "freedom" (R §7). Hegel explains the relation between the will and its concept bringing in an interesting analogy with the body. Freedom is the "substance" or "substantiality" (R §§4, 7) of the will. But in explaining how freedom really accomplishes this both substantial and conceptual function, Hegel adds that it constitutes the gravity or the weight (*Schwere*) of the will, "just as gravity constitutes the substantiality of the body." Freedom is precisely what carries the abstractness of the will down to earth, down to concrete existence and to all the "practical" problems that this existence implies. It is a "naturalistic" model that Hegel is proposing here: freedom determines the development of the will in the same manner as gravity determines the movement of the body. In that way Hegel sketches out the "scene" that the *Philosophy of Right* is going to animate with its figures.

Carried by its weight down to the objective world, the will is determined by freedom to seek a *Dasein* in which to be embodied. Hegel's perspective here is very far from Plato's: the embodiment of the subject (soul or free will) is for Hegel the first act of an actual freedom, not the negative sign of its finitude. "Right" is the first, more abstract and general figure of that *Dasein* (R §29). In the sphere of "abstract right," because of its initial immediacy, the free will is first of all in the conceptual moment of its *individuality*. As such, it is the "*individual* will of a subject." Moreover, in its *particularity* the will is projected toward an immediately given outside world in which it finds the manifold content of its purposes and activities (R §34). The *universal* moment of the will is captured by a self-relation that posits the subject as "*Person*." "Personality" recollects now all previous structures of the will, and establishes "that as *this* person I am completely determined in all respects (in my inner arbitrary will [*Willkür*], drive, and desire, as well as in relation to my immediate external existence—*Dasein*), and that I am finite, yet totally pure self-reference, and thus know myself in my finitude as *infinite, universal, and free*" (R §35).

The whole development that led to this situation tells us, first, that the notions of "person" and "personality" apply here for Hegel to a strictly juridical context—that is, they are derived as logical implications from the idea of "right" as *Dasein* of the free will. In other words, 'person' cannot be, for Hegel, a category that voices a content which is in the first instance *moral*. Moreover, supporting the necessity of introducing the term "person" as opposed to that of "subject," Hegel argues that here the term "subject" would not have been adequately determined[9] in order to express the specific set of relations that personality has to face—as the subject represents for Hegel only the "possibility of personality."[10] Second, we have to stress that a person is always "this" (*Dieser*) person, is always empirically designated (pointed out for some empirical features and characters),[11] and finally, that precisely this *empirical individuation* is what makes the *juridical universality* and the freedom of the subject in its pure self-relation. Evidently enough, it is this latter paradoxical point that needs to be explained. The complete determination that renders the subject a *free person* involves from the very beginning two different sides: the *bodily* side and the absolute aspect of *pure self-reflection*. The first side includes one's capacity of choice, one's empirical and physical drives, impulses, and desires as well as the whole connection of one's external existence. The body is here at the same time what governs and is governed by an empirically conditioned *arbitrium*, and the center of the "being in the world" proper to a particular subject.

From this analysis we can conclude that the idea of a reflexive self-relation through the mediation of empirical external existence is constitutive of the concept of "*Person*" introduced by Hegel at the very beginning of the sphere of "abstract right." Furthermore, it is evident that it is not the general notion of an external world that is crucial, in the first instance, to the self-reference of the person, but rather the idea of a complete determinate totality of empirical conditions that makes of the person a subject existent as "*this* person." This totality is precisely the person's own body. The body is therefore constitutive of the concept of person: it is not simply its external correlate, but is rather one of its fundamental *conceptual* elements. The whole movement of the first sphere of objective spirit arises from the relation between will and body immanently established by the notion of person. Confronted with an external nature, and in search for an earthly existence of its own, the will strives in order to pull that existence away from natural objects and to transform that existence into its own. In this process, the relation to the body remains the model or the rational basis (*Grundlage*). After the appropriation of the body, every further appropriation takes on this same form: I declare something to be my property when I put in it a purpose that originally it did not have, *when I put in it another soul than the one that originally animated it*, "when I put in it my own soul" (R §44Z). Thereby is established not only the statement "my body is my property," but also the claim "my property is/becomes my body."

At this point, however, a further condition must be added to the picture. Hegel repeatedly insists on the fact that the 'personality' with which we have to deal at the level of the "spirit which is in and for itself" means not the same as the "self-consciousness" of the "spirit in its appearance" (R §35A). What has to be specifically developed from the concept of person is a whole structure of *juridical relations*. In this perspective, both the *natural* attitude that binds the subject to its body and the body's natural priority over other external objects are not enough to ground the *juridical* structure of the "person." This is the reason why the body, as well as all other objects in the world, needs to become a person's first object of "*property*," wherefore it needs to be *appropriated* by a special act of the will.

2. THE PERSON AND THE "EXTERNAL SPHERE" OF HIS/HER FREEDOM

Still reasoning in terms of the "imperative" of freedom that pushes the will toward its realization in the forms of Dasein, Hegel's logic carries us one step further. The first step was to acknowledge that in the realm of right the free will has a concrete existence in the juridical figure of the person. The second step consists in showing that the person, in turn, can have a juridical existence as subject of rights only in and through his/her body—that is, as *owner of his/her body*. Precisely this relation is the ground for the concept of "property."

According to Hegel's presentation, the notion of 'person' is not simply *descriptive* of a set of given juridical relations. It rather entails the "*commandment* of right" (R §36) that Hegel expresses in two clauses. "Be a person" is the first provision, directed to each free individual subject as such. "Respect others as persons" is the second provision that Hegel addresses to each individual that, as person, necessarily relates to other persons through his/her "being-for-others"—namely, through the body as his/her immediate and first object of property. In this second clause of the *Rechtsgebot* Hegel translates Kant's categorical imperative in the sphere of right. In order to fulfill the twofold commandment of right the person "must" provide for him/herself an "external sphere of freedom." This is going to be, once again, a form of *Dasein*. Because of its initial abstractness, that *Dasein* is qualified, this time, as *external* to the will and therefore as "immediately different" and "separable" (R §41) from it. The "sphere of freedom" that results from that exteriorization is the determination of "property." Person is for Hegel the owner of property. Property is so essential to the juridical status of a person that a person without property would be a *contradictio in adjecto*.

"Exteriority" (*Äußerlichkeit*) is the first feature of what needs to become the property of the person in order for him to really be free as a person. Immediate exteriority is an "otherness" that necessarily remains "other" through the possibility of separating oneself from it. The first, and most general, form of exteriority for spirit is nature. Moreover, *Äußerlichkeit* is what can become the object of an act of *Äußerung*. We can distinguish three different types of *Äußerlichkeit*: (1) that which things reveal by their being immediately set out "*against me*"—a kind of *Dasein* that reacts harshly *against* the subject in its being different from it; (2) the *Äußerlichkeit* of a simple *natural* existence that is exterior precisely *because it belongs immediately to nature*, and that, at the same time and for that very same reason, belongs to me without exercising any opposition against me—this is evidently the exteriority that belongs to my naturally given body. (3) The third kind of exteriority characterizes spiritual things (*Geistiges*): they are exterior because they are made exterior by the will's own act of *Äußerung*.

This classification remains at the basis of Hegel's development of "property." The first moment of the process is characterized by the natural existence of the person. This form of existence has two sides: one that is inwardly related to the person, the other that reaches out to an external world (R §43). The subject can and must first of all take possession of the sphere of its 'natural existence' in order to become a person. Hegel explains the traditional distinction between possession (*Besitz*) and property (*Eigentum*) by saying that possession is the simple capacity of having something under the control of "my external power" (*Gewalt*), whereas property is the true juridical determination of my will as an effectively actual will (R §45). There is a sense here in which the appropriation of the body is even a condition for the simple possession of other things, as my external power that allows me to take possession of things is nothing but the physical force of my body.

Yet, the true *juridical* relation between body and person is introduced by Hegel as a relation of *property*. The first "thing" (*Sache*) that becomes property of the person is the body. The body is a natural form of existence that is exterior simply because it belongs to nature. In its exteriority the body is immediately *mine* without opposing any resistance to me as its legitimate owner. The body as property is now raised from its *natural determination* to its being the *juridical Dasein* of the person—it becomes that by means of which the individual subject can be viewed as a subject of rights. But every *Dasein*, for the logical determination expressed by this category, is "being-for-other."[12] Thereby the body becomes the appearance through which the person is a person *for other individuals*. Precisely in this determination of the bodily possession of the person, the two provisions given by the commandment of right receive their first concrete fulfillment (or the possibility of their infringement).

If my will becomes "personal" in property, and if the person is always necessarily *this* individual person, then property constitutes what is essentially personal of this specific will. Property is therefore "private property." It expresses not just an external, more or less accidental, addition to the person but it is rather what constitutes the personality of the person in its singular individuality—in its proper *Dieses*. Precisely because of this necessary individuation of the person, the first object of property must be the body. In the sphere of right, the very meaning of my individuality is that "I am *alive* in this *organic body*, which is my *undivided* external existence [*Dasein*], *universal* in content, the real possibility of all further determined existence. But as a person, I at the same time possess *my life and body*, like other things, *only in so far as I so will it*" (R §47). As a *living* being, my body *is* immediately my own objective being. The organic nature of the body requires, however, that it should be an *"undivided"* (*ungeteiltes*) unity or totality—an aspect which is going to be very significant in the juridical context given that this determination of the body remains the "real possibility" of all successive forms of existence that the subject is going to present at the different levels of the development of objective spirit. Contrasted to my simply natural existence is my existence as a person. In this case, to all that precedes should be added that *"I have"* my life and my body in my possession. This is an immediate consequence of an act of free decision.

3. TO BE FREE IN ONE'S OWN BODY

What Hegel presents in this way is the *transition from my naturally being alive in the body to my being really free in it*. Whereas it is common to all living beings to be alive in a body, only human beings can and must acquire a *"right to their own body"*[13]—a right to be free in their natural body. This right must represent a step further even in relation to the simple possibility or capacity proper of human beings of depriving themselves voluntarily of the whole or of parts of their body. Suicide or mutilation are only acts of a purely negative, subjective, and abstract *arbitrium* so that to this kind of liberty *no right* can be claimed in the sphere of abstract right. Consequently, to be actually free in one's own body and life cannot simply mean to have the possibility of destroying or mutilating oneself. According to Hegel, I am not really free in my body—and I am not a person at all—if I decide to take my life or to mutilate my body although my having the possibility of this choice is the condition for me to be a person.

It has been observed[14] that in his formulations of R §47 Hegel seems to cancel the fundamental distinction between two radically different acts: the *free renunciation* of life and body on the one hand, and the *free acquisition* of life and body on the other. I think that while this difference is going to be discussed by Hegel later, what he presents in the passage that we are presently analyzing is the systematic condition that grounds the possibility of that very distinction. In order to understand what is the difference, *as far as right is concerned*, between the free decision of renouncing life or the body, and the free decision of acquiring a body, Hegel needs to introduce the distinction between my simply *natural* being in the body and my *having* a body as person. The important point is that this distinction is going to be a *spiritual* and a *physical* distinction at the same time.

Because of the immediacy and abstractness of their relation, the will and its external sphere of freedom are initially separable and not yet adequate to each other. But what the organic body is not commensurate to is not the natural existence of the subject but rather its objective spiritual appearance (R §48). The body is placed in a twofold relation with the person: it is, at the same time, what is inwardly and outwardly mostly "mine." In the perspective of spirit, however, the body cannot simply be something given. This is the reason why, at this point, the person must strive for the appropriation and spiritual transformation of his/her body. It is the first provision of the *Rechtsgebot* that commands one to become a person. What previously was presented as the organic "undivided external existence" of a simple living human being must now be transformed into the "spirit's willing organ (*williges Organ*) and soul-inspired instrument (*beseeltes Mittel*)" (R §48).

Hegel is exhibiting here the *spiritual* difference between two forms of *physical* existence of the subject. Since precisely this is the ground for the ontological and axiological distinction between the body of a living creature and the body of a person—and not the fact that a human being can simply decide to renounce his/her life—Hegel's point is not to indicate the difference between the two acts of appropriating one's body and life on the one hand, and destroying one's body or physical life on the other. His argument is rather to show that in order to exist as a free subject in his/her body, the person must willingly take possession of that body, at the same time radically transforming its physical function and existence. The free act of becoming a person implies a physical metamorphosis of the organic body. To push Hegel's argument even further, we can say that, to a certain extent, the free will of the subject striving toward personality does not have a real choice of whether to appropriate or to renounce its body or life. The subject can either renounce life and not be a person, or appropriate its body, radically transforming it and becoming a person. But a person as a person cannot destroy or renounce his/her body or life—and this because of a juridical, not a moral ground. The intimation of right, "Be a person," gives the normative support to Hegel's claim.

4. TO BE FREE FOR THE OTHERS IN ONE'S OWN BODY

The double relation between body and person according to which the person needs to be embodied in an undivided and indivisible organism, while the body becomes the organic instrument of the person's will, is the basis from which Hegel infers both a *limited right* for the person to dispose of his/her body and an *unlimited right* for each person to be respected in his/her body by the other persons.

The sphere of property develops along three stages: (1) the act through which the person 'takes possession' of the external world and its objects; (2) the "use of things" as far as they are objects of property; and (3) the "alienation of property." The act through which the person takes possession of his/her body sanctions the beginning of the collaboration between the will and the body in the progressive appropriation and use of all other external objects. "Physical seizure"—*körperliche Besitzergreifung* (R §55)—is the first mode of appropriation. The body represents the immediate presence (*Gegenwart*) of the person in the objective world, constitutes the individuation of the subject in *this* space and time (R §56). Now, the physical act through which the person establishes his/her bodily presence in a sphere of objects guarantees his/her first right to property. This process shows, at the same time, the *use* that the will makes of the body as its own "soul-inspired instrument." Furthermore, the person as owner of external objects can alienate them. Alienation affects what is *Äußerliches* by its own nature (R §65). On the basis of the foregoing process, Hegel sets the *limits* of one's right to dispose of his/her body—both in the use and in the alienation of it. The imperative of right, "Be a person," functions here as the normative principle that forbids one to misuse one's body (R §48A), to mutilate oneself, to commit suicide, to give oneself in slavery, and to alienate all that belongs to the essential nature of the person. Since life and body are the necessary conditions of personality, the right to life and to a free use of the body can never be alienated, can never become the object of a contract or of market relations.[15] "In so far as I am alive, my body and my soul . . . are not separated. *My body is the existence (Dasein) of freedom.*"[16]

If the body is the immediate form of the person's own *Dasein* this, in turn, always implies a "being-for-other"—the relation of the person to other persons. I am free in my body when I willingly take possession of it and thereby become a "person." But "*for others* I am essentially a free being according to the way in which I am in immediate possession of my body" (R §48A). How I relate to my body, how I concretely act as its owner—by using or misusing it, by temporarily alienating its functions or its parts, and so on—tell the others if, and how, I am a free person in my body. While for me my naturally being in my body and my juridical appropriation of it represent two different actions, for the others my being in the body and my acting as a person in it are one and the same reality. My body is the existence of freedom not only for myself but also for the others. "For others I am in my body. I am free for the other only in so far as I am free in my existence (*Dasein*)" (R §48A). It is only by an act of abstract subjective freedom that I can consider myself free even if I am in chains, even if my body is abused or subjected to the power of an other. In the sphere of right, however, my freedom is not separable from my body. I cannot retire in myself from my external existence and be free. In the realm of objective spirit, I am free for others only in what I feel and live in my body. As person I am nothing but my body. "Violence done *to my body* by others is violence done *to me.*" It is precisely from these relations that Hegel infers the unlimited right of the person to be respected by others as person in and through his/her own body. Thereby the second provision of the *Rechtsgebot*, "Respect others as persons," is addressed.

NOTES

1. In speaking here of two conflicting "models" I am obviously not meaning to be in any sense historically accurate, but only to present in a sketchy way two theoretically opposed possibilities of thinking about the relation between body and person.

2. For the role played by the "category" of "recognition" in the development of the *Philosophy of Right*, cf. Robert R. Williams, *Hegel's Ethics of Recognition* (New York, 1998).

3. The first general meaning of this terminological distinction proper to the German language can be expressed by the opposition in which the two terms

respectively appear: *Leib* is opposed to *Seele* (soul), whereas *Körper* is opposed to *Geist*. For an excellent analysis of these terms in relation to Hegel's anthropology section of the *Enzyklopädie*, cf. M. Wolff, *Das Körper-Seele Problem. Kommentar zu Hegel, Enzyklopädie (1830)*, §389 (Frankfurt a.M.: Klostermann, 1992).

4. For an analysis of the problem of the "body" in Hegel's *Phenomenology*, cf. John E. Russon, *The Self and Its Body in Hegel's Phenomenology of Spirit* (Toronto: University of Toronto Press, 1997).

5. R (= *Grundlinien der Philosophie des Rechts*) §4.

6. R §2A (Anmerkung = Remark).

7. *Enzyklopädie der philosophischen Wissenschaften in Grundrisse* (= Enz.), §§481–482.

8. R §1 and the Remark that contains Hegel's first methodological statement for the *Philosophy of Right*. On the problem of the "logic" of Hegel's *Philosophy of Right*, cf. A. Nuzzo, *Rappresentazione e concetto nella 'logica' della "Filosofia del diritto" di Hegel* (Napoli: Guida, 1990), and A. Nuzzo, *Vorstellung und Begriff zwischen Logik und Realphilosophie bei Hegel*, in *Hegel Studien*, 25, 1990, pp. 41–63.

9. For the difference between "person" and "subject," see the handwritten remarks to R §35 and the Addition.

10. R §35Z (Zusatz = Addition).

11. Both in the *Phenomenology of Spirit* and in the *Logic* Hegel insists on showing that the form of the *Dieses*—the individuality of the "this"—can only be designated by an extralinguistic *Zeigen*, by our pointing it out; for the relation of this Hegelian doctrine to Wittgenstein, cf. the interesting remarks in M. Forster, *Hegel's Idea of a Phenomenology of Spirit* (Chicago: University of Chicago Press, 1998).

12. See also the handwritten remark to R §58: the "being-for *other*" is here specifically said to be the "other of *my* personality."

13. R §47, handwritten remark.

14. See L. Siep, *Leiblichkeit, Selbstgefühl und Persönlichkeit in Hegels Philosophie des Geistes*, in *Praktische Philosophie im Deutschen Idealismus* (Frankfurt a.M.: Suhrkamp, 1990), pp. 195–217, especially p. 212.

15. See the important handwritten remarks to R §66A, where Hegel excludes a right to suicide, mutilation, castration, and even to the didactic activity in surgical operations; see also R §70.

16. R §48A (my emphasis).

CHAPTER 6

Hegel on the Justification of Punishment

Dudley Knowles

My claim in this essay is that Hegel's theory of punishment is a very near miss. It is fair to say that the theory is complex and unclear—what else could account for the variety of interpretations it has provoked, the amount of good work directed to its exegesis and evaluation? But I think a clear path can be traced through the textual thickets. Unfortunately, when clarity dawns, we are left with a conclusion that I believe cannot serve to justify punishment: the claim that the criminal himself cannot complain if he is treated in roughly the way he has treated others. I want to end the essay on a provocative note by suggesting that Hegel's purpose, the justification of punishment within the normative framework of "Abstract Right,"[1] could best have been fulfilled had he espoused a hypothetical social contract theory. Hegel's refusal to do so is explicit. I suggest that he was confused.

Hegel wrote about punishment throughout his career; he discusses the problem in his early essay on *The Spirit of Christianity and its Fate*, in the essay on *Natural Law*, in the Jena manuscripts and the Nuremburg *Propaedeutic*. But the text on which I concentrate is the *Philosophy of Right*. His final statement of the principles of just punishment occurs at *PR* §220:

> When the right against crime takes the form of *revenge* (see §102), it is merely right *in itself*, not in a form that is lawful [*Rechtens*], i.e. it is not just [*gerecht*] in its existence [*Existenz*]. Instead of the injured party, the injured *universal* now makes its appearance, and it has its distinctive actuality in the court of law. It takes over the prosecution and penalization of crime, and these thereby cease to be the merely *subjective* and contingent retribution of revenge and are transformed into

the genuine reconciliation of right with itself, i.e. into *punishment*. Objectively, this reconciliation applies to the *law*, which restores and thereby *actualizes itself as valid* through the cancellation [*Aufheben*] of the crime; and subjectively, it applies to the criminal in that *his law*, *which is known by him* and is *valid* for him and *for his protection*, is enforced upon him in such a way that he himself finds in it the satisfaction of justice and merely the enactment of what is *proper to him* [*des Seinigen*].

A sound interpretation of Hegel's views will clarify the conclusion he reaches here and outline the arguments that sustain it. The burden of argumentation is effected earlier in the book, in subsection 3, "Wrong" of "Abstract Right." Let us turn in that direction.

CONTEXT: PERSONS AND RIGHTS

"Abstract Right" elaborates the moral perspective of persons, taking "person" to be a technical term denoting our first-shot (immediate) conception of ourselves as discrete, atomic individuals. The "person" is the familiar protagonist of modern liberalism, the agent conscious of himself merely as distinct from other individuals, the most skeletal, universally applicable mode of self-ascription. In the classical literature of political philosophy, Hegel's concept of the person best articulates the target of modern communitarian writings. The category is almost as empty and formulaic as these critics of liberalism suggest.[2]

Sparse though the concept of the person may be, it has an appropriate normative content—the capacity for rights—and an appropriate normative expression—the language of rights, summarized in the command or imperative of right as '*be a person and respect others as persons*' (PR §36). As they say nowadays, the right has priority over the good. At this stage of the dialectic, Hegel has nothing to say concerning characteristic human goals or ends.[3] "In formal right, therefore, it is not a question of particular interests, of my advantage or welfare" (PR §37). The rules of right are Nozickian side-constraints on action: "The necessity of this right is limited to the negative—*not to violate* personality and what ensues from personality. Hence there are only *prohibitions of right*" (PR §38).[4] "Abstract Right" therefore delineates the contours of a rights-based morality. The details are filled out in three movements: "Property" explains the necessity of rights to property and physical integrity; "Contract" advances the analysis to explain the structures of will manifest in interpersonal transactions; "Wrong" advances the analysis still further by explaining that rights are enforceable—and, in the particular case of criminal wrongs, how punishment is the appropriate response.[5] Hegel's account of punishment is thus lodged in a theory of rights. The point of the discussion of punishment is to show what is entailed by our concept of the person and its attendant doctrine of personal rights.

Of course, *our* prime interest may be in the philosophical problem of punishment; Hegel's chief aim, by contrast, is to show how our thinking about punishment informs our understanding of ourselves as rights-bearers.[6] His specific thesis is that "through this process of mediation [the righting of wrong, generally the infliction of punishment] whereby right returns to itself from its negation, it determines itself as *actual* and *valid*, whereas it was at first only *in itself* and something *immediate*" (*PR* §82).[7] The righting of wrong, whether it is effected in civil law by adjudication or compensation, or in criminal law by punishment, establishes the rights that persons characteristically claim as actual and valid in a way that their mere assertion, howsoever universal, could never achieve.

It is tempting to read Hegel's doctrine of punishment as the response to a difficult problem which all rights theorists face and which some have tackled explicitly.[8] Rights theorists, minimally, demand respect for physical integrity, territorial mobility, and private property. Such rights demand protection and enforcement by coercive legislation that sanctions the punishment of offenders. Punishment standardly takes the form of capital or corporal punishment, imprisonment, fines, or compulsory social service—all of these being measures that in the normal case would constitute rights violations. Hence rights theorists propose, as protective of rights, coercive instruments that standardly would violate rights. Rights theorists, then, have a *special* problem concerning the justification of punishment and we should expect their discussion of both rights and punishment to reflect this.

That said, I am unclear whether Hegel himself notices the point. He certainly does not address the problem directly as a problem concerning rights—in fact, read naively, his claim that punishment is the criminal's right suggests the opposite: punishment, far from constituting an incipient violation of the rights of the criminal, serves to respect them. On the other hand, exactly the same form of the problem emerges when it is couched in terms of the value of freedom. Rights are necessary to promote and protect freedom. The coercion of the criminal looks to diminish his freedom in just the way that the criminal limits and repudiates the freedom of his victim. As injuries to the criminal's will, the standard modes of punishment promise to infringe on his freedom. As soon as we insist that rights are enforceable—in Hegel's terms, "Abstract Right is a coercive right" (*PR* §94)—paradox threatens.[9]

THE STRUCTURE OF THE ARGUMENT

Let us extract from *PR* §220, quoted above, several theses that will form the agenda of our discussion:

> *First*, punishment, as imposed by courts of law, is the genuine reconciliation of right with itself.

> *Second*, this reconciliation has an objective characterization: summarily, the restoration of right.

> *Third*, this reconciliation has a subjective characterization: it is applied to the criminal on the grounds that he endorses its application. As expressed at *PR* §100, punishment is *"his* right . . . a *right for the criminal himself,* that is, a right *posited* in his *existent* will, in his *action."*

How are these theses related to each other? Each of them postures as a justification of punishment, so one might say: punishment is legitimate as the reconciliation of right with itself, and/or the restoration of right, and/or the recognition of right on the criminal's part. It is fair to say that the variety of *good* (and some bad!) interpretations of Hegel's discussion of punishment reflect the ambiguities of the "and/ors." Some readers have concentrated on one or another of these items; some have discussed two, or maybe three. I try to make sense of all three, defending the following theses.

The first claim, that punishment is the reconciliation of right with itself, is programmatic: it announces that the justification of punishment that is to follow is an implication of the theory of rights that has preceded it. As I suggested above, the notion of rights, their universal assertion and moral force, frames the context for the discussion of punishment that follows.

The second and third claims, concerning objectivity and subjectivity, may be viewed as distinct arguments. I argue that, although each may be (and have been) advanced independently as distinctive of Hegel's contribution to the philosophical problem of punishment, they work better in harness. This, of course, is Hegel's intention; this is how 'objectivity' and 'subjectivity' work for him. I shall outline the arguments severally, point out their limitations, and explain how these limitations are overcome when they are understood to imply each other. This is a nicely dialectical procedure, and, for Hegelians, it should be good news, supposing that the complex account is defensible. The bad news is that this defense is faulty. Were the flaws to be rectified, Hegel would be required to accept a version of contract theory that he did not fully understand, and which, to the extent that he did understand it, he positively rejected!

THE RECONCILIATION OF RIGHT WITH ITSELF

Mention of reconciliation calls to mind Michael Hardimon's recent discussion of Hegel's social theory.[10] Reconciliation is achieved when those susceptible to the tensions of fulfilling both individual and social projects—tensions that may amount to alienation—find themselves at home in the world, and a world that is a home for its members is a world of freedom.

One might doubt that Hardimon's analysis can have any grip on Hegel's discussion of punishment. "Abstract Right" does not delineate a properly social world. But the persons who inhabit this hypothetical[11] moral structure recognize norms of property and physical integrity that are interpersonally valid and engage in transactions that express a common, though contingently fixed, will. If the institutions of ethical life comprise the actual social world, we can think of "Abstract Right" as a quasi-social world. It is not the pre-social world of solitary individuals that Rousseau conjectures in the *Discourse on the Origin of Inequality*. As in the states of nature encountered in Hobbes's *Leviathan* and Locke's *Second Treatise of Government*, persons like us (rather than our ancestors) confront each other with a social problem: how to manage interactions so as to avoid conflict and effect cooperation. It establishes in the foreground of discussion the fact that persons like us tend to assert conflicting claims of right—hypostatized as "Wrong," whether unintentional (nonmalicious wrong, *PR* §§84–86) or intentional (Fraud, *PR* §§87–89, or Crime, *PR* §§90–103)—which require arbitration or adjudication. Not only is "Abstract Right" a social world in this weak sense; as in Locke's natural state, its members have a distinctive moral status; as persons, they have a capacity for rights on the basis of which they make claims to respect from each other. So "Abstract Right" is enough of a social world to make talk of reconciliation apt, if it has features that call for reconciliation.

Furthermore (and this is the point of my citation of the conclusion of Hegel's discussion of punishment at *PR* §220), the hypothetical or abstracted construction of "Abstract Right" is integrated into the structures of ethical life chiefly in the first two figures of "Civil Society"—the "System of Needs" and the "Administration of Justice." At this level of analysis, members of "Civil Society" identify their social world as one in which the rights that they claim as persons, as atomic, discrete, individuals (albeit integrated into families—male heads of families, for the most part) find institutional expression and recognition.

We can attempt an understanding of the reconciliation of right with itself by first exploring the conditions under which such a reconciliation is necessary. Formally, it is the fact of wrongdoing that calls for reconciliation. Wrongdoing is characterized as a show or semblance of right. Some sort of false claim concerning the principles of right is made by the wrongdoer. The wrong may be an unintentional error, calling for adjudication. Or it may be a fraud, wherein deception parades as respect for right, mutton is sold as lamb. Or it may, in the particular case of crime, involve a rejection of the principles of right. Hegel announces: "The initial use of coercion, as force employed by a free agent in such a way as to infringe the existence [*Dasein*] of freedom in its *concrete* sense—i.e. to infringe right as right—is *crime*" (*PR* §95).

The implication is twofold: the criminal's use of coercion violates the particular right of the victim to the object of his legitimate claims, and hence his freedom, and in addition, denies his moral status as a person, his capacity for rights.[12] The criminal, say a car thief, harms the victim, if not twice-over, then in two related domains, failing to respect both his specific right to the car he steals and the victim's moral status as an owner, a person with rights.

There is a contradiction at the heart of crime or, if not exactly a contradiction, then a couple of competing claims. The victim is a person, asserting a capacity for rights and making a specific claim to be, for example, the owner of this car. The thief, who has driven it away, rejects the victim's rightful claim and, by implication, his moral status as a person, a bearer of rights.

Unfortunately, at this stage in the argument of the *Philosophy of Right*, Hegel's analysis looks as though it collapses into a string of metaphors that darken rather than clarify the position. Crime is a nullity as manifested by the subsequent nullification of the infringement when punishment is effected. Punishment is the negation of a negation, the actuality of right, the necessary mediation of right with itself as it achieves the cancellation (annulment, negation, *Aufhebung*) of its infringement. This is the sort of rhetoric that has given Hegel a bad name with impatient critics. As Wood points out, if this language is taken at face value, some very bad arguments are being sketched.[13]

If these phrases are to have any purchase on reality, they must be construed loosely as trailers for the closer arguments to follow.[14] We must read Hegel as insisting that persons cannot be, know, or feel themselves to be at home in a world where conflicting claims are made regarding each other's moral status and specific rights. The demand for the reconciliation of right with itself is the demand that the conflict or contradiction be sorted out—and, evidently, the way to do this is to vindicate one of the conflicting claims, advancing the analysis of rights by ascribing to them a force which was hitherto unperceived or unrecognized (as we shall see, on the part of the criminal). Better still, we can seek to demonstrate to one of the contending parties that they themselves must accept the decisive judgment as an implication of other things they affirm. *This how Hegel proceeds.* Mercifully, we can abandon the rhetoric and attempt to track down the arguments.

THE RESTORATION OF RIGHT

Hegel tells us explicitly that punishment is the restoration of right. The claim is first made at *PR* §99: "Thus, an injury to the latter [the criminal] as an existent will is the cancellation [*Aufheben*] of the crime, *which would otherwise be regarded as valid,* and the restoration of right." It is repeated, as we have seen, at *PR* §220, where the "genuine reconciliation of right with itself" is effected objectively by legal punishment, which "restores [the law concerning rights] and thereby *actualizes itself as valid.*"

This reading of Hegel's theory of punishment has produced a dense and useful literature in recent years. In 1971, David Cooper explained Hegel's talk of punishment restoring the right as the assertion of a logical or conceptual thesis. It is a necessary condition on rights being successfully asserted that their violation be punished. "Unless people are generally apprehended and punished for preventing others doing *x,* there is reason to suppose that the latter do not have the right to do *x.*"[15] Although Cooper stresses the conceptual connection between the assertion of rights and the application of just punishment, Peter J. Steinberger argues that the conceptual connection has not been drawn tightly enough. Since it relies on empirical judgments to the effect that only the *punishment* of offenders (i.e., hard treatment, and not, for example, public denunciation) can vindicate the rights which the criminal challenges, it misrepresents the logical or conceptual groundings of Hegel's defense of punishment.[16] Allen Wood notices Hegel's talk of restoring the right and associates it with Feinberg's expressivist theory.[17] He is ambivalent about attributing this theme to Hegel, claiming that Cooper's explication fails on all grounds: it is not explicitly stated in the texts, and, if it were, it would be a poor argument.[18] Stephen Houlgate has challenged Wood's rejection of a conceptual thesis, claiming that "a [criminal] violation cannot therefore be allowed to stand but must be negated so that the necessary validity of right is restored."[19] In the same volume, Wood replies forcefully, challenging the 'conceptual' interpretation of the restoration of right theme and rejecting the argument, once more, as "*just no good.*"[20]

We can begin to adjudicate these disputes by paraphrasing Hegel's statement of the position at *PR* §97. If an ostensible right is violated and the violator is not punished (supposing him to be known and available for punishment, etc.), we must regard his deed as innocent; if he has taken some property, we must regard that property as his. *Contrariwise*, if the criminal is punished, the status quo ante crime is publicly restored; both the victim's moral status and his specific rights are vindicated. The deed cannot be both a crime and right.[21] It is either not a crime or not right—and the response, by way of condonation or punishment, demonstrates one's judgment of it. Are these conceptual claims? As they used to say, it all depends what you mean by "conceptual." Cooper amplifies his interpretation by the employment of the Austinian apparatus of performative utterances, so perhaps this argument is best seen as the application of conceptual analysis of the 'ordinary language' variety.[22] This kind of analysis evidently takes on board ground-level empirical beliefs (or "presuppositions") on the part of those whose discourse is being analyzed—which is why Steinberger feels Cooper's account is mistaken. (Steinberger's own contribution is an even more pernickety employment of this philosophical genre.) Wood gestures toward Feinberg's expressivist theory as a close relation, but, so far as I can see, does not endorse this reading, since he believes that a consequentialist concern for the restoration of rights cannot be reconciled with other, central, propositions of Hegel's theory, including notably the claim that punishment is retributive in intent. (Other critics have claimed that Hegel's account becomes teleological if the purpose of punishment is to restore the right—a version of rights- or freedom-consequentialism, perhaps.)[23] Houlgate believes that Hegel adduces a conceptual rather than a causal connection between punishment and the actualization or validation of rights, claiming that it is that of the form of logical necessity integral to Hegel's speculative practice.

It should be evident by now that these issues cannot be sorted out, at the level of interpretation, without the commentator's coming to some explicit conclusions concerning the methodology of Hegelian argumentation. It looks as though no advance is possible without exploring the deepest veins of Hegelian scholarship. If what we are faced with is conceptual analysis of a familiar sort, as Wood points out, the conclusion will be parochial and conservative—but then perhaps "we" can find agreement about how "we" think in "our" parish, and maybe this enterprise can afford "*comprehension* of that truth concerning *right, ethics, and the state* [which] is *as old* as its *exposition and promulgation* in *public laws and in public morality and religion*" (PR Preface ¶5).

If, by contrast, we are tracking the path of a speculative logic, we still have to unpack the metaphors that fill the conceptual space of "the reconciliation of right with itself," and what better way of doing this can there be than to find a valid argument? One point should be agreed on by all: that Hegel's argument, even as paraphrased lengthily above, is elliptical. As such, we should expect any plausible reconstruction of it to read the texts at their most capacious and go beyond them if the argument requires supplementation. And, *pace* Wood, a plausible reconstruction of the filling Hegel's argument evidently requires need not, of itself, amount to the reconstruction of a plausible argument or one that is consistent with everything else Hegel says on the topic.

It is on these grounds that I am content to endorse the drift of Cooper's original reading. Following my earlier remarks about Hegel's focus on our understanding of rights and his interest in what a philosophical examination of our practice of punishment contributes to that enterprise, I state the conceptual truth at the heart of the restoration of rights argument as follows:

> Rights are not properly recognized (actualized) as valid claims, binding on others, unless their violation is met with punishment wherever possible.

As conceptual truths go, this is, as Wood implies, parochial. It applies to *our* world, supposing that alternative responses would not serve the purpose of public recognition. For all I know, there are other worlds wherein a public judgment of wrongdoing may suffice to restore the right. But then, I suspect (and this is suggested by Tunick's example),[24] public judgment would amount to denunciation, and this in turn would be regarded as hard treatment and hence as a measure of punishment. I speculate, on the basis of the sort of common sense that is acknowledgedly fallible, that in our world rights cannot be protected, right cannot be restored, by nonpunitive communications.

This reading can be supported in a way that Cooper does not attempt. Punishment can only restore the right if the institutions whereby punishment is effected constitute the means of public recognition of rights. Plausibly, if not speculatively or logically or conceptually-in-all-possible-worlds, public recognition requires public institutions. And so it proves. In the institutions of "Civil Society" that administrate justice, "Abstract Right" is posited objectively as law, universally promulgated and intelligibly codified, publicly dispensed in open court following trial by jury.[25] The practice of punishment, following court proceedings that have established the fact of criminal behavior, makes it clear to all parties (victim, criminal, and the general public) that the rights of the matter are as the law states them to be. The fact that the restoration of right is achieved *objectively*, in a public institutional process, emphasizes one element of the reconciliation of right with itself. In Hardimon's language, the social world is, and is known, felt, and affirmed to be, a home for rights-bearers. The victim's rights are vindicated, his moral (now legal) status as a person with the capacity for rights is affirmed, the public's interest in countering a danger to society is satisfied (*PR* §218). But what of the poor criminal?

If the criminal is left out of the picture, the objection I mentioned earlier to the restoration of rights theory of punishment, that it is, at bottom, consequentialist, is telling. Even if, instead of the usual suspects (happiness, pleasure net pain, preference satisfaction, objective list), the value to be maximized is conformity to rights, or freedom, it is hard to see Hegel's account as distinctively retributivist. This is not because retributivism and consequentialism are inherently incompatible. Retributivism is too broad a philosophical church to permit this inference.[26] Rather, it is because the restoration of rights thesis seems to articulate the social functionality of punishment and seems to ignore that aspect of punishment which is directed toward the particularity of the specific violation. The dealings that the punitive agency has with the criminal seem to be secondary to the efficacy of punishment as the instrument of social purposes. If we read Hegel in the fashion that Cooper recommends and I have reconstructed, we must conclude either that the theory, as articulated thus far, does not accomplish its retributive intent, as Wood argues,[27] or that it is incomplete. This latter is my claim. The restoration of right *is* a public function: the objective face of the reconciliation that the fact of crime necessitates. The subjective aspect of the reconciliation of right with itself is revealed in the response of the criminal. To repeat: "reconciliation applies . . . subjectively . . . to the criminal in that *his law, which is known by him* and is *valid* for him and *for his protection*, is enforced on him in such a way that he himself finds in it the satisfaction of justice and merely the enactment of *what is proper to him*" (*PR* §220). We need to understand these ambitious claims. And we need to show how they amplify, rather than contradict, Hegel's concern for the restoration of right.

THE CRIMINAL'S RIGHT TO PUNISHMENT

The criminal objectively denies the right of the victim to his property, rejects his moral status as a person with a capacity for rights, and, in "Civil Society," repudiates the regime of rights as this is actualized, that is, institutionalized in the workings of the economy and the justice system by which it is regulated. Whatever the criminal *says* he is up to, this is what his action bespeaks. This is what Hegel calls, teasingly, "the right of the *objectivity* of the action . . . to assert itself as known and willed by the subject as a *thinking agent*" (*PR* §120), as distinct from the moral subject's right of intention. The rational agent knows that his actions disclose his intentions since he employs the same rational schema as others do to understand the actions of his fellows. And he knows how they will interpret his actions when he commits a crime. Irrationality (and, consequently, absent or diminished responsibility) is the cost of dislocation between the specification of his own intention given by the agent and the description of his action given by fully informed observers. So the criminal, if he is a real criminal, either knows or is culpably ignorant of the fact that he is striking both at his victim's rights and those recognized by his society. Whether or not he is alienated, he is in conflict with his society and reconciliation is called for.[28]

Let us return to Hegel's treatment of punishment in "Abstract Right" to see how these facts are treated there. To focus discussion, I cite the paragraph we shall dissect:

> The injury [*Verletzung*] which is inflicted on the criminal is not only just *in itself* (and since it is just, it is at the same time his will as it is *in itself*, an existence [*Dasein*] of his freedom, *his* right); it is also a *right for the criminal himself*,[29] that is, a right *posited* in his *existent* will, in his action. For it is implicit in his action, as that of a *rational* being, that it is universal in character, and that, by performing it, he has set up a law which he has recognized for himself in his action, and under which he may therefore be subsumed as under *his* right. (*PR* §100)

This argument suggests a variety of characterizations that have both a classical provenance and contemporary support. Punishment is justified since the rights violator has forfeited his rights.[30] Punishment is justified on the basis of the criminal's consent.[31] Punishment is justified as the issue of a social contract.[32] None of these positions, as outlined by their ancient and modern protagonists, quite captures Hegel's approach. But their variety alerts us to the possibility of rewriting his argument through this tradition. A successful reconstruction will conclude, as each of the above approaches attempts to do, that the criminal accepts the necessity of his own punishment. Thus it will present a process of practical reasoning that can successfully be imputed to the criminal.

The clearest way of reading the argument of *PR* §100 is stated carefully by Wood. It works back from the statement that the criminal's action sets up a law under which the criminal is himself brought. Through his action, the criminal is saying (in the sense of *PR* §120) and knows or ought to know that he will be taken as saying (*mens rea*), "It's fine to violate the rights of the victim." The implication of the law implicit in the action is that it is fine to violate the rights of the criminal in the same measure. The punitive response is justifiable *ad hominem*, in accordance with the principle of his own actions, a principle which, as a rational agent, he cannot reject. This conclusion is stated explicitly in the

Propädeutik: "It [the principle or law of the criminal's action] is valid only for the one who committed it because he alone recognizes it by his action and no one else. He himself, therefore, is essentially subject to this principle or 'Law' and it must be carried out upon him."[33]

The difficulty, or rather, one difficulty,[34] with this argument is that it does little more than dress up the thought that the criminal himself cannot complain if he is treated in the same fashion that he treats the victim. As put, this thought has much to be said for it, but it is hard to see how it can be acceptable to the punishing agency. The criminal's act, we recall, also has the dimension of a 'negatively infinite judgment'; he denies the victim's capacity for rights—and, in "Civil Society," the whole regime of right, as this applies to its members. The punishing agency cannot be thought to assert *this* as the principle of *its* action, and, explicitly, it does not. Punishment recognizes the criminal's own right; through it he "is honoured as a rational being" (*PR* §100R). If this is true, how can the criminal's law be applied validly by the victim or the courts? One might say: because his law is valid *for* him alone, it is applied *to* him alone. But this is to lose the validity of the license which the criminal act yields to the punisher. And in "Civil Society," it would not be applied to him alone. It would be applied to any criminal, in accordance with the law and its proper procedures. The last thing the punishing agency should be doing is adopting the moral perspective of the criminal.

This response to Hegel also dresses up an old saw: two wrongs don't make a right. If this play on the universal character of the criminal's deed is all that Hegel manages at *PR* §100, it should be judged a weak and unconvincing argument. I think we can find an alternative that is stronger and more satisfactory.

A HYPOTHETICAL CONTRACT MODEL OF PUNISHMENT

To do this we return to the perspective of "Abstract Right" and note that all rational agents claim the moral status of person, assert their capacity for rights, and endorse the imperative of right commanding them to be persons and respect the personality of others. Respecting the personality of others requires one to respect their rights claims. All of this is clear to the criminal. If it is not, he is not a rational agent responsible for his actions. I claim that we can develop from these initial postulates a full justification of punishment on the hypothetical contract model. Thus:

1. Individuals claim rights against each other and recognize that others claim equivalent rights against themselves.

2. They see no prospect of others respecting their rights while they themselves are immune to the rights claims of others.

3. They suspect that others may attempt to become free riders on the convention of respect for rights, since they understand that the attractions of wrongdoing with impunity on their own part is enhanced by the predictability of others' behavior—which they may be able to exploit.

4. Hence, they demand a guarantee of good faith in the principles of rights from those others who avow them, and they are willing to give such a guarantee themselves.

5. The guarantee which is universally offered and taken up is a recognition of the legitimacy of punishment exacted against criminals; a guarantee taken up against criminals on the part of all contractors, against themselves, of course, should they turn out to be criminals.

6. They accept that punishment may take the form of actions which, in other contexts, would amount to a violation of their rights.

7. Hence, those who wish their rights to be promoted and protected are willing to alienate their rights should they, themselves, violate the rights of others.[35]

How much of this argument can we recognize in Hegel's texts? At first sight, admittedly, not much. Point 1 certainly is a Hegelian thesis, and so is the conclusion at point 7. This explicates the thought that, both in itself and explicitly, punishment is the right of the criminal. In some sense, the criminal consents to his punishment. What of the steps in between? I would be prepared to defend point 2 as a Hegelian position. Besides being one of the sources of the universality explicit in the imperative of right, it is a clear implication of the demand that law be universally valid and universally known through its promulgation in a public legal code and its prosecution in transparent legal processes (*PR* §§209–211, 215–217). We can take it, too, that the rational agent will endorse the principles of "Abstract Right" on which the administration of justice is, in part, founded. Similarly, I think point 6 can be defended as an implication of the Hegelian texts, which stress that the appropriate measure of punishment will be equal to the crime in point of its value (*PR* §§101, 214). But that is as far as the texts will take us.

Why did Hegel reject the sort of argument that Beccaria, and following him, Rousseau, had provided (although they disagreed on the specific issue of capital punishment)? Why was he so hostile to a contract argument in favor of punishment? The answer to these questions is that he was hostile to the social contract model of the ontology of the state, of the relation between the state and its constituent citizens, and could not separate the philosophical problems of the legitimacy of sovereign authority and the legitimacy of state punishment. See how swiftly Hegel's discussion of Beccaria on punishment at *PR* §100 modulates into a discussion of the social contract account of the state.[36] Hegel may well be correct in his criticism of the implications of contract theory for an acceptable social and nation-state ontology, and by implication for an acceptable account of political obligation. But his central doctrines concerning *punishment* are lodged, as we have seen, in his discussion of our moral nature as persons, distinct and discrete bearers of rights. Thinking of ourselves as persons, as Hegel insists that we must, we may have quite sufficient cognitive-cum-rational resources to work out, from the perspective of the rational agent who turns out to be a criminal, that his liability to punishment, her legitimate punishability, is the inevitable normative consequence of his criminality.

All that is necessary for each person to reach this conclusion is that he review the claims he (and, by implication, each other person) is prone to make, the duties he (and all others) are likely to demand (and they and he to accept on their own part), together with some tariff of punishment as the recognized normative consequence of *anyone's* actual failure to respect the claims made and fulfill the duties they entail.[37] This argument does not rest on a contract theory of the state or a contract theory of rights. In principle, it is quite open to anyone to reject contract theories in these fields (and contract theories of justice and morality, too) and still endorse a contract theory of punishment.

The contract is, of course, hypothetical. It binds not as a real contract might, but solely in virtue of the independent persuasiveness of the premises it contains.[38] The version of the contract argument that I give above details the major elements of such a deduction as is available to the criminal contemplating his punishment, and, so far as I can see, it can be advanced without reference to our political standing as citizens of a nation-state. If this is right, Hegel was quite wrong to disallow this model of practical reason as germane to the deduction of our duties in respect of punitive institutions. His own favored argument, which has criminals, through their actions, laying down a law under which they in turn are brought, employs premises that are no less *individualistic*, although it exhibits the striking flaw of reaching the wrong conclusion.

Disregard for the moment Hegel's obliviousness to the resources of this model of practical reason when defending punishment. Ask instead: What is its plausibility, what are its limitations? I will not defend its plausibilty here, but its usefulness is clear. It displays how the criminal, on condition of his rational agency, must accept as legitimate the punishment his actions call forth. This is exactly the conclusion Hegel's argument strains for. Its weakness is exactly the same as the weakness

Wood notices in respect of the incompleteness of the consent version of Hegel's theory as he interprets it: Hegel's argument does not give "a *positive reason* why the state should actually inflict punishment. That is, granting that punishment does no injustice, we might still ask if there is any good reason for the state to punish."[39] Now this *is* a limitation on Hegel's theory following Wood's interpretation. If, on the other hand, Hegel were to have employed the contract theory I have recommended, he would have a perfectly straightforward reply. At this point in the dialectic he could bring together the 'objective' and 'subjective' strands of argument.

THE ALIGNMENT OF "OBJECTIVITY" AND "SUBJECTIVITY"

I have defended the claim that punishment is justified as restoring the right, but argued that this insight is not distinctively retributivist and, in any case, may be lost on the criminal.[40] Next, I claimed that the criminal may be made to accept the legitimacy of his punishment through a contract argument, but suggested, following Wood, that the argument is incomplete. Two things are needed to remedy these putative defects. In the first place, the contract argument requires a lemma to the effect that the criminal must recognize that his punishment is legitimate *insofar as it procures the restoration of right*—a goal that he himself endorses as appropriate for the law to effect. All citizens accept the validity of the goal of the restoration of rights, not because this is a valuable social function of punishment, but because it is necessary for the protection of the rights that they themselves claim. So the state *must* punish criminals if it is to serve the purpose of protecting rights.[41] *Pace* Wood, this amounts to a positive reason for the state to punish, and not merely a license. Second, viewing the matter from the perspective of the concern to restore the right, this becomes a properly retributive function just as soon as it is realized that the specific institutions that effect the restoration do so in a manner that enlists the rational endorsement of citizens. The transparency that is at the heart of the administration of justice serves to embed the reasoning of the contractor in the institutions that identify, prosecute, and punish criminality. The restoration of right is accomplished by social mechanisms that demonstrate to all, honest and criminal citizens alike, the nature of their rights, their concomitant duties, and the penalties to be imposed for noncompliance. The institutions make explicit, through their laws, processes, and punitive regime, the rights for which persons demand protection. Notoriously, this knowledge, explicit in the alignment of subjectivity and objectivity, is not available to the criminal in "Abstract Right" where punishment takes the form of revenge and revenge breeds vendetta (*PR* §102). But it *is* available in "Civil Society."

The restoration of right is achievable wherever the administration of justice is so structured as to make transparent to citizens the rights they may justly claim, the duties they must fulfill, and the penalties they will incur for noncompliance. In "Civil Society," the reconciliation of right with right, which is necessitated by the fact of crime, is achieved by the rule of law, serving ends which all citizens endorse as promoting their interests and dispensed in courts of law which make that endorsement evident to reflective, rational agents. The hypothetical contract device explicates the structure of practical reason by which all rational agents, criminals included, can be presumed to accept the legitimacy of punishment. By embedding the necessity of the restoration of right within the practical reason of all rational agents, and by describing how the administration of justice articulates the self-understanding acquired by these practical reasoners, we deflect the outstanding objections. Against all his instincts, but following through on his most convincing arguments, Hegel should have employed a hypothetical contract argument to defend the institution of punishment.[42]

NOTES

This essay has been improved through my having to reflect on the criticisms of the Hegel Society of America referees. They may disagree! But thanks are due for their detailed comments. Thanks are also due to those who helped me improve the essay following its presentation at the HSA meeting. Mark Tunick, Robert Berman, Robert Williams, and Stephen Houlgate were particularly helpful in getting me to change and clarify the argument.

1. I stress "the normative framework of 'Abstract Right'," meaning by this the concept (*Begriff*) of "Abstract Right," ignoring Hegel's conclusion that the concept cannot be actualized since a positive realm of "Abstract Right" would be riven by vendetta (*PR* §§102–103). As we shall see, the concept of "Abstract Right" *is* actualized within "Civil Society." Citations of *PR* refer to G. W. F. Hegel, *Elements of the Philosophy of Right,* ed. Allen W. Wood, tr. H. B. Nisbet (Cambridge: Cambridge University Press, 1991).

2. I have in mind the views of Charles Taylor and Michael Sandel, among others. See Charles Taylor, "Atomism," in *Philosophical Papers,* vol. 2 (Cambridge: Cambridge University Press, 1985), and "Cross-Purposes: The Liberal-Communitarian Debate," in *Liberalism and the Moral Life,* ed. N. Rosenblum (Cambridge, Mass.: Harvard University Press, 1989); Michael Sandel, *Liberalism and the Limits of Justice* (Cambridge: Cambridge University Press, 1982).

3. This is one reason why "Abstract Right" is *abstract.*

4. Allen W. Wood fails to notice the careful logic of Hegel's initial presentation of his theory of rights, and this infects his reading of Hegel on pun-

ishment. Discussing David Cooper's interpretation, he writes, "In the theory of abstract right developed in *PR* §§34–80, he regards abstract right as conferring on persons both a permission and a warrant to exercise arbitrary choice within a limited sphere (*PR* §§38, 41). Only later does he focus attention on the claim that others should respect this sphere (cf. *PR* §49R)." Allen W. Wood, *Hegel's Ethical Thought* (Cambridge: Cambridge University Press, 1990), p. 111. *PR* §38, as quoted above, with its characterization of the rules of right as negative, as *prohibitions*, shows that this is a mistake—as does the imperative of right itself (*PR* §36), enjoining us to "respect others as persons," which *PR* §38 glosses in negative terms. The 'permission or warrant' Hegel characterizes at *PR* §38 is not merely correlative to the duty of noninterference; the "positive form of commandments of right is, in its ultimate content, based on prohibition."

5. It is not a coincidence that this structure mirrors that of Nozick's entitlement theory of justice, which consists of principles governing acquisition, transfer and rectification. See R. Nozick, *Anarchy, State and Utopia* (Oxford: Blackwell, 1974), pp. 150–51. In "Abstract Right," Hegel is presenting the core doctrines of atomistic liberalism. Although he traces the origins of this style of morality to the Roman world, in effect he is presenting a digest of modern, that is, post-Reformation, rights theory as one (but *pace* Nozick et al., only one) element of the way moderns think about ethics. *Pace* the communitarians, by contrast, although rights theory is not the whole story concerning our ethical obligations, it is ineliminable. Hegel insists, surely correctly, that we just *do* claim rights nowadays, seeing ourselves as distinct individuals. The metaphysical blankness of the concept of 'person' is remedied by its amplification, as rights are specified, and as other modes of self-identification are added. It is certainly not rejected as conceptually inchoate.

6. Robert R. Williams notices this point. See *Hegel's Ethics of Recognition* (Berkeley, Los Angeles, and London: University of California Press, 1997), pp. 155–57. "Wrong clarifies the substantial nature of right" (p. 155). See also I. Primoratz, *Justifying Legal Punishment* (Atlantic Highlands, N.J.: Humanities Press, 1989), p. 74.

7. The point is repeated in Hotho's notes: following punishment, "right acquires the determination of something fixed and valid. . . . Whereas right previously had only an immediate being, it now becomes *actual* as it returns out of its negation; for actuality is that which is effective" (*PR*, Addition to §82).

8. Locke and Rousseau tackle the problem head on. See J. Locke, *Second Treatise of Government*, §§6–9, 16–19, 87–88 and elsewhere; J.-J. Rousseau, *The Social Contract*, bk. II, ch. V. Nozick notices the difficulty and skates over it quickly, suggesting that perhaps a social contract argument promises a solution. *Anarchy, State and Utopia*, pp. 137–38. In "Punishment and Rights," *Punishment and Political Theory*, ed. M. Matravers (Oxford: Hart, 1998), I discuss a range of solutions to this problem.

9. Lewis P. Hinchman claims that Hegel is addressing this problem. See "Hegel's Theory of Crime and Punishment," *The Review of Politics*, vol. 44, 1982, p. 543. Allen W. Wood hints at such a reading. See *Hegel's Ethical Thought*, pp.109–10, as does Robert Williams, *Hegel's Ethics of Recognition*:

"Although in general coercion is a violation of right, sometimes coercion is necessary, and if necessary, then justified. Our question is, How is coercion of freedom—which is strictly speaking impossible—nevertheless possible?" (p. 158).

10. Michael O. Hardimon, *Hegel's Social Philosophy: The Project of Reconciliation* (Cambridge: Cambridge University Press, 1994), pp. 95ff.

11. "Hypothetical" gives us yet another meaning of *abstract* in "Abstract Right." The norms of "Abstract Right" require a "Civil Society" for their actualization.

12. Crime "constitutes a *negatively infinite judgement*'" (PR §95). In the paragraph cited, this is taken as a claim that crime negates not merely my will embodied as it is in property, but also "the universal and infinite element in the predicate 'mine'—i.e. my *capacity for rights*."At PR §218, where crime is considered in the context of "Civil Society," the scope of the infinite judgment is widened, so that we are to see the criminal act as striking at society, presumably at the whole normative regime. In consequence, criminal action is viewed as "a *danger* to society." Which actions constitute a danger to society beyond violations of individual rights? This issue is discussed by Mark Tunick, *Hegel's Political Philosophy* (Princeton, N.J.: Princeton University Press, 1992), pp. 110–13.

13. Allen W. Wood, *Hegel's Ethical Thought*, pp. 112–13.

14. It may be objected that these sayings are not metaphors, that they characterize the structure of Hegel's argument in terms of his distinctive speculative logic. I have no doubt that this is what Hegel *thought* he was doing. At this point, I don't want to pick a fight with those who insist that there is a distinctive and genuine logic here that constitutes good argument. On the other hand, I do want to insist that the argument which is being sketched is *unpacked* in the detail of the discussion that follows. I want to allow Hegel the opportunity to be persuasive to those for whom the speculative logic is a mystery, since this was a dialectical strategy he himself was ready to exploit, in both the text and the lectures on the *Philosophy of Right*. (I make this comment in order to address objections strongly put at the University of Georgia meeting.)

15. David E. Cooper, "Hegel's Theory of Punishment," in *Hegel's Political Philosophy: Problems and Perspectives*, ed. Z. A. Pelczynski (Cambridge: Cambridge University Press, 1971), cited at pp. 162–63.

16. Peter G. Steinberger, "Hegel on Crime and Punishment," *American Political Science Review*, 1983, vol. 77, pp. 858–70.

17. Joel Feinberg, "The Expressive Function of Punishment," in *Philosophical Perspectives on Punishment*, ed. Gertrude Ezorsky (Albany: SUNY Press, 1972).

18. Allen W. Wood, *Hegel's Ethical Thought*, pp. 111–13.

19. Stephen Houlgate, "Hegel's Ethical Thought," *Bulletin of the Hegel Society of Great Britain*, no. 25, 1992, cited at p. 12.

20. Allen W. Wood, "Reply," *Bulletin of the Hegel Society of Great Britain*, no. 25, 1992, cited at p. 44.

21. "It would be impossible for a society to leave a crime unpunished—since the crime would then be posited as right" (PR §218A). Mark Tunick illustrates this point with a good story from the Upper Congo, concluding that

"without the old woman's response [of denunciation] there would have been no crime: not because if nobody discovers it happened it didn't happen, but because if nobody declares it's wrong, it's not." For further details, see M. Tunick, *Hegel's Political Philosophy*, pp. 78–80. Likewise, if technical violations of the law go openly unpunished, as was the case in Scotland before the law on consensual homosexual acts was brought in line with the reforms effected in English law, we may judge that no wrong is committed. Where prosecution is capricious and arbitrary—this is the early history of boxing in Britain; sometimes the magistrates stopped the fights, sometimes they sat in the front row—the law is an ass because the right is indeterminate.

22. Allen Wood notices this, commenting that the methodology is as defunct as Hegelian speculative logic! Later, he claims, intriguingly, that the "conceptual argument" "deliberately leaves unasked the critical qestion whether 'our' talk, and the 'form of life' it reflects, can be given any rational justification . . . [hence] it embodies a fundamentally *Anti-Hegelian* attitude toward philosophy." See "Reply," pp. 43–45.

23. For another example of this line of criticism, see S. I. Benn and R. S. Peters, *Social Principles and the Democratic State* (London: George Allen and Unwin, 1959), p. 177.

24. See n. 21.

25. For these details (and more), see *PR* §§209–229.

26. In conversation, Mark Tunick convinced me of this.

27. Allen Wood, *Hegel's Ethical Theory*, pp. 110–12.

28. There is a general difficulty in the background here concerning Hegel's characterization of the content of the mind of the criminal. What exactly must we be able to claim about what he knows about what he is doing? Crime is not, after all, nonmalicious wrongdoing. Is it enough that we make true judgments concerning what the criminal ought to know? These are standard problems in applying the doctrine of *mens rea*, and I shall have more to say about this later.

29. Stephen Houlgate puts it to me that "a *right for the criminal himself*" mistranslates "ein *Recht an den Verbrecher* selbst." The Knox translation, reading "a right *established* within the criminal himself" (G. W. F. Hegel, *Hegel's Philosophy of Right*, tr. T. M. Knox (Oxford: Clarendon Press, 1952), is better because it does not carry the implication that "a right *for* [my italics] the criminal himself" is a right of which the criminal is fully aware, or, perhaps, even stronger, actively demands. I can't say whether the translator's "for" carries the implication of full self-knowledge which is distinctive of Hegel's *für sich*.The precise point is that the criminal's *action* bespeaks his existing will. Neither the original nor its translation should be taken to entail that the criminal explicitly asserts the law of his action, as it were giving a running commentary on what he is doing. It is implied that he ought to accept such a law in accordance with the "right of *objectivity* of the action" (*PR* §120). Such an implication can properly be represented as the conclusion of a hypothetical contract argument, of which more later. See n. 28 *supra*.

30. John Locke, *Second Treatise of Government*: "[The criminal] so far becomes degenerate, and declares himself to be quit the Principles of Human Nature and to be a noxious creature" (§10); "In so revolting from his kind to

that of Beasts and by making Force which is theirs, to be his rule of right, he renders himself liable to be despised . . . as any other wild beast or noxious brute" (§172). For a modern argument to the effect that the rights of the criminal, which would otherwise prohibit boundary crossings, are forfeit, see Alan H. Goldman, "The Paradox of Punishment," *Philosophy and Public Affairs* 9 (1979).

31. J.-J. Rousseau, *The Social Contract*: "the death penalty inflicted upon criminals may be looked on in much the same light [as conscription]: it is in order that we may not fall victims to an assassin that we consent to die if we ourselves turn assassins" (bk. II, ch. IV). For a modern treatment, see C. S. Nino, "A Consensual Theory of Punishment," *Philosophy and Public Affairs* 12 (1983).

32. Cesare Beccaria, *On Crimes and Punishments, and Other Writings*, ed. R. Bellamy (Cambridge: Cambridge University Press, 1995). For a modern treatment, see Jeffrie Murphy, "Marxism and Retribution," *Philosophy and Public Affairs* 2 (1973).

33. G. W. F. Hegel, *The Philosophical Propaedeutic*, ed. M. George and A. Vincent, tr. A. V. Miller (Oxford: Blackwell, 1986), p. 31. G. W. F. Hegel, *Philosophische Propädeutik, Sämtliche Werke*, ed. H. Glockner (Stuttgart: Frommann Verlag, 1971), vol. 3, p. 68. This argument is emphasized by Igor Primoratz in *Banquos Geist. Hegels Theorie der Strafe. Hegel-Studien*, Beiheft 29, 1986, and fully endorsed in *Justifying Legal Punishment* (Atlantic Highlands, N.J. and London: Humanities Press, 1989), ch. 4, especially pp.76–79. Robert Williams, *Hegel's Ethics of Recognition*, also follows this line: "Hegel believes that retribution is just because retributive punishment is simply the reversal of the offense; that is, it demands that the principle of the transgression be applied to the offender" (p. 168). Neither Hegel nor his interpreters see that this is a very bad argument. If the principle of the transgression endorses the violation of rights, that should disqualify it as a principle to be applied by any other agency. The act of punishment should make this disqualification explicit rather than employ the invalid principle to vindicate punishment. By contrast, the thought that the criminal cannot legitimately complain is very useful when it is the appropriate *measure* of punishment that is being considered, as Primoratz sees (*Justifying Legal Punishment*, chs. 4.5, 5.2).

34. There are others. How do we get over the problem of the criminal who explicitly disavows the imputed saying? If we answer that he ought to recognize that he will be taken to be saying this, we are adducing his *hypothetical* consent to the proposition: he would accept it if he were rational, fully informed, sincere, and apprised of the logical consequences of other propositions he affirms. This takes us halfway down the road of hypothetical contract, wherein rational agents take into account what others, as well as themselves, may reasonably reject as the basis for agreement on principles.

35. I defend this argument in "Punishment and Rights," where I argue that it shores up weaknesses in both forfeiture and consent arguments to the conclusion that the criminal wills his own punishment.

36. Contract theories of the state are criticized in *PR* at §§75 and 258 in addition to the above.

37. If this claim is hard to stomach, remember that Hegel himself insists that the justice of punishment can be demonstrated on the basis of the very limited normative resources available to the person under "Abstract Right." "The state is not a necessary condition of justice in itself," Hegel claims at §100R.

38. Famously, this point is made by Ronald Dworkin, "The Original Position," in *Reading Rawls*, ed. N. Daniels (Oxford: Blackwell, 1975), p. 18. Despite Hegel's knowledge of the contract tradition, especially as employed by Rousseau, Kant, and Fichte, I don't think he managed to unravel the striking differences between the actual and hypothetical forms of the argument. Had he done so, he would have seen the aptness of the hypothetical contract structure for modeling the arguments of "Abstract Right" and the sections of "Civil Society" that discuss the protection of persons' rights under the "Administration of Justice." The version of hypothetical contract theory I employ here derives from T. M. Scanlon, "Contractualism and Utilitarianism," in *Utilitarianism and Beyond*, ed. A. Sen and B. Williams (Cambridge: Cambridge University Press, 1982). For an application of this style of normative ethics that is useful in thinking about punishment, see T. Nagel, *Equality and Partiality* (Oxford: Oxford University Press, 1991), ch. 4.

39. Allen Wood, *Hegel's Ethical Theory*, p. 116.

40. To be specific, the implication is not that this is a bad argument. I believe it's a good one. Rather, it looks inconsistent with other claims that Hegel makes about the retributive intent of punishment.

41. To deflect objections: this is not the only purpose of the state. Rather it is just the best way of securing that freedom which is required by the fact of our personhood.

CHAPTER 7

War, Slavery, and the Ironies of the American Civil War: A Philosophic Analysis

Lawrence S. Stepelevich

On November 22, 1864, exactly four years to the day after a Confederate meeting at Abbeville, South Carolina, had initiated the "War for Southern Independence," the inexorable progress of the Union Army was momentarily halted. On that day, an irregular force of outnumbered Confederate militia and work battalions had gathered to face Sherman's veterans near Macon, Georgia, at a place named Griswoldsville. In seven heroic but vain charges the Confederate force was finally destroyed. After the battle, the Union victors were appalled by the slaughter they had inflicted. The Southern dead, fallen by the hundreds before the Union lines, were all young boys and old men, some few still holding onto their obsolete weapons. This battle, in proportion to the numbers involved, was the bloodiest battle of the American Civil War. It was, as the Civil War itself, but another bloody mark on what Hegel had termed "the slaughter bench"[1] of history. Over six hundred thousand lives were lost in that war, more than the combined total of American losses in both World Wars, Korea, and Vietnam—and with these losses drawn from a population base of about one-tenth that of today.[2]

Nevertheless, despite its terrible impact on American history, this war has been almost completely ignored by the philosophic academy— even by American Hegelians. The silence of this school, given Hegel's philosophy of history and his own extensive treatment of such categories as war, freedom, slavery, and nationality, seems even more inexplicable than the academy in general. Perhaps because of the Eurocentric turn of American philosophers, or, more likely, because any discussion of the

147

American Civil War would have to confront such embarrassing topics as slavery and sectionalism—both scandals to the image of a nation proclaimed as a paradigm of universal freedom and political unity.

In the present, after a century of war, both "hot" and "cold," the academy and most everyone else envision war as a dreadful, but avoidable, historical contingency, which—given a sufficient amount of good will and resolve—can and should be eliminated. In this view, held by such as Kant and most politically correct activists of the present, the American Civil War (as most) should not have be called, as it was, "an irrepressible conflict." Such political despair is presently unacceptable. However, for Hegel, as with Plato, war and peace are locked into an unavoidable logic. In this view, war in general, as well as the American Civil War, can be the subject of philosophic consideration, and not merely dismissed as a dreadful contingency. But if this essay takes up that war, it can make no claim to being more than a first sketch, a collection of limited philosophic observations, more suggestion than argument. It will likely prove neither fully satisfying to the historian, being too philosophic, nor, for the opposite reason, to the philosopher, nor, for that matter, to anyone else, as it seems too brief for such grand speculations. Nevertheless, that war will be addressed, if only to serve as a small memorial for those who died in it.

For Hegel, war was the necessary counterpart of peace, the violent consequence of two factors generated in times of peace—a fixed national identity and a unifying moral aspiration. In times of peace, the *Volksgeist*, the spirit of a people, the nation, would solidify its own distinctive legal, political, religious, and cultural matrix into what might be termed a national habit. This distinctive national character would resist all foreign threats to its established identity, and no international "league of peace" could claim sovereignty over it—as the nation was formed to express and defend the particular interests of its people. Its boundaries, both geographical and cultural, would be inviolate, and war would become ever more likely the more these boundaries were tangential to nations holding other definitions that could threaten national sovereignty. Mere threats to those boundaries would be cause of war, and that war would come should not be surprising. What Hegel terms an "anthropological principle" is expressed in every nation, wherein the nation perceives itself and is perceived as a concrete individual. When, for example, it is said that "Italy" and "Austria" are determined to resolve a trade or boundary issue, or when it is said that "the United States is or is not willing to do this or that," we unconsciously recognize the nation as an individual. It is of interest to note that prior to the Civil War the United States, as its name suggests, was taken as a plural entity. But after the war, the "United States are . . ." became the "United States is. . . ." The same reduction of the "are" to the "is" occurred after Bismarck—when "the Germanies" became "Germany."

As to the moral aspirations underlying war, the young and old who died in the charges at Griswoldsville fought for their nation, which they understood to be a spiritual entity in whose defense they were willing to sacrifice all. Those who did not hold that moral aspiration and chose to remain at home to protect their family, their property, or their lives were viewed as moral cowards. Here, the nation is understood as a moral individual holding a higher spiritual meaning than those whom it putatively protects.

Now, I suspect most nonacademics, and indeed most academics as well, who know of Hegel, would probably reduce their knowledge of his philosophy to the simple rubric of "the dialectic of thesis-antithesis-synthesis." Expanded upon, this can be taken to mean that *if* something is given (a thesis)—be it an idea or an objective actuality—*then* that something will find itself confronted by an opposite which it has itself generated out of the limits of its own definition, out of the ever-present inner contradiction which dictates the limits of that something. This self-generated opposition can be, and has been, termed the "antithesis." The resolution of the opposition will contain both antithetical sides within a higher union, a reunion of the antithetical elements, termed a "synthesis." Certainly, this expansion would not satisfy any fully developed view of Hegel's dialectic, but nevertheless, even in this simple formation, it can find a historical expression in the American Civil War. In the briefest outline, if the American Constitution be taken as a thesis, as the original form of union, this form contained an inner contradiction: the contradiction between state rights and federal sovereignty. This inner contradiction ultimately found its actuality violently expressed in the Civil War, in which the original union sundered itself into the two antithetical nations of the North and the South. The postwar history of the United States can be taken as a synthesis, as a reunion, as, in Lincoln's terms, a "new birth of freedom"—a restored union which not only had resolved its inner contradiction but a new nation whose internal struggles seem to have been largely forgotten in the external excitement of a rapid expansion to the Pacific and its enjoyment of international power. But perhaps such a simple dialectical framework is too facile to convince anyone of the relevance of Hegel's philosophy toward the comprehension of the American Civil War—a comprehension which, as earlier mentioned, holds little interest among academic philosophers.

However, this academic silence is not found in public life. This is evident in the loud displays of what I might call "bad conscience" now taking place—an ever-growing and almost obsessive general interest in the Civil War. The continuous theatrical restaging of that war, the thousands who gather to reenact the events of that war, and the innumerable studies of it, the gathering of artifacts, the debates over the display of the Confederate flag, and the growing strength of those who would memorialize and preserve the sites on which the war was fought, suggests that our national consciousness remains unsatisfied as to its resultant meaning. These reenactments and retellings of that war of "brother against brother" suggest that our nation might well be engaged in a therapeutic recollection, a public psychodrama acted out in the hope that the internal contradiction that found expression in the self-inflicted wounds of the Civil War can somehow be resolved, that its results were commensurate with its destruction. Hegel well understood the need for a nation's recollection, of an *Erinnerung*, of a historical "inward going," for, as he noted, "the external existence of the state . . . is an incomplete present which cannot understand itself and develop an integrated consciousness without reference to the past."[3] Just as with the subjective spirit of the individual, a retelling of the experiences of that consciousness is, for a national spirit, the necessary condition for the securing of a coherent self-consciousness. The recalling of its own past fulfills that which Hegel terms the "highest impulse" of a nation," which is "to comprehend itself and to realize in every area of its existence the concept it has formed of itself."[4]

As Lincoln understood it, the Civil War was an "irrepressible conflict," and as such, is rightly described as a "national tragedy." But as today's public reenactments of that drama suggest, the tragedy of that war did not seem to have provided a satisfactory catharsis for the self-estrangement of the national spirit, and Lincoln's promised "new birth of freedom" has proven to be an insufficient resolution. As to the term "tragedy," which is often used to describe the war, it was indeed just that, and in the precise meaning that Hegel gives that term. The war was not an unfortunate accident, a pathetic event, but a moral struggle, in which two antithetical national spirits, derived from the same spirit, sought recognition not only from each other, but from the world-spirit itself. This world-spirit, which is always, for Hegel, "striving to grasp itself in its highest form," presents itself to us as a "divine tragedy, where spirit rises above pity, ethical life, and everything that is otherwise sacred to it."[5] The Civil War, as the self-contradiction of a national spirit that had not yet been fully formed, was indeed a tragedy, and beyond the comprehension of a finite understanding locked in dichotomies seeking merely to determine who was right and who was wrong. In this regard, as Hegel said, "in what is truly tragic there must be valid moral powers on both the sides which come into collision. . . . Two opposed rights come into collision, and the one destroys the other. Thus both suffer loss and yet both are mutually justified; it is not as though the one alone were right and the other wrong."⁶ It might well be that the wide public interest in the recalling and reenacting that war is but an effort to resolve a historic mystery as to its meaning, a meaning that seems to transcend the mere assignment of that "either-or" of victory or defeat.

Recently, historians have once again began to perceive the war between the North and the South as an international conflict.⁷ Even their common designation, as *North* and *South*, which sets them into the actuality of opposing climatic condition and geographic place, suggests that these two spirits are more than mere abstractions of national ideals. A century before Rudolf Kjellén had coined the term "geopolitics."⁸ Hegel had already treated of the relationship holding between geographic form and political ideal. A national spirit was more than a mere ideal. To actually exist it must also claim, and be claimed, by a specific time and place. It must have a homeland, and so find itself in a landscape "separated in time and space" from other national spirits.⁹ The State of Israel is a recent example of a national ideal rendered incarnate. As to the United States, its physical homeland, from its colonial beginnings well into the last century, suggests the existence of two national spirits, separated by both geography and climate—the North and the South. But, at the start of their history, when the American Revolution signaled their birth and separation from England, their aptly named "mother country," these two latent national spirits had the luxury of unimpeded development, and nothing seemed seriously to threaten the internal complacency of these developmental years—the so-called Era of Good Feelings.¹⁰ As Hegel wrote in 1830,

> North America cannot yet be regarded as a fully developed and mature state, but merely as one which is still in the process of becoming; it has not yet progressed far enough to feel the need for a monarchy. It is a federal state, but such states are in the worst possible position as regards external relations. Its peculiar geographical situation has alone prevented this circumstance from bringing about its complete destruction.¹¹

The luxury of this "peculiar geographical situation," in which a political federation, once established within a virtually uninhabited continent, protected in both east and west by large oceans and unthreatened by its weaker neighbors, has allowed it, no matter how insecure in itself, to rest secure from others within its own private and comfortable geopolitical room. A recent book concerned with the history of American foreign relations bears the fitting title *Promised Land, Crusader State*.¹² In it, the author argues that the natural geopolitical advantages enjoyed by the United States have allowed it not only to hold the high *economic* ground, but to assume, in consequence, that it also stood on the highest *moral* grounds. From its onset, the federation took its security and its natural wealth as a sign of divine favor, and it took on itself the mission to save the world—which meant to form the world in accord with its ideals. In considering the foreign policy of the United States, Hegel's description of the adolescent consciousness suggests itself. This reforming mentality "fancies himself called and qualified to transform the world, or at least to put the world back on the right path from which, so it seems to him, it has strayed . . . he feels that both his ideal and his own personality are not recognized by the world, and thus the youth, unlike the child, is no longer at peace with the world."[13] The early militant moral enthusiasm of the United States set on putting the world on the right path, that is, its own path, has remained almost undiminished, and although its recent good intentions of setting up voting booths in such distant places as Vietnam and Somalia were unwelcome, it still keeps trying.

But if its continental geography had protected the youthful nation from those foreign threats which Hegel takes as stimulating the maturity of national self-consciousness, its internal geography suggested internal divisiveness. Of North America,

> we first of all encounter a broad coastal strip along the eastern seaboard, beyond which a mountain range—the Blue Mountains or Appalachians, with the Allegheny Mountains to the north—extends. The rivers which flow from these water the coastal regions, which are admirably suited to the needs of the free North American states which first grew up in this area.[14]

What is of interest here is that although Hegel's brief description is accurate, he has not pointed out that there is only *one* of these rivers watering the coastal regions which breaks through the mountain ranges and opens a link between the east and the west. This is the Potomac. President Washington, always sensitive to the need for the symbols of a new nation, well understood the symbolic need to establish a national center, the national city, on that river.

Unlike the Nile, which, for Hegel, stabilized Egyptian political unity, the Potomac River was a natural separation between the North and the South—the natural parallel to the Mason-Dixon Line. It is of interest to note that at the start of the war, the Confederacy moved its center of government to Richmond, Virginia, to mark its claim to northern Virginia and the Potomac. In the narrow space between these two capitols most of the well-known battles of the Civil War occurred— from John Brown's Raid to the Surrender at Appomattox.

But if the Potomac was the geographical boundary between North and South, it also marked their climatic boundary. Of course, as Hegel noted, climate and season merely condition the natural human soul; they do not, as with plant and animal, determine its life. Nevertheless, as Hegel noted, "winter disposes to withdrawal into oneself, to collecting one's thoughts, to family life, to the worship of the *penates*. In summer, on the other hand, we feel more inclined to travel, feel drawn into the open air, and the ordinary folk are moved to go on pilgrimages."[15] The contrast between a wintery withdrawal into thought and the social gatherings of summer, between a somber and silent Northern religiosity and a loquacious Southern gentility drawn more to the Romantic than the biblical, can easily be overdrawn to a caricature—but yet there is some truth in caricature.

Still, if only in regard to productive resources, climatic differences alone would have inclined the South to agriculture and the North to industry. And to all these provocations to difference there would have to be added the not inconsiderable linguistic differences between the two incipient nations, differences of syntax and accent that were, at the time of the Civil War, more extreme than today. And finally, for some historians, there was also a profound ethnic divide between the two nations.[16] This would be the ancient antagonism between the Celts and the English, since, for these historians, "Yankee culture was in large part transplanted English culture; southern culture was Celtic—Scottish, Scotch-Irish, Welsh, Cornish, and Irish."[17] The wars of Celts against English have been restaged again and again, and might still be said to continue in Northern Ireland. If the brave but vain charge of Southern irregulars at Griswoldsville can be said to have echoed Pickett's charge at Gettysburg, then this was itself only an echo of earlier failed Celtic charges against the English lines at such places as Flodden Field and Colloden.

Fractured by geography, climate, accent, and ethos, the North and the South established their own respective founding myths and ideal images—myths and images that were often more literary than literal, more heritage than history. The North recalled the virtues of past Puritanism, and the South looked back on a noble inheritance. In the first year of the Civil War, George Bancroft's comparison of the national differences was reprinted in the popular Northern journal, *Harper's Magazine*. It reads:

> Historians have to eulogize the manners and virtues, the glory and the benefits, of chivalry. Puritanism accomplished for mankind far more. If it had the sectarian crime of intolerance, chivalry had the vices of dissoluteness. The knights were brave from gallantry of spirit; the Puritans, from the fear of God. The knights obeyed the law of honor; the Puritans harkened to the voice of duty. the knights were proud of loyalty; the Puritans of liberty . . . etc., etc.[18]

As one commentator on this passage observed: "*Harper's* apparently did not question whether a portrayal of seventeenth-century Puritans, composed in the heyday of romanticism's reconstruction of Puritan tradition, accurately characterized the nineteenth-century radical bearing the same name almost thirty years later. The presumption of linkage was indicative of how confident the North was of its destiny in 1862."[19]

The Northern myth flourished during the so-called Great Religious Awakening of the 1850s. It was a Romantically reconstructed Puritanism that derived its new content from the secular abstractions of the Enlightenment. Divine Providence was restored as human progress, and the angry God of Cotton Mather returned as the wrathful God of "The Battle Hymn of the Republic," whose Providence directed the progress of human history toward universal freedom and equality. This compelling doctrine was set forth by such Transcendentalists as Theodore Parker, whose conflation of faith and progress formed, as one writer noted, "the core of the theological liberalism that dominated northern American Protestantism by the Civil War." As to the South, as Edmond Wilson wrote,

> [it] had a reciprocal myth which it pitted with equal fanaticism against the North's Armageddonlike vision, derived from its traditional theology, of the holy crusade which was to liberate the slaves and to punish their unrighteous masters. If the Northerners were acting the Will of God, the Southerners were rescuing a hallowed ideal of gallantry, aristocratic freedom, fine manners and luxurious living from the materialism and vulgarity of the mercantile Northern society.[21]

Cultural historian William Taylor has proposed that in the initial formation of the United States, two foundational and antithetical ideals had already emerged: in the North the acquisitive Yankee, in the South the aristocratic Cavalier. As for the Southern ideal,

> the equalitarian character of life in the North provided an unsuitable terrain in which to locate, even in fantasy, an aristocracy. . . . By the eighteen thirties the legendary Southern planter . . . began to seem almost perfectly suited to fill the need. His ample estates, his spacious style of life, his Cavalier ancestry and his reputed obliviousness to money matters gained him favor in the eyes of those in search of a native American aristocracy. More and more, he came to be looked upon as *the* characteristic expression of life in the South. Meanwhile, the acquisitive man, the man on the make, became inseparably associated with the North and especially with New England, In the end, the Yankee—for so he became known—was thought to be as much the product of the North as the planter-Cavalier of the South. By 1850 these two types—the Cavalier and the Yankee—expressed in the pop-

ular imagination the basic cultural conflict which people felt had grown up between a decorous, agrarian South and the rootless, shifting, money-minded North.[22]

In the decades just prior to the war, Southern literary taste, in expected contrast to the North, ran to chivalric romances rather than Puritan stories and Old Testament readings, and in the South, no author was more popular than Sir Walter Scott. As Mark Twain saw it,

> He [Scott] did measureless harm; more real and lasting harm, perhaps, than any other individual that ever wrote. Most of the world has outlived a good part of these harms, though by no means all of them; but in our South they flourish pretty forcefully still. . . . It was Sir Walter Scott that made every gentleman in the South a major or a colonel, or a general or a judge . . . it was he who created rank and caste down there, and also reverence for rank and cast, and pride and pleasure in them. . . . Sir Walter had so large a hand in making Southern character, as it existed before the war, that he is in great measure responsible for the war.[23]

In the aesthetics of nationalism, it is, as Hegel noted, "in song that particular national differences . . . are most completely in evidence."[24] This was the case in the Civil War. The antithetical images of the North and the South were cast into the poetry of popular song, into two songs that remain their unofficial anthems—"The Battle Hymn of the Republic" and "Dixie." In this same aesthetics, the unsingable "Star-Spangled Banner" has proven to be a unsatisfactory synthesis. The well-known first verse of "The Battle Hymn of the Republic" reads:

> Mine eyes have seen the glory of the coming of the Lord;
> He is trampling out the vintage where the grapes of wrath are
>   stored;
> He hath loosed the fateful lightning of His terrible swift
>   sword;
> His truth is marching on.

The first lines of Dixie read:

> I wish I was in the land of cotton, old times there are not
>   forgotten,
> Look away, look away, look away, Dixie land.

The contrast in both lyric and music is complete. "The Battle Hymn" is a crusading march, as one writer noted, "an exhortation to action which would have created no surprises had its numbers sounded through the ranks of Cromwell's Ironsides."²⁵ On the other hand, "Dixie" is drawn from a traditional and cheerful minstrel dance. "The Hymn" looks to a future "coming of the Lord," "Dixie" looks away to a past, to a pleasant and unforgotten "old times."

On the side of the North, one need only read Lincoln's Gettysburg Address to hear echoes of that same messianic nationalism and admonitory Old Testament tonalities as found in the "Battle Hymn." On both sides a God-given mission: to create a new nation or to restore an old nation. And both found their heroes, the two greatest being the messianic Lincoln and the chivalrous Lee—both exemplars of the spirits that infused their nations. Both, as Hegel wrote of heroes, "swallowed up the fulness and seriousness of meaning and the inner character of the spirit which bears the particular life, the demands the needs, and customs of his nation."

As for Lee, Hegel's remark, that "the handsome warrior is indeed the glory of his particular nation,"²⁶ seems perfectly fitting. In his dignified bearing, lineage, and noble conduct he embodied the Southern ideal. Lee was, as one historian has said, "the absolute symbol of the Confederacy."²⁷ As "The Marble Man," Lee, although in some respects sharing the characteristics of Hegel's classical hero, nevertheless manifested a bravery that was of "a totally different complexion" than that of the classical hero. It was the bravery of the Romantic hero, which was "the outcome of the secret wealth of the soul, its honor and chivalry, and is in the main a creation of the phantasy, which undertakes adventures that have their origin in . . . the impulses of mystical piety , and we may add generally the personal attitude of the individual."²⁸

Lincoln in almost all respects, presented the antithetical image of Lee. And if he be taken as a hero, then he is more the modern hero, confronted more by an inner than an outer enemy. Lincoln is better described, and was described, as "The Man of Sorrows"—an image deepened by his assassination on Good Friday. Nevertheless, despite his public awkwardness and his tormenting inner depression, he realized his purpose. He does seem to deserve, more than Lee, Hegel's title of "world-historical individual." He surely understood and expressed "what the age requires," and his age required national unity.²⁹ He was quite willing, for the sake of expediting that unity, to suspend, without legal authority, several hallowed constitutional guarantees, and in this he was one with such of his contemporaries as Cavour (1810–60) of Italy and Bismarck (1815–96) of Germany. Of course, Lincoln, as such an individual, did not share in the American mandate to pursue happiness. As Hegel noted, such individuals

cannot be said to have enjoyed what is commonly called happiness.
They did not wish to be happy in any case, but only to attain their end,

and they succeeded in so doing only by dint of arduous labors. They knew how to obtain satisfaction and to accomplish their end, which is the universal end. With so great an end before them, they boldly resolved to challenge all the beliefs of their fellows.[30]

Of this, John Hay, Lincoln's secretary, made it clear that "[it was] absurd to call him [Lincoln] a modest man. No great man is ever modest. It was his intellectual arrogance and unconscious assumption of superiority that men like Chase and Sumner could never forgive."[31] Forgiven or not, Lincoln was resolved to secure the future stability of the original national union—even if it meant war.

The war itself was immanent, as it had long germinated within the ambiguities of the Constitution, but its actual birth had to await the emergence of some external provocation, and in this case it was the geography of the continent itself.

In 1848, just fourteen years before the outbreak of the Civil War, the end of the Mexican War marked the acquisition of Texas, New Mexico, Arizona, and Upper California. With this, the present continental boundaries of the United States were framed. In that same year, its physical limits explored by the California Gold Rush, the frontier had reached its term at the Pacific Ocean, and the "manifest destiny" of the nation had been obtained. Hegel had anticipated what this geographical closure might portend. For Hegel,

> A state cannot truly exist as such until it has ceased to direct its energies into constant emigration; . . . North America is still at the state of cultivating territories. Only when, as in Europe, it has ceased merely to augment its farming population will the inhabitants press in upon each other to create town-based industries and communications instead of moving outwards in search of new land; only then will they set up a compact system of civil society and feel the need for an organic state.[32]

After 1848, it was understood that the "constant emigration" into free land was no longer without limit. This understanding, which rested on "the need for an organic state," precipitated a debate as to who would have use of that land, the slave-based agriculture of the South or the so-called free-soilers of the North.

Lincoln, in order to win election to the presidency of the Republic, could not avoid addressing the issue of slavery, which, as a nationalist, he took to be "the only thing which threatens the Union."[33] For him, the slavery issue was reduced to being only an obstacle to national union. As he wrote to Horace Greeley in 1862, "My paramount object in this struggle is to save the Union, and is not either to save or destroy slavery."[34] During his campaign, he first advocated that the institution of slavery should only be tolerated within the states where it had been established, but not permitted to expand into the new territories. But although Lincoln's moderate policy, which included a weak support of the Fugitive Slave Law, narrowly won the election for him, neither the social interests of the South nor the moral imperatives of the Northern abolitionists were satisfied. Southern radicals, compelled to respond to the moral issue of slavery, presented it as a necessary good. However, for an ever-growing number of Northerners, it was an absolute evil. Hegel had earlier laid out these two antithetical attitudes:

> The alleged justification of slavery (by reference to all its proximate beginnings through physical force, capture in war, saving and preservation of life, upkeep, education, philanthropy, the slave's own acquiescence, and so forth), as well as the justification of slave-ownership as simple lordship in general, and all historical views of the justice of slavery and lordship depend on regarding man as a natural entity pure and simple, as an existent not in conformity with its concept (and existent also to which arbitrariness is appropriate). The argument for the absolute injustice of slavery, on the other hand, adheres to the concept of man as mind, as something inherently free.[35]

Hegel's position is clear enough in regard to any "alleged justification of slavery." For him, "the very status of slave . . . is an outrage on the conception of man."[36] However, Hegel would likely not have joined the radical abolitionists, as in his words, although "slavery is in and for itself *injustice*, for the essence of humanity is *Freedom*; but for this man must be matured. The gradual abolition of slavery is therefore wiser and more equitable than its sudden removal."[37] In regard to slavery, the views of both Jefferson and Lincoln seem more in accord with Aristotle's doctrine of the natural slave than with Hegel rejection of this "outrage." Lincoln was clear about the matter:

> I have no purpose to produce political and social equality between the white and the black races. There is a physical difference between the two which, in my judgment, will probably forever forbid their living together upon the footing of perfect equality; and inasmuch as it becomes a necessity that there must be a difference, I, as well as Judge Douglas, am in favor of the race to which I belong having the superior position. . . .
>   I agree with Judge Douglas that he [the black] is not my equal in many respects,—certainly not in color, perhaps not in moral or intellectual endowment.[38]

Whoever visits the Jefferson Memorial in Washington will see the inspirational words of Jefferson inscribed on its wall, one reading, "Nothing is more certainly written in the book of fate than that these people [the black slaves] are to be free." However, what is not inscribed is Jefferson's next sentence: "Nor is it less certain that the two races, equally free, cannot live in the same government."[39] The Enlightenment mind found itself at home in Jefferson's world, a world of utility and precise mathematical measurements. There is also, in Jefferson, more than a bit of the cynical nephew of Rameau. Practice and theory were seldom so separated. As one historian recorded, "Jefferson was relentless in tracking down his own fugitive slaves, and severe—even gratuitously harsh—in administering punishment to runaways."[40] Of this frame or shape of consciousness, Jefferson can well fit what Henry Harris has termed the "Contemptuous Consciousness" which is "the whole world of the Enlightenment."[41] Jefferson's world was that of both the aristocrat of Montecello and the revolutionary leader. In time, as Hegel noted, from the "inner revolution" generated by the Enlightenment there "emerges the actual revolution of the actual world, the new shape of consciousness, *absolute freedom*."[42] The lawyer Jefferson, just as his French contemporaries whom he admired, had no problem in dealing with the heady abstractions of Liberty, Equality, Fraternity—which, as Karl Marx correctly observed, were soon replaced by Infantry, Artillery, Cavalry.

To submit that Hegel, on the matter of racial equality, might even be more open-minded than either Jefferson or Lincoln is not at all implausible. Hegel accepted it as a fact the report that freed slaves in South America had demonstrated themselves quite capable of civic equality, among them being "the black physician Dr. Kingera, who first acquainted the Europeans with quinine." Others had proved themselves to be "skilled workers and tradesmen, and even clergymen and doctors, etc."[43] Considering that Hegel died two years before the English even decided to free their 780,000 colonial slaves, his stance regarding their equality seems remarkably liberal.

As Hegel had indicated, reasons for slavery, even if it were an "outrage upon the conception of man," could nevertheless be adduced, and so they were. For radical Southern apologists the "peculiar institution" found justification not only as an economic necessity but as a consequence of a rational social order. For them, justifications for slavery were to be found everywhere—even, as it happened, if only to serve a defiant sign to the North. Indeed, even Hegel's statements concerning Africa, carefully edited, were called up before the U.S. Congress in an attempt to justify the cause of slavery.[44] And finally, on this, even the Hegelian theologian Philip Schaff, a major figure in the so-called Mercersburg School, found biblical reasons to support Hegel's advice that slavery should only be gradually abolished.[45] But this less radical view, although it found support among many in both North and South, did not prevail, and the debate soon reached the battlefield.

With Lincoln, and the North, the stringent religious codes of the Old Testament sustained the most radical proposals of the Enlightenment—universal freedom and equality. The God of Abraham, as understood by the abolitionists, gave his support to the *Philosophes* and the clarity of simple arithmetic. As Hegel wrote in his *Phenomenology*, "Enlightenment . . . holds an irresistible authority over faith."[46] The abolitionist conception of freedom accords itself to Hobbes's definition of freedom, which was "an absence of restraint," a simple release from external bondage, independence, separation, and liberty from others. Needless to say, Hobbes's notion of equality was not taken up—which is simply that individuals are equal when it comes to killing one another. The abolitionists seemed not to have considered that freedom from external constraint is not an end in itself, but only a condition for the exercise of concrete freedom, for rational self-determination.

The simple linking of abstract freedom and abstract equality, so evident to the Enlightenment mind, rests on quantitative abstractions. In the abstract realm of the mathematical understanding, any qualified being can be abstracted and considered as a separate, free, and independent unit, a simple quantum equatable to every other. Qualitative diversity can easily be reduced to quantitative identity. As Hegel noted in regard to mathematical thought, "it is easy to discover a guiding principle, and that is the immanent principle of analytic identity, which appears in the diverse as *equality*; [and] progress consists in the reduction of the unequal to an ever greater equality."[47] For the mathematical mind, which defined Enlightenment intentions, mathematical progress was to find itself embodied in social and political ends as the reduction of the unequal to an ever greater equality, of total democratization. It was perceived as a moral imperative to press society toward reducing qualitative diversity into numerical plurality. Henceforth, only the unqualified numerical majority would be allowed to determine the course of government. Majority rule would ensure social and political unity—even if only as a matter of statistics and polls. In its more revolutionary mode, the same mind would demand that all qualitative diversity be forcibly abolished for the sake of quantitative identity—in short, the establishment of a mathematical society in which "progress consists in the reduction of the unequal to an ever greater equality." John Calhoun's proposal that a "concurrent majority" was preferable to a numerical majority ran absolutely contrary to the democratic vision, which could not, in principle, introduce any qualitative factor in political determinations. It is of interest to note that it has been argued that Hegel would have agreed with Calhoun on this matter of a "concurrent" majority.[48]

Not surprisingly, the Enlightenment understanding of individual freedom and social equality, embodied in such politically sacred documents as the Declaration of Independence and the Gettysburg Address, have proven not only difficult but even dangerous to effect in the actual world. As Hegel had noted:

> Liberty and Equality are the simple rubrics into which is frequently concentrated what should form the fundamental principle, the final aim and result of the constitution. However true this is, the defect of these terms is their utter abstractness: if stuck to in this abstract form, they are principles which either prevent the rise of the concreteness of the state, i.e. its articulation into a constitution and a government in general, or destroy them. . . . As regards, first, equality, the familiar proposition, All men are by nature equal, blunders by confusing the "natural" with the "notion." It ought rather to read: By nature men are only unequal.[49]

Hegel's cautionary principle was, if somewhat embarrassing to abolitionists, always implicit in Northern political policy. Egalitarian declarations, no matter how loudly voiced, were not the ultimate reason for the war. In this regard, in a recent study entitled *Two Nations: Black and White, Separate, Hostile, Unequal* sociologist Andrew Hacker writes: "Had white America really believed in its egalitarian declarations, it would have welcomed former slaves into its midst at the close of the Civil War. Indeed, had that happened, America would not be two racial nations today."[50]

Slavery, with its attendant issues of universal freedom and equality, provided the North with a moral justification for bringing about a war which had always been latent in the ambiguities of the original Constitution and the myriad differences of geography, language, ethos, and heritage that separated North from South. As Hegel observed about the nature of war, since the contending states act as autonomous individuals, "a state may regard its infinity and honor as at stake in each of its concerns."[51] The seizure of Fort Sumpter provided that concern.

Since the Enlightenment enthusiasm for universal welfare, more in evidence in the North than the South, toward the advancement of such abstract causes as "freedom" and "equality" often ran counter to the concrete intentions of the nation to advance its own particular welfare, its own nationalistic *Realpolitik*, the Civil War brought forth some terrible ironies. One of the many possible examples of these ironies which surfaced in this war of national recognitions and universal ideals occurred during that same march through Georgia which saw the loss of all but honor among those who fought at Griswoldsville. Here, even honor was lost.

On December 3, 1864, just eleven days after the battle of Griswoldsville, the XIV Corps of Sherman's Army drew close to Savanna. In its destructive course through Georgia it had been followed by a ever-growing number of freed slaves. These displaced thousands trailing in the wake of the Union Army had been given to believe that they would be afforded protection. The commander of the XIV Corps bore, ironically, the exact name of the Confederate president, Jefferson C. Davis. From the beginning of its career through Georgia, General Davis was disturbed and angry about being forced to provide for these freed slaves while being threatened by General Wheeler's Confederate cavalry. But Davis soon found a way to rid himself of the refugee problem. Just before reaching Savanna, the corps set up a pontoon bridge to cross the swollen and icy waters of Ebenezer Creek. The frightened refugees were held back from crossing the bridge until the whole XIV Corps had crossed. Then, by order of General Davis, and without warning, the bridge was suddenly dismantled. The helpless former slaves were then faced with the oncoming Confederate cavalry. As close as could be estimated, there were anywhere between five thousand and ten thousand refugees left stranded and unprotected. As Wheeler's corps descended on these former slaves, a slaughter ensued. As one Union officer who commanded the rear guard wrote, "I witnessed a scene the likes of which I pray my eyes may never see again." The refugees, with many women and children among them, "raised their hands and implored from the corps commander [Davis] the protection they had been promised . . . but the prayer was in vain and, with cries of anguish and despair, men, women and children rushed by the hundreds into the turbid stream and many were drowned before our eyes." Of the refugees who did not enter the creek, as that same officer wrote, "their fate at the hands of Wheeler's troops was scarcely to be preferred." Those that survived the swords of the cavalry on the banks of Ebenezer Creek were returned to their masters.[52] Here, Hegel's remark that " the World Spirit is unsparing and pitiless" might come to mind.[53]

General Davis, who was never punished for his act, was part of an army that had, at least as its moral justification, the purpose of freeing the slaves. He had certainly "freed" the slaves by allowing them to be completely independent. In a less striking but equally terrorizing irony, the abolitionists did the same as General Davis. This moral faction, whom Hegel might characterize as "beautiful souls," had never doubted themselves, nor had they reflected on the nature of either freedom or equality or the possibility of a link between them. The abolitionist movement came to an end when the war ended. The emancipation of the slaves, contrary to what Hegel might have wished, was equally sudden. For the abolitionists, it was a happy conclusion. For the former slaves, impoverished and now left without either property or place, and unprepared or forbidden to participate in the established civil society, it was not such a happy conclusion. They found themselves, for many generations, isolated within the angry ruins of the South or simply ignored in a prospering North, which drew on Europe to satisfy its need for labor. The Union had been saved and the slaves freed by such as General Davis, but the hopeful expectations of the former slaves, expectations shared by the refugees at Ebenezer Creek, had been fulfilled in the same terrible irony.

For the unreconstructed Southern mind, that Lee's brilliant chivalry had not prevailed against the Northern invaders was due not only to the loss of Jackson and the betrayal of Longstreet,[54] but also to the ruthless willingness of Grant and Sherman to sacrifice their men. Here is how one Southern apologist evaluated Grant: "He contained no spark of military genius; his idea of war was to the last degree rude—no strategy . . . ; he had no conception of battle beyond the momentum of numbers. Such was the man who marshaled all the material resources of the North to conquer the little army and overcome the consummate skill of General Lee."[55] Nevertheless, Lee, from the moment he took command, seemed unable to accept the fact that the Confederacy was outproduced and outnumbered. In his dashing raids into the North, at Antietam and Gettysburg, the Confederacy lost over sixty thousand men—a crippling loss. As one military historian wrote,

> The acid fact is that Lee lost the war. His Southern chivalry and virtuoso tactical footwork were ultimately overwhelmed by novel forces which Southern society . . . was ill equipped to meet. . . . For many commentators . . . the war has become a parable in the futility of such romantic notions as "nobility" or "officer-like behavior." It was those officers who broke away from their professional code of chivalry who finally came out on top, not those like Lee who remained loyal to it.[56]

After Gettysburg, it became evident that the Southern military was simply unable to deal with the new age of warfare, which was utilitarian in nature. Of this new age of warfare, as Hegel wrote,

> The principle of the modern world—thought and the universal—has given courage a higher form because its display now seems to be more mechanical . . . it seems to be turned not against single persons, but against a hostile group, and hence personal bravery appears impersonal. It is for this reason that thought has invented the gun, and the invention of this weapon, which has changed the purely personal form of bravery into a more abstract one, is no accident.[57]

The industrial North, with its mass production and its population, coupled with a moral indignation driven by Enlightenment ideals, proved too much for the agrarian and Romantic South. The "momentum of numbers" and the definite mathematical ballistics of the Northern rifle proved more powerful than Southern smoothbores and Celtic charges. As one study has argued, "the Confederate generals . . . fought in the past. The Union leaders fought in the future."[58] The World-Spirit had moved on, and the South was left only with the sad memory of the "Lost Cause." The Celtics who comprised the Confederate Army once again heard what was said of their forefathers a century earlier, after the battle of Culloden: "it is for their bravery and loyalty in 'a lost cause' that they are chiefly remembered today."[59]

In tracing the dialectical path of self-alienated spirit as a historical passage, a reason suggests itself as to why the Southern cause was a "lost cause." In this phenomenological history, the noble consciousness, called forth out of the Romantic memory of Southern chivalry, could not but be overcome by the advent of a later "shape" of the world-mind, the Enlightenment. Among Southern apologists, the "roundheads"[60] of the North were scorned for their materialist utilitarianism, for their pragmatic Puritanical bustle, but nevertheless, it was just this scorned aspect which enabled the North to win the war.

The American Civil War was indeed, given the myriad natural and moral differences that then divided the original federation of states, an "irrepressible conflict." It was also, in the exact sense that Hegel uses the term, a "tragedy."

NOTES

1. G. W. F. Hegel, *Lectures on the Philosophy of World History: Introduction*, tr. H. B. Nisbit (Cambridge: Cambridge University Press, 1975), p. 69.

2. Samuel Eliot Morison, *The Oxford History of the American People* (New York: Oxford University Press, 1965). p. 480 n.

3. Hegel, *Philosophy of World History*, p. 136.

4. Ibid., p. 112.

5. G. W. F. Hegel, *Lectures on Natural Right and Political Science*, tr. J. M. Stewart and P. C. Hodgson (Berkeley: University of California Press, 1995), p. 306.

6. G. W. F. Hegel, *Lectures on the History of Philosophy*, tr. E. S. Haldane (London: Routledge and Kegan Paul, 1955), vol. I, p. 446.

7. See James M. McPherson's *For Cause and Comrades: Why Men Fought in the Civil War* (New York: Oxford University Press, 1997).

8. Kjellén's 1916 work, *Staten som Lifsform*, translated as *The State as Organism*, bears signs of being influenced by Hegel's treatment of the geographic influences on political policy.

9. Hegel, *Philosophy of World History*, p. 152.

10. Morison, *Oxford History of the American People*, p. 400ff.

11. Hegel, *Philosophy of World History*, p. 169.

12. Walter A. McDonald, *Promised Land, Crusader State: The American Encounter with the World since 1776* (New York: Houghton Mifflin, 1997).

13. G. W. F. Hegel, *Philosophy of Mind*, tr. W. Wallace (Oxford: Clarendon Press, 1973), pp. 61–62.

14. Hegel, *Philosophy of World History*, p. 162.

15. Hegel, *Philosophy of Mind*, p. 39.

16. Grady McWhiney and Perry D. Jamieson, *Attack and Die: Civil War Military Tactics and the Southern Heritage* (Tuscaloosa: University of Alabama Press, 1984).

17. Ibid., p. 172.

18. Cited in Jan Dawson, *The Unusable Past: America's Puritan Tradition, 1830–1930* (Chico, Calif.: Scholars Press, 1884), p. 74.

19. Ibid., p. 74.

20. Ibid., p. 18.

21. Edmond Wilson, *Patriotic Gore: Studies in the Literature of the American Civil War* (New York: Oxford University Press, 1962), p. 436.

22. William R. Taylor, *Cavalier and Yankee: The Old South and American National Character* (Cambridge, Mass.: Harvard University Press, 1979), p. 335. This distinction between Cavalier and Yankee is still alive and well and manifested in a divided U.S. foreign polity. See Michael Lind's "Civil War by Other Means," in *Foreign Affairs*, vol. 78, no. 5 (September–October 1999), pp. 143–42.

23. Cited in Wilson, *Patriotic Gore*, p. 445.

24. G. W. F. Hegel, *Aesthetics: Lectures on Fine Art*, tr. T. M. Knox (Oxford: Clarendon Press, 1975), II, p. 1143.

25. M. E. Bradford, *A Better Guide than Reason: Studies in the American Revolution* (LaSalle, Ill.: Sherwood Sugden, 1979), p. 188.

26. G. W. F. Hegel, *Phenomenology of Mind*, tr. A. V. Miller (Oxford: Clarendon Press, 1997), p. 439.

27. Thomas L. Connelly, *The Marble Man: Robert E. Lee and His Image in America Society* (Baton Rouge: Louisiana State University Press, 1990), p. 16.

28. G. W. F. Hegel, *The Philosophy of Fine Art*, tr. F. P. B. Osmaston (New York: Hacker Art Books, 1975), vol. II, p. 331.

29. Hegel, *Philosophy of World History*, p. 84.

30. Ibid., p. 85.

31. Cited in Wilson, *Patriotic Gore*, p. 119.

32. Hegel, *Philosophy of World History*, p. 170.

33. Arthur Charles Cole, *The Irrepressible Conflict: 1850–1865* (New York: Macmillan, 1934), p. iv.

34. Letter to Horace Greeley, August 22, 1962. Cited in Morison, *The Oxford History of the American People*, p. 616.

35. G. W. F. Hegel, *Philosophy of Right*, tr. T. M. Knox (Oxford: Oxford University Press, 1967), p. 48.

36. Ibid., p. 15.

37. Hegel, *Philosophy of History*, p. 99.

38. John T. Morse Jr., *American Statesmen: Abraham Lincoln* (Cambridge, Mass.: Riverside Press, 1893), vol. I, p. 136.

39. Cited by Hadley Arkes in "Jefferson on Race and Revolution," *The New Criterion*, vol. 15, no. 5 (January 1997), p. 29.

40. Ibid.

41. *Hegel's Ladder II: The Odyssey of Spirit* (Indianapolis: Hackett, 1997), p. 277.

42. Hegel, *Phenomenology*, p. 356.

43. Hegel, *Philosophy of History*, p. 165.

44. Michael H. Hoffheimer, "Does Hegel Justify Slavery?" *Owl of Minerva*, vol. 25, no. 1 (Fall 1993), pp. 118–19.

45. Cole, *The Irrepressible Conflict*, p. 256.

46. Hegel, *Phenomenology*, p. 348.

47. *Hegel's Science of Logic*, tr. A. V. Miller (Atlantic Highlands: Humanities Press, 1989), p. 790.

48. Gunner Heckscher, "Calhoun's Idea of 'Concurrent Majority' and the Constitutional Theory of Hegel," *The American Political Science Review*, vol. 23, no. 4 (August 1939), pp. 585–90.

49. Hegel, *Philosophy of Mind*, p. 265.

50. Andrew Hacker, *Two Nations: Black and White, Separate, Hostile, Unequal* (New York: Ballantine Books, 1992), p. 12.

51. Hegel, *Philosophy of Right*, p. 214.

52. Edward M. Churchill, "Betrayal at Ebenezer Creek" *Civil War Times* (October 1998), p. 259.

53. Hegel, *Lectures on Natural Rights*, p. 306.

54. See William Garrett Piston's *Lee's Tarnished Lieutenant: James Longstreet and His Place in Southern History* (Athens: University of Georgia Press, 1987).

55. E. A. Pollard, *The Lost Cause* (New York: Gramercy Books, 1994; facsimile of the original 1886 edition), p. 510.

56. Paddy Griffith, *Battle Tactics of the Civil War* (New Haven: Yale University Press, 1987), p. 23.

57. Hegel, *Philosophy of Right*, p. 212.

58. Thomas B. Buell, *The Warrior Generals: Combat Leadership in the Civil War* (New York: Crown, 1997), p. 12.

59. McWhiney, *Attack and Die*, p. 144.

60. Emory M. Thomas, *The Confederate Nation: 1861–1865* (New York: Harper and Row, 1979), p. 24.

CHAPTER 8

Social Contract Theory and the Politics of Recognition in Hegel's Political Philosophy

Alan Patten

Freedom is the value which Hegel most greatly admires and the central organizing concept of his social philosophy. He holds that freedom is the "worthiest and most sacred possession of man" (PR §215A) and thinks that the entire normative sphere, or "system of right," can be viewed as "the realm of actualized freedom" (PR §4; cf. §29).[1] In taking freedom to be the fundamental principle of his political philosophy, Hegel acknowledges an important debt to Rousseau, Kant, and Fichte. "It was the achievement of Rousseau," he writes, "to put forward the *will* as the principle of the state" (PR §258). "It is a great advance," he adds in discussing Kant's practical philosophy, "when the principle is established that freedom is the last hinge on which man turns, a highest possible pinnacle, which does not allow itself to be impressed by anything, so that man allows no authority, or anything else, to be valid if it goes against his freedom" (VGP III 367/459).[2]

But, although Hegel agrees that freedom constitutes the fundamental axiom of moral and political argument, he strongly rejects the contractarian account of social and political legitimacy which Rousseau and his followers take to be an implication of that axiom: neither marriage, nor the state, he asserts, should be "subsumed under the concept of contract" (PR §75). This attitude toward his predecessors provokes a question that I want to explore in this essay: How can Hegel both accept the starting point of social contract theory (the commitment to freedom) and reject what social contract theorists take to be an obvious implication of that starting point (the contractarian account of legitimacy)?

The main aim of the chapter is to give a clear and precise account of why Hegel thinks he can reject social contract theory without abandoning its commitment to the principle of human freedom. In developing this account, I focus mainly on the published texts and recorded lectures of Hegel's mature social and political philosophy. My ambition is to add to the existing literature on Hegel and social contract theory in two ways.[3] First, I emphasize and explain the role played by Hegel's account of recognition in his judgment on, and alternative to, social contract theory. Second, by stating Hegel's position clearly and precisely, and by fully appreciating the role played in it by recognition, I hope to persuade at least a few readers that Hegel's position is less vulnerable to certain obvious objections than is often supposed.

1. HEGEL'S CRITIQUE OF SOCIAL CONTRACT THEORY

Hegel shows some awareness of the diversity within the social contract tradition that he criticizes. In the *Philosophy of Right*, for instance, he invokes the distinction between the view that the state is a contract of all with all and the view that it is founded on a contract of all with the sovereign (PR §75).[4] He also distinguishes between the contractarianism of "earlier times," which he associates with the aristocratic reactionaries of his own day (who view political rights and duties as the "immediate private property of individuals" to be bartered with the state)[5] and the social contract theories of "more recent times" (PR §75). Hegel does not, at paragraph 75, mention any particular social contract theorists by name but seems to assume either that his criticisms would apply to a range of different formulations of social contract theory or that his intended audience would be familiar with the theories he discusses and would know from the context which particular claims, by which particular thinkers, he was attacking.

At PR §258 Hegel singles out Rousseau and Fichte for criticism, and it seems likely that their versions of social contract theory are foremost in his mind. It is less clear whether he would include Kant's theory of the social contract among the targets of his criticisms. As will become apparent from the discussion to follow, Hegel's main criticism of social contract theory does not really work against Kant's "hypothetical" formulation of the theory. Unlike Rousseau and Fichte, Kant agrees with Hegel's contention that we have a duty to belong to a rational state whether we have consented to such an arrangement or not.[6]

The central claim of social contract theory, as Hegel interprets it, is that the state is "based on," or "grounded in," the individual (or "principle of the individual will").[7] The following, for instance, is a fairly typical characterization of social contract theory for Hegel: "According to Rousseau, self-sufficient individuals, as atoms, constitute the foundation of the state" (Henrich 82). More specifically, he takes social contract theorists to be grounding the state in the *Willkür* (choice, discretion) of the individual as this is expressed in the decision to give or withhold consent to a social contract. This characterization of social contract theory remains extremely vague, however, to the extent that it fails to specify which aspects of the relationship between individual and state are said to be grounded in individual consent.

A survey of passages in which Hegel discusses social contract theory reveals at least three different ways in which he further specifies what precisely is being grounded in individual consent: (1) whether or not a "state" ("union within the state," "government," "people") is to be "established" ("founded," "brought into existence"); (2) whether or not the individual has a duty to become and remain a member of the state (or simply "to be in the state"); (3) whether or not "the sovereign and the state" are to be regarded as having (certain) rights.

Noticeably absent from these formulations is any explicit recognition of the claim—central to much social contract theory—that consent determines: (4) whether or not the individual has a duty (or obligation) to obey the law (and perhaps to support the state in other ways). It is reasonable to suppose, however, that Hegel does intend formulations (1) to (3) to imply (4). For one thing, the idea of a duty of membership referred to in (2) is itself vague and needs further filling out (as does the idea of a state "existing" referred to in [1]). It could mean something fairly minimal, like a duty to reside on a territory in which an effective state is up and running, or it could, more demandingly, involve having a duty (or obligation) to obey the state (and perhaps to support it in other ways). The second, stronger interpretation is supported by Hegel's discussion of membership in part III of the *Philosophy of Right* (and the corresponding lectures), where the notion of membership in ethical institutions (including the state) is strongly associated with having certain duties to those institutions (§§148, 149, 155, 261). The latter include "the duty to submit to the court's authority" (§221) and duties to perform certain "services and tasks—on behalf of the state" (§261), including military service if the state's independence is at risk (§§324–326). Formulation (3) is also frustratingly vague insofar as it fails to specify what kinds of rights the state is said to acquire through the consent of individuals. The most obvious right that Hegel may have in mind, however, is the right to make authoritative rules and decisions—a right that is traditionally thought to correlate with the individual subject's duty to obey. If this is what Hegel means—and he clearly does accord such a right to the state—then he does indeed recognize something like formulation (4) in his account of social contract theory, and we should read him as offering a critique of it.

Hegel's most general objection to social contract theory is that it misapplies the norms and principles of the bourgeois sphere of civil society to the normative theory of the state. "The intrusion of this relationship [of contract], and of relationships concerning private property in general, into political relationships has created the greatest confusion in the normative theory of the state (*Staatsrecht*) and in actuality" (PR §75; cf. Hotho 266, 269). There is, for Hegel, an important distinction between the spheres of *Privatrecht* and *Staatsrecht*: the norms and values which it is appropriate to appeal to in one sphere are not those of the other.

On its own, however, this objection is not very persuasive unless Hegel can tell us why it is inappropriate to treat *Staatsrecht* as continuous with *Privatrecht*. A social contract theorist might argue that there is nothing wrong with applying the norms and principles that prevail in civil society to the political sphere: an ideal of consensual exchange is essential to both, it might be contended, because this ideal is grounded in the principle of respecting human freedom.

Against this view, Hegel argues that because social contract theory makes political legitimacy dependent on individual choice (*Willkür*) and consent, membership in the state, and the precise set of institutions and arrangements that comprise the state, become a matter of individual discretion (PR §75,A and §258; Wannenmann 58). Individuals may choose to enter the state, or they may not; they may legislate some set of institutions for the state, or they may not. Against this implication of social contract theory, Hegel cites Aristotle's dictum that "a man who could live alone would either be an animal or a god" (Henrich 210; cf. VGP II 227/208) and asserts that "it is the rational destiny (*Bestimmung*) of human beings to live within a state, and even if no state is yet present, reason requires that one be established" (PR §75A). "It is not optional (*ein Belieben*) for men, whether they enter into a state or not, but rather it is their absolute duty to do so" (Henrich 210; cf. Homeyer 232). Hegel's argument, then, is that since contracts are the product of individual choice or *Willkür* (they are entered into at the discretion of the contracting parties), they provide too capricious (*zufällig*) and unreliable a foundation on which to build the legitimacy of the rational state. Or, to return to the earlier formulation, his claim is that it is inappropriate to apply the norms and principles of contractual relationships to the political sphere, since, unlike a commercial transaction, there is nothing optional or discretionary about being a member of a rational state: some political arrangements are reasonable and legitimate, and therefore owed allegiance, whether or not they are agreed to.

Hegel is thus taking issue with passages such as the following from Fichte's *Grundlage des Naturrechts*:

> That I must adapt myself to just these particular men arises because I live with them in society; but I live with them in society because of my free resolution, and in no way out of an obligation. This is applicable because of the civil contract (*Bürgervertrag*): it is originally in the free choice (*in der freien Willkür*) of every man whether he wills to live in this particular state, although, if he wishes to live with men [in general], then it is not a free choice whether to enter into some state or other. . . . But, as soon as he expresses his will to enter into a particular state, and is accepted into it, he is thereby, through this mere mutual declaration, completely restricted by all the laws required of this group of men. . . . Through these few words—I will to live in this state—he accepts all of the laws. . . . [The material of the law is given by the law of right]. . . . But the form of the law, its binding power, is given for the individual only through his consent.[8]

Against the view expressed in this passage—that the binding or obligatory power of law and state derive from the actual consent of the individual—Hegel's argument is that the state is not based on a contract because individuals already have a duty to belong to, and obey, the state whether or not they have given their consent.

To this challenge, contractarians might respond by conceding that they do view the nature and legitimacy of the state as ultimately a matter for individual choice (albeit a choice that is constrained by certain rational norms and principles). This does indeed mean that there is a theoretical possibility that individuals will decide not to enter or recognize the authority of the state at all or will stubbornly decide to establish a state that is irrational or unstable. But leaving open this possibility is necessary if an account of political legitimacy is to show respect for the value of individual freedom. It is because freedom is the first principle of political legitimacy for contractarians that they insist that the decision to enter a state on certain terms is ultimately a matter of individual choice. The implication of Hegel's claim that the rational state is necessary, and that individuals have a duty independently of their consent to belong to and obey it, is to deny the value of freedom and to belie Hegel's claim to have grounded his view in freedom.

This formulation of the contractarian view brings us to the crux of what divides Hegel and social contract theorists. For against the argument put in this form Hegel is ready with two different replies. The first is a point that commentators sometimes seize on as evidence of the weakness of Hegel's critique.[9] To the extent that social contract theory equates freedom with the capacity for individual choice (*Willkür*), Hegel maintains that it is working with a false and unattractive conception of freedom (PR §258; VGP III 307/402; VG 117–18/99). Whereas contractarians tend to operate with a relatively, if not completely, open-ended conception of freedom, Hegel thinks freedom can be tied to specific rational ends and duties, including the duty to be a citizen of a rational state. Contractarians may conclude from this that the Hegelian challenge to social contract theory is grounded in too controversial a premise to be of much concern. They might even go so far as to argue that Hegel can only claim to have grounded his communitarian alternative to social contract theory in the value of freedom by perversely adopting a conception of freedom which is the very opposite of how that term is ordinarily understood.

I think more can be said in defense of Hegel's account of freedom than this suggests, but for the purpose of this essay let me focus on Hegel's second point, which has independent force.[10] A major assumption of social contract theory, as Hegel understands it, is that agents are free and rational in the state of nature. It is because free and rational individuals in the state of nature give their consent to be members of the state that the legitimacy of the state can be said to be grounded in the freedom of the individual. Hegel questions, however, whether individuals in the state of nature can be expected to have and maintain even the most minimal capacities for free and rational reflection presupposed by this assumption. Against the view that they do have these capacities, Hegel argues that the state of nature is not a state of freedom at all but of animal impulse and savagery. "We are accustomed to starting from the fiction of a state of nature, which is certainly no state of spirit (*Zustand des Geistes*), of rational will, but of animals amongst one another. The true state of nature is a war of all against all, as Hobbes very correctly remarked" (VGP II 92/108; cf. PR §194; VG 117/99; Enz III §502; Wannenmann 38; Homeyer 212; LPR 215).

Now on the face of it this seems a rather odd criticism, since (as Hegel's own reference to Hobbes suggests) it is contractarians themselves who tend to emphasize the uncertainties and inconveniences of the state of nature. Hegel's point, however, cannot be so easily deflected. His claim is not just that the state of nature would be an inhospitable place to live, but that the very capacities for freedom and reason that are presupposed by the idea of individuals freely choosing to set up social institutions would not be present in the state of nature. The attitudes and capacities that make up free and rational agency cannot reliably be developed and sustained in the state of nature, but only in the context of social institutions, including the rational state.

The claim is most explicitly made in a passage from VG:

Freedom . . . does not itself possess an immediate and natural existence. It still has to be earned and won through the endless mediation

of discipline acting upon the powers of cognition and will. For this reason, the state of nature is rather a state of injustice, of violence, of
uncontrolled natural impulses, and of inhuman deeds and emo-
tions. . . . Restrictions . . . are part of that process of mediation
whereby the consciousness of freedom and the will to realize it in its
true (i.e. rational and essential) form are engendered. . . . Such restrictions are the indispensable conditions of liberation; and society and the
state are the only situations in which freedom can be realized. (VG
117–18/98–99)

Hegel's view is that human beings in the state of nature are, in effect, like
children: they have the potential for freedom and reason but that potential has not yet been realized.[11] For that potential to be unleashed they
must undergo an often arduous process of self-formation and education,
which Hegel usually refers to as *Bildung* (PR §57 and §187). *Bildung* is
the general term used by the German *Aufklärer* to designate both the
process of education and acculturation that an individual or people must
go through to achieve freedom and rationality and the result of that process. An individual undertakes *Bildung* in the schoolroom and at the
knee of his parent or *précepteur*, but also, Hegel is claiming, in the
broader context of his social, cultural, and even political experience.[12]

Hegel's most interesting objection to social contract theory, then, is
that it operates with an excessively instrumental view of state and society. It imagines that human beings with fully developed capacities for
free and rational agency choose to adopt major social institutions in
order to advance their ends and interests. For Hegel, this picture makes
the "common error of taking crude peoples to be free" and thus ignores
the "absolute worth of *Bildung*" (Henrich 64–65). In the absence of
social institutions such as the rational state, human beings could not
develop and maintain capacities for freedom and reason and thus could
not possibly be in a position to give their free consent. As Hegel puts it
in his *Lectures on the History of Philosophy*, social contract theory
assumes that the "universal" can be separated from the "individual"—
"as if the individual could on its own (*an und für sich*) be what it
presently is, and the universal did not make it that which it is in truth"
(VGP II 108/93). Put more plainly, contractarian thought forgets or
ignores the important role that social institutions play in constituting the
free and rational individuals whom they take for granted.[13]

If Hegel's argument can be sustained, then it follows that, far from
being the only account of political legitimacy which takes seriously the
value of individual freedom, contractarianism risks undermining the
very attitudes and capacities that make up free agency. To the extent
that social contract theory allows that it is optional for individuals to
contract into the rational state, the possibility opens up that the individ-

ual freedom which contractarians so greatly cherish will not be realized at all. Hegel, by contrast, can argue that, because "society and the state are the only situations in which freedom can be realized" (VG 118/99), we have reasons grounded in the value of freedom to affirm and accept social institutions even if we have not given them our consent. He clearly envisages an alternative to social contract theory that will seek to articulate the social and political arrangements that provide the context in which the capacities for freedom and reason can develop and flourish. Thus, whereas social contract theorists start by asking "What arrangements, if any, have free and rational individuals consented to be part of?"—leaving open the possibility that they did not consent to be part of the arrangements required to nourish their capacities for freedom and rationality—Hegel, by contrast, can be thought of as asking a somewhat different question: "What social arrangements must be in place if individuals are to develop and sustain their capacities for freedom and rationality?"

Although there are a number of possible rejoinders to Hegel's critique, limited space forces me to move directly to the one I think is the most serious. An important assumption of Hegel's argument is that the state is one of the social institutions that is necessary for the development and maintenance of free and rational agency. Without this assumption, Hegel's argument is effective only against those contractarian theories which assume a state of nature that is not just pre-political but also pre-social. However, it is not at all obvious that the assumption is defensible. It is plausible to say that the capacity for free and rational agency is a product of some social institution or other (and hence that any view that assumes a pre-social view of the state of nature is likely to be unsustainable). But why should we accept Hegel's claim that the rational state is necessary for the *Bildung* of the free individual? Only if he can provide an adequate response to this question can his critique be of real concern to contractarians.[14]

2. RECOGNITION AS THE FOUNDATION OF HEGEL'S ALTERNATIVE TO SOCIAL CONTRACT THEORY

The foundation of Hegel's attempt to show the necessity of certain practices and institutions is his theory of recognition. The theory of recognition provides the bridge between the concern for the development of individual freedom and the focus on the social institutions and practices that make up a community of free individuals. It constitutes Hegel's explanation of why the development of free and rational agency is ultimately a social and political process.

For Hegel, developing and reinforcing a capacity for free and rational agency is primarily a problem of arriving at and sustaining the right sort of self-understanding. When an agent is unfree, or a "slave," this is usually due not to his chains but to his underdeveloped self-conception or self-understanding. The problem with the slave, Hegel claims, lies in his will, which "does not yet know itself as free and is consequently a will with no will of its own" (PR §26A; cf. Henrich 73). "The basic principle of all slavery," he thinks, "is that man is not yet conscious of his freedom" (VG 225/183; PR §57). If the slave could only think, or take, himself to be free, then he would become free: "It is the sensation of freedom alone which makes the spirit free" (VG 56/48; cf. Wannenmann 55). Individuals remain unfree in the state of nature, Hegel claims, because they lack this "sensation" or "thought" of their freedom (Wannenmann 38).

The suggestion seems to be that the possession of a certain set of goals, attitudes, and capacities is an indispensable condition of free and rational agency. Hegel mentions some of these different capacities and attitudes in a passage in his *Lectures on the Philosophy of World History*: the individual achieves *Bildung*, he says, when he is "accustomed to adopt a theoretical attitude," "to control himself," "to renounce particularity and act in accordance with universal principles," "to analyze the situation before him," and to 'isolate' different aspects of that situation and 'abstract' from them (VG 65–66/57). Unless an agent has this set of attitudes, goals, and capacities, which together form a distinctive self-understanding, he could never engage in the kind of reflective choice that is the hallmark of free and rational agency.

Hegel's account of recognition seeks to explain how individuals could come to have, and to reinforce, this self-understanding or consciousness of their freedom. It is in the account of recognition that Hegel investigates the conditions under which agents can gain a sense of their own agency or achieve what he calls "self-certainty." The struggle for recognition, he says, is "a necessary moment in the *Bildung* of all men" and represents "the *beginning* of true human freedom" (Enz III §435A).

The broad outline of Hegel's account of recognition should be familiar to most readers.[15] Hegel assumes that an agent can only achieve self-certainty, or confirmation of his freedom and independence, through interacting with his environment, and he considers three possible ways in which an agent might do this: (1) by negating nature; (2) by extracting recognition from others; (3) by enjoying the freely given recognition of others. Through an analysis of the master/slave relationship, Hegel arrives at the conclusion that only model 3 is workable: "I am only truly free," on this view, "when the other is also free and is recognized by me as free" (Enz III §431A). His claim is that the only way in which an agent can conclusively affirm his own sense of agency and independence is as part of a community of mutually recognizing free agents.

This conclusion helps to show more precisely why Hegel thinks it is so problematic for social contract theory to assume that individuals have the capacities for freedom and rationality in the state of nature. The possession of these capacities presupposes that individuals have a certain self-understanding—that they have what Hegel terms a "consciousness of their freedom." The acquisition of this self-understanding, in turn, requires that individuals participate in stable patterns of mutual recognition. But because the state of nature is a condition of war of all against all, it is a condition in which the struggle for recognition has not yet been resolved. As Hegel puts it in his 1817–18 lectures on *Rechtsphilosophie*:

> When [the individual] does not freely enter into [the state], he places himself in the state of nature, where his right is not recognized and the natural process whereby he becomes recognized, through the struggle for recognition and through power, must still come about. . . . If the individual has the particular will not to be in the state, then he wills an immediate existence, and he puts himself against the state in the state of nature. . . . The free agent must have his knowledge in another self-consciousness; this is his higher existence. . . . The individual can only have this existence in the will of another, whom he recognizes. (Wannenmann 145–46)

For Hegel, the mistake made by contractarians is overlooking the fact that it is only through the state that the struggle for recognition can be resolved and that agents can thus acquire the very capacity for free and rational agency that social contract theory presupposes. "Only in the state is the recognition of freedom complete" (Henrich 74).

3. SOCIAL INSTITUTIONS AS MEDIATING AND STABILIZING RECOGNITION

What remains unclear is just how Hegel proposes to derive the necessity of particular social and political arrangements from the general requirement that a community of mutual recognition be established and maintained. It seems especially unclear why the state should be considered a necessary feature of such a community. Yet Hegel is committed to showing that it is if his critique of social contract theory is to be valid against versions of the theory that assume a pre-political but not a pre-social state of nature. Otherwise contractarians can argue that the state of nature is sufficiently constituted as a community of mutual recognition for the capacities to be developed which allow individuals to make an intelligent and free choice about entering the state.

The crucial step in Hegel's argument that mutual recognition has specific institutional implications is his idea that mutual recognition needs to be *mediated* by institutions and practices. Hegel's claim is that two or more individuals can recognize each other as free and rational agents only *through* specific institutions and practices in which they are participating. To this extent, a community of mutual recognition can only be realized if it has a certain objective institutional structure.

To locate this idea in Hegel's thought it is helpful to examine an unresolved problem inherited from his initial treatment of recognition. In the struggle for recognition, agents are led by a need to affirm their sense of agency to attempt, through force, to extract the recognition of their fellows (I referred to this earlier as model 2). This attempt involves the risking of life in a deadly combat with the other, a struggle which arises, in part, because neither agent is willing to give up the goal of liberation without putting up a fight.

But the risking of life in combat is important for Hegel's account for another reason as well. In order to *attract* the recognition of the other, the agent needs to do something to *show* the other that he is free: each self-consciousness has, as Hegel puts it, the "drive to *show* (*zeigen*) itself as a free self, and to be as such for the other" (Enz III §430). The other's recognition that I am free needs to be *mediated* by some demonstration by me of my freedom and independence. Risking my life in combat is this kind of demonstration: it shows that I am indifferent to, and not dependent on, my natural existence. "At this stage," Hegel explains, "man demonstrates his capacity for freedom only by risking his own life and that of others" (Enz III §421A; cf. PhG 149/114).

The violent struggle between agents is clearly of limited duration. It leads eventually either to the death, or to the surrender, of one of the combatants, the latter case setting up the master/slave relationship. This relationship raises an important problem: Now that the combat is in the past, what mediates the recognition of the master by the slave? Now that he is no longer risking his life, what *existence* does the master give his freedom, such that the slave can recognize him as free? How does he *demonstrate* his freedom to the slave?

The answer of course is that the master does *not* adequately demonstrate his freedom, and this is exactly the defect of the master/slave relationship: having won the battle, he slips back into a passive life of consumption and sensuous pleasure. The slave recognizes the master because he is forced to, not because there is something indicative of free agency in the master's activity. It is the slave, if anyone, who gives an objective, recognizable existence to his agency through his disciplined activity of formative work (PhG 153–55/117–19).

The failure of the master/slave relationship is resolved by the transition to 'universal self-consciousness' (model 3) (Enz III §436), which is Hegel's term for a community of mutually recognizing free agents. It is important to note, however, that even in this community the need for recognition to be mediated still arises. Given that agents are no longer risking their lives in battles with one another, they need to find some alternative means of demonstrating to one another that they are free. They need to manifest their agency in ways that can attract the recognition of the other. Hegel acknowledges this problem and gestures at the solution in a lecture version of his account of recognition. The individual, he claims, "makes himself worthy of . . . recognition" by showing himself to be a rational being: he does this by obeying the law, by filling a post, by following a trade, and by other kinds of working activity (Enz III §432A).

Hegel claims that the standpoint of the *Philosophy of Right* is beyond the stage at which spirit must attain a consciousness of its freedom through the struggle for recognition (PR §57). However, it would be a mistake to conclude from this that the derivation of social arrangements in the *Philosophy of Right* will have nothing to do with recognition. In the *Philosophy of Right*, and the associated lectures, Hegel returns to the theme of recognition time and time again, emphasizing in particular the ways in which the institutions and practices he discusses work to mediate mutual recognition and thus reinforce individuals' consciousness of their freedom.

For instance, in the published version of "Abstract Right," Hegel notes that "I am free for the other only in so far as I am free in my existence" (PR §48) and explicitly relates this assumption to his accounts of property and contract (PR §71; cf. §40 and §51). He makes much the same point in his 1819–20 lectures ("In order to become recognised as free, I must also show myself to be free in my existence" [Henrich 73–74]) and is even more explicit there and elsewhere about the ways in which this requirement underlies his accounts of property and contract (Enz III §§490–491; Wannenmann 48 and 56–57; Homeyer 231).[16] Hegel also sees crime as a form of negative recognition in which the criminal denies, rather than affirms, that his victim is a free and rational being and thinks that punishment is a way of negating this negation (Wannenmann 68, 71, and 130). He holds that civil society is the domain in which mutual recognition is most fully realized (PR §238; Wannenmann 125 and 130; Homeyer 264; Henrich 72), in part because it secures the freedoms of property and contract, but also because it is the sphere in which individuals can attract the recognition of others by taking a position in an estate and showing industriousness, skilfullness, rectitude, honor, and so forth, in performing the functions of that position (§§244, 253; Wannenmann 124; Henrich 194–96). He thinks that the rule of law is another way in which the validity of the rational will is recognized by others (PR §217A); he maintains that love and friendship are forms of mutual recognition (PR §158A); and he even claims that fashion and imitation are ways in which individuals attract the recognition of others (Wannenmann 113; Homeyer 260–61).

Thus it seems that one way in which Hegel proposes to move from the general idea that a community of mutual recognition must be established to the affirmation of specific social and political arrangements is by arguing that certain particular arrangements are required to mediate recognition and, to that extent, to make a community of mutual recognition possible.[17] A social world without property, contract, punishment, love, fashion, civil society, the state, and so on, could not be a community of mutual recognition, since it would lack the necessary mechanisms by which individuals attract and express recognition. Someone who agrees with Hegel that human freedom ought to be the principle of all moral and political justification thus has reason to endorse and affirm these institutions and practices whether or not they have been consented to: if Hegel's claims are correct, then these arrangements are necessary for mutual recognition and for the development and maintenance of free and rational agency.

Of course this is only a partial reconstruction of Hegel's alternative to contractarianism in that it fails to explain what might be called the "developmental structure" of the argument of the *Philosophy of Right*: the fact that it presents a sequence of shapes or determinations of spirit, each of which is supposed to develop necessarily out of the previous one. There isn't space for detailed consideration of this (for Hegel, very important) aspect of the argument here, but it is worth mentioning something briefly to complete the argument of this chapter.[18] The method by which the book attempts to identify and elaborate the necessary structure and content of a community of mutually recognizing free agents is the speculative method borrowed from Hegelian logic. The argument begins by specifying a conception of what such a community would be like whose basic features seem indispensable or minimally necessary. By "basic features" I mean, for example, the self-understandings of agents in the community, the institutions and practices in which agents interact together, and the rights, duties, and virtues that make up the normative framework in which they operate.

The argument then proceeds with a kind of thought experiment which attempts to reconstruct the experience of a social world having those features. The aim of this reconstruction is to show that a social world with just those features would not, in fact, be self-sufficient (*selbständig*) but rather would in some sense be self-defeating, unless it also had certain additional features. Since the features of the initial conception are indispensable for mutual recognition, and they turn out to depend on a richer conception with additional features for their possibility, these further features can be regarded as indispensable as well. The argument then examines whether the newly characterized social world would, on its own, be self-sufficient, and so on. The outcome, if Hegel can sustain the argument, is a complex and highly differentiated picture of the necessary structure and content of a community of mutual recognition—one which he thinks would correspond in its essentials with the modern European social world in which he lives. If we are willing to affirm the first, simple social world as necessary for the mediation of mutual recognition, then we have reason to affirm and feel reconciled with our own social world as well.

We might summarize the main steps in Hegel's alternative to the social contract theory of political legitimacy, then, as follows:

1. Human freedom is the basis of all rights and duties.

2. The capacity for freedom is not something which every adult human being automatically has but is only developed and sustained in the context of a community of mutual recognition: it is the recognition by other free agents that reinforces the idea of oneself as free that is essential to being free.

3. A community of mutual recognition is only possible if it contains certain mediating institutions and practices: it is through these institutions and practices that individuals attract and express recognition.

4. The set of institutions which make up the modern social world, and which include the state, represent the minimum self-sufficient institutional structure that is capable of mediating mutual recognition.

Like social contract theory, Hegel's alternative approach seeks to ground the legitimacy of the major institutions of the social world in freedom. For social contract theory (as Hegel understands it) this is done by imposing a requirement that those institutions enjoy the consent of all of their members. For Hegel, however, this argument presupposes that individuals outside institutions such as the state could have and maintain the capacity to make a free and rational decision about joining the state—an assumption he disputes. Rather, he argues that it is ultimately only in a social world containing the state that individuals develop and sustain these capacities because such a social world is the minimum self-sufficient social world that is capable of mediating mutual recognition. For Hegel, then, we have a reason grounded in freedom to affirm and endorse the modern state whether or not we have consented to it.

NOTES

This essay is a shortened version of chapter 4 of my book, *Hegel's Idea of Freedom*, Oxford University Press, 1999. Reprinted by permission of Oxford University Press.

1. For a key to abbreviations used for citations, see Works by Hegel Cited following the notes section.

2. Hegel also acknowledges his debt to Rousseau, Kant, and Fichte at VGP III 306–8/400–402 and 413/503.

3. Good discussions of Hegel and social contract theory include: J. W. Gough, *The Social Contract* (Oxford: Oxford Unversity Press, 1957), ch. XI; Patrick Riley, *Will and Political Legitimacy* (Cambridge, Mass.: Harvard University Press, 1982), ch. 6; Seyla Benhabib, "Obligation, Contract and Exchange: On the Significance of Hegel's Abstract Right," in *State and Civil Society: Studies in Hegel's Political Philosophy*, ed. Z. Pelczynski (Cambridge: Cambridge University Press, 1984); Domenico Losurdo, *Hegel et les libéraux*, tr. François Mortier (Paris: Presses Universitaires de France, 1992); Bruce Haddock, "Hegel's Critique of the Theory of Social Contract," in *The Social Contract from Hobbes to Rawls*, ed. by David Boucher and Paul Kelly (London: Routledge, 1994).

4. For a good discussion of this distinction, see Gough, *The Social Contract*, pp. 2–3.

5. This variant of contractarianism is discussed most extensively by Hegel in his 1822–23 and 1824–25 lectures, Hotho 265–72 and Griesheim 251–54 respectively. See Losurdo, *Hegel et les libéraux*, ch. 3, for a good treatment of Hegel's account. As Losurdo points out, those who take Hegel's anti-contractarianism to be a mark of his conservatism tend to overlook the fact that Hegel directs his criticisms at radical democrats such as Rousseau and reactionary German conservatives who had taken up the rhetoric of contractarianism in defense of their feudal privileges.

6. See Kant, "Metaphysical First Principles of the Doctrine of Right," in *The Metaphysics of Morals*, tr. Mary Gregor (Cambridge: Cambridge University Press, 1991), §42; and *Political Writings*, tr. H. B. Nisbet, ed., Hans Reiss, 2nd ed. (Cambridge: Cambridge University Press, 1991), p. 79.

7. Hegel's main discussions of social contract theory can be found at: PR §75,A and §258; Wannenmann 58; Homeyer 267–68; Henrich 82, 212–13; Hotho 265–72; Griesheim 251–54; VG 116–18/98–99, 145–46/122; and VGP II 107–8/92–93, 226/208. My characterization of Hegel's interpretation of social contract theory in this paragraph and the next draws on these sources.

8. Johann Gottlieb Fichte, *Grundlage des Naturrechts*, in *Johann Gottlieb Fichtes sämmtliche Werke*, ed. I. H. Fichte, vol. 3 (Berlin: Veit und Co., 1845–46), pp. 14–16. (Cf. p. 107.) The translation is my own.

9. See, for instance, Riley, *Will and Political Legitimacy*, pp. 167, 173, 182, 191–93.

10. For further discussion of Hegel's account of freedom, see my *Hegel's Idea of Freedom*.

11. Hegel draws the analogy between the state of nature and childhood at Homeyer 205 and 212. For further passages in which Hegel asserts the necessity

of society and state for the development of free and rational agency, see Wannenmann 38 and Henrich 210.

12. Hegel describes *Bildung* at PR §187 and Henrich 57 and 63. For two good discussions of the concept, with specific reference to Hegel, see Hans-Georg Gadamer, *Truth and Method*, ed. Garrett Barden and John Cumming (London: Sheed & Ward Ltd., 1975), pp. 9–19; and G. A. Kelly, *Idealism, Politics and History* (Cambridge: Cambridge University Press, 1969), pp. 341–48.

13. For a forceful recent statement of this argument, see Charles Taylor, "Atomism," in *Philosophy and the Human Sciences: Philosophical Papers* 2 (Cambridge: Cambridge University Press, 1985).

14. Gough objects in *The Social Contract* (p. 185) that Hegel "fails to distinguish between society and state, and attributes to citizenship what is more truly due to membership of society."

15. Excellent discussions in the secondary literature include: G. A. Kelly, "Notes on Hegel's Lordship and Bondage," in *Hegel: A Collection of Critical Essays*, ed. Alisdair MacIntyre (New York: Doubleday, 1972); Charles Taylor, *Hegel* (Cambridge: Cambridge University Press, 1975); Allen Wood, *Hegel's Ethical Thought* (Cambridge: Cambridge University Press, 1991); Robert R. Williams, *Recognition: Fichte and Hegel on the Other* (Albany: SUNY, 1992); Robert Pippin, "You Can't Get There From Here," in *The Cambridge Companion to Hegel*, ed. Frederick C. Beiser (Cambridge: Cambridge University Press, 1993).

16. I discuss Hegel's justification of property in *Hegel's Idea of Freedom*.

17. For a similar formulation, see Benhabib, "Obligation, Contract and Exchange," p. 173.

18. For a fuller discussion, see my *Hegel's Idea of Freedom*.

WORKS BY HEGEL CITED

In references to works by Hegel, I have used the abbreviations listed below. Where an abbreviation refers to both the German original and an English translation, I give the page references for both, with the German first and the English second, separated by a slash (/). Where possible I have used standard English translations, but I have occasionally amended these to make them more literal or to standardize terminology. Where no suitable English translation is available, translations are my own. References to lecture materials not published during Hegel's lifetime are made, where possible, directly to the transcription from which they were taken. However, where these materials are included as 'Additions' or *Zusätze* to standard editions of Hegel's published works, I have cited the paragraph number of the relevant work together with an 'A'. Thus 'PR §7,A' refers to paragraph 7 of the *Philosophy of Right* and the Addition to that paragraph.

Enz III   *Enzyklopädie der philosophischen Wissenschaften*, vol. III (1817, revised 1827, 1830). *Werke X*. Cited by paragraph number (§).

Hegel's Philosophy of Mind, tr. William Wallace and A. V. Miller (Oxford: Oxford University Press, 1971). Cited by paragraph number (§).

Greisham   *Vorlesungen über Rechtsphilosophie*, vol. IV, ed. K.-H. Ilting (Stuttgart: Fromman Verlag, 1974). Transcription of Hegel's 1824–25 lectures by K. G. von Greisham. Cited by page number.

Henrich   *Philosophies des Rechts: Die Vorlesung von 1819/1820*, ed. Dieter Henrich (Frankfurt: Suhrkamp Verlag, 1983). Anonymous transcription of Hegel's 1819–20 lectures. Cited by page number.

Homeyer   *Die Philosophie des Rechts: Die Mitschriften Wannenmann (Heidelberg 1817–1818) und Homeyer (Berlin 1818–1819)*, ed. K.-H. Ilting (Stuttgart: Klett-Cotta Verlag, 1983). Transcription of Hegel's 1818–19 lectures by C. G. Homeyer. Cited by page number.

Hotho   *Vorlesungen über Rechtsphilosophie*, vol. III, ed. K.-H. Ilting (Stuttgart: Fromman Verlag, 1974). Transcription of Hegel's 1822–23 lectures by H. G. Hotho. Cited by page number.

LPR   *Lectures on the Philosophy of Religion: The Lectures of 1827*, ed. Peter C. Hodgson, tr. R. F. Brown, P. C. Hodgson, and J. M. Stewart with the assistance of H. S. Harris (London: University of California, 1988). Cited by page number.

PhG   *Phänomenologie des Geistes* (1807). *Werke III*. Cited by page number.

                 Phenomenology of Spirit, tr. A. V. Miller (Oxford: Oxford University Press, 1977). Cited by page number.

PR   *Grundlinien der Philosophie des Rechts* (1821). *Werke VII*. Cited by paragraph number (§) except where otherwise indicated.

                 Elements of the Philosophy of Right, tr. by H. B. Nisbet, ed. Allen W. Wood (Cambridge: Cambridge University Press, 1991). Cited by paragraph number (§) except where otherwise indicated.

VG   *Die Vernunft in der Geschichte*, ed. J. Hoffmeister (Hamburg: Felix Meiner Verlag, 1955). Cited by page number.

                 Lectures on the Philosophy of World History: Introduction, tr. H. B. Nisbet (Cambridge: Cambridge University Press, 1975). Cited by page number.

VGP   *Vorlesungen über die Geschichte der Philosophie*. 3 vols. *Werke XVIII–XX*. Cited by volume and page number.

Hegel's Lectures on the History of Philosophy, tr. Elizabeth Haldane (Lincoln: University of Nebraska Press, 1995). 3 vols. Cited by volume and page number.

Wannenmann   *Die Philosophie des Rechts: Die Mitschriften Wannenmann (Heidelberg 1817–1818) und Homeyer (Berlin 1818–1819)*, ed. K.-H. Ilting (Stuttgart: Klett-Cotta Verlag, 1983). Transcription of Hegel's 1817–18 lectures by P. Wannenmann. Cited by page number.

Werke   *Hegel: Werke Theorie Werkausgabe* (Frankfurt: Suhrkamp Verlag, 1970). 20 vols. Cited by volume number.

CHAPTER 9

Hegel's Implicit View on How to Solve the Problem of Poverty: The Responsible Consumer and the Return of the Ethical to Civil Society

Joel Anderson

Hegel clearly struggled with his views on poverty. His brilliant analyses of pauperization in industrial England and his expression of heartfelt concern for its victims, especially in his lectures on the *Philosophy of Right,*[1] stand in stark contrast to his near silence regarding a solution to the problem of poverty. Unlike, for example, the category of crime, poverty is not presented as a necessary evil that is *aufgehoben* as part of realization of a rational social order. According to Shlomo Avineri's now classic assessment, "on the problem of poverty, [Hegel] ultimately has nothing more to say than that it is one of the 'the most disturbing problems which agitate modern society'. On no other occasion does Hegel leave a problem at that."[2]

The lack of an explicit solution to poverty in Hegel's social philosophy has evoked widely varying responses. Some have followed Avineri in viewing this as evidence of Hegel's ability to recognize the unavoidable difficulties for welfare state capitalism.[3] Others have seen it as highlighting the exclusionary character of his social philosophy.[4] In contrast, I argue that there is a very interesting approach to fighting poverty implicit in Hegel's social philosophy and suggested by many of his explicit claims.

I argue that Hegel held the following view: (1) that the chronic poverty endemic to industrial capitalism can be overcome only through changes that must include a transformation in practices of consumption;

(2) that this transformation must lead to more *sittlich* (ethical) and self-conscious practices of consumption; and (3) that the institution best suited to enable the development of these more *sittlich* and self-conscious practices of consumption is the associational institution that Hegel called the *Korporation*. I am not claiming that Hegel believed that this transformation of consumer practices could actually be brought about. He certainly made no proposal for doing so. My more limited claim is that the best way to make sense of his writings on poverty is by attributing to him the view that such a transformation was necessary for ending poverty.

To understand the case for this interpretation, it is important to focus on the systematic structure of Hegel's economic and social philosophy. Accordingly, I focus on two key dialectical transitions in Hegel's *Philosophy of Right*. The first is the transition in the notion of "resources" (or *Vermögen*) from the economic system based on the "family principle" to that based on the principle of civil society. The second transition is the moment at which civil society's attempts to solve the problem of poverty through colonization, international trade, welfare policies, and industrial regulation reach a point of exhaustion in a moment of "bad infinity." Hegel's account of these transitions provides crucial support for attributing to him the view that ending poverty requires a "return of the ethical [*das Sittliche*]" into civil society and, especially, into practices of consumption.

1. MODERN POVERTY AND THE
RELATIONAL CHARACTER OF "RESOURCES"

In discussing Hegel's view of poverty, it is perhaps best to begin with his rather cryptic summation of the problem of modern poverty: "[D]espite an *excess of wealth*, civil society is *not wealthy enough*—i.e., its own distinct resources [*ihr eigentümlichen Vermögen*] are not sufficient—to prevent an excess of poverty and the formation of a rabble" (§245). This formulation highlights what Hegel sees as the paradox of modern poverty: destitution in the midst of unprecedented wealth. In trying to understand Hegel's position—and his puzzling contrast between "wealth" and "resources"—one should begin by noting that Hegel traces the form and causes of modern poverty (that is, very roughly, poverty under conditions of capitalism) to the fact that, in civil society, one must earn one's livelihood by producing for the ever-changing needs of others. If one cannot find buyers in the marketplace—or if one's employer cannot—then one will not be able to satisfy one's own needs. As a result of this interdependence, civil society is a domain of profound and universal vulnerability for individuals.

This is in sharp contrast to the economic order out of which civil society emerges, that based on the "family principle." Hegel uses the concept of "family" to designate a form of social relation characterized by immediate, relatively undifferentiated solidarity, particularly economies based on agriculture. There, one consumes what one produces and produces what one needs. In the economic order based on the family principle, one is naturally still vulnerable, but primarily to the vicissitudes of the weather and the soil. The basic productive unit—say, the extended family—is not dependent on others' desires for its produce.[5] In the familial economic order, what is needed for livelihood—the "family resources"—is something "permanent and secure," typically, "soil" (§170; cf. §§203, 247). Once this is in place, families can provide for their simple needs.

The concept of civil society entails something wholly different. For although a member of civil society is in many ways freer and more independent (*selbständig*), "he cannot accomplish the full extent of his ends without reference to others" (§182A).[6] In part, this has to do with the industrial mode of production, with the way in which the division of labor puts individuals in a fragile network of interdependence (§198). But the more fundamental shift is systemic, and has to do with change in the *Vermögen* that is required for a family to provide for itself: "For the families in civil society, property takes on forms other than land, for the needs belonging to civil society become the resources out of which the family creates its satisfied needs" (VPR III: 540). Since members of civil society no longer produce for their own consumption, they cannot provide directly for their own needs. They have to rely on others to produce the means for the satisfaction of their needs, which they can only obtain if they have something to offer that others need.

As the basis for earning a livelihood, the successful mediation of needs and labor constitutes what Hegel terms the "resources" (*Vermögen*) distinctive of civil society.[7] Hegel distinguishes further between the "particular" resources of an individual (or family) within a society and the "general" resources of the society as a whole. An individual's resources are a function of being appropriately situated within the network of production and consumption, of plugging into this network, of integrating oneself into the interdependent web of supply and demand in such a way that the products of one's labor end up meeting the needs of others. From this perspective, it becomes clear that Hegel's definition of the resources of individuals as "the possibility of sharing in the general resources" (§200) is *not* to be read in terms of getting one's slice of the economic pie, for that would deny the relational element of *Vermögen*.[8] Rather, the resources of individuals are constituted by the degree to which they have the opportunity to participate in a well-functioning economy.

Accordingly, the *general* resources (*das allgemeine Vermögen*) represent the capacity of a society to provide individuals with the opportunity to earn a living, which depends on the coordination of a fragile network of interdependencies, the "all-round mutual effects of everyone on one another" (VPR IV: 594). In the *Encyclopedia*, Hegel speaks of *Vermögen* as a societal constellation, stating that "this mediation of satistisfaction by the labor of all constitutes the general resources" (*Werke* 8: §524). For my purposes, it is important to emphasize that these interconnections comprising societal resources also depend on patterns of *consumption*: "The endless multiplication of the needs of others is a lasting general resource for everyone" (VPR I: 313). And more strongly and more optimistically: "No one can take a bite of bread without thereby providing bread for others" (VPR III: 614). In this relational sense, the needs of others (and, more concretely, their consumer practices) are a resource for all. The point I wish to stress here is that Hegel saw very clearly that the ability of civil society to provide individuals with the opportunity to earn a livelihood depends on the patterns of *consumption* as much as on the patterns of production. The *Vermögen* of a society is adequate just in case production and consumption fit into a coherent pattern.

It is in light of this idea that we can make sense of §245, quoted earlier: what is needed in order to avoid mass and chronic unemployment is not wealth as such but rather the dynamic balance of production and consumption that Hegel terms "the resources [*Vermögen*] distinctive to civil society." Thus, the problem of poverty—or, more precisely, the emergence in wealthy countries of masses of able-bodied people who are unable to provide for themselves and their families—is a problem of *coordination*. Rather than being generated by shortages or disasters, as is the case in premodern economies, the form of poverty with which Hegel is concerned results from the normal functioning of an "unrestricted" (§243) free market economy.

2. ECONOMIC LIBERALIZATION AND VULNERABILITY TO THE CONTINGENT

There is an additional step in Hegel's argument, which has not yet been mentioned, namely, that in order to achieve a high level of general resources, a society must introduce economic liberalization and allow more room for subjective freedom—precisely the developments that generate the economic instability that causes modern poverty. Increased subjective freedom and increased individual vulnerability are linked within civil society, in that the primary causes of modern poverty are chronic overproduction and severe imbalances of consumption and production—all of which can be linked to the fact that civil society is the realm of contingency and arbitrariness (*Zufälligkeit*). As a result of the liberalization and industrialization of economic relations, there is no longer any guarantee that either the individual producer will be able to participate adequately in the economy or that the overall balance of consumption and production will provide enough jobs.

This raises the thorny issue of the status of subjective freedom within Hegel's economic philosophy. Although much has been made of his commitment to economic liberalization as creating a realm of subjective freedom and individuality,[9] Hegel has serious misgivings, as we shall see, about giving subjective freedom free rein, *even in the economic domain*. Indeed, everything in the systematic logic of the *Philosophy of Right* points toward an eventual *Aufhebung* of the contingency on which subjective freedom is based.[10] And what drives civil society to this supersession of contingency is the travesty of poverty.

Because of their dependence on markets, it is a matter of luck (*Zufälligkeit*) whether even hard-working individuals can earn a living in civil society. But it is at the collective level that arbitrariness generates the most problems, in terms of the vicissitude of the market. For it is here, in the delicate web of interdependencies, that arbitrariness and contingency generate the mass unemployment and poverty that concerns Hegel.

> The contingency of the satisfaction [of needs] is present in the most diverse manner in the mechanics of society's necessity, both with regard to the changeability of the needs themselves and as a result of . . . the errors and illusions that can be introduced into individual parts of the whole mechanism and can bring it into disarray. (*Werke 8:* §533)

Here contingency of consumer demand becomes relevant in its effect on the smooth operation of the economy. Free trade policies leave the coordination of supply and demand to market forces. In principle, Hegel favors loosening contemporary restrictions on trade and employment practices, but he argues that the contingencies of production and consumption generate economic disequilibria in civil society, leading to the collapse of firms and the loss of jobs. "When a branch of industry does especially well, many individuals enter it. But the need for products has its limits, and even if such an industry becomes overfilled, the individuals cannot see it; they join in and are ruined" (VPR III: 698). What Hegel is describing here is the blindness and haphazardness of boom-and-bust market cycles.

As Hegel was well aware, laissez-faire economics treats the painful consequences of disequilibria as the market's way of correcting itself. Despite his appreciation for the analytic power of this economic perspective (§189A; VPR IV: 487), Hegel has nothing but sarcastic scorn for laissez-faire talk of "market self-correction," as his analogy with the plague makes clear: "The plague ends too; it rights itself. But hundreds of thousands have perished of it; they're all dead. Everything has thereby also been straightened out again" (VPR IV: 625). These market shifts occur so quickly that workers have little time to adapt, especially as a result of the specialization of their training, and they are thrown out of work and lose their livelihood. Hegel also saw causes of unemployment and poverty in long-term trends toward mechanization, heavily capitalized competition, and general market saturation, but it is the periods of disequilibrium that are, rightly, his focus.

Whatever the causes, the resulting poverty generates a prima facie demand for serious change. This is true for impoverishing inadequacies at both the individual and the collective levels, but I shall be focusing here on the collective level of the economy as a whole. At the individual level of the *besonderes Vermögen,* Hegel seems to favor a familiar welfare package including public provision of minimal needs, assistance in locating work, and job training and education, especially as these are provided through the *Korporation.*[11] Hegel sees the only genuine anti-poverty approach as one of ensuring that the economy provides jobs that pay a living wage, which is the task of ensuring that the collective *Vermögen* is adequate.[12]

There is, then, a need for intervention in the economy, according to Hegel. Put in systematic terms, the dialectic generated by poverty in civil society leads away from the blindness and *Zufälligkeit* of unregulated market relations:

> [T]he more blindly [the particular interest] immerses itself in its selfish ends, the more it requires such regulation to bring it back to the universal, and to shorten and moderate both the dangerous convulsions and the length of the intervening period during which these collisions are supposed to return, by a process of unconscious necessity, to equilibrium. (§236R; translation revised)

The problem, then, is contingency—blind chance. Within the individualistic framework of civil society, economic actors lack the necessary awareness of the interdependencies within which they are entwined (§236). The need, in essence, is for what Hegel calls "self-consciousness." And in the process of achieving greater self-consciousness, the emergence of the public authority (*Polizei*) plays an important transitional role, for it is only at that point that the economy can be surveyed (VPR IV: 591, 600).

3. THE FAILURES OF THE PUBLIC AUTHORITY:
EXTERNALITY AND BAD INFINITY

In his discussion of efforts on the part of the governmental bureaucracy (*Polizei*) to solve the problem of poverty, Hegel focuses on two broad strategies: direct intervention in the domestic economy and the development of foreign markets. Hegel saw both strategies destined to fail, and the reasons he had for thinking this failure inevitable suggest what, for him, a genuine solution to the problem of modern poverty would have to look like.

The first strategy involves a wide range of programs familiar from the history of Keynesianism and state socialism: production regulations, price controls, jobs programs, protectionism, and, more generally, measures aimed at regulating and moderating the vicissitudes of the marketplace (§§231–249). Although Hegel was a staunch defender of certain regulatory practices (and very clearly of the public authority's responsibility for the infrastructure), he argues that the public authority's way of overcoming the blindness and extreme particularity of civil society is "external" to the will of participants in the market (§231, 236). Individuals experience the public authority the way people often seem to experience taxation and regulation: as a bureaucracy whose purpose and policies are not understood or recognized as an expression of their will, even if they sometimes benefit from them. In part, this experience may disappear as members of civil society become reconciled with their society as a result of coming to understand that it is rational to have differentiated economic and political roles.[13] But it is also clear that Hegel is thinking of a set of public agencies that, by their nature, must operate on the basis of elite expertise and will thus always be somewhat alien to ordinary members of society. On this reading, Hegel is arguing that bureaucratic institutions are *necessarily* ineffective in combating poverty because of their essential *externality*. Given the motivational problems involved, a command economy is not the best strategy for fighting poverty.[14] What this shows, in terms of the logic of Hegel's overall argument, is that poverty cannot be eliminated through external interventions, that is, by having the universal imposed. Hence the need, as we shall see, for the intermediate and more *internal* institution of the *Korporation*.

The second strategy is to find new markets, especially by encouraging international trade and colonization (§§246–248). As a structural solution, this approach is initially more promising, for it is aimed at increasing society's "general resources" by addressing what Hegel sees as the fundamental problem, namely, a lack of consumers: "The poverty of workers consists precisely in the fact that there are no takers for what they produce. There is too much capital present, and so more is produced than the nation can consume" (VPR 19: 199). Like Marx, Hegel saw the development of the forces of production as in the driver's seat: in civil society, productivity "increases in an unendingly large proportion to consumer need, and thus in the end even those who work hard cannot earn their bread" (VPR IV: 612). The only way out seems to be to find consumers in less-industrialized countries:

> This inner dialectic of society drives it—or in the first instance *this specific society*[15]—to go beyond its own confines and look for consumers, and hence the means it requires for subsistence, in other nations which lack those means of which it has a surplus or which generally lag behind it in creativity, etc. (§246)

As Hegel emphasizes, the asymmetry is crucial. Colonies and other less industrialized countries function as new markets only insofar as they are not able to produce the goods of which the mother country has a surplus. With regard to the American colonies, for example, Hegel thought that because American independence left the asymmetry of industrial development intact, it actually was all to the advantage of Britain.[16] Colonization is thus not a generalizable solution to the problem of poverty, and it is clear, despite commentators' claims to the contrary, that Hegel realized this.[17]

Hegel goes on to argue that international trade in general will not solve the problem of overproduction behind modern poverty. This may be surprising, since we can easily imagine symmetrical trading relations in which equally highly industrialized countries export "excess" goods and yet still provide consumer niches for the "excess" goods of other countries. And there is even some evidence that Hegel saw the internationalization of economies as offering some stability (VPR IV: 507f.). Ultimately, however, he thought that this only postponed the crisis. Given that civil society is oriented toward limitless expansion, even a successful scenario, in which new markets *are* found, provides only the illusion of a solution: a country finds an export market for surplus products; this enables economic growth, which again leads to overproduction, and a new border must be crossed in order to secure a new market. And this matter of endlessly "going beyond oneself" (*Übersichhinausgehen*) is precisely the sort of fallacious thinking that Hegel condemns as "bad infinity." The discussion of bad infinity in the *Enzyklopädie* contains a description of "flight" that perfectly describes the futile attempt to export the problem of overproduction:

> A limit is set, then surpassed, then yet another limit, and so on forever. We have here nothing but a superficial alternation that remains stuck in the finite. When one thinks one can free oneself from the finite by

stepping into that infinity, then that is in fact merely the liberation of flight. But the one who flees is still not free, for in fleeing he is still determined by that from which he is fleeing. (*Werke* 8: §94A)[18]

Similarly, attempts to solve the problem of poverty by boosting growth through trade ultimately remain trapped within the pointless pursuit of infinite expansion. The problem keeps returning.

Thus, despite the undeniable importance of the public authority in many regards, neither expert regulation of the economy nor growth in foreign markets can ensure that the general resources of a society will be adequate to prevent poverty. Within the logic of Hegel's account, the failure of the public authority is the failure of economic policy that lacks the internality and self-restraint essential to full ethical self-consciousness. And this is precisely what the *Korporation* provides.

Before turning to the role of the *Korporation*, it is worth taking stock of the plausibility of Hegel's views on the economy. It must be acknowledged that Hegel's talk of "overproduction," as a feature of an entire domestic economy, is at best misleading. For as long as money is included as a commodity (which it is), overproduction as such is impossible. As Say's Law states, "Goods constitute the demand for goods."[19] If I make more shovels than anyone in my community wants, the price drops and suddenly shovels are a lot more affordable, so that more people will then buy them. The problem is thus not overproduction per se but rather the depression of prices in a given market and the resulting fact that I do not earn enough to live on. But that simply means that I should make something other than shovels—because otherwise, I'm just making something that no one really wants (unless the price drops close to zero). Price, after all, is a mechanism for determining what people think ought to be produced.

Of course, the disruption in my life is serious, and that is really where the suffering comes in. In line with this, it seems safe to say that Hegel's strongest point comes from saying that rapid fluctuations in supply and demand generate unacceptably high costs for those who are displaced by the fluctuations in employment.

4. THE *KORPORATION* AND THE *GEBILDETE* CONSUMER

Although its precise nature is much disputed, the *Korporation* can be thought of as an intermediate institution or *association* that provides a form of community between that of the family and that of the nation. In Hegel's discussion, membership in a *Korporation* is typically a function of one's participation in a branch of industry—although not of one's class—but the activities of the *Korporation* include political and social activities alongside the economic ones. Several historical models are available, including the medieval guilds, the Sozialdemokratische Partei Deutschlands in the early 1900s, and the Dutch confessional *zuilen* ("pillars") of the century preceding the Second World War.[20] As these models suggest, the *Korporation* is supposed to provide a context for everyday cooperation and discursive interaction that generate a feeling of belonging as well as a heightened understanding of the rationality of one's social world.

Because of this more "internal" relation between the *Korporation* and its members, Hegel views the *Korporation* as better able to address the needs of the poor. This has often been noted,[21] but the focus is usually on the way in which this more internal relation provides a respectful and supportive context for solidary aid: "Within the corporation, the help which poverty receives loses its contingent and unjustly humiliating character" (§253R; cf. VPR19: 203, 206; VPR III: 709). This is merely a matter of *ameliorating* poverty, however. If the *Korporation* is going to play a role in actually addressing the causes of poverty, there has to be more going on here. And there is.

The moment of the *Korporation* marks the return of the ethical to civil society, for, as members of a *Korporation*, individuals have a heightened consciousness of shared goals and mutual interdependence:

> The *Korporation* initially has the same function, the same purpose as the public authority, namely, the particular interest—not, however, as the object of a merely external ordering activity (as is the case with the public authority), but rather as the object of an activity that wills the universal, but in such a way that the individual himself participates in this activity. (VPR IV: 621; see also §255A)

In addition to the oft-noted transformation of ethical disposition this involves, this shift to more reflective participation of individuals in determining their conditions of life has significant politico-economic implications as well. And this is the crucial point. For the emergence of this new awareness raises the possibility of increased rationality of the economy by introducing attitudes toward production and consumption in which individuals participate with greater understanding of how they are contributing to the common good (*das Allgemeine*).[22]

One way in which this happens is by the *Korporation* restricting the number of people who can enter its ranks and thus be productive in a particular industry. The basic idea here is that, in consciously limiting the number of people producing certain goods or services, the *Korporation* prevents wild fluctuations in both employment and production. Thus, when Hegel asserts that "the corporation has the right . . . to admit members . . . in numbers determined by the universal context"

(§252), he is assigning the *Korporation* the task of assessing, within the framework of the economy as whole, how many people the industry can sustain. Stephen Houlgate formulates Hegel's point as follows:

> [A] corporation can not only limit the number of people producing a certain type of product within society as a whole, but can also ensure that within the corporation production opportunities are equitably distributed and that manufacturers and traders do not try to undercut one another. In this way, the measures needed to prevent overproduction are taken by the producers themselves, rather than by the state. This ensures not only that decisions about production are taken by people who understand it, but also that controls on the productive activity of members of civil society are self-imposed.[23]

Here it becomes clear in what sense the *Korporation* is able to accomplish what the public authority failed to do. By intervening in the economy "internally" and with an awareness of their place in the networks of production and consumption, members of *Korporationen* are better able to avoid impoverishment that results from producing more than the market can bear at decent prices. And they can do so, according to Hegel, without violating the principle that individuals have a right to choose an occupation that makes good use of their talents.[24]

There are limits to this approach, however, for simply restricting the *number of employees* in an occupation is not enough to regulate the uncontrolled expansion of production, particularly since Hegel traced the tendency toward overproduction not only to periodic swells of hiring, but also—even especially—to efficiency measures and mechanization (VPR IV: 612; VPR17: 138). More important for my purposes, it does not guarantee sustained consumer demand.

Again, as we have seen repeatedly, we come back to the issue of ensuring stable and adequate consumer demand so that the collective *Vermögen* remains high, thus guaranteeing enough jobs that pay a living wage. And here too the *Korporation* can play a role, in this case, by providing the context for the formation of more responsible consumer practices. Although this has not, to my knowledge, been discussed in the literature, I believe that Hegel thought that, as members of *Korporationen,* individual consumers can promote the common good—they "will the universal"—by *spending their money in ways that increase the general resources (allgemeine Vermögen), thereby alleviating poverty.*

There are several places where Hegel suggests this. To begin with, he emphasizes the economic importance and *rationality* of certain modes of consumption. "We can distinguish here between consumption that also contributes to the general resources and consumption that reduces the general resources" (VPR III: 618). Or again "A big spender benefits civil society more than someone who contributes the same amount to charity, because the first way is tied to the activity of others, the employment of their understanding" (VPR III: 615). Especially in light of his criticism of conspicuous consumption, it becomes clear that Hegel has in mind an ethic of responsible consumption, one which involves the form of self-consciousness that, as we saw at the end of the previous section, is needed for moving beyond the limitations of the public authority. Among *ungebildeten Völkern* (uncultured peoples), he emphasizes, "there is a lack of consciousness of the way the use of my property is disadvantageous for others" (VPR IV: 591; see also the especially strong language at VPR IV: 475–77). By contrast, the model of the rich doing good by consuming more is an example of a more general, responsible attitude toward consumption: responsible consumers understand their consumption as contributing to economic welfare and—to extend Hegel's thought here—in times of overconsumption and capital shortage, these responsible consumers would presumably spend less and save more. The general principle, however, is that a society with stable employment patterns will be a society in which consumers put their money where the jobs are.

Hegel does not offer many examples, but contemporary experiences with heightened consumer consciousness shed some light on the possibilities. We are most familiar with consumer groups that are motivated by *moral* objections to brutal political regimes (divestiture from South Africa in the 1980s), inhumane labor practices (child labor in the handmade carpet industry), environmental degradation (tropical hardwoods), cruelty to animals (especially veal or frois gras), moral turpitude (movie studios that produce pornographic films), and so on. The model I see suggested in Hegel is different, however, for it focuses not on a moralization of consumer practices but rather on a concern with the universal in a more purely economic mode. The point is that consumer preferences themselves would have to be mediated by an understanding of what current production patterns are and how one's consumer practices affect them. For example, if I am aware that a favorite restaurant is having trouble attracting business, I may frequent it more often to help keep it afloat. If a craze for this Christmas season's "hot" toy is leading to wild retail and production fluctuations, I may choose a different gift for a child. Or I may purchase goods that are produced by laborers earning a living wage, so as to resist the downward pressures on wages that come from uncertainty and fierce competition. In small ways, these choices help to support rational and stable growth in consumer demand, and *insofar as this occurs, the general resources are increased.*

There is a danger here of what could be called a "productionist" bias. This involves assuming current production patterns as given, and then requiring individual's tastes to adapt to the production. This is not only psychologically implausible, it is clearly much too one-sided for Hegel. A much more Hegelian picture is to say that both the productionist model and the economic liberal's model (according to which production patterns ought to adapt immediately and constantly to changes in consumer preferences) are each only half right. Although there is no point in producing something no one wants, there is also no point in disposing of the accumulated knowledge of established production patterns—and generating unemployment, displacement, and poverty in the process—for the sake of consumers' whims. For example, in a society in which many people are employed in building wooden houses and are highly skilled at it, it might make sense—as part of "willing the universal"—for consumers not to give in to a new fashion for brick houses. To dismiss the relevance of the existing production practices (as economists tend to do in treating these as irrational attachments to "sunk costs")[25] and to insist that production must always do the bidding of given preference is to succumb to a form of one-sided thinking.

Whatever the details of how this ought to be done, it is clear that this attitude of what we could call the "responsible consumer" perfectly fits Hegel's model of the advance in rationality that he terms "self-consciousness," an advance that can only result from the transformative learning process he calls *Bildung*. The concept of *Bildung* is crucial for understanding why self-conscious consumer practices are part of the development of civil society, and not a simple forfeiture of gains of subjective freedom. In the opening sections of "Civil Society," Hegel describes civil society as a process by which particularity is "educated" to and brought in line with universality through economic activity.

> [In civil society], the individual is initially for himself; he is his own end; yet the satisfaction of his needs also involves others; in this way, the individual is dependent on the others, and must be oriented toward them; he must often sacrifice his particular will, for what matters is [not only] his own will but of bringing himself in accordance with others who are likewise situated [*selbstische Anderen*]. That is, he must distance himself from the particular. In civil society, the process [of education] is this eradication of the particular. . . . [T]he uneducated [*ungebildetel*] man always reveals his particularity—now injuring, now offending. To behave in a universal manner entails having consideration for what is appropriate to the nature of the relations. (VPR IV: 484; cf. §187R, A; VPR III: 581–85)

But to say that, in civil society, the particular is educated to will the universal is not to say that individuals are swallowed up into a general will at the expense of their individuality, originality, and particularity. Especially with regard to matters that are of relatively little importance to society and the state, the "formal freedom" of caprice and personal projects has its place (§289R). What this formative process does put an end to, however, is individuals' insensitivity to the welfare of others and to the common good, as well providing an understanding of how to avoid the bad infinity of the "indeterminate multiplication of needs, means, and pleasures" (§195).[26] Central to Hegel's account, then, is the idea that education produces an *awareness* of the impact of one's actions, including economic activities, on others. This consciousness of one's situation within webs of interdependence and the sense of responsibility that comes with it emerge only in a formative process. And the development within civil society that we have followed—whereby the interdependence demanded by the market leads through a crisis of poverty and overproduction to the conscious willing of the universal (first by the public authority and then by members of *Korporationen*)—represents just such a developmental process (*Bildungsprozeß*).

For Hegel, the *Korporation* is the appropriate institution for this transformation of consumption practices for several reasons. In part, the *Korporation* can play the role it does because of the community context it provides. Once an individual is assured recognition within the *Korporation*, the economically destabilizing need to prove himself through conspicuous consumption vanishes,[27] and he must instead show his worth "through the manner in which he uses his wealth for his cooperative [*Genossenschaft*]" (VPR 19: 207). How one spends one's money thus becomes an ethical matter. In this sense, the *Korporation* represents the "return of the ethical to civil society" (§249). More generally, however, the *Korporation* provides the context for ongoing, intersubjectively mediated socialization of individuals as responsible agents, in particular, the conscious attention on the part of individuals themselves to the networks of interdependence within which they move. Within the ethical framework of the *Korporation*, the distinction between the sort of consumption that contributes to the common welfare and the sort that does not becomes the basis for a principle that members of the *Korporation* can use in guiding their own lives and in according recognition to others. What we have here, then, is a subjective appropriation of the logic of *Vermögen* ("resources") and, thus, an "internalization" of the coordinating function that the public authority tried to achieve externally. It is the *Korporation* that makes this possible, for it is only with the emergence of that form of community that individuals in civil society become able to relate to their own needs and desires in a way that is mediated by shared concerns. None of this needs to involve explicit, moral deliberation about what the right thing to do is. As an instance of the ethical substantiality that constitutes ethical life, it would come to be second nature or habitual (cf. §§151, 151A) that responsible consumers consider the impact of their practices. And that second nature is acquired and sustained through the socializing context of the *Korporation*.

The notion of the *gebildete*, responsible consumer I have been describing can be clarified with a parallel in contemporary discussions of the role of political associations and the public sphere within a model of deliberative democracy.[28] In the context of political will-formation, the role of intermediate institutions is to offer a context in which arbitrary, subjective political opinions of individuals are educated or *gebildet* in a way that allows for both stability and flexibility. The rationality afforded by a reflexive moment of public deliberation provides protection against both the wild political vacillations of plebiscitary democracy (the political corollary of laissez-faire economics) and the rigidity of expert-driven democracy (the political corollary of a command economy run by the public authority). This is not something that happens by itself. It requires a public context. And thus we can imagine the *Korporation* playing a parallel role in shaping responsible practices of consumption.

One difficulty for the interpretation I have been offering is that, while the control of production naturally falls to the *Korporation*, given that its membership is based on shared connection to a specific branch of industry, the same cannot be said for consumption.[29] One response is to say that even if we assume that corporate membership must be industry-based or profession-based, the *Korporationen* serve as *general* schools of virtue, inculcating practices of consumption that are good for the whole economy, rather than only for one's own *Korporation*. On this model, the *Korporationen* function to instill a sense of economic citizenship and civility, just as they do for the political realm. Alternatively, the *Korporationen* can be understood more broadly, as including social and cultural associations, something suggested by Hegel's discussion of churches (§270R). This would then allow for membership in multiple *Korporationen*: one is a Catholic *and* a lawyer *and* a member of a co-op for buying organic food *and* a user of Apple computers, each of which offers an institutional context of ethical socialization (*Bildung*), but in a way that is geared toward protecting specific interests that one shares with the interests of one's *Korporation*. Either way, we can certainly envision associations that serve to develop, inculcate, and reinforce patterns of action—in this case, of consumption—that have the potential to help stabilize the economy.

5. CONCLUSION

Whether a transformation in practices of consumption could actually be realized and whether it would end poverty is a very open question.[30] My claim here, however, is that Hegel had more of a sense than is usually thought of what the components of a solution to poverty would have to be. His published texts are clearly pessimistic about the prospects for such a solution, but particularly in the lectures that he gave toward the end of his life, he seemed to hold out a vision of a world in which poverty would no longer do the damage that he saw it doing in England.

Even as a proposed reading of Hegel, however, there are several issues yet to be resolved. First, more would need to be said about the model of the responsible consumer, its psychological feasibility, its compatibility with the decentralized, complex conditions of market economics, and its relation to the form of ethical freedom that Hegel calls "autonomy." Second and relatedly, more would need to be said about the character of the *Korporation* in which this responsible consumer would be found and formed, particularly regarding the *discursive* and *deliberative* character of this form of associational life. Finally, and perhaps most important, the residual particularity of the *Korporation* needs to be addressed.[31] Hegel saw the *Korporation* as in danger of becoming mired in the myopic defense of its own interests and as thus in need of integration into more universal moment of ethical life, namely, what Hegel calls the "state" (§289A). The key, then, is to show that the logic of Hegel's argument demands a model according to which the *Korporation* internalizes some of the self-consciousness and universality of the moment of the state without returning to the *external* controlling mechanisms of the *Polizei* or exclusively top-down control by the state.[32]

However much may still remain unclear at this point about the details, what I hope to have made plausible is that, on Hegel's view, any solution to the problem of poverty would have to pay attention to practices of consumption and that one of the potentials for increased rationality afforded by the *Korporation* is for the formation of more self-conscious, *sittlichen*, and responsible consumers.

ABBREVIATIONS OF WORKS USED

References that include a section number—for example, "(§245)"—are to Hegel's *Rechtsphilosophie*. English translation: *Elements of the Philosophy of Right*, tr. H. B. Nisbet and ed. Allen W. Wood (New York: Cambridge University Press, 1991). Citation is by paragraph number and, when relevant, "R" for Hegel's marginal "Remarks" and "A" for the "Additions" drawn from lecture notes. Note that the orthography and spelling of the lecture notes is often nonstandard. All translations from the lecture notes are mine.

Werke   *Hegel: Werke: Theorie Werkausgabe* (Frankfurt: Suhrkamp, 1970), volume and page number.

VPR17   *Die Philosophie des Rechts: Die Mitschriften Wannenmann (Heidel-berg, 1817–18) und Homeyer (Berlin, 1818–19)*, ed. K.-H. Ilting (Stuttgart: Klett-Cotta, 1983).

VPR19   anonymous transcription of the lectures from 1819–20, published as *Philosophie des Rechts: Die Vorlesung von 1819/1820*, ed. Dieter Henrich (Frankfurt: Suhrkamp, 1983).

VPR III H. G. Hotho's transcription of 1822–23 lectures, published in *Vor-lesungen über Rechtsphilosophie*, vol. III, ed. K.-H. Ilting (Stuttgart: Frommann-Holzboog, 1974).

VPR IV   K. G. von Griesheim's transcription of the 1824–25 lectures, pub-lished in *Vorlesungen über Rechtsphilosophie*, vol. IV, ed. K.-H. Ilt-ing (Stuttgart: Frommann-Holzboog, 1974).

NOTES

For comments on and discussion of earlier drafts, I would like to thank Rüdiger Bittner, Jim Bohman, Susan Buck-Morss, Will Dudley, Raymond Geuss, Joe Heath, Axel Honneth, Stephen Houlgate, Pauline Kleingeld, John McCum-ber, Kevin Olson, Thomas Schmidt, Kevin Thompson, Allen Wood, and members of the audience at the Hegel Society of America meeting in Athens, Georgia.

1. The recently published notes from Hegel's lectures on the *Philosophy of Right* (VPR I–IV; VPR17; VPR19) provide crucial evidence for the interpretation defended here, and I shall be making extensive use of them. These student tran-scriptions represent a reliable source for Hegel's views and are, unlike the ver-sion published during Hegel's lifetime, free from the mark of government cen-sors. Although some of this material has been available in the "Additions" that Hegel's student Eduard Gans included in his posthumous edition of the *Philos-ophy of Right*, Gans's selections are partial and frequently do not contain cru-cial passages. This is not to say that the views expressed in the notes cannot be found in the published text, but rather that they can sometimes be discerned best in light of the articulations found in the lecture material. (Note that the transla-tions of the lecture material quoted here are mine.)

2. Shlomo Avineri, *Hegel's Theory of the Modern State* (Cambridge: Cam-bridge University Press, 1972), 154. For further discussion of the uniqueness of poverty as a problem that Hegel does not solve, see Michael Hardimon, *Hegel's Social Philosophy: The Project of Reconciliation* (New York: Cambridge Uni-versity Press, 1994), 236–50.

3. In addition to Avineri, see also Allen W. Wood, *Hegel's Ethical Thought* (New York: Cambridge University Press, 1990), 242; and J. Donald Moon, "The Moral Basis of the Welfare State," in *Democracy and the Welfare State*, ed. Amy Gutman (Princeton, N.J.: Princeton University Press, 1988), 28–30.

4. Raymond Plant, "Hegel on Identity and Legitimation," in *The State and Civil Society: Studies in Hegel's Philosophy*, ed. Z. A. Pelczynski (Cambridge: Cambridge University Press, 1984), 239–43; Thomas E. Wartenberg, "Poverty

and Class Structure in Hegel's Theory of Civil Society," *Philosophy and Social Criticism* 8 (1981): 169–82; and Bernard Cullen, *Hegel's Social and Political Thought* (New York: St. Martin's Press, 1979), 85–96.

5. "As such, the family is initially closed in on itself, without a need for outward integration." ("Die Familie als solche ist zunächst in sich beschlossen, hat kein Bedürfniß der Vereinbarung nach Außen") (VPR III: 623).

6. In light of Hegel's own views on women, I use "he" as the pronoun for such terms as "citizen" and "individual."

7. It is important not to think of "resources" (*das Vermögen*) necessarily in terms of financial or property assets. Unfortunately, the earlier Knox translation uses "capital" or "wealth," which, for starters, blurs Hegel's distinction among "*Vermögen*," "*Kapital*," and "*Reichtum*." Nisbet's recent translation corrects this by using "resources" throughout, but even this can still mistakenly suggest that it is something that can be possessed in the form of income or wealth. One interpreter who understood this well is Paul Vogel: "The lasting general resources of society are thus not the sum of the natural treasures and exchangeable goods, not at all anything material and dead, but rather the sum of living laboring energies that are guided by a rational intellectuality and which, in mutual dependence, enhance one another's productivity" (Vogel, *Hegels Gesellschaftsbegriff und seine geschichtliche Fortbildung durch Lorenz Stein, Marx, Engels, und LaSalle* [Berlin: Pan-Verlag Rolf Heise, 1925], 25).

8. For this reason, Nisbet's translation is misleading here. In the passage "The possibility of sharing in the universal resources—of holding particular resources" (§200), the phrase "of holding" is neither contained in nor required by the original German. It has the unfortunate effect of forcing a reading of *das besondere Vermögen* as akin to property.

9. Manfred Riedel, *Bürgerliche Gesellschaft und Staat bei Hegel* (Neuwied: Luchterhand, 1970), and Joachim Ritter, *Hegel und die französische Revolution* (Frankfurt: Suhrkamp, 1965).

10. See especially §185. For an excellent recent discussion of how Hegel's notion of freedom demands an approach to economics that goes beyond arbitrary choice, see Will Dudley, "Freedom and the Need for Protection from Myself," *The Owl of Minerva* 29 (1997): 39–67.

11. In this connection, it is important not to misunderstand some of Hegel's harsher claims, such as "leave the poor to their fate and direct them to beg from the public" (§245R; Hegel's most revealing discussion of this is at VPR IV: 612). What Hegel wishes to prevent is able-bodied individuals—and men in particular, who are assumed to be the breadwinners—developing the attitude that they have claim-rights to assistance without any correlative duties: "Since society is obliged to feed its members, it also has the right to urge them to provide for their own livelihood" (§240A; on duties and rights, see §155). The refusal to recognize this is what Hegel calls the "rabble mentality" (see esp. VPR IV: 609). Note that the rich can also have this mentality (VPR IV: 608).

As long as aid is not unconditional, it is not clear that Hegel must see direct aid to the poor as a problem. See also Nobert Waszek, "Hegels schottische Bettler," *Hegel Studien* 19 (1984): 311–16; Hardimon, *Hegel's Social Philosophy*, 238–39; and Wood, *Hegel's Ethical Thought*, 250–54.

12. The more direct approach of providing government jobs is rejected by Hegel, on the grounds that they only exacerbate overproduction (§245). But Hegel is too quick here, for this objection is true only of jobs programs that increase production in a market that is saturated. The situation was quite different, for example, for WPA programs of Depression-era America, which put people to work doing things that would not otherwise have been done, like building trails in national parks and producing public artwork.

13. Hardimon, *Hegel's Social Philosophy*, 206–9.

14. Wolfgang Kersting, "Polizei und Korporation in Hegels Darstellung der bürgerlichen Gesellschaft," *Hegel-Jahrbuch 1986*, 378.

15. There is reason to think that the reference to "this specific society" is a reference to Britain. Hegel traced Britain's prosperity to her unique circumstance as the dominant industrial economy in the world. In an insightful remark on the use of England as an example in defense of laissez-faire economics, Hegel points out that "comparisons are often distorted, and rarely are all factors considered; England has the whole world as a market and as a basis for colonization—that is the major factor" (VPR IV: 625; cf. VPR III: 711). See also A. S. Walton's discussion of this passage in "Economy, Utility, and Community in Hegel's Theory of Civil Society," in Z. A. Pelczynski, *The State and Civil Society*, 259.

16. "North America, for example, liberated itself, and this turns out to have been of greatest advantage to England, for although North America has made itself into a state, it still has many needs that it cannot provide for on its own, since it is still largely an agricultural state" (VPR III: 707; cf. §248A; VPR19: 199; VPR IV: 615f.; *Werke* 12: 114). Independence did, of course, release the Americans from what Hegel saw as unjust restrictions on industrialization and trading relations (VPR19: 198).

17. It is striking how many commentators attribute to Hegel the view that colonization is a solution to the problem of poverty. Raymond Plant, for example, states that "Of course it is well known that in the *Philosophy of Right* Hegel argued that the problem of poverty required a solution which involved imperialism" ("Hegel on Identity and Legitimation," 240f.). The fact that colonization involves a "return to the family principle" makes it undeniable that this is at best a postponement of the problem, since the family principle always gives way to civil society.

18. With regard to the "infinite" economic expansion of civil society, see VPR IV: 612. This point has also been noted by Paul Chamley: "According to Hegel, interdependence creates serious dangers for the provision of consumers as well as the income of workers. The principle vice of this system is the lack, within itself, of a principle of its equilibrium. Its law is that of bad infinity, of linear progress toward infinity" (Paul Chamley, "La doctrine économique de Hegel d'après les notes de cours de Berlin," in D. Henrich and R.-P. Horstmann [eds.], *Hegel's Philosophie des Rechts: Die Theorie der Rechtsformen und ihre Logik* [Stuttgart: Klett-Cotta, 1982], 135).

19. For an excellent overview, see Mark Blaug, *Economic History in Retrospect*, 4th ed. (Cambridge: Cambridge University Press, 1985), ch. 5.

20. On the social democrats, see Carl Schorske, *German Social Democracy 1905–17* (Cambridge, Mass.: Harvard University Press, 1983). On the Dutch

confessional "pillars," see, for example, Siep Stuurman, *Verzuiling, kapitalisme en patriarchaat* (Nijmegen: SUN, 1983). Regarding Hegel's attitude toward the guilds, which were typically much more than economic organizations, it is important to note that, although he had criticisms of the guilds, the most damning lines on the topic ("the miserable guild system," and the last two sentences of §255A) are not actually found in the lecture notes from which that "Addition" is supposedly taken, and cannot be found in any of the published lecture notes.

21. For a good discussion of this point, see Robert R. Williams, *Hegel's Ethics of Recognition* (Berkeley: University of California Press, 1997), ch. 11.

22. For a discussion of this shift as a matter of grasping connections that were already in place but not fully understood, see Raymond Plant, "Hegel on Identity and Legitimation," op. cit. My own sense is that Plant's reading puts too much weight on the shift in thinking and not enough on the transformation of customs and practices established in the *Korporation*, although these are arguably inseparable for Hegel.

23. Stephen Houlgate, *Freedom, Truth, and History* (London: Routledge, 1991), 117.

24. VPR IV: 624. For Hegel, the freedom of occupational choice is the freedom to choose a manner of participating in the economy that allows one to fit into a complex network of interdependent relations: "The individual will pursue what he can and the choice is up to him, as a matter of his arbitrary choice [*Willkür*]; on the other hand, he will not only do what he can, but has the essential end of thereby securing subsistence for himself; that's supposed to be the outcome. . . . One often gets stuck on the formal matter of the desire to pursue [a particular occupation]; what is crucial, however, is the other side, that the goal be met; and that is what the *Korporation* does" (ibid.).

25. For an interesting discussion of "sunk costs, see Elizabeth Anderson, *Value in Ethics and Economics* (Cambridge, Mass.: Harvard University Press, 1993), 34–36.

26. In this passage, Hegel says that just as this indeterminate expansion of needs "has no limits," the same can be said of "the distinction between natural and educated interests" (§195). In his translation of this passage, Nisbet follows Ilting (VPR II: 644) in reading (for the word translated as "educated") "gebildetem" rather than the Suhrkamp edition's "ungebildetem." Both readings are, however, mistaken. The passage should read "eingebildetem" (artificial or fanciful), which is the phrase found in the parallel passage in the Griesheim notes [VPR IV: 493]. One reason for preferring this reading is that it more easily explains lexigraphically Gans's misreading of "un-" for "ein-." For my purposes, however, the important point is that this keeps open the space for understanding *educated* needs as the *Aufhebung* of natural and artificial needs, and as a form of consumer desires that is not subject to "bad infinity."

27. *Philosophy of Right*, §253R; VPR19: 206f. For good discussions of this point, see Dudley, "The Need for Protection from Myself," 52f.; Iring Fetscher, "Zur Aktualität der politischen Philosophie Hegels," in *Hegel-Bilanz: Zur Aktualität und Inaktualität der Philosophie Hegels*, ed. Reinhard Heede and Joachim Ritter (Frankfurt: Vittorio Klostermann, 1973), 212; and Robert Williams, *Hegel's Ethics of Recognition*, ch. 11.

28. See, for example, Jürgen Habermas, *Between Facts and Norms: Contributions to a Discourse Theory of Law and Democracy*, tr. William Rehg (Cambridge, Mass.: MIT Press, 1996); James Bohman, *Public Deliberation* (Cambridge, Mass.: MIT Press, 1996); and James Fishkin, *Democracy and Deliberation* (New Haven: Yale University Press, 1991).

29. I would like to thank Stephen Houlgate for raising this issue.

30. Wood, for example, suspects that it is "utopian" to think that corporate civil society can stabilize the economy without undermining the subjective freedom made possible by market-based civil society (Wood, *Hegel's Ethical Thought*, 242).

31. There is, of course, a very real issue of how the *Korporationen* are to relate to one another, and in this sense they are not fully concerned with the universal. This objection is pressed, for example, by Richard Teichgraeber, "Hegel on Property and Poverty," *Journal of the History of Ideas* 38 (1977): 59–62.

32. In this connection, Robert Williams proposed reading of the state as a "social organism" is particularly fruitful (Williams, *Hegel's Ethics of Recognition*, ch. 13).

CHAPTER 10

Law, Culture, and Constitutionalism: Remarks on Hegel and Habermas

Andrew Buchwalter

In his *Faktizität und Geltung*[1] Jürgen Habermas draws a distinction between law and culture. Questions of law are matters of justice that concern rules adopted by citizens to regulate their communal life and in principle define the structure of any validly constituted legal community. Questions of culture, by contrast, bear on the ethical self-understanding of a particular community and pertain to the values that define that community and its sense of what is desirable. Habermas, to be sure, acknowledges that a system of law is tied to the values of a community in the way that, say, a moral account of justice is not. It is in thus distinguishing law from morality that he expands on and even revises earlier versions of his "discourse-theoretic" approach to normative issues. Nonetheless, Habermas maintains that as regards meaning and legitimacy legal questions possess a formality and generality that distinguish them from the substantive particularism of ethical-cultural considerations. Nor could it evidently be otherwise. Paradigmatically committed to structures of communication rather than modes of consciousness, the discourse-theoretic approach is arguably obliged to down play attention to those orientations, attitudes, and motivations that more centrally comprise the focus of a cultural approach to law.

In this chapter I question Habermas's pointed distinction between law and culture, a distinction replicating his Neo-Kantian juxtaposition of the right and the good. I shall not, however, dispute Habermas's contention that cultural matters bear on the ethical values of a community or, conversely, that legal questions concern general rules and principles governing communal conduct. Instead, I challenge the assumption—certainly not unique to Habermas—that the relationship of law and culture must be construed in terms of the static oppositions sketched in *Faktiz-itüt und Geltung*. I do so by recalling arguments advanced by Hegel in his *Philosophy of Right* [or Law],[2] where he calls for the superssesion (*Aufhebung*) of law in ethical life (*Sittlichkeit*). In particular, I argue that legitimate law presupposes for its validity and, with special attention to constitutional law, for its meaning appeal to the type of ethico-cultural considerations connoted by the concept of Sittlichkeit. Additionally, I argue, *pace* Habermas, that Hegel's culturalist approach to law entails neither a subordination of law to ordinary politics nor a denial of the emphatic normative concerns this approach is often presumed to jetti-son. I conclude by noting the significance of Hegel's culturalist approach to law and constitutionalism.

I. LAW, PUBLIC CULTURE, AND CIVIC VIRTUE

Hegel's account of the indispensability of culture to legal validity centers on his view of the place in legal philosophy of attitudes, motivations, values, and what generally he calls sentiment (*Gesinnung*). This empha-sis on the concept of *Gesinnung* is traceable to Montesquieu, whose *De l'esprit des lois* identified the social and cultural presuppositions of for-mal legal and political theory. In the *Philosophy of Right*, Hegel devel-ops Montesquieu's insight along several different tracks. Most impor-tant for present purposes is his view of the dependence of a genuine political order on the civic virtue or public sentiment of its citizens. In asserting this dependence, however, Hegel does not embrace the repub-licanism of those for whom civic virtue simply consists in engagement for the common values of a particular community.[3] Habermas may fol-low those who equate republicanism with a defense of a communal ethos, yet, for Hegel, recourse to republicanism is inseparable for a mod-ern commitment to rights, liberties, and the rule of law.[4] In his view, the legal-procedural institutions necessary for a modern political order can-not properly function unless supplemented by attitudes that evince com-mitment to uphold and sustain those institutions.

This point is central to Hegel's account of the dependence of prin-ciples of abstract right and morality on *Sittlichkeit*.[5] While asserting the indispensability of general principles of right and duty for a modern political order, Hegel maintains that those principles must be embedded within a public culture characterized by a general willingness on the part of citizens to accept and defend public norms. Without being thus situ-ated, general principles are easily manipulated for ends inimical to the public goals they are assumed to serve. Thus in his discussion of "Abstract Right," Hegel demonstrates how, in the absence of a commitment to such values as agreement, impartiality, and truthfulness, individuals will commonly enter into contracts which they have no intention of honoring and which they may breach when it is in their interest to do so. Similarly, if contractual relations must be supplemented by a sense of moral duty, duties themselves, in the absence of a corresponding commitment to the value of accepting and honoring obligations, can likewise be manipulated for private advantage. This of course is central to Hegel's discussion of the hypocrisy characteristic of individuals who cloak their conduct in the garb of principles in order to pursue ends that are only too self-serving. In his method of presentation, Hegel specifies the nature and conditions of a public ethos only after having first examined the principles of right and morality. However, his substantive position, as he often notes, is that these principles have neither meaning nor reality unless embedded in a public culture characterized by an *antecedent* commitment on the part of individuals to those principles.[6]

The same point can be made with regard to the theory of positive law—for Hegel, as for Habermas, the central means of social integration in modern industrial societies. Anticipating Habermas, Hegel accords normative dimension to the concept of positive, coercive law, going so far as to perceive in positive law a type of postmetaphysical continuation of the aims of natural law theory.[7] With Habermas (who builds on H. L. A. Hart), Hegel maintains that positive law rests on general claims to recognition (*Annerkantsein*),[8] whose institutional viability both requires securing individual liberties and mandates that law find acceptance by the community as a whole. For Habermas, to be sure, this takes the form of an account of the dependence of positive law on a theory of democracy, one in which those subject to the law ("the addressees of law") can simultaneously understand themselves as authors of law. For Hegel, the public dimension is of a more mediated character: legitimate law is rooted in a system of justice (*Rechtsplege*) and a structure of public authority (*Polizei*) committed to the common good.[9] Whatever the differences, though, Hegel anticipates Habermas in discerning in the concept of valid positive law simultaneous commitment to general principles of public as well as private autonomy.

Where Hegel does differ from Habermas is in rejecting any conceptual relationship, or "internal connection," between positive law on the one hand and justice and autonomy on the other.[10] In his view, the relationship between positive law and more emphatically normative principles is at best contingent. Indeed, given the roots of positive law in modern commercial societies, where the common good is achieved, if it is achieved at all, not directly but as an incidental by-product of individuals pursuing private ends, positive law, for Hegel, is compatible with growing injustice, social inequity and what, generally, he calls a *Verlust der Sittlichkeit*. Hegel's *Philosophy of Right* does include institutions of public welfare designed to counteract the injustices associated with an economic construal of positive law. Yet he also knows that legally sanctioned forms of state intervention into social relations can be counterproductive, as they tend to undermine the very liberties and forms of dignity they are intended to protect. In a welfare system, "the needy might be given subsistence directly, not by means of their work, and this would violate the principle of civil society and the feeling of individual independence and self-respect in its individual members."[11] In this regard, positive law, in Hegel's view, tendentially assumes the forms of legal regulation, or juridification (*Verrechtlichung*), that Habermas so astutely analyzed in *The Theory of Communicative Action*,[12] yet is less inclined to address in his present theory.[13] Whether expressed in market relations or state interventionism, positive law, for Hegel, remains in the grip of a dichotomy of universal and particular, public and private, that undermines its claims to freedom, equality, and mutual recognition.

Habermas, to be sure, is no less aware than Hegel of the pathologies that can result when law is subordinated to the exigencies of monetary and administrative subsystems. Indeed, the discourse theory of law is, notably, conceived precisely as an effort to fashion an alternative to both bourgeois-liberal and welfare state paradigms of law, neither of which can do justice to the public autonomy central to an account committed to conjoining constitutional and democratic theory. Still, the differences are significant, since for Hegel the limitations of positive law stem not from its economic or statist construal but from the structure of positive law itself.[14] Because positive law does not address matters of sentiment, because it is only posited or imposed (*nur gesetzt*), because it is governed by a procedural formality or, what Hegel calls, "lawlikeness" (*Gesetzmässigkeit*) designed only to regulate external behavior, it can accommodate and even foster conduct inimical to civic life.[15] This point has been made by Peter Dews, who notes the potentially disintegrative dimension of a notion of law that permits anything not explicitly forbidden.[16]

Thus while Hegel may share Habermas's commitment to the rationality of a system of positive law, he also recognizes that the salutary values associated with such a system cannot be assured via the resources of positive law itself. Instead, positive law, like abstract right and formal morality, must be embedded in a public culture characterized by a commitment on the part of citizens to the principles implied by the rule of law. This is the point of his celebrated supersession of civil society in state. At issue is not the denial of the legal institutions of civil society but the accommodation of the attitudes and sentiments required for their sustainability. In the ethical community (*das sittliche Universum*) that defines Hegel's theory of the state, individuals attend to the ends of public life not coincidentally, as in civil society, but directly and deliberately. In this way they are able to defend and nurture those principles of law that are rendered pathological when law is autonomized in the form of markets, the "external" welfare state, or even formal procedures. For Hegel, the principle of justice implied by civil society is dependent on a political culture committed to justice as a good. The procedural model of justice entailed by a rational concept of positive law rests on the civic republicanism of an ethical community.[17]

II. *VERFASSUNG* AND *VOLKSGEIST*

It may seem that Habermas's position has been done a disservice, for he certainly does not ignore the ethical-cultural considerations that Hegel claims are essential for sustaining an institutionalized system of positive law. Indeed, he asserts that, via the deliberative politics that conditions its legitimacy, a valid system of positive law is connected to a rationalized lifeworld that "it meets halfway" (*entgegenkommen*), a political culture characterized by commitment to the values associated with the rule of law.[18] In this respect, Habermas holds that law depends on what, following Albrecht Wellmer, he calls a "democratic *Sittlichkeit*":[19]

> Law can be preserved as legitimate only if enfranchised citizens switch from the role of private legal subjects and take the perspective of participants who are engaged in the process of reaching understanding about the rules for their life in common. To this extent constitutional democracy depends on the motivations of a population *accustomed* to liberty, motivations that cannot be generated by administrative measures.[20]

Yet this appeal to *Sittlichkeit* on Habermas's part is problematic for several reasons. On a general level there is something dubiously circular about the appeal itself, for, after all, Habermas champions positive law as a source of social integration precisely because the modern world, decentered and pluralistic in structure, has rendered implausible appeal to an ethos as a credible source of social integration. If law is invoked to counteract the deficiencies of appeal to an ethos, it cannot itself appeal to ethos as the condition for its legitimacy.[21]

Even apart from this problem, however, Habermas's appeal to *Sittlichkeit* remains problematic from a Hegelian perspective. When Habermas relates a valid system of positive law to the ethos of an existing political culture, he is not following Hegel in asserting that cultural embeddedness conditions the meaning and validity of law. Instead, he maintains only that cultural contextualization is needed to *apply* principles whose validity has been exogenously determined—via analysis of the formal pragmatic conditions of communication.[22] Legal norms are indeed matters of justice and thus "are not related from the outset to a specific collectivity and its form of life."[23] It is true that, unlike moral norms, which claim transcultural status, juridical rules, for Habermas, "also give expression to the particular wills of members of a determinate legal community."[24] Still, as regards validity, legal norms possess a context-transcending dimension, one requiring that they "be compatible with moral tenets that claim universal (*allgemeine*) validity going beyond the legal community."[25] In this way, Habermas advances what Georgia Warnke has called a "top-down" account of the relation of norms to culture, where cultural values are molded to accommodate already justified norms and principles. While he may appropriate certain features of Hegel's *Aufhebung* of morality and law in *Sittlichkeit*, Habermas's juxtaposed understanding of the relationship of justification and application, procedure and ethos, the right and the good, precludes any systematic appropriation of the basic principle, nicely formulated by Warnke (although invoking Charles Taylor rather than Hegel): "cultural values and orientations must be acknowledged not just as elements of the concrete situations to which principles of justice apply but as codeterminers of their meaning."[26]

From a Habermasian perspective, it may be countered that, in his attention to cultural considerations, Hegel has departed from the very domain of law, jettisoning the question of the norms that citizens adopt to regulate their common life for what in fact are only the cultural assumptions of a particular community. Neo-Kantian legal scholar Ingeborg Maus has argued along these lines when dismissing as "legal nihilism" efforts to "sublate" law in *Sittlichkeit*.[27] Habermas himself levels similar charges against republican legal scholars like J. G. A. Pocock, who draw "on the language of classical ethics and politics rather than on a legal vocabulary."[28]

But these concerns, however warranted as regards communitarian republicans, are unjustified as regards Hegel, for whom notions of cultural value and civic sentiment are implied by the very concept of law. He does not follow Kant, who, he notes, defined right, or law (*Recht*), as "the limitation of my will or freedom of choice (*Willkür*) in such a way that it may coexist with the will or free choice of everyone else in accordance with a universal law."[29] Instead, *Recht* is defined by Hegel as the *Dasein des freien Willens*.[30] In this way he repudiates Kant's effort—evidently continued in Habermas[31]—to define law in terms of external considerations, be it observable behavior, objective institutions, or formal procedures. By focusing on the existence of the moral will rather than free choice, on *Wille* rather than *Willkür*, Hegel announces at the outset that law encompasses internal as well as external considerations.[32] As the "Idea of Freedom"[33]—and, of course, an Idea here connotes the unity of concept and existence—right denotes a relationship of subjective orientations and objective conditions.[34] Hegel's *Philosophy of Right* is indeed a Theory of Objective *Spirit*. This expanded notion of law can be better appreciated by considering Hegel's concept of the constitution, *die Verfassung*.

Again with Montesquieu, Hegel claims that a constitution must not be viewed exclusively or even primarily in terms of formal-legal institutions. Such an approach is indeed captured by an account of what Hegel calls the "political constitution,"[35] or *Konstitution*,[36] and while such an account is essential to constitutional theory, the constitution itself must accommodate the broader cultural values and practices of a people. A constitution can have binding value for a people only to the extent that it expresses "the customs and consciousness of the individuals who belong to it."[37] Without this specific reference to sentiment, the constitution remains an abstraction (*Gedankending*), and so "will have no meaning or value, even if it is present in an external sense."[38] For a constitution to hold constitutive value for a culture, it "must embody the nation's feelings for its rights and conditions."

In keeping with this commitment to the centrality and even priority of culture and sentiment, Hegel links his constitutional theory to the idea of a *Volksgeist*, the spirit of a nation or people. He calls the *Volksgeist* the foundations or "cause" of a nation's constitution, something he intends in a double sense. First, he asserts that the constitution must be in "agreement with the *Volksgeist*."[39] It must express "the living customs present in the nation."[40] Second, he maintains that a *Verfaßung* is itself the *Volksgeist*.[41] Here the constitution is conceived as the organizing principle that sustains and indeed constitutes a people, the principle that both expresses and shapes its identity.[42] A *Staatsverfaßung*, he writes in *Natural Law*, is "the constituting of the absolute ethical identity"[43]— that principle of collective self-definition that animates the laws and institutions of a nation.[44] In both respects, the very idea of a constitution incorporates, for Hegel, the cultural considerations that Neo-Kantians like Habermas strictly demarcate from legal principles.

In emphasizing the relationship of a constitution to the spirit of a people, Hegel clearly rejects the Enlightenment tendency to regard the constitution as a product of formal political-legislative enactment. As he never tires of arguing, a constitution cannot be regarded as a construction (*ein Gemachtes*). This approach—evidently reaffirmed by Habermas[45]—is ruled out if for no other reason than that it fails to recognize the degree to which a people is always already constituted. The notion that a constitution could be an explicit act of creation is part and parcel of the liberal conviction that, outside formal institutions, individuals are isolated atoms related to one another in the formless "shape" of an aggregate (*Haufen*). Yet this view, aside from the injustice it may do to a concept of human nature, misconstrues political action (constitution-making included), which is unintelligible unless individuals are already related to one another in some preconstituted manner.[46]

At the same time, however, denial of the formal constructability of a constitution is not to imply that, for Hegel, constitutionalism is not linked to an emphatic notion of political action. Hegel's point is not the Burkean one that renders a constitution just a matter of tradition, custom, and historical evolution. Precisely because the constitution is an expression of a public culture, it must, if it is to retain validity, regularly be refashioned to accommodate, and adapt to, changing values and circumstances. While a constitution can never be formally made, it must nonetheless be routinely renewed or rejuvenated (*verjüngert*)[47] if it is to continue to embody adequately and constitute the *spirit* of a people. Indeed, Hegel's constitutional theory in this respect assigns a greater and more demanding role to constitutional politics than does the liberal counterpart. In its assumption that a constitution can be the product of self-sufficient individuals who adopt rules to protect their subjective liberties, liberal thought presumes that a constitution is a type of contract, one that, once finalized, acquires a binding force that renders unnecessary further recourse to constitutional politics. By contrast, a more historically sensitive approach to constitutional theory depends on the continued and ongoing involvement on the part of the individuals governed by it. Precisely because a constitution is never only a legal structure but an organizing principle of an existing people, because it is a principle of collective identity rather than contractual relation,[48] it can retain meaning and validity only inasmuch as it is reconsidered and reappropriated to accord with changes in the conditions of a people's self-definition. If the constitutional language of choice for liberalism is construction (*Machen*), Hegel invokes that of interpretation (*Auslegung*).[49] Understood as a transmitted legacy whose vitality requires renewal, a constitution depends on a community of interpreters who reappropriate and clarify legal traditions, principles, and institutions in light of present realities.[50]

In this respect, Hegel's constitutional historicism, as it might be called, is not a paean to tradition but a call for civic virtue or patriotism, one in which civic engagement and public virtue play a central role in defining and indeed constituting the constitution. Adapting an expression of Frank Michelman,[51] we might say that Hegel advances a notion of *jurisgenerative* patriotism, one accounting for the very meaning and reality of the constitution. This follows from the fact that a constitution is understood by Hegel not as a fixed and formal construction, but as a complex of values and institutions that depends for its continued vitality on the activity of a citizenry prepared to reinterpret and reapply received principles and traditions in light of changing social circumstances. Hegel, to be sure, notes the extent to which patriotism also denotes an attitude of loyalty via-à-vis existing institutions and as such is "merely a consequence of the institutions within the state."[52] Yet the dependence of constitutionalism on interpretive appropriation and revalidation mandates that patriotism also have a constructive role.[53] "Patriotism is the result of the institutions of the state, just as this sentiment is the source through and out of which the state has its activation and its preservation."[54] We find such constitution constitutive patriotism in the participation of individuals in those corporations or intermediate associations whose vitality is central to a constitutional order defined through the unity of legal institutions and the subpolitical domains of family and sociality—those crucibles of civic sentiment termed by Hegel "the pillars of public freedom."[55] And it is also discernible in his account of the participation of individuals in public debate, principally in legislative assemblies where the constitution acquires "new and further determination."[56] In both respects civic virtue is essential to the continued meaning and reality of a constitution.

III. CONSTITUTIONAL POLITICS
AND CONSTITUTIONAL LEGITIMACY

It may again seem that we have done Habermas an injustice. While his is a procedural account of the constitution, it is one that seeks to accommodate the motives and attitudes of citizens.[57] "The principles of the constitutional state can become the driving force for the dynamic project of actualizing an association of free and equal persons only if they are contextualized in the history of a nation of citizens in such a way that they connect with these citizens' motives and fundamental beliefs (*Gesinnungen*)."[58] Moreover, Habermas stresses, as does Hegel, the importance of collective interpretation and reinterpretation for the meaning and even reality of the constitution. "Every constitution is a project that can *endure* only as an ongoing interpretation continually carried forward at all levels of law-making."[59] In this respect Habermas distinguishes his constitutional theory from Rawls's constructivist approach, which, like contract theory, binds political will-formation to the requirements of an originary agreement.[60] As he notes in arguing for the co-originality of private and public autonomy, constitutional stipu-

lation regarding basic rights cannot be dissociated from political processes of debate and action. Furthermore, Habermas underscores the
extent to which this dynamic vision of the constitution relies on the public engagement of citizens:

> From this long-term perspective, the constitutional state does not rep-
> resent a finished structure but a delicate and sensitive, above all, falli-
> ble and revisable enterprise whose purpose is to realize the system of
> rights anew in changing circumstances, i.e., to interpret the system of
> rights better, to institutionalize it more appropriately, and to draw out
> its contents more radically. This is the perspective of citizens who are
> actively engaged in realizing the system of rights.[61]

Finally, Habermas follows Hegel in asserting that this form of civic
engagement must also be understood as a type of "constitutional patriotism," one that is animated by an effort to interpret and reinterpret
basic rights and principles.[62]

Still, the place of collective interpretation and civic engagement in
Habermas's constitutional theory remains ambiguous. While he clearly
seeks to incorporate such components into his account, he does so at a
secondary level. Such activity is necessary for realizing an abstract system of rights whose validity is secured independently—in the analysis of
formal pragmatic conditions for discourse. No less sympathetic a critic
than Thomas McCarthy has noted the dualism between cultural clarification and normative validation in *Faktizität und Geltung*: "Habermas'
hermeneutic self-clarification does not function as the basic level of justification in his theory of justice. Rather, it is theoretically subordinate
to his derivation of an 'abstract system of basic rights' through an analysis of the presuppositions of democratic self-determination."[63] Indeed,
Habermas himself makes this point in the book's 1994 "Postscript,"
something noted by Rawls in defending himself against Habermas's
charges.[64] Not unlike Rawls, with whom his differences, he says,
"remain within the bounds of a family dispute,"[65] Habermas asserts that
the realization of rights is achieved through the institutionalization of
rights against the state, not the rights individuals initially cede one
another as persons—rights that must be presupposed in subsequent realization processes.[66] At most Habermas appears to argue that a constitution facilitates the process of its realization, but that realization process
itself presupposes core principles whose validity is already determined.
Nor is it clear how it could be otherwise. Anything else would call into
question the basic distinction between justification and application that
informs Habermas's practical philosophy—a distinction, he writes, that
is no less appropriate for legal than for moral theory.[67] It would also call
into question his fundamental distinction between the right and the

good as well as his prioritizing the former. If "[u]nlike ethical questions, questions of justice"—and Habermas construes legal norms as matters of justice—"are not related from the outset to a specific collectivity and its form of life,"[68] then efforts at contextualizing rights remain categorically distinct from conditions of their validation.

In this respect, then, Habermas's position remains manifestly distinct from that of Hegel. In Hegel's view, matters of justification cannot be fully demarcated from those of application.[69] Precisely because constitutional principles are inextricably intertwined with the values of a culture, issues of constitutional validation are always linked to their contextualization—just as, conversely, matters of contextualization can never be fully removed from those of justification. Hegel would agree with Frank Michelman, who asserts that "[c]onstitutional law is institutional stuff from the word go," and who accordingly accentuates the "substantial-ethical character of originary-justificatory discourse."[70]

It is thus not surprising that Habermas's idea of constitutional patriotism does not assume the jurisgenerative form it has with Hegel. While he follows Hegel in formulating a notion of patriotism based on interpreting basic principles in light of changing circumstances, interpretation remains at the level of the affirmation of principles whose validity can be determined independently of the conditions of their appropriation by a particular community.[71] The efforts of the constitutional patriot, in Habermas's account, remain directed to the "best interpretation of the same basic rights and principles"[72]—those "equally constitutive (*konstitutiv*) for every body of citizens."[73] His is therefore not Hegel's constitution constitutive patriotism, where republican engagement is part and parcel of an activity through which the meaning and validity of a constitution are shaped and defined.[74]

None of this implies that Hegel conceives constitutional politics as merely a feature of popular will. Although Hegel does accentuate the place of legislative activity in constitutional politics,[75] that very fact assures that the process is governed by constraints—the "constitutional laws" (*Verfaßungsgesetze*) that govern ordinary legislation.[76] In addition, any autochotonous notion of parliamentary action is ruled out by the "organic" nature of the constitution. Precisely because a people is always already constituted, any popular change of the constitution itself presupposes the constitution and therefore can occur "only in a constitutional manner."[77] Moreover, commitment to "entrenched" constraints also flows from Hegel's equation of the constitution with the *Volksgeist*. Because a constitution, for Hegel, is understood as the spirit of a people, constitutional change consists in the change in a people's identity. Yet because the object of change is also the source of the change, any act of change is simultaneously an affirmation of principles of constitutional continuity.[78] In this respect, Hegel is as opposed to wholesale transformation as he is to binding precommitments. "Individual components can be changed, but not the whole, which shapes itself gradually."[79] Hegel could well sympathize with Thomas Jefferson's concerns about the dangers to civic life posed by adherence to constitutional structures that no longer express the concerns of the "living," yet his own notion of constitutional renewal is governed by cross-generational constraints whose elimination is neither possible nor desirable.[80]

In this respect Hegel's theory can be instructively compared to that of Bruce Ackerman.[81] Like Ackerman, Hegel advances an emphatic notion of constitutional politics, one accounting for systematic alteration of constitutional principles via ongoing processes of popular self-constitution. With Ackerman, Hegel also recognizes that an account of constitutional change must accommodate larger cultural forces and cannot be restricted to any formal amendment process. On the other hand, Hegel would reject Ackerman's contraposition of constitutional to ordinary or everyday politics. He would, in particular, reject Ackerman's Kuhnian-inspired view that change occurs through radical, episodic shifts operating outside ordinary political and legislative life. Claiming instead that constitutional change transpires through gradual transformations in a culture's self-understanding, Hegel would argue that everyday politics also thematizes constitutional issues, and any difference between the two is more of degree than kind. Hegel thus anticipates Michelman, who construes constitutional change "more like a movement from margin to center—a shift of attention—than . . . the total replacement of one 'world' by another."[82] Conversely, Hegel would insist that even constitutional politics must be subject to the legal constraints that govern ordinary legislation and administration. While constitutionalism cannot be defined in terms of rights foundationalism, it also cannot be abandoned to the whims of subinstitutional populism. In a philosophy of law understood at once as *Naturrecht und Staatswissenschaft*, a political culture is sustainable only if ordinary legislation is capable of broaching constitutional questions *and* constitutional politics is not exempt from the formal constraints regulating ordinary parliamentary activity.[83]

IV. NORMATIVITY AND THE
CULTURIST CONCEPTION OF LAW

Even if Hegel's notion of constitutional theory may be governed by juridical constraints that preclude either constitutional populism or parliamentary supremacy, its commitment to exigencies of a particular legal community may still leave it incapable of thematizing those "higher" norms and principles whose accommodation is, for Habermas, the task of any legitimate modern constitution. Indeed, by defining law in terms of a notion of *Volksgeist*, Hegel would seem to abandon law to the customs and habits of a particular culture, and thus forfeit the normativity and reflexivity claimed by nonculturist conceptions of law. What Habermas says of communitarian theories might still apply to Hegel: he reduces law "to the ethos of an already integrated community" and "the substantial ethical life of a background consensus assumed as unproblematic."[84]

In the foregoing I have already indicated the general problem with this view: in situating law within the context of a particular culture, Hegel's point is not to foreclose but to initiate critique. The very demand that constitution express the culture of a people mandates that received traditions be constantly challenged and refashioned so as to accommodate changing practices and circumstances. The same point can be made with regard to Hegel's concept of the *Volksgeist*. For Hegel, a *Volksgeist* only subsists through such reflectivity. It is not some prereflective *factum brutum*; it is, *qua* spirit of a people, sustained only through the arguments through which agreements and forms of collective self-interpretation are defined and redefined over time.[85] It is no coincidence that Hegel identifies Volksgeist with a deliberative public sphere (*Öffentlichkeit*), for it is only in public deliberation about ends of communal life that a people "establishes its identity"; the public sphere "ist der Geist der sich geltend macht,"[86] the domain in which the spirit of a people is validated.

A similar point can be made by noting the sense in which, for Hegel, the *Volksgeist* denotes a structure of collective *self*-interpretation. Here two matters are of import. First, in line with his social theory, Hegel maintains that the identity of a culture presupposes an openness to other cultures, including a *limine* other interpretations of its own culture. He makes the point when arguing that, as regards the nation-state, constitutional law (*das innere Staatsrecht*), presupposes international law (*das äussere Staatsrecht*). "The legitimacy of a state . . . is essentially to be completed through the recognition of other states." As he also writes: "Without relations with other states, the state can no more be an actual individual [*Individuum*] than an individual [*der Einzelne*] can be an actual person without relationship with other persons."[87] While Hegel does define a constitution in terms of communal self-interpretation, his account of the logic of such interpretation incorporates and requires a pluralist openness to other perspectives, perspectives that can challenge rather than reinforce the self-understanding of a given cultural context.

Second, in line with his metaphysics and his logic of self-knowing subjectivity, Hegel maintains that the process of self-reflection is governed by certain context-transcending norms. To be successful, processes of self-interpretation must conform to a normative concept of selfhood; they must also adequately accommodate structures of correspondence, self-congruence, reflective appropriation, and other criteria permitting differentiation between genuine and spurious forms of self-definition. What precisely these norms are and how they are to be determined is, naturally, a difficult matter. Clear, though, is that in asserting that the process of self-definition connoting *Volksgeist* must express the "shape of universality,"[88] Hegel proffers a culturist notion of a legal community able to challenge a community's particularist self-understanding.[89]

Thus there *is* a normative-critical dimension to Hegel's culturalist and even communal interpretation of law and the constitution. A legal community, for Hegel, is defined in terms of processes of self-interpretation that require reflexivity, adhere to mechanisms of public deliberation, remain open to plurality of perspectives, and acknowledge norms and ideals able to scrutinize an existing social structure. Habermas repudiates a culturalist conception of law because he assumes that all (ethico-cultural) values are normatively particularist. "Valid norms obligate their addressees equally and without exception to satisfy general behavior expectations, whereas values are to be understood as intersubjectively shared preferences."[90] Yet the uniqueness of Hegel's culturalist approach to law lies precisely in its effort to fashion what might be called a normative-critical *logic of ethicality*. Against static oppositions between concepts like norms and values, Hegel's position furnishes the parameters for a normative account of the reproduction and self-reproduction of a culture.[91]

V. CONCLUSION

Appreciation of Hegel's cultural concept of law is inter alia important as it contributes to current debates in constitutional theory itself, triggered anew by recent developments in Canada and Eastern Europe. It demonstrates, for instance, how, *pace* Ackerman, constitutional and ordinary politics can be conjoined without vitiating their important differences; how processes of constitutional revision can, *pace* Rawls, thematize "constitutional essentials" rather than just their application; how, *pace* Habermas, constitutional patriotism can have a truly constitution-constitutive, or jurisgenerative, function; how, *pace* Dworkin, constitutional hermeneutics can assume the form of a community-wide rather than just a judicial interpretation; how, *pace* Michelman, constitutional culturism can be understood as much through reference to a future as to a past or present identity. Similarly, appreciation of Hegel's position demonstrates that constitutionalism need not be distinct from popular sovereignty and that liberal commitment to the rule of law is not antithetical to conditions for collective identity and mutual trust. Or again, Hegel's claim that constitutionalism focuses on an always already constituted people whose vitality is maintained through continued, collective processes of self-(re)interpretation renders his position hospitable to the pluralistic assumptions less easily accommodated in constitutional theories committed to an originary contractual agreement.[92] Finally, Hegel's account of constitutional formation demonstrates why constitution-founding is always a matter of reconstitution, how a constituted people can also claim constitutive power (*un pouvoir constituant constitués!*), and how by fashioning constitutional politics as a legally governed parliamentary process, Hegel provides a method for navigating a course between rights foundationalism and legal populism.

Hegel's account of law is also significant for more generally philosophical reasons. In particular, it can serve as a model for a normative theory at once nonfoundational and immune to charges of contextualism. Indeed, by deriving normativity from the conditions for historical embeddedness itself, Hegel advances a critique of contextualism arguably more consequential than a version that simply contraposes norms to history and tradition. At the least, the principle of self-congruence governing his account of collective self-formation demonstrates how constitutional theory can attend to the exigencies of a particular culture and still champion an emphatic account of normativity without necessitating recourse to a general theory of language, rationality, or autonomy.

NOTES

1. *Faktizität und Geltung: Beiträge zur Diskurstheorie des Rechts und des demokratischen Rechtsstaats* (Frankfurt: Suhrkamp, 1992) [hereafter *FG*]. A English translation has been published under the title *Between Facts and Norms* (Cambridge, Mass.: MIT Press, 1996).

2. *Elements of the Philosophy of Right* (Cambridge: Cambridge University Press, 1993) [hereafter *PR*], §3. Unless otherwise noted, I use this version of the English translation.

3. Here I follow Habermas's possibly one-sided characterization of Rousseau.

4. See Andrew Buchwalter, "Hegel's Concept of Virtue," *Political Theory* 20/4 (November 1992): 548–83. For Machiavelli and modern political theory, see Quentin Skinner, "On Justice, the Common Good and the Priority of Liberty," in Chantal Mouffe (ed.), *Dimensions of Radical Democracy* (London: Verso, 1992), pp. 211–24.

5. *PR* §141Z.

6. *Encyclopaedia of the Philosophical Sciences* III (Oxford: Clarendon Press, 1971) [hereafter *Enc.*] §408.

7. Hegel's concept of positive law, *Recht als Gesetz*, is found principally in *PR* §§209–229.

8. *Enc.* §484.

9. See Wilhelm R. Beyer, "Norm-Probleme in Hegels Rechtsphilosophie," *Archiv für Rechts- und Sozialphilosophie* 56 (1964): 561–80.

10. "On the Internal Relation between Law and Democracy," *European Journal of Philosophy* 3/1 (April 1995): 12–20.

11. *PR* §245. Here I employ the translation by Knox (Oxford: Clarendon Press, 1967). See Raymond Plant, "Hegel on Identity and Legitimation," in Z. A. Pelczynski (ed.), *The State and Civil Society* (Cambridge: Cambridge University Press, 1984), p. 240.

12. *Theory of Communicative Action* 2 (Boston: Beacon Press, 1987), p. 387.

13. In this regard it is perhaps telling that, more so than some other contemporary democratic theorists (e.g., Ingeborg Maus), Habermas grants a larger role to the judiciary in preserving and nurturing deliberative democracy. See *FG*, p. 340.

14. For a different account of Hegel's assessment of the limitations of positive law, see Paul Bockelmann, *Hegels Notstandslehre* (Berlin: de Gruyter, 1935), p. 42ff.

15. *PR* §212.

16. See his "Law, Solidarity and the Tasks of Philosophy," MS. Related criticisms of the concept of formal law have been advanced by both Carl Schmitt and proponents of Critical Legal Studies. For a discussion of Habermas's relation to such views, see John P. McCormick, "Three Ways of Thinking 'Critically' about the Law: Schmitt, CLS, & Habermas," MS.

17. Charles Taylor has advanced these types of argument. See "Hegel's Ambiguous Legacy for Modern Liberalism," *Cardozo Law Review* 10/5–6 (March 1996): 857–70; and "Cross-Purposes: The Liberal-Communitarian Debate," in Nancy L. Rosenblum (ed.), *Liberalism and the Moral Life* (Cambridge, Mass.: Harvard University Press, 1989), pp. 159–82.

18. *FG*, p. 366.

19. "Bedingungen einer demokratischen Kultur," in Micha Brumlik and Hauke Brunkhorst (eds.), *Gemeinschaft und Gerechtigkeit* (Frankfurt: Fischer, 1993), pp. 173–96. Richard J. Bernstein has argued similarly from a Deweyan perspective: "The Retrieval of the Democratic Ethos," *Cardozo Law Review* 17/4–5 (March 1996): 1127–46.

20. "Postscript to *Faktizität und Geltung*," *Philosophy and Social Criticism* 20/4: 147. (*FG*, p. 504). See also *FG*, pp. 434 and 504; and "Citizenship and National Identity: Some Reflections on the Future of Europe," *Praxis International* 12/1 (April 1992): 6f.

21. This point has been astutely made by Peter Dews in the essay already cited: "Law, Solidarity and the Tasks of Philosophy." Here we leave aside the question of whether Habermas may also beg the question when he relates a system of law to a lifeworld whose "rationalized" character itself is defined by

validity claims expressive of the formal-pragmatic conditions of communication. On the general issue of the relationship of lifeworld and proceduralism, see J. M. Bernstein, *Recovering Ethical Life: Jürgen Habermas and the Future of Critical Theory* (London and New York: Routledge, 1995).

22. This point is especially clear as regards *moral* rules: "Universalist moralities are dependent on forms of life that are rationalized in that they make possible the prudent application of universal moral insights and support motivations from translating insights into moral action." See *Moral Consciousness and Communicative Action*, p. 109.

23. *FG*, p. 344.

24. Ibid., p. 188.

25. Ibid., p. 344.

26. "Communicative Rationality and Cultural Values," in Stephen K. White (ed.), *The Cambridge Companion to Habermas* (Cambridge: Cambridge University Press, 1995), p. 135.

27. "Liberties and Popular Sovereignty. On Jürgen Habermas' Reconstruction of the System of Rights," *Cardozo Law Review* 17/4–5 (March 1996): 829.

28. *FG*, p. 325.

29. *PR* §29, translation amended.

30. Ibid.

31. It may be noted that in earlier writings Habermas advanced a notion of law that seemed to focus not just on procedural mechanisms but on the "broader political, cultural, and social context" in which "[t]hey are embedded." He called this law "as institution" rather than law "as medium." "By legal institutions I mean legal norms that cannot be sufficiently legitimized through a positivistic reference to procedure. Typical of these are the bases of constitutional law, the principles of criminal law and penal procedure, and all regulation of punishable offenses close to morality (e.g., murder, abortion, rape, etc.). As soon as the validity of *these* norms is questioned in everyday practice, the reference to their legality no longer suffices. They need substantive justification, because they belong to the legitimate orders of the lifeworld itself and, together with informal norms of conduct, form the background of communicative action." Although Habermas here adopts the type of dyadic approach to law foreign to Hegel's position, his notion of law as institution does capture the sociocultural considerations that, for Hegel, are part of a comprehensive definition of right. See *The Theory of Communicative Action II*, p. 365f.

32. See Miguel Giusti, *Hegels Kritik der modernen Welt* (Würzburg: Königshausen & Neumann, 1987), pp. 178–85.

33. *PR* §29

34. See Bruno Liebrucks, "Recht, Moralität und Sittlichkeit bei Hegel," in Manfred Riedel (ed.), *Materialien zu Hegels Rechtsphilosophie* (Frankfurt: Suhrhamp, 1975), 13–51.

35. *PR* §271; as he also terms it, "the political state proper and its constitution" ("der eigentlich politische Staat und seine Verfassung") [*PR* §267].

36. *Vorlesungen über Naturrecht und Staatswissenschaft*, tr. P. Wannenmann, ed. Claudia Becker et al. (Hamburg: Meiner, 1983) [hereafter *Wa*]. *Wa* §163.

37. *PR* §274.

38. *PR* §274A.

39. *Wa* §134.

40. *Natural Law* (Philadelphia: University of Pennsylvania Press, 1975), p. 116; hereafter *NL*.

41. *Wa* §134.

42. See Sheldon S. Wolin, "Collective Identity and Constitutional Power," in *The Presence of the Past: Essays on the State and the Constitution* (Baltimore: Johns Hopkins University Press, 1989), pp. 8–31.

43. *NL*, p. 116.

44. Heinz Kimmerle, "Die Staatsverfassung als 'Konstitutierung der absoluten sittlichen Identität' in der Jenaer Konzeption des 'Naturrechts,'" in Hans-Christian Lucas and Otto Pöggeler (eds.), *Hegels Rechtsphilosophie im Zusammenhang der europäischen Verfaßungsgeschichte* (Stuttgart-Bad Canstatt: Frommann-Holzboog, 1986), pp. 129–48.

45. As he writes: "My reconstruction of the meaning of a legitimate legal order begins with the original resolution (*Entschluss*) that any arbitrary group of persons must make if they want to constitute themselves as a legal community of free and equal members. Intending to legitimately regulate their life by means of positive law, they enter into a common practice that allows them to frame a constitution." See "Reply to Symposium Participants," *Cardozo Law Review* 17/4–5 (March 1996): 1504.

46. *PR* §273f.

47. *Wa* §134. In arguing that a constitution can and must be renewed, Hegel is obviously ascribing to political action something he denies to philosophy, for which a shape of life that has grown old "cannot be rejuvenated but only known" ("lässt sich nicht verjüngen, sondern nur erkennen") [22, translation amended].

48. For an overview of different concepts of constitutionalism, see E.-W. Böckenförde, "Geschichtliche Entwicklung und Bedeutungswandel der Verfassung," in *Staat, Verfassung, Demokratie* (Frankfurt: Suhrkamp, 1991), pp. 29–52.

49. *PR* §344.

50. For an illuminating discussion of the general relationship between tradition and renewal in constitutional theory, very similar to Hegel's, see Sheldon S. Wolin, "Contract and Birthright," in *The Presence of the Past*, pp. 137–50. Hegel's position also finds rearticulation in the legal hermeneutics of Ronald Dworkin, although Hegel would not accept, *inter alia*, Dworkin's restriction of the interpretive process to the judiciary. For Habermas's reception of Dworkin's hermeneutic of law, see *FG*, pp. 258–72.

51. "Law's Republic," *The Yale Law Journal* 97/8 (July 1988): 1493–1537.

52. *PR* §268, translation emended.

53. Cf. Harry Brod, *Hegel's Philosophy of Politics* (Boulder, Colo.: Westview, 1992), p. 121.

54. *Vorlesungen* 4:641.

55. *PR* §265.

56. *PR* §298.

57. Such contextualization is also in keeping with his account of the degree to which law is self-referential as regards its own institutionalization.

58. *FG*, p. 226.

59. Ibid., p. 163.

60. See "Reconciliation through the Public Use of Reason," especially 126ff. See also Thomas McCarthy, "Constructivism and Reconstructivism," *Ethics* 104/1 (October 1994).

61. *FG*, p. 464.

62. "Struggles for Recognition in the Constitutional State," in Charles Taylor et al. (eds.), *Multiculturalism* (Princeton, N.J.: Princeton University Press, 1994), p. 144.

63. "Legitimacy and Diversity: Dialectical Reflections and Analytical Distinctions," *Cardozo Law Review* 17/4–5 (March 1996): 1100.

64. "Reply to Habermas," *Journal of Philosophy* 92/3 (March 1995): 164f.

65. "Reconciliation through the Public Use of Reason," p. 110.

66. "Postscript," p. 43f.

67. "Remarks on Discourse Ethics," *Justification and Application*, p. 88.

68. *FG*, p. 344.

69. An interesting illustration of this point can be found in Hegel's history of philosophy and in particular his account of the transition from Greek to Christian worldview. Although the "Christian" principle of subjectivity makes its conceptual appearance already in Greek thought with the decline of the *polis*, the relationship of the Greek to the Christian period cannot be understood as merely the historical concretization of an existing principle. Rather, the realization process itself presupposes a procedure by which the conceptual categories are transformed and revalidated. See Oscar Daniel Brauer, *Dialektik der Zeit*, pp. 186–91.

70. Frank Michelman, "Family Quarrel," *Cardozo Law Review* 17/4–5 (March 1996): 1175.

71. *The New Conservatism: Cultural Criticism and the Historian's Debate* (Cambridge, Mass.: MIT Press, 1989), p. 261.

72. "Struggles for Recognition in the Constitutional State," p. 122.

73. *FG*, p. 372.

74. In this respect Hegel's notion of civic engagement resembles the "communal democracy" that Wolfgang Kersting juxtaposes to Habermas's idea of constitutional patriotism. What I argue here, though, is that what Kersting champions in opposition to a notion of constitutional patriotism is for Hegel a form of constitutional patriotism itself. See "Verfassungspatriotismus, kommunitäre Demokratie und die politische Vereinigung der Deutschen," in Petra Braitling and Walter Reese-Schäfer (eds.), *Universalismus, Nationalismus und die Einheit der Deutschen* (Frankfurt: Fischer, 1991), and "Verfassung und kommunitäre Demokratie," in Günther Frankenberg (ed.), *Auf der Suche nach der gerechten Gesellschaft* (Frankfurt: Fischer, 1994), pp. 84–102.

75. Here Hegel would clearly disagree with Rawls, for whom the supreme court exemplifies the "public reason" central to constitutional politics. See *Political Liberalism* (New York: Columbia, 1996), p. 231ff.

76. *Wa* §§131, 146. See Rolf Grawert, "Verfassungsfrage und Gesetzgebung in Preussen. Ein Vergleich der vormärzlichen Staatspraxis mit Hegels rechtsphilosophichen Konzept," in Hans-Christian Lucas and Otto Pöggeler (eds.), *Hegels Rechtsphilosophie*, especially p. 294.

77. *PR* §273.

78. A current version of this thesis has been formulated by Frank Michelman, "Can Constitutional Democrats be Legal Positivists? Or Why Constitutionalism?" *Constellations* 2/3 (January 1996), especially 298–303.

79. *Wa* §134.

80. In this regard Hegel would likely agree with Philip Selznick, who has characterized constitutionalism "as a style of decision. It is a way of upholding principles while recognizing the demands of a changing social reality. Constitutionalism provides a perspective of continuity and a resource for the future, but it also insists that each generation be its own master." See "The Ethos of American Law," in Irving Kristol and Paul Weaver (eds.), *The Americans: 1976* (Lexington, Mass.: D. C. Heath, 1976), p. 222.

81. *We The People 1: Foundations* (Cambridge, Mass.: Harvard University Press, 1991).

82. From a Hegelian perspective as well, political jurisgenesis is "a constant, not an episodic, activity." See "Law's Republic," pp. 1523, 1525.

83. For a contemporary notion of parliamentary constitutionalism within a context of legal continuity, see Stephen Holmes and Cass Sunstein, "The Politics of Constitutional Revision," in Sanford Levinson (ed.), *Responding to Imperfection: The Theory and Practice of Constitutional Amendment* (Princeton, N.J.: Princeton University Press, 1995), pp. 275–306.

84. *FG*, pp. 338, 340.

85. Cf. Alasdair MacIntyre, *Whose Justice? Which Rationality?* (Notre Dame, Ind.: University of Notre Dame Press, 1988), p. 12.

86. *Vorlesungen* IV, p. 722ff.

87. *PR* §331R, amended. Nor is the recognition at stake merely a legal or formal one. Arguing that genuine international relations repose on "the mutual recognition of free national *individualities*" (emphasis added) , Hegel adverts to a form of internal reciprocity directed to the cultural identify expressed in a nation's constitution. See *Enc.* §547; see also Klaus Vieweg, "The Principle of Recognition in Hegel's Theory of International Law," MS.

88. *PR* §187R.

89. For a related discussion of Hegel's application of a logic of equivalence and self-equivalence to his social theory, see Andrew Buchwalter, "Hegel, Marx, and the Concept of Immanent Critique," *Journal of the History of Philosophy*, 29/2 (April 1991), especially 260–64.

90. *FG*, p. 310f.

91. For a related attempt to fashion a normative theory more context-sensitive than Habermas's, see Alessandro Ferrara, "The Changing Paradigm of Justice. Reflections on Justice and Judgment," MS of a paper delivered at the April 1997 Columbia University conference "Democratization and Justice." Ferrara's discussion is significant not just because he seeks to supplant a context-transcending account of normative theory with one focused on conditions for

cultural self-congruity; it is also significant because he formulates his account via a characterization of constitutionalism—a historically based account of "higher law"—consonant with the nonfoundationalist normative theory thematized in this essay.

92. Compare James Tully, *Strange Multiplicity: Constitutionalism in an Age of Diversity* (Cambridge: Cambridge University Press, 1995).

CHAPTER 11

The End(s) of the State in
Hegel's Philosophy of Right

David C. Durst

In an essay entitled "The Political Technology of Individuals," Michel Foucault asserts that the overriding objective of modern "governmentality" is to "strengthen the state."[1] The method used to achieve this goal is what Foucault terms a double bind strategy, by which the "integration of the individuals in a community or in a totality results from a constant correlation between an increasing individualization and the reinforcement of this totality."[2] The state is strengthened by fostering the development of societal relations, in which the individual's desire for happiness is linked to institutional power. In light of this political economization of life, the happiness of the modern individual no longer represents the highest end of the modern state; instead, it enters into the calculations of this new governmentality to the extent that the well-being of citizens becomes a factor in the solidification of state power. For Foucault, then, the state now takes individual human happiness into consideration "not only as a simple effect. Happiness of individuals is a requirement for the survival and development of the state. It is a condition, it is an instrument, and not simply a consequence. People's happiness becomes an element of state strength."[3] The end of the state is no longer, then, in good liberal manner simply the well-being of each individual (e.g., Humboldt); instead, a sort of reversal takes place in which what is claimed to be a means to individual human happiness, the state, now becomes the determinate end.

In the following, I attempt to show in what way Foucault's functionalist interpretation of the modern state may be used to problemize Hegel's political philosophy. In Hegel's *Philosophy of Right*, the goal of state action remains potentially ambiguous. For although Hegel unequivocally asserts that "the end of the state is the happiness of its citizens," the ground he gives to justify this statement seems to potentially subvert its own intent: "The end of the state is the happiness of its citizens. This is certainly true, for if their welfare is deficient, if their subjective ends are not satisfied, and if they do not find that the state as such is the means to this satisfaction, the state itself stands on an insecure footing" (*PR* §265A). The law of reason must coalesce with that of subjective freedom so that the ends of individuals promote the "stability" of the state; "otherwise," as Hegel argues, "the state will hang in the air" (*PR* §265A). What constitutes here the means, and what the end? Does Hegel's state target individual human happiness as a means to promote its own stability, as Foucault would seem to have us insist, or do individuals use the state as a means to their own satisfaction? Or, in good dialectical gesture, are these two ends to enlist the service of each other reciprocally, reconciling each other in an act of mutual functionality?[4]

In order to begin to take up this question, I first attempt to show the pragmatic grounds governing Hegel's introduction of a paradigm change in the principles of modern political rationality. In his philosophy of ethical life, Hegel recognizes the functional limitations of the economy of coercive power at work in abstract legality and morality. Because they coercively intern the difference of individual desire, the repressive interventions of abstract legality and morality lead not to reconciled but instead to "forced" (*gezwungen*) social identities (*D* 115). As a result, these repressive practices only exacerbate the conflict and fragmentation of individuals pervading modern life. In response to the functional limitations of this logic of repressive control, Hegel advances his philosophy of ethical life by developing a new, what I term *productivistic form of functional reason (Vernunft)*. This productivistic reason is designed to more effectively reconcile the conflicts of the day by disciplining subjective desires of individuals to actively affirm state power. Instead of repressing the nature of man, this new form of productivisitic reason seeks to reintegrate the individual into the state by promoting the actualization of the free will as "sheer restless activity," that is, by mobilizing self-motion, producing productivity in a mutually useful fashion: it is a matter of realizing in concrete action the abstract concept of the Idea of the will, which Hegel defines in the *Philosophy of Right* as *"the free will which wills the free will"* (*PR* §108A, §27).[5] Under the hegemonic sway of ethical life, the reconciling of individual rights with social duties is to promote a more normalized, habituated, and spontaneous affirmation of the general imperatives of the ethical totality.[6] By doing so, ethical life promises to augment the coercive mechanisms of abstract legality and morality in the modern state; to be sure, the goal is by no means an inflated dependence of individuals on the coercive laws of the state, but instead, as the younger Hegel already states, the governing of individuals in a way that renders abstract state "laws superfluous by the ethical norms (*Sitten*)" of a community (*D* 146).

In Hegel's *Philosophy of Right*, it is not the critical use of reason by the general public, but—alongside practices such as the family, the division of labor, the solidifying role of corporations, the universal orientation of public servants, and the cultivation of a patriotic spirit in the identification of the individual with the ethical totality—institutions such as schools and the police (or public authorities) that are to play a pivotal role in securing the sociocultural conditions necessary for the stabile reproduction of the state apparatus by "(breaking) the resistance of the subject" (*PR* §151A). Education, as Hegel, for instance, writes, is "the art of making human beings ethical" (*PR* §151A): it gentrifies individual human desire in a way that the individual finds his own habituated enjoyment in serving as a means to the enjoyment of all others in the ethical community (*PR* §151A). The simultaneous individualization and universalization of man in ethical life contributes in no small degree to the reinforcement of the state, for, as Hegel himself formulates it in §265A of the *Philosophy of Right*, the state's "stability consists in the identity of the two aspects." Against the backdrop of this functionalist interpretation of Hegel's philosophy of ethical life, the idealistic claim to a reconciled identity between individual freedom and political power will yield, I suggest, to a more fundamental ambiguity over the relative priority of the end(s) of the modern state.

In the *Philosophy of Right*, Hegel constructs his dialectical critique of abstract right and morality along the knowledge/power axis by questioning both the rules of veridiction as well as the subsequent rules of jurisdiction at work in such practices. In his critical appropriation of the theoretical basis of abstract legality and morality, Hegel explicitly takes up the transcendental philosophy of Fichte (*PR* §§6, 7, 15, 16, 29, 30). Dialectical critique measures a philosophical practice not on some principle external to it, but on its endowment to turn its principle into pragmatic consummation.[7] Accordingly, Hegel's discursive strategy is to reveal how the coercive interventions of abstract legality and morality, taken alone, systematically preclude the realization of the principle to which they claim to aspire. In the *Philosophy of Right*, Hegel defines the fundamental principle of political philosophy as the reconciled identity of thought and will, form and content, the rational and the actual, or the concept of right and its actualization in the free will of individuals of a state; it constitutes the true "philosophical Idea" (*PR* §4, *PR* Preface, p. 22). In Fichte's *Theory of Knowledge* (*Wissenschaftslehre*), the goal of a reconciliation of intelligence and will is articulated as the absolute identity of ego as reason and ego as nature (*PR* §6A).

As elsewhere, in the *Philosophy of Right* Hegel argues that Fichte commits a grave error in the elaboration of his philosophical system. By rendering the true philosophical Idea into an object of pure reflection, Fichte defines this identity of intelligence and will according to the formal law of contradiction, an analytic unity the Understanding posits in abstraction from determinate difference. As a result of this determination, as Hegel mentions at the outset of §5, the will contains "the element of *pure indeterminancy* or of the 'I' 's pure reflection into itself, in which every limitation, every content, whether present immediately through nature, through needs, desires, and drives, or given and determined in some other way, is dissolved; this is the limitless infinity of *absolute abstraction or universality*, the pure thinking of oneself." Although Fichte takes this formal identity of intelligence and will as the positive, rational, spontaneous self-causation of the individual will to be the "truth" (*PR* §6A), in reality, as Hegel correctly argues, "only one aspect of the will is defined here—namely this absolute possibility of abstracting from every determination in which I find myself or which I have posited in myself, the flight from every content as a limitation" (*PR* §5A).

Because the freedom of the will cannot satisfy itself in this abstract determination, Fichte is forced to posit a second moment. In this second moment, however, Fichte merely compounds his problems. By analytically separating thought from will, not only is intelligence reduced to a formal unity of Understanding without expression in the determinate difference of reality; in the second proposition of Fichte's philosophy human nature itself is now defined according to the law of difference barring inner unity. Hegel explains this when he states, for instance, in §22 that in the second proposition of Fichte's transcendental philosophy, Understanding posits its object not as itself but as an "other or as a limitation," that is, as something absolutely opposed and alien to the "pure activity" of the ego.[8] Degraded to a being lacking inner purposiveness and self-emerging power, nature—as this other of reason—reflects an absolute limit to the spontaneous activity of the free will. Hegel thus argues that Fichte's transcendental philosophy posits a structurally fixed "opposition" (*PR* §8) between the subjective and the objective, a rigid "*dualism of infinity and finitude*" (*PR* §6R). In this way, human nature lacks the capacity for rational, self-determined activity; it is passively dependent on an other, determinate cause. As a result, Hegel can claim in §15R that "to the certainty of this abstract self-determination, *determinism* rightly opposed the *content*, which, as something encountered, is not contained in that certainty and therefore *comes to it from the outside*—although 'outside' here denotes drive or representation, or simply the fact that the consciousness is filled in such a way that

it content is not derived from its own self-determining activity as such."
Paradoxically, then, the self-determination of the abstract subject finds
its limitation in its opposite: the mechanically determined nature of its
very own objective content.

Hegel argues that the theoretical dualism between reason and nature
reappears in Fichte's practical philosophy in the form of a mechanically
causal relation between abstract (moral) law and contingent human
desire. According to Fichte, the rational will can exercise practical freedom first by acting as a determining cause that sets its own body (*Leib*)
in motion. In the *System der Sittenlehre von 1798*, for instance, Fichte
writes that there is a "drive of nature concentrated" in the empirical
body of man, "which, however, has in itself no causality. Yet as a direct
consequence of our [rational] will, it has causality; our will (*unser Wille*)
becomes immediately the cause in our body. We only need to will, and
there results in the body what we will."[9] In the sphere of morality, the
causality of freedom demands that the will must restrict contingent
desires in order to effect human action in strict accordance with universal moral law. And in politics, Fichte's concept of right (*Rechtsbegriff*)
commands that the freedom of each individual is limited by the lawful
freedom of all others; it is this political relation of mutual limitation that
reflects the vital precondition for the "co-existence of freedom" in the
modern liberal state.[10] By displacing the principle of mechanically
causality to the fields of morality and legality, however, a fixed opposition between abstract (moral) law and contingent human desire is
posited which for Hegel blocks the path to unity.

That Fichte's philosophy systematically obstructs the path to reconciliation is not just documented, however, by the logical deficits dis-
closed in the theoretical foundations of moral and legal formalism; in
the *Philosophy of Right*, Hegel links this logic of moral and legal formalism to the practice of moral and legal coercion.[11] On the one hand,
Fichte's moral philosophy leads to a demand for the individual to exercise self-constraint (*Selbst-Beschränkung*), that is, in effect placing one's
own internal nature under the subordinate control (*Botmässigkeit*) of
the rational will.[12] On the other hand, Fichte's theory of right demands
that citizens must be subject to the prohibitive, coercive law (*Zwanges-
gesetz*) of the state; this relation of external coercion reflects in turn a
relation of reciprocal constraint among citizens: each individual must
restrict his own realm of natural freedom wherever necessary in order to
respect the freedom of others in the polity.[13] In this way, Fichte's conception of legality and morality remains overly reliant on the coercive
marginalization of contingent human nature.[14]

In consequence, the individual will continues to harbor within himself a contradiction that makes its appearance, according to Hegel, "as

a dialectic of drives and inclinations which conflict with each other in such a way that the satisfaction of one demands that the satisfaction of the other be subordinated or sacrificed" (*PR* §17). For Hegel, the practices of abstract legality and morality thus lead at best to the production of forced social identities, in which the antagonism between individual and community interests is not dissolved but simply repressed (*D* 115, 119). There remains an inexorable difference between abstract law and determinate will that precludes the reconciliation of individuals in the community. In such a state of contingency, the individual will is forced to arbitrarily choose between two contradictory ends, abstract law or determinate desire. According to Hegel, what one must reckon with by leaving the arbitrary will of the individual the freedom of such a choice is less the effective mitigation than the perpetuation of evil in the world. As he states in the *Philosophy of Right*, to "merely will the good and to have a good intention in one's action is more like evil than good, in that the good is willed only in this abstract form so that its determination is left to the arbitrary will of the subject" (*PR* §140R). Hence, it should come as no surprise that the younger Hegel identified such an arbitrary will with the "principle of the Unethical" (*NL* 78).

In response to the threat of political contingency perpetuated by the impoverished pragmatics of legal and moral formalism, Hegel advances his philosophy of ethical life (*Sittlichkeit*). In his critique of formalism, Hegel asserted that the coercive economy of abstract legality and morality in no way alone can reconcile the increasing antagonisms pervading modern life. By tracing the coercive nature of legal and moral formalism back to the ineluctable opposition between universal reason and individual human desire, Hegel realized that if one is to transcend such a repressive economy of power, one must abandon its rigid dualistic logic of "either/or" (*NL* 89, *PR* §6R). In what constitutes nothing less than a fundamental paradigm change in modern political philosophy, Hegel abandons the idea of an irreducible opposition between universal reason and individual human nature. In its stead he "speculatively" posits the potential for the progressive mutual absorption of reason and human nature in the reconciled relations of ethical life.[15] The ethical apotheosis of human nature, however, has less to do with Hegel's normative concerns than political expediency. For it is first by redefining reason as the innermost potentiality of human nature that Hegel can hope to elude the dysfunctional effects of coercion.[16] In arguing that the struggles between rational law and human nature are not absolute but relative to the existing *modi* of societal control, Hegel opens the way for the progressive political reunification of reason and nature.[17]

By raising human nature to the highest ethical potential of man, it now no longer makes sense to demand in the name of the universal (moral) law simply and solely the mortifying self-abnegation or coercive repression of individual human desires. Instead, the hitherto hidden ethical potential of human nature is to be positively enlisted to support the state. Mobilization of the ethical potential in modern man, not its mortification, is the ruse of Hegelian reason. Hence, Hegel can assert in reference to Aristotle that "the Ethical" (*das Sittliche*) is "the Unmoved, which moves" (*das Unbewegte, welches bewegt*) all things human (*VPR* 19, 127). The strategy of ethical life no longer places its entire weight on repressive marginalization but instead seeks to augment law by productively enjoining individual human desire to actively affirm the political imperatives of the state. Rather than constrict the contingent desires of the individual, the norms and customs (*Sitten*) of the ethical community seek to promote the positive support of individual material interest in order to better advance mutually productive forms of human activity. Indeed, Hegel posits the activation of each individual's motion as the precondition for social stability in ethical life.[18] For Hegel, the strategic gain proffered by this new productivistic economy of ethical power (*sittliche Macht*) is clear: once in effect in the habituated activity of the ethical subject, the mediating institutions of ethical life must no longer intervene ever anew into the field of human practice in order to guarantee an essentially tenuous legal order. Ethical norms function instead in a continuous, individual, and anonymous fashion in the very being of ethical subjects to secure their 'spontaneous' consent to the imperatives of the state.

In Hegel's view, the reconciliation of individuals in modern life is to be achieved by first rendering the actions of each serviceable to all others in civil society. It is first by utilizing human desire in this fashion that governmental practices can produce the conditions desired for the reproduction of a strong state. Indeed, it is one of Hegel's most consequent insights into the nature of the modern social order that the true actualization of the universal can only take place in the concrete actions of individuals who directly pursue their own particular interests, albeit in a mutually productive fashion. In a functionally interdependent order so characteristic of complex modern societies, an individual is for himself by being for others. In other words, ethical life can come to full expression only on the basis of a civil society, in which the principle of functional reciprocity reigns. The individual must serve all others to serve himself; he must render himself a useful instrument for the enjoyment of all others in order to have all others serve as means to the end of his own enjoyment: "In this dependency and reciprocity of work and the satisfaction of needs, subjective selfishness turns into a contribution towards the satisfaction of the needs of everyone else. By a dialectical movement, the particular is mediated by the universal so that each individual, in earning, producing, and enjoying on his own account, thereby earns and produces for the enjoyment of others" (PR §199).[19] Paradoxically, then, the injunction of the idealist Hegel to individuals is in effect—*Enjoy yourself!* I say paradoxical, for it involves an enjoyment of the self predicated on the reduction of the self to an active means for the enjoyment of others.[20]

Against this backdrop it seems, then, that reconciliation in mutual recognition of individual interests is *at its basis* a function of reciprocal utility. It is not until a person has rendered himself utilizable to others of the community, has made himself into an active instrument of the social totality by desiring what others desire of him, that he is worthy of full recognition. The circle of exchange must be closed before the way to mutual recognition can be opened. The recognition granted by the community is dependent on satisfaction of its material interests through the actions of the individual; it reflects nothing other than the fulfillment derived from the utilization of individuals as means to the ends of enjoyment. In short, reciprocal functionality is the precondition for mutual recognition and not vice versa. Once we gain insight into the functional nature of Hegel's productivistic reason the notion of reciprocity loses something of its normative quality and becomes more fundamentally an economic category of the political community.

By constructing this functionability on a strictly reciprocal basis, the actions of individuals dialectically contribute to the 'spontaneous' reproduction of the societal whole. Because individuals act in a fashion less antagonistic to the interests of others, the mutually productive beings find themselves submerged in an ever more spontaneously self-reproducing cycle of exchange at all levels of social life; moreover, such a spontaneous order promises to effectively transcend the coercive strategies of abstract morality and legality Hegel criticizes.[21] Of course, in order to move from the difference of civil society[22] to the true ethical identity of the state, as Hegel terms it, individuals must first "discover their essential self-consciousness in social institutions as that *universal* aspect of their particular interests which has being in itself, and by obtaining through these institutions an occupation and activity directed towards a universal end within a corporation" (PR §264).

This awareness is manifest not only in the spirit of legally recognized corporations, but also in patriotism, piety, individual virtue, the customs of a nation, the universal orientation of public officials, and the public knowledge of the constitution of the ethical totality: "Spirit is actual only as that which it knows itself to be, and since the state, as the spirit of the nation, is both the law which permeates all relations within it and also the customs and consciousness of the individuals who belong to it" (PR §274).[23] However, far from abolishing relations of mutual functionality, the movement from the difference of civil society to the unity of the state implies the recognition of their relative ubiquity. The principle of reciprocity is to govern the actions of individuals in the economic, political, and all other realms of ethical life. To restrict the need for reciprocal relations to simply the economic activities of individuals would be to reduce the modern state to what Plato's Glaucon once so wittingly termed a "city of pigs"[24]; instead, as the basis for the identity of individual desire and universal law the principle of reciprocity is to be embodied in the entirety of human practices.

Whereas Hegel perceived in this state of mutual enjoyment the precondition for a reconciled ethical community, Foucault sees this same process as the result of a "really demonic" force in modern life.[25] The constant correlation of individualization and totalization increasingly reduces socially acceptable forms of individual human behavior to those bearing the stamp of social utility. Foucault's "hyper-pessimism" may have some legitimacy here.[26] In the *Philosophy of Right*, the spirit of mutual productivity was not primarily to be a product of an open discursive struggle for recognition in a democratic will-formation process of private individuals. Although attempting himself in the 1960s to retrieve out of the younger Hegel's theory of mutual recognition a theoretical basis for his own notion of communicative action, in *The Structural Transformation of the Public Sphere* Habermas pointed out Hegel's at best ambiguous relationship to public reason as a mechanism for the reconciliation of the growing antagonisms found in modern societies.[27] Although in the *Philosophy of Right* Hegel does indeed to his credit argue that "whatever is to achieve recognition today no longer achieves it by force and only to a small extent through habit and custom, but mainly through insight and reasoned argument," such reasoned argument is not to be the creation of the critical use of reason by a broad public (*PR* §316A). His distrust of public opinion was simply too great to allow him to place his hope for social reconciliation primarily in the hands of the masses he saw as potential "rabble"; instead, it seems that the true use of reason beyond the contingency of public opinion was to be reserved for informed scientists and public officials (*PR* §§316–319).[28]

In the stead of critical public debate, Hegel believed that—among other institutions—both education (*Bildung, Pädagogik, Erziehung*) and the positive interventions of the police (or the public authorities) would play a central role in the promotion of social integration. On the one hand, Hegel placed great trust in the power of education to "iron out [the] particularity" of the subject (*PR* §187A). This is to be achieved by transforming the original nature of individuals into a "second, spiritual nature so that this spirituality becomes *habitual* to them. In habit, the opposition between the natural and the subjective will disappears, and the resistance of the subject is broken" (PR §151A). For Hegel, then, "education" (Pädagogik) constitutes nothing less than "the art of making human beings ethical" (PR §151A), which "in its absolute determination, is therefore liberation and work towards a higher liberation; it is the absolute transitions to the infinitely subjective substantiality of ethical life, which is no longer immediate and natural, but spiritual and at the same time raised to the shape of universality" (PR §187R). This "liberation" is to find its concretization in the socially productive activity of the individual; in its practical sense, education thus has the function not only of providing individuals with a technical skill but also of instilling in these same individuals an ethic of occupation: "The barbarian is lazy and differs from the educated man in his dull and solitary brooding, for practical education consists precisely in the need and habit of being occupied" (PR §197A).

That Hegel is disquieted by such wasteful idleness is documented further, on the other hand, by the disciplinary role he assigns to the positive interventions of the police or public authorities. In the Philosophy of Right, Hegel argues that the public authorities are to fulfill an important function in "actualizing and preserving the universal which is contained in the particularity of civil society" (PR §§231–249).[29] The public authorities manage the dislocations between individual interest and public utility not only negatively in the administration of justice by preventing crimes and abuses related to the exchange of goods but also positively in the fostering of the public weal by "supervising and influencing" the health, education, and moral-religious attitudes of citizens (PR §239). In this latter field of positive interventions, the public authorities are to focus on societal disruptions stemming from what Hegel termed the "permissible arbitrariness of inherently rightful actions"; here, we are dealing with a broad spectrum of human conduct in civil society not explicitly proscribed by the laws of the state but nevertheless antithetical to social stability. In these "spheres of contingency," as Hegel calls them, individuals do not enter into the scope of the public authorities so much as abstract juridical agents or formally equal legal subjects than as concrete individuals embedded in materially unequal economic milieus with their correspondingly different sociocultural orientations; on this dark side of abstract individual rights, where the public authorities are to concern themselves with citizens not yet worthy of sociocultural recognition, it is above all a matter of adapting individuals to the imperatives of "public utility" by soliciting from them a concrete cultural habitus as it relates to their work ethic, health, morals, and religion (PR §§231, 235).[30]

By closer inspection, then, what Hegel refers to as the general "right" of every individual to "particular welfare" in many ways resem-

bles more the particular duty of each individual to serve the general welfare (*PR* §230). Drawing here apparently on Sir James Steuart's theory
of political economy,[31] Hegel argues that the public authorities should
have the "duty and right to act as a guardian on behalf of those who
destroy the security of their own and their family's livelihood by their
extravagance (*Verschwendung*), and to implement their end and that of
society in their place" (*PR* §240).[32] As an example of the public authorities' guardian care of individuals in protecting them from their own
wastefulness, Hegel seems to indicate that the public account of each
individual's means of support may be necessary in order not only to prevent individual starvation but also "the wider viewpoint" of the "need
to prevent a rabble from emerging" (*PR* §240A).[33]

Especially with respect to the poor Hegel sees an important function
for the public authorities: in order to ensure that the impoverished do
not degenerate into a rabble population—which for Hegel clearly results
from the adoption of a specific moral or cultural disposition (*Gesinnung*) of inward rebelliousness against the rich, society and government[34]—the public authorities should see to it that the poor are not
deprived of "the consolation of religion," as is apparently often the case
(*PR* §241). "For the poor," as Hegel concludes, "the universal authority" (*Macht*) must therefore assume often "the role of the family with
regard not only to their immediate deficiencies, but also to the disposition of laziness, viciousness, and the other vices to which their predicament and sense of wrong give rise" (*PR* §241). And although these positive interventions into the moral and cultural attitudes of the poor
indeed cannot really solve the economic problem of poverty, they
promise to contribute to the reduction of the sociopolitical dislocations
resulting from it in a law-governed state.[35]

The positive interventions of educational institutions and the public
authorities therefore do not just simply break the resistance of the subject or instill in citizens a work ethic necessary for the functioning of
modern civil societies; more broadly, these disciplinary institutions play
an important role in erecting the sociocultural hegemony of ethical life
over the individual, which—in the Gramscian sense—augments the negative or repressive interventions of the state by cultivating in individuals
interests that promote their more habituated, normalized, and 'spontaneous' support for the state.[36] Seen in this light, the disciplinary power
of these mediating ethical institutions may lead less to the "liberation"
(Hegel) of the individual than to an increasing dependence on the habituated and hegemonic relations of ethical life. Indeed, in this context
Hegel himself warns against excessive habituation in ethical life, for it
tends to mentally and physically blunt the individual; paradoxically, the
progressive realization of an ethical community in mutually functional

relations may bring about the progressive exhaustion of the human spirit (*PR* §151A).[37] But even in their nonexhausted state, the ethical relations Hegel has in mind are not the product of a detached individual conscience reasoning over contingent paths of human conduct (*NL* 66).[38]

Throughout his writings, Hegel criticized the notion of autonomy as the product of an arbitrary will that deliberates between two contingent ends of action (*NL* 75, 89). In ethical life, individuals are enmeshed in concrete, habituated relations governed by the normalizing rules of the community. Yet by thus drawing the "individual back into the fold of normality," the hegemonic force of ethical life may actually hinder critical moral reflection.[39] Against this backdrop, one may better understand the grounds for the critique Jürgen Habermas levels against Rüdiger Bubner in their debate over the relationship between morality (*Moralität*) and ethical life (*Sittlichkeit*). In his response to Bubner's Neo-Aristotelian support of ethical life, Habermas defends the universal principles of Kant's ethical philosophy by underscoring the critical function they serve in "de-motivating" or "distancing" the individual from otherwise "self-explanatory" values of ethical life. The importance of such universal rules rests at least in part in their capacity to provoke a critical questioning of the often more parochial norms of ethical life, which otherwise, according to Habermas, go "unquestioned."[40]

In recognizing the functional grounds of reason's unrest it appears more difficult to identify the shift of emphasis away from the coercive strategies of legal and moral formalism toward the productivistic politics of ethical life as a clear-cut path to reconciliation. Hegel's theory of ethical life anticipates not simply the "decline of (repressive) law" (Hayek) so characteristic of our liberal societies today, but the historical ascent of societal techniques designed to heighten man's hegemonic control over man by rendering the happiness of each individual into an instrument for the reinforcement of the modern state. In order for Hegel's "project of reconciliation" (Hardimon) to deflect these concerns and avoid the "tyrannizing syntheses"[41] of modern social institutions, of which Foucault speaks, the processes managing social dislocations need to be based above all on the critical use of public reason. Forms of reconciliation worthy of the name are reflected not simply in the capacity to overcome societal conflict by the functional reintegration of individuals into reciprocal relations of ethical life.[42] Without a doubt, as Hegel clearly argues, the reciprocity of human interests forms a fundamental principle of the modern age; it constitutes a vital precondition for rational consensus. But to ensure the legitimacy of such relations, processes of reconciliation must be linked to critical rational debate opened to all concerned parties and involving the sociocultural recognition of individuals not already acting in what is considered to be publicly useful ways; they must be a manifestation of what Habermas terms communicative reason. Only in this way can one better secure the reduction of institutional violence to which Hegel himself claims to aspire.

To close on perhaps a different note, although I have argued that Hegel's philosophy of ethical life may tend to render the happiness of the individual into a political factor for the reinforcement of the modern state, it is just such a strong state rooted in the ethical life of a nation that has the inner stability to practice what Hegel refers to as toleration. For "only if the state is strong in other respects," as Hegel writes in a note in the *Philosophy of Right*, "can it overlook and tolerate anomalies," such as the religious allegiances of the "Quakers and Anabaptists" or the national allegiances of the "Jews," which otherwise may act counter to the principles of the modern state, and "rely above all on the power of custom (*Sitten*) and the inner rationality of its institutions to reduce the discrepancies" (*PR* §270, Hegel's Note). Paradoxically, it is first by rendering the well-being of individuals into means for its strength that the modern state is secure to recognize the individual as an end beyond the strictures of functional reciprocity, beyond the need for its own reinforcement.

ABBREVIATIONS

References to works of G. W. F. Hegel are to the following editions:

D   *The Difference between Fichte's and Schelling's System of Philosophy*, tr. H. S. Harris and Walter Cerf (Albany: SUNY Press, 1977).

FK   *Faith and Knowledge*, tr. Walter Cerf and H. S. Harris (Albany: SUNY Press, 1977).

NL   *Natural Law: The Scientific Ways of Treating Natural Law, Its Place in Moral Philosophy, and Its Relation to the Positive Sciences of Law*, tr. T. M. Knox (New York: University of Pennsylvania Press, 1975).

PR   *Elements of the Philosophy of Right*, ed. Allen W. Wood, tr. H. B. Nisbet (Cambridge: Cambridge University Press, 1991). In passages of *PR* cited by paragraph (§), Remarks are indicated by 'R', Additions by 'A'.

PS   *Phenomenology of the Spirit* (Oxford: Oxford University Press, 1977).

VPR IV   *Vorlesungen über Rechtsphilosophie*, ed. K.-H. Ilting, vol. IV (Stuttgart: Frommann Verlag, 1974). Including notes and transcriptions from Hegel's lectures of 1831 (transcription by D. F. Strauss).

242   DAVID C. DURST

VPR 19   Philosophie des Rechts: Die Vorlesungen von 1819/1820, anonymous
transcription or transcriptions edited by Dieter Henrich (Frankfurt
a.M.: Suhrkamp Verlag, 1983).

NOTES

1. M. Foucault, "The Political Technology of Individuals," in *Technologies of the Self*, ed. L. Martin, H. Gutman, and P. Hutton (Amherst: University of Massachusetts Press, 1988), 150; Foucault, "The Subject and Power," in *Michel Foucault: Beyond Structuralism and Hermeneutics*, ed. H. Dreyfus and P. Rabinow (Chicago: University of Chicago Press, 1983), 216; M. Foucault, "Governmentality," in *The Foucault Effect*, ed. G. Burchell, C. Gordon, and P. Miller (Chicago: University of Chicago Press, 1991), 87; M. Foucault, "Politics and Reason," in *Politics, Philosophy, Culture: Interviews and Other Writings 1977—1984*, ed. L. D. Kritzman (London: Routledge, 1988), 58–85.

2. Foucault, "Political Technology," 160f.

3. Ibid.," 158.

4. This reflects the general argument made by Franz Grégoire in his defense of Hegel's political philosophy. See F. Grégoire, "Is the Hegelian State Totalitarian?" in *The Hegel Myths and Legends*, ed. Jon Stewart (Evanston, Ill.: Northwestern University Press, 1996), 104–8. For a detailed study of Hegel's politics of reconciliation, see Michael Hardimon, *Hegel's Social Philosophy: The Project of Reconciliation* (Cambridge: Cambridge University Press, 1994).

5. A working assumption of this essay is that what Foucault defined as the difference between a repressive and a positive economy of power is systematically reflected in Hegel's critical movement from the coercion of abstract legality and morality toward the productivistic politics of ethical life. See M. Foucault, "Truth and Power," in *Power/Knowledge*, ed. C. Gordon (New York: Pantheon, 1980), 119. In his essay on the political thrust of Hegelian thought, W. E. Connolly posits a similar opposition between a politics of "repression" and Hegel's "philosophy of reconciliation" (W. E. Connolly, "Hegel: The Politics of Inclusivity," in *Political Theory and Modernity* [Ithaca: Cornell University Press, 1993], 88).

6. For the central role of habit in Hegel's *Philosophy of Right*, see PR §151.

7. For the young Hegel's understanding of immanent or dialectical critique, see G. W. F. Hegel, "Über das Wesen der philosophen Kritik überhaupt und ihr Verhältnis zum gegenwärtigen Zustand der Philosophie insbesondere," in *Werke 2* (Frankfurt a.M.: Suhrkamp, 1986), 171–87.

8. See also PR §7A, where Hegel writes that the "'I' as such is primary pure activity, the universal which is with itself; but this universal determines itself, and to that extent is no longer with itself but posits itself as an other and ceases to be with the universal." And in PR §6A Hegel writes: "This second moment appears as the opposing one. The 'I' here emerges from undifferentiated indeterminacy to become differentiated, to posit something determinate as its content and object. I do not merely will—I will *something*. A will which wills

only the abstract universal wills *nothing* and is therefore not a will at all. The particular thing which the will wills is a limitation, for the will, in order to be a will, must in some way limit itself. The fact that the will wills *something* is the limit or negation. Thus particularization is what as a rule is called finitude. Reflective thought usually regards the first moment, namely the indeterminate, as the absolute and higher moment, and conversely regards the limited as a mere negation of this indeterminancy."

9. J. G. Fichte, *System der Sittenlehre nach den Principien der Wissenschaftslehre von 1798*, in J. G. Fichte, *Fichtes Werke IV* (Berlin: Walter de Gruyter, 1971), 214 (my translation).

10. J. G. Fichte, *Die Grundlage des Naturrechts nach Prinzipien der Wissenschaftslehre von 1796*, in J. G. Fichte, *Fichtes Werke III* (Berlin: Walter de Gruyter, 1971), 92.

11. With respect to legality, for instance, Hegel writes unequivocally in the *Philosophy of Right*: "Abstract right is a coercive right" (*PR* §94).

12. Fichte, *Die Grundlage des Naturrechts*, 166; Fichte, *System der Sittenlehre*, 214.

13. Fichte, *Die Grundlage des Naturrechts*, 139ff. For Kant's statements on "reciprocal coercion," see I. Kant, *Metaphysics of Morals*, 134f.

14. Hegel writes in §38A of the *Philosophy of Right* that "there are only *prohibitions of right*, and the positive form of commandments of right is, in its ultimate content, based on prohibition."

15. In the *Philosophy of Right*, Hegel comments: "The first two moments—that the will can abstract from everything and that it is also determined (by itself or by something else)—are easy to accept and grasp, because they are, in themselves, moments of the understanding and devoid of truth. But it is the third moment, the true and speculative (and everything true, in so far as it is comprehended, can be thought of only speculatively), which the understanding refuses to enter into, because the concept is precisely what the understanding always describes as incomprehensible" (*PR* §7).

16. In §7 of the *Philosophy of Right*, for instance, Hegel writes unequivocally that the first two moments of the abstract self-determination of the 'I' and the determinate and limited self, when taken alone, are "only abstractions; what is concrete and true (and everything concrete is true) is the universality which has the particular as its opposite, but this particular, through its reflection into itself, has been reconciled (*ausgeglichen*) with the universal."

17. In the *Difference* essay, Hegel argues in the following fashion: "through this antinomy reflection points towards an absolute synthesis of freedom and natural impulse; and in doing so, it has not maintained but annulled the opposition and the standing of the two terms or of either of them, and it has not maintained but annulled the claim that it is itself the Absolute and the eternal; it has thrown itself into the abyss of its perfection" (D 140).

18. Hegel's understanding of the relationship between individual motion and social stability reveals his indebtedness to the science of political economy. In his *Theory of Moral Sentiments*, Adam Smith, for instance, writes that "the man of system . . . seems to imagine that he can arrange the different members of a great society with as much ease as the hand arranges the different pieces

upon a chessboard. He does not consider that the pieces upon the chessboard have no other principle of motion besides that which the hand impresses upon them; but that, in the great chessboard of human society, every single piece has a principle of motion of its own, altogether different from that which the legislature might choose to impress upon it. If those two principles coincide and act in the same direction, the game of human society will go on easily and harmoniously, and is very likely to be happy and successful. If they are opposite or different, the game will go on miserably and the society must be at all time in the highest degree of disorder" (Adam Smith, *Theory of Moral Sentiments* [Indianapolis: Liberty Press, 1976], pt. 6, ch. 2).

19. In *PR* §182A Hegel writes: "In civil society, each individual is his own end, and all else means nothing to him. But he cannot accomplish the full extent of his needs without reference to others; there others are therefore means to the end of the particular person. But through its reference to others, the particular end takes on the form of universality, and gains satisfaction by simultaneously satisfying the welfare of others."

20. In the *Phenomenology of Spirit* Hegel argues: the "distinction between duty to the individual and duty to the universal is . . . not something definitely fixed. The truth is rather that what the individual does for himself also contributes to the general good; the more he has made provision for himself, not only is there a greater *possibility* of his being of service to others, but his *actual* existence itself consists only in his being and living in contact with others. His individual enjoyment essentially has the meaning of putting what is his own at the disposal of others and of helping them to obtain *their* enjoyment. Therefore, in the fulfillment of duty to individuals and so to oneself, the duty to the universal is also fulfilled" (*PS* 392).

21. To my mind, it is in this critique of coercion that we find one of the strongest tendencies linking Hegel to the tradition of modern (neo)liberal thought. In *The Road to Serfdom*, F. A. Hayek states, for instance, that "The fundamental principle (of liberalism) is that in the ordering of our affairs we should make as much use as possible of the spontaneous forces of society, and resort as little as possible to coercion" (F. A. Hayek, *The Road to Serfdom* [Chicago: University of Chicago Press, 1980], 17).

22. In *PR* §186 Hegel writes that "in the very act of developing itself independently to totality, the principle of particularity passes over into universality, and only in the latter does it have its truth and its right positive actuality. The unity is not that of ethical identity, because at this level of the division, the two principles are self-sufficient; and for the same reason, it is not present as freedom, but as the necessity whereby the particular must rise to the form of universality and seek and find its subsistence in this form."

23. In recognition of the utility of the government in securing the individual's educated interests, the particularistic aspect of civil society is drawn back into the universality of the state. As Hegel argues, this is the secret grounds of patriotism: once the corporations gain "legal recognition," their spirit is "inwardly transformed into the spirit of the state, because it finds in the state the means of sustaining its particular ends. This is the secret of the patriotism of the citizens in the sense that they know the state as their substance, for it sup-

ports their particular spheres and the legal recognition, authority and welfare of these. In so far as the *rooting of the particular in the universal* is contained *immediately* in the spirit of the corporation, it is in this spirit that such depth and strength of disposition as the state are to be found" (*PR* §289R)

24. Plato, *Republic*, 372. For a discussion of the notion of reciprocal functionality as the principle of justice in the Platonic *polis*, see G. Vlastos, "Social Justice in the Polis" and "The Rights of Persons in Plato's Conception of the Foundations of Justice," both in G. Vlastos, *Studies in Greek Philosophy* (Princeton, N.J.: Princeton University Press, 1995), 2:78ff. and 110ff.

25. The significant passages read: "Our societies proved to be really demonic since they happened to combine those two games—the city-citizen game and the shepherd-flock game—in what we call the modern states. . . . Political rationality has grown and imposed itself all throughout the history of Western societies. It first took its stand on the idea of pastoral power, then on that of reason of state. Its inevitable effects are both individualization and totalization. Liberation can only come from attacking, not just one of these two effects, but political rationality's very roots" (M. Foucault, "Politics and Reason," 71, 85).

26. M. Foucault, "On the Genealogy of Ethics," in Dreyfus and Rabinow, *Michel Foucault*, 231–32.

27. J. Habermas, *The Structural Transformation of the Public Sphere* (Cambridge, Mass.: MIT Press, 1989), 117–22.

28. See Habermas, *Structural Transformation*, 118.

29. For an insightful analysis of the function of the public authorities in Hegel's *Philosophy of Right*, see D. Cornell, M. Rosenfeld, and D. G. Carlson, eds., *Hegel and Legal Theory* (New York: Routledge, 1991), 216f.

30. Let there be no misunderstanding. Hegel vehemently rejects the idea of a police-state as the term is often understood today. It is a well-documented fact that already the young Hegel sharply criticized Fichte's conception of a police-state that attempts to monitor every action of its citizens. At the same time, however, it must be clear that what Hegel found disturbing about Fichte's police-state is above all the fact that, while the external actions of individuals are to be supervised by a costly and ultimately ineffective state apparatus of surveillance, the "inner life [of each citizen] is not to be inspected" at all (*VPR IV*, 617). Hegel felt that what should replace the inefficient, because wholly negative, interventions of external state surveillance is the publicly useful action of individuals, which is first achieved by making the "universal essentially not external but an inward, immanent end, the activity of individuals themselves" (*VPR IV*, 617).

31. For a discussion of the young Hegel's indebtedness to Steuart's *Inquiry into the Principles of Political Economy* (1767), see Laurence Dickey, *Hegel: Religion, Economics, and the Politics of Spirit 1770–1807* (Cambridge: Cambridge University Press, 1987), 199–204; see also Raymond Plant, "Hegel and Political Economy I & II," in *New Left Review*, nos. 103 and 104 (May–June 1977 and July–August 1977): 79–92 and 103–13.

32. Although I cannot pursue here Hegel's relation to the *Polizeiwissenschaft* of the eighteenth century, the potential parallels are not insignificant. For Foucault's discussion of the *Polizeiwissenschaft* of the cameralist tradition

in Germany and France, see his essay "The Political Technology of Individuals." Here, Foucault argues that the "integration of individuals in the state's utility is . . . obtained in this new political rationality by a certain specific technique called then . . . the police. . . . When people spoke about police . . . , they spoke about the specific techniques by which a government in the framework of the state was able to govern people as individuals significantly useful for the world. . . . The police (*Polizei*) have a positive task. . . . The aim of the police is the permanently increasing production of something new, which is supposed to foster the citizens' life and the state's strength. The police govern not by the law but by a specific, a permanent, and a positive intervention in the behavior of individuals" (Foucault, "Political Technology," 153–54, 159). See also Marc Raeff, *The Well-Ordered Police State* (New Haven: Yale University Press, 1983).

33. Hegel defines *rabble* as a disposition associated with poverty reflecting an "inward rebellion against the rich, against society, the government, etc." (*PR* §244A). And although this disposition can be found in the rich (*PR* §454), Hegel does not foresee a need for the public authorities to make provisions to ensure that the rich also benefit from the consolation of religion; they apparently have the financial means to do so on their own volition.

34. In *PR* §244A, Hegel writes: "Poverty in itself does not reduce people to a rabble; a rabble is created only by the disposition (*Gesinnung*) associated with poverty, by inward rebellion against the rich, against society, the government, etc. It also follows that those who are dependent on contingency become frivolous and lazy, like the *lazzaroni* of Naples, for example."

35. This is not to imply that Hegel supports the idea that religion is to be instrumentalized for tyrannical purposes. In the *Philosophy of Right*, Hegel explicitly argues that "if the proposition [that the state needs religion as its foundation] means that individuals must have religion in order that their fettered spirit can be more effectively oppressed within the state, the meaning is a bad one" (*PR* §270A). Hegel also comments that it is a "mockery to dismiss resentment towards tyranny by declaring that the oppressed should find consolation in religion" (*PR* §270R). Nevertheless, Hegel does believe that in a constitutional state the consolation of religion can play a positive role in preventing the rise of a rabble population by deterring individuals from developing beliefs, such as disrespect for the rich, society, and government (*PR* §241). For insightful discussions into the economic and cultural problems as well as the proposed solutions of poverty in Hegel's political philosophy, see S. Avineri, *Hegel's Theory of the Modern State* (Cambridge: Cambridge University Press, 1972); A. Wood, *Hegel's Ethical Thought* (Cambridge: Cambridge University Press, 1990), 247–54; and M. O. Hardimon, *Hegel's Social Philosophy: The Project of Reconciliation* (Cambridge: Cambridge University Press, 1994), 236–50.

36. A. Gramsci, *Selections from the Prison Notebooks* (London: International Pub., 1971).

37. For further discussion of the exhaustion of a nation's ethical spirit in habit, see G. W. F. Hegel, *Reason in History* (Englewood Cliffs, N.J.: Prentice Hall, 1953), 90f.

38. In a further clarification of the qualities of this relation of mutual productivity in the *Phenomenology of Spirit*, Hegel writes: "Any weighing and com-

paring of duties which might be made here would be tantamount to calculating the advantage accruing to the universal from an action. But firstly, the result would be that morality would be made dependent on the necessary *contingency of insight*, and secondly, it is precisely the essence of conscience to have no truck with this calculating and weighing of duties, and to make its *own* decision without reference to any such reasons" (PS 393). See also Hegel, *FK* 184ff.

39. Connolly, "Politics of Inclusivity," 90.

40. See J. Habermas, "Über Moralität und Sittlichkeit—Was macht eine Lebensform 'rational'?" *Rationalität*, ed. H. Schnädelbach (Frankfurt a.M.: Suhrkamp, 1984), 222, 225f.; Rüdiger Bubner, "Rationalität, Lebensform und Geschichte," in *Rationalität*, 198–217.

41. M. Foucault, *Madness and Civilization* (New York: Random House, 1965), 36.

42. In "Traditional and Critical Theory," Max Horkheimer states similarly that the purpose of a critical theory of society "is not . . . the better functioning of any element in the structure. On the contrary, it is suspicious of the very categories of better, useful, appropriate, productive, and valuable, as these are understood in the present order. . . . There is no naturally limited or necessary role for the individual in society" (Max Horkheimer, "Traditional and Critical Theory, " in Max Horkheimer, *Critical Theory* [New York: Continuum, 1992], 207).

CHAPTER 12

Hegel, Rawls, and the Rational State

Stephen Houlgate

I

John Rawls and G. W. F. Hegel are often held to represent two distinct, indeed diametrically opposed, traditions of political philosophy. Rawls is understood to advocate a liberal individualism, according to which, as Alasdair MacIntyre puts it, "individuals are . . . primary and society secondary."[1] Hegel, on the other hand, is understood to be one of the fathers of the communitarian view that human individuality is itself socially constituted. As Sibyl Schwarzenbach has pointed out, however, Rawls recognizes as well as Hegel that human nature is "fundamentally social," and Hegel recognizes as well as Rawls that a rational modern society must protect basic individual rights.[2] Both have a claim to being regarded as liberal communitarians, therefore, and are by no means as different from one another as is often believed.

My purpose in this essay is to claim, with Schwarzenbach, that there are indeed striking similarities between Hegel and Rawls. But it is also to point to certain fundamental differences between the two philosophers' respective conceptions of the rational modern state. These differences, in my view, are inextricably bound up with their respective methods of philosophizing.

Let us turn first to the similarities. Rawls, like Hegel, believes that individuals *find* themselves located within a given society and that society is thus not to be regarded as produced by the agreement of "presocial" individuals.[3] Not even the parties in Rawls's hypothetical "original position" are agreeing to form a new society together. They are, rather, agreeing on fair terms of cooperation which are to govern the society to which they *already* belong. Indeed, this is one of the reasons why those parties must be placed behind a "veil of ignorance"—because fair terms of cooperation can only be agreed if the parties considering them are deprived of information about their existing position in society and so are unable to arrange the terms of their cooperation to their own advantage. If the parties in the original position are not already socially situated, one principal reason for invoking the veil of ignorance is lost.[4]

Rawls also agrees with Hegel that human interests are (largely, if not exclusively) "fashioned" by our interaction with others and are not given independently of, or "prior" to, society.[5] Furthermore, Rawls and Hegel both note that an individual's sense of self-respect is dependent on the recognition accorded to him by others—both in the voluntary associations to which he belongs and in society as a whole.[6]

The most striking similarity, however, is between Rawls's conception of a well-ordered society and Hegel's conception of the rational modern state. Like Hegel's state, Rawls's well-ordered society is held together, not by mere force or economic power, but by publicly recognized principles and laws.[7] Furthermore, in Rawls's well-ordered society, as in Hegel's state, "basic social institutions generally satisfy and are generally known to satisfy these principles." Indeed, for both Rawls and Hegel, a rational state owes much of its stability to the fact that its basic institutions are just and so "fashion a climate within which . . . citizens acquire a sense of justice inclining them to meet their duty of civility."[8]

Hegel and Rawls also agree that the principles of justice governing the modern state should be founded on the concept of rational freedom, not on any particular *religious* beliefs. Furthermore, both believe that participants in public political debate, especially in the legislature, should be guided solely by such principles of justice. That is to say, participants should argue for a particular law or policy because it is just, not because it is what a Christian or a Muslim should do.[9]

Rawls and Hegel also agree, however, that principles of justice cannot be wholly separate from religious belief: our religious beliefs must lend support to the principles of justice if those principles are to be properly grounded. A conception of justice is stable, therefore, when it is realized in society's institutions *and* when individuals endorse such a conception from their own religious and moral points of view.[10]

The obvious difference between Hegel and Rawls is that, whereas Rawls thinks that principles of justice suitable for a free state can be endorsed by a wide variety of "reasonable" religious beliefs, Hegel thinks that such principles require the support of Christianity in particular. Moreover, whereas Rawls maintains that "the state can favor no particular religion" but must treat all alike, Hegel maintains that the state is entitled to give the Christian church "every assistance and protection in the pursuit of its religious end . . . , since religion is that moment which integrates the state at the deepest level of the disposition [of its citizens]."[11] Yet, although Hegel and Rawls do differ in this respect, they are in my view not quite as far apart as it may appear.

The distance between them begins to diminish when one realizes that, for Hegel, the religious beliefs of citizens in a modern state do not need to be absolutely homogeneous. A rational modern state should rest on the broad foundation of Christian—preferably, Protestant—belief, and the state, accordingly, may provide assistance to the church to further its religious ends. But Hegel also recognizes that individual citizens have the right to belong to whichever particular church community they choose. Citizens may belong to various different Protestant denominations, or the Catholic Church, or even—in a strong, liberal state that "may completely overlook individual matters"—marginal groups, such as the Quakers, which refuse to recognize all the duties of citizenship.[12] Indeed, Hegel argues, it was precisely the division of the church into different sects after the Reformation, and the resulting fragmentation of religious power, that allowed the state finally to free itself from the authority of the church and become an independent "self-conscious configuration of right, [and] of free ethical life." Consequently, Hegel remarks, "far from it being . . . a misfortune for the state if the Church is divided, it is *through this division alone* that the state has been able to fulfil its destiny as self-conscious rationality and ethical life."[13]

In *Political Liberalism* Rawls puts forward a strikingly similar view, when he claims that the religious pluralism that resulted from the Reformation, and the ensuing debates about toleration, led to "something like the modern understanding of liberty of conscience and freedom of thought." Moreover, Rawls explicitly acknowledges his debt to Hegel in making this claim: "as Hegel saw, pluralism made religious liberty possible."[14] The degree of religious diversity that Hegel deems to be compatible with the modern rational state is clearly less than that found in Rawls's well-ordered society. But it is important to note that Hegel and Rawls nevertheless agree that the modern state permits—indeed, in one sense requires—the existence of *different* religious communities.

One should also remember that Hegel and Rawls are looking to religion to perform the same role in society: to provide support for the publicly recognized principles of justice and right that unite citizens. Hegel believes that a modern state should be founded on Christianity because Christianity is the only major religion that actively promotes the "freedom of personality."[15] Thus, even though a modern state can incorporate non-Christian minorities,[16] Christianity must predominate if the state as a whole is to be committed to freedom and right. Rawls agrees that any religious faith that is to provide support for the principles of justice must—in addition to being "reasonable"—have "an account of free faith." He supposes, however—by his own admission, "perhaps too optimistically"—that, except for some kinds of fundamentalism, all the main historical religions admit of such an account.[17] Rawls thus has no reason to want to base a free and rational society primarily on Christian belief, because he holds that all the main historical religions can equally well support a conception of political freedom and justice. But what if his optimism were in fact misplaced? What if certain religions do not have an account of "free faith" and do not in fact support the concept of the free and rational person? Would not Rawls then have to say of them, as he says of unreasonable comprehensive doctrines generally, that, although they may exist in a well-ordered society, they should "not gain enough currency to undermine society's essential justice"?[18] Would this not mean that a Rawlsian well-ordered society might have to favor some religions more than others, after all? And would not such a move bring Rawls close to Hegel? If this is the case, then perhaps there is no *fundamental* difference between Hegel and Rawls concerning the relation between the state and religion. Hegel may simply be less optimistic than Rawls about the ability of religions other than Christianity to support the principles of justice to which they are both committed.

II

In my remarks so far I have tried to show that Hegel and Rawls share a similar vision of a rational, well-ordered society. I do not wish to deny, however, that there are nevertheless certain fundamental differences between Rawls's well-ordered society and Hegel's modern state. These differences become apparent when we focus specifically on the various rights, liberties, and opportunities which each regards as important.

The citizens of Hegel's modern state and Rawls's well-ordered society enjoy many of the same rights and liberties. They all enjoy equal protection under the law, the right to own and use personal property, freedom of movement, and freedom from slavery and personal injury. They also all enjoy liberty of conscience, freedom of thought, and freedom of speech and the press. Rawls's well-ordered society and Hegel's rational modern state are thus clearly representatives of the same *kind* of state: a liberal modern state governed by laws and principles of justice that are recognized as binding by all free and rational citizens.[19] Yet, certain rights recognized by Rawls, but restricted by Hegel, indicate that there are some fundamental differences between the two philosophers, and that they actually offer two *alternative* visions of the liberal modern state. What I propose to do now is to examine three of these differences and consider how they are related to differences between the philosophers' methods.

The first fundamental difference between Hegel and Rawls concerns the freedom of choice of occupation. Rawls believes that this freedom is basic and must be upheld, whether the economy is founded on the private or public ownership of the means of production. In order to safeguard this freedom, Rawls maintains, labor and production should be kept free from "direct planning" and should be determined by the demands of the market alone. Individuals should thus be entitled to pursue whatever career they choose, provided that a market can be found for their goods or services (and that they abide by the basic principles of justice). They should be able to compete freely for jobs that are on offer and, if there are not sufficient positions available, they should be able to set up new businesses of their own (although in a socialist economy, of course, ownership of any new business may be required to pass into public hands—either those of the state or the local community or cooperative). Rawls recognizes that a market economy can lead to damaging inequality, but he would compensate for this by redistributive government transfers—welfare payments—rather than by the rational planning and management of production by public bodies.[20]

As I understand it, this right freely to choose one's own occupation would be violated by a command system in which individuals were conscripted to do certain kinds of work against their will. But it would also be violated by a planned system in which, for the sake of controlling the amount of output produced, individuals with the requisite skills and motivation were prevented by public bodies from exercising those skills and trying to find (or create) a market for their goods. A private-property or socialist economy based on the principles of justice would thus, according to Rawlsian theory, have to avoid either kind of "direct planning."[21]

Hegel also recognizes the right of individual citizens to choose their occupation,[22] but, unlike Rawls, he thinks this right can legitimately be restricted for the sake of rationally planned production. Production is to be planned, not so much by the state but by modern-day guilds or *corporations*; and corporations have the right to manage production, in Hegel's view, because, in so doing, they secure for their members the *satisfaction* to which they are entitled. According to Hegel, citizens not only have the right to *pursue* satisfaction (a right recognized by Rawls), they also have the right to satisfaction itself.[23] In the pursuit of material wealth, however, there is no point at which we can say that we have reached our goal and finally achieved satisfaction, because there is always more wealth that can be accumulated. In the pursuit of *recognition* from our peers, on the other hand, there is a point at which we can say that we have reached our goal—namely, once the work we do is recognized as worthy of respect by those qualified to judge. Corporations thus enable citizens actually to achieve the satisfaction they seek by teaching them to find it in reciprocal recognition and respect, rather than material consumption.[24]

If corporations are to secure satisfaction for their members, however, they must not only provide them with peer recognition, but also safeguard the activities through which they are to gain such recognition. That is to say, corporations must protect the jobs of their members (in a way that is consistent with the overall health of the economy). This does not mean guaranteeing its members jobs for life, however badly they perform, but rather regulating the number of people who can produce certain goods so that production of a given product does not greatly exceed demand and plunge people into unemployment. Hegel recognizes that the right of a corporation to "determine the number of its members" restricts the freedom of choice of occupation; but he believes that this right of corporations is essential if the production of goods is to be rationally managed, overproduction avoided, and the members of every branch of the economy guaranteed the opportunity to work and gain the satisfaction of having their work recognized.[25]

Here, therefore, we have a fundamental difference between Hegel and Rawls. For Hegel, citizens of a rational modern state have the right to secure actual satisfaction in their activity. If citizens are to achieve such satisfaction, they must be taught to find it not primarily in material wealth, for which the desire is limitless, but in recognition by one's peers in a corporation. To secure their members the work through which they are to gain recognition, corporations must be able to regulate the numbers of people who are able to produce certain goods. But this is seriously to restrict the equal right of all individuals to choose their own occupation in the name of the rational management of production by organized groups of producers.

Rawls, by contrast, understands the freedom to choose one's occupation to be an inalienable liberty, but recognizes no right to satisfaction itself. There is thus no place in his well-ordered society for organizations, such as corporations or guilds, which restrict citizens' freedom of choice of occupation in the name of securing satisfaction for their members. Indeed, Rawls would surely reject Hegel's corporations as imposing unjustified "monopolistic restrictions" on modes of productive activity (or service) which should by right be open to all who believe that a market can be found (or created) for the goods concerned.[26]

The second fundamental difference between Hegel and Rawls concerns the political process, and voting in particular. Rawls adheres to what he calls the "principle of (equal) participation," according to which "all citizens are to have an equal right to take part in, and to determine the outcome of, the constitutional process that establishes the laws with which they are to comply."[27] Rawls acknowledges that in a modern society laws must be made by a representative body, rather than the people as a whole. But the principle of equal participation means that each (sane, adult) citizen has an equal voice in choosing those representatives, that is, that each elector has one vote. Furthermore, it means that all citizens are to be represented equally in the legislature itself, that is, that each member of the legislature must "represent the same *number* of electors" (assuming single-member territorial constituencies).[28]

Rawls recognizes, however, that universal suffrage has been rejected by most writers until recent times and that persons have not even been regarded as the proper subjects of representation. "Often it was interests that were to be represented," Rawls notes, "for others it is regions that are to be represented, or forms of culture, as when one speaks of the representation of the agricultural and urban elements of society." At first sight, Rawls comments, "these kinds of representation appear unjust"; and, he adds, "how far they depart from the precept one person one vote is a measure of their abstract injustice."[29]

Hegel is famously one of those who reject the idea that all citizens must be able to participate in deliberations concerning the laws and policies of the state. That idea appears to be plausible, Hegel says, only because "it stops short at the *abstract* determination of membership of the state and because superficial thinking sticks to abstractions."[30] For Hegel, however, citizens of a modern state are not only abstract persons, each of whom is formally equal to everyone else, but they are also concrete social and economic beings, who have different *particular* interests in common with others in their trade or profession. These interests are not merely the contingent interests of single individuals, but the rational interests of the various branches of society in which people earn their livelihood and in terms of which they primarily define who they are: the interests of engineers or clothing manufacturers. Such interests are given publicly recognized institutional embodiment in the various corporations in the state. Since the stability of the modern state rests partly on the trust that citizens have that their particular interests are indeed protected by the state, it is essential that the interests of the various trades and professions to which citizens belong be seen to be represented in the legislature. This means that the members of the lower house in Hegel's state must represent the *corporations* that embody those interests, rather than numerically defined territorial constituencies, as Rawls advocates.[31] Local communities (*Gemeinden*) may elect deputies to the lower house, in Hegel's view, but such communities must themselves be regarded as corporations with recognized common interests, and should not just be collections of individuals residing in a certain area.[32]

Hegel notes in his Heidelberg lectures on the philosophy of right that requiring votes to be channeled through corporations is not in itself incompatible with universal suffrage. "If it is for associations to send deputies, and all citizens must be members of an association, then every active citizen can also take part in the election."[33] It is clear, however, that Hegel does not consider it *necessary* that all citizens have the vote or that all participate equally in the political process: "for it is not essential that the individual should have a say as an abstract individual entity; on the contrary, all that matters is that his *interests* should be upheld in the assembly which deals with universal issues."[34] For this reason, Hegel's rational state *may* restrict the right to vote which Rawls considers to be universal and inalienable.

The third significant difference between Hegel and Rawls again concerns the political process. In this case the constitutional structure of Hegel's state unquestionably restricts rights to which Rawls gives high priority. In Rawls's view, the first principle of justice requires, as an equal basic political liberty, that all citizens have an equal right to run for and hold political office (and that that right is *worth* the same to all citizens who wish to take advantage of it). The second principle of justice supports this political right by guaranteeing to all citizens fair equality of opportunity. This means that all citizens, whatever their income or social status, must have an equal chance of securing any position of authority in society, provided that they have the requisite talent and motivation.[35]

Now Hegel accepts that positions in the civil service should be open to all those qualified to fill them.[36] But he does not deem it necessary that *all* positions of political power should be open to everyone. In particular, he believes that seats in the upper house of parliament should be reserved for members of the agricultural or landowning estate who inherit their property through primogeniture. The reason for this is that, if laws are to safeguard all the interests and needs of citizens, they must be debated and enacted not only by representatives of the corporations in civil society, but also by citizens who are "independent of . . . the quest for profit . . . [and] of the favour of the executive power and of the masses," and who are informed above all by an abiding sense of dependence on, and gratitude toward, *nature*.[37] The role of the upper house is thus to make sure that legislation is determined not just by commercial interests and the interests of the executive, but also by the interests of those who work, and care for, the land. And it should be emphasized that although Hegel expects only wealthy landowners to enter the upper house because only they will have the wherewithal to guarantee their political independence, he insists that those landowners have to be involved in actually working the land in some way, if they are to represent the interests of their estate. "There is," he says, "no longer any room for a nobility that lacks all recognized employment and is proud of the fact."[38]

As Rawls points out, the upper house of the Hegelian legislature clearly violates the principle of fair opportunity and restricts the right of all citizens to run for every political office. What Rawls fails to note, however, is that Hegel imposes this restriction because he wants to ensure that ecological intuition plays as much of a role in the legislative process as commercial understanding.[39]

We have seen that in three important ways Hegel's rational modern state restricts (or may restrict) certain rights and opportunities that Rawls's well-ordered society secures for everyone. What I now wish to suggest is that Hegel departs from Rawls, not out of any nostalgic medievalism, but because he employs a different *method* to determine the principles that should govern a rational state based on free will.

III

Rawls proceeds by setting out various conditions which he believes such principles must meet. The first is that the principles of justice are not to be derived a priori through an analysis of the concept of right, but are to be "*selected* as the outcome of a process of rational deliberation."[40] The second is that the principles of justice are to be selected by reflective persons who regard themselves as free and equal. This means that each person must be regarded as having an equal interest in what those principles prescribe and so must have an equal voice in determining them. The process of choosing the principles of justice must thus be *fair* to all and allow no one "to design principles to favor his particular condition."[41]

The way to guarantee such fairness, Rawls believes, is by depriving all involved of any invidious information about their particular condition. They may know about the general conditions of life and moral psychology, but they may not know anything about their own natural talents, social circumstances or personal beliefs, and so must choose the principles of justice behind a "veil of ignorance."[42] This condition is fair to all because all are similarly situated and no one has any advantage or disadvantage with respect to anyone else.[43] *All* are to be involved in choosing the principles of justice, and all are to be involved as *equals*. Rawls acknowledges that we can never actually be placed in such a situation of ignorance, but he claims that we can work out which principles persons in such a hypothetical situation *would* choose. The principles of justice that are to govern a modern society based on freedom are thus those that would be chosen by free and equal rational persons in an "original position" of fairness.[44]

Rawls argues that persons in that position would choose principles which give equal protection to the basic liberties of all citizens (and their associations).[45] The specific content of these liberties is determined by the two fundamental "moral powers" free and equal persons are assumed to have: the capacity for a sense of justice and the capacity for a conception of the good. The first moral power is more specifically the power to cooperate with others according to principles of justice chosen by all. The second moral power is more specifically the power to choose one's own life-plan. "The basic rights and liberties of a constitutional regime," Rawls writes, "are to assure that everyone can adequately develop these powers and exercise them fully over the course of a complete life as they so decide."[46]

The first moral power underlies the equal political liberties in particular.[47] All persons, in Rawls's view, are assumed to have an interest in exercising their capacity to cooperate with others according to principles that would be chosen by all under fair conditions. Indeed, all are assumed to have an interest in cooperating with others *to choose* the very principles and laws that are to govern their cooperation. To guarantee that everyone can actually exercise this capacity fully, if they wish, the parties in the original position would thus choose principles of justice that protect the equal right of all to run for and hold political office and to elect those who seek such office.[48]

The rights to liberty of conscience and freedom of association similarly guarantee that all persons can exercise their second moral power to form and revise their own conception of the good. Further basic rights— such as the right to security of property and person, freedom of movement and of choice of occupation, and the right to equal protection under the law—serve, Rawls maintains, to "support" the first two sets of (political and personal) liberties.[49]

The first priority of persons in the hypothetical original position would thus be to agree to principles that give *all* citizens the *equal* right to develop and exercise their fundamental moral powers. Accordingly, they would choose Rawls's first principle of justice:

> Each person has an equal right to a fully adequate scheme of equal basic liberties which is compatible with a similar scheme of liberties for all.[50]

After considering the equal rights to be enjoyed in a well-ordered society, Rawls then notes that *inequalities* in such a society (for example, in power or income) would also have to be *equally* acceptable to everyone. Inequalities will thus only be agreed to, if they do not infringe the equal basic rights protected under the first principle and if everyone has an equal—or fair—opportunity to attain the more influential or well-paid positions. But, of course, each person must also accept that he has an equal chance of ending up with the *smallest* share of wealth or power. Free and equal persons would accept inequality under this condition, however, if the situation of the least advantaged would actually be better than it would be under an equal division of resources. Thus, Rawls says, "the parties [in the original position] arrive at the difference principle."[51] The requirement that inequality be equally acceptable to all in the original position means, therefore, that persons in that position would choose Rawls's second principle of justice:

> Social and economic inequalities are to satisfy two conditions. First, they must be attached to offices and positions open to all under conditions of fair equality of opportunity; and second, ["the difference principle"] they must be to the greatest benefit of the least advantaged members of society.[52]

That is to say, the worst off must be better off under an unequal division of income and power than they would be under an equal division of income and power.

Note that Rawls determines which principles of justice should govern a free, rational society by working out what free and equal persons behind a veil of ignorance would all rationally *agree* to and *choose*. The persons concerned are not free to choose any principles whatsoever, because the principles must be equally acceptable to all, given their presumed interest in exercising their moral powers. But principles of justice—however much reason may recommend them—can never be forced onto free citizens either, because such citizens regard themselves as "rational beings with a *liberty to choose*."[53] The parties in the original position are thus to be envisaged as *selecting* principles of justice through a process of rational deliberation. Moreover, the main aim of the principles to which they agree will be to protect the equal right of all persons to *choose* their own life-plan and to *choose* those who will govern them.

Hegel also believes that the rights, laws, and "principles of justice" that hold the modern state together must be grounded in the free will.[54] But he does not endeavor to determine what free and equal persons would select or agree to; he seeks to establish what follows *necessarily* from the very idea of the free will. "An immanent and consistent theory of duties," he says, "can be nothing other than the development of *those relations* which are necessitated by the Idea of freedom."[55]

Hegel begins by showing that freedom necessarily entails choice, but more important, the right to own and exchange property, to find satisfaction through one's actions, and to determine through one's own free reason what is to count as the good. Freedom also entails living in a relationship of love within a family, engaging in economic activity to meet one's needs, enjoying the protection of the law and the police, being recognized by one's peers, and living in a state whose laws take account, not only of the interests of the whole, but also of the various branches of society and of our indebtedness as free beings to nature.

I do not propose here to explain in detail why Hegel believes that these things are required by the very idea of freedom. I have discussed three of them briefly above and several of the others elsewhere.[56] All that needs to be understood here is that, in Hegel's view, freedom by its nature *necessitates* these rights, activities, and institutions.

This, I believe, explains why Hegel is prepared to restrict certain freedoms to which Rawls gives the highest priority. What is of primary importance, in Hegel's view, is not that all persons be able to choose their occupation in complete freedom or be able to choose who should govern them, but that all the *requirements* of freedom be met. These requirements do indeed include the freedom to choose one's occupation and the right of members of corporations to elect their political representatives (as well as various equal legal and moral rights); but they also include the requirement that individuals find satisfaction in their activity and that the laws under which citizens live be formulated in light of their numerous economic interests and freedom's dependence on nature. And, as we have seen, these requirements of freedom establish the right of corporations to restrict the free choice of occupation by restricting the numbers of people producing certain goods. They also establish the need for certain constitutional arrangements, such as a lower house elected from the corporations and an upper house drawn (without election) from the agricultural class, which may be or indeed are at variance with the equal right of all citizens to vote and to gain access to all political offices. Hegel's distinctive method of seeking to determine what is required by the idea of freedom, rather than what free and equal persons would choose, thus leads him, in contrast to Rawls, to a conception of the state in which choice, equality, and fairness, while important, are not the principal values, and in which certain *unfair inequalities*, above all in political representation, are understood to be in the deeper interests of freedom.[57]

It is important to note that the necessity Hegel believes determines the structure of the modern state is not external to the free will. Hegel is not a "rational intuitionist" in Rawls's sense, for whom the principles of justice reflect "an independent moral order."[58] The necessity that determines the structure of the modern state is immanent in the free will itself: it is freedom's *own* necessity—that which is required by the very nature of the free will itself. Like Rawls, Hegel insists that the laws and institutions under which citizens live must "be justifiable to all citizens." In contrast to Rawls, however, Hegel does not think that this means all citizens must have an equal share in choosing those institutions and laws. It means that they must be able to recognize—whether or not they have the vote—that those institutions and laws fulfill the requirements of freedom itself.[59]

With its lower house elected through the corporations and its unelected upper house (and indeed monarchy), Hegel's rational modern state is clearly less *democratic* than Rawls's well-ordered society. But it is important to remember that it is less democratic because of what Hegel believes is necessitated by the very idea of *freedom*, not because of any desire to preserve the premodern privileges of corporations and the aristocracy. From Hegel's point of view, Rawls's well-ordered constitutional democracy would itself be open to criticism, therefore, because it is not based on a full understanding of what freedom itself requires.

IV

In this essay I have tried to show that Hegel and Rawls share very similar conceptions of the modern state, but that there are nevertheless significant differences between them. Both Hegel and Rawls conceive of the modern state as governed by principles of justice rooted in the free will, but Hegel's state—in the interests of freedom itself—places restrictions on liberties which Rawls holds dear, such as the freedom of choice of occupation and the equal political liberties. The question facing readers of these two philosophers is: Which of their conceptions of the rational state is to be preferred? This is not an easy question to answer, because Hegel and Rawls can each offer significant criticisms of the other's political theory.

The strongest Hegelian critique of Rawls, I believe, is that Rawls fails to identify the principles of justice appropriate for a free will in a manner that is itself fully free and self-determining.[60] For Hegel, a free, self-determining political philosophy is one that is not *bound* in advance to any specific principles of justice: its task is not to decide between principles that are already given, nor does it assume that the principles chosen will be suited to one kind of free society—for example, democracy—rather than another. It begins, rather, from nothing more determinate than the bare idea of the free will and allows that bare idea itself to determine the requirements of freedom. In the course of this process, philosophy *discovers* which principles of justice are suited to freedom (and, indeed, learns that freedom has a social and historical character). A free, self-determining political philosophy is thus a presuppositionless philosophy in which nothing determines what is just apart from the immanent—and therefore necessary—development of the idea of freedom with which one begins.[61]

Rawls's political philosophy falls short of Hegel's ideal in two ways. First, Rawls identifies the principles of justice suited to freedom by working out which principles persons in the original position would select from a "short list of traditional conceptions of justice" that they "simply take as *given*."[62] Second, as Richard Winfield has pointed out, Rawls takes for granted from the start the priority of fairness and equality and the idea that free persons are essentially rational choosers. He is thus not engaged in a free, presuppositionless attempt to *discover* which principles of justice are required by the free will, but is committed from the outset to presenting "a conception of political and social justice which is congenial to the most deep-seated convictions and traditions of a modern *democratic* state."[63] From Hegel's point of view, therefore, Rawls's political thought is not insufficiently historical, but rather *too* historical: for it is bound in advance to principles of justice that are suited to a particular historical social form—namely, democracy (with its ideals of fairness, equality of choice, and well-ordered cooperation)—rather than to freedom as such. And a philosophy that allows itself to be governed by what is *given* in history in this way is not itself self-determining and free.[64]

This criticism of Rawls strikes me as correct—from a *Hegelian* point of view. The problem is that it does not meet Rawls on his own ground. Rawls's goal in *A Theory of Justice* and *Political Liberalism* is ultimately a practical one: to find principles of justice that can be *agreed on* by reasonable citizens of a modern, pluralist democratic state.[65] There is no need to seek an account of justice that is free or true, in his view, because, even if one were found (for example, by Hegel), it could not provide a basis for agreement among citizens of fundamentally different philosophical views.[66] Only principles of justice based on fair choice can do that. Rawls thus does not see any need to meet Hegel's rigorous standards for a free and true political philosophy. Nor does he see it as a failing of his theory that it seeks principles of justice suited to democratic society in particular: for it is precisely pluralist, *democratic* society that raises the specific problem of agreeing on common principles that Rawls seeks to solve.

The Hegelian critique of Rawls sketched above is undoubtedly decisive from Hegel's point of view, but from Rawls's point of view it appears to miss the point. Moreover, for Rawls, Hegel's own conception of the rational state is not one on which free and equal citizens could agree. But if, as it appears, Rawls and Hegel approach justice and right from such incommensurable perspectives, how do we determine whose theory is to be preferred? Is it possible to offer an immanent critique of one theory that leads us to favor the other? I will end this essay by suggesting that at least a *quasi-immanent* critique of Rawls can be offered by the Hegelian.

Rawls explains that the conception of justice he puts forward is "freestanding" in that it rests, not on any particular philosophical, moral, or religious worldview, but on an independent *political* conception of the person as free and equal. But he also insists that, if a well-ordered society is to be stable, that freestanding conception of justice should be endorsed by all citizens from their own philosophical, moral, and religious point of view in an "overlapping consensus."[67] For such a consensus to be possible, the personal beliefs of citizens do not need to be true; they just need to be "reasonable" and to lend support to justice as fairness. Insofar as such beliefs are indeed reasonable in this way, they can be left alone by the political theorist. Only when they are unreasonable and "reject all variations of the basic essentials of a democratic regime" does the political theorist have to take a stand against them and work to ensure that they "do not gain enough currency to undermine society's essential justice."[68]

Now, taking a stance against an "unreasonable" and undemocratic worldview in the name of justice as fairness is itself a perfectly reasonable thing to do, provided that that undemocratic worldview is not actually true. If it is true, however, the political theorist finds himself in the awkward position of recommending that citizens turn their backs on the truth (or keep it to themselves) for the sake of supporting justice as fairness. But this hardly seems *fair* to those who have found the truth (nor indeed is it very honest). Alternatively, the political theorist can acknowledge that those citizens who have the truth have the right to proclaim it to others. But if this truth is incompatible with justice as fairness or with parts of it, then no completely overlapping consensus will be possible and justice as fairness will be unstable.

Note that the issue here is not how the Rawlsian political theorist should react to an undemocratic comprehensive view that is merely *claimed* to be true. In that case, the political theorist can simply refuse to accept that claim and, with good conscience, can recommend that certain measures be taken against the proponents of the view concerned, in the interests of justice as fairness.[69] The issue here is how the political theorist should react to an undemocratic comprehensive view that is *in fact* true. It is in this case, as I see it, that the position of the Rawlsian political theorist becomes problematic, whichever course of action he elects to pursue.

My suspicion is that Rawls does not think the situation I have described would actually ever arise. He does not believe that a true comprehensive doctrine would necessarily command the assent of all citizens; but neither does he believe that a true doctrine would be *at variance* with justice as fairness. Yet, as I have tried to show, Hegel's political theory does not accept the moral primacy of fairness and equality and restricts certain rights and liberties secured by justice as fairness. If Hegel's theory is not true, Rawls will not in any way be discomfited by it. If, however, Hegel's theory is true and does tell us what freedom in truth requires, then Rawls is placed by his *own* theory in a decidedly uncomfortable position. For either he must work (unfairly) against the truth in the name of justice as fairness, or he must allow the truth (and its public expression) to work against justice as fairness by undermining the possibility of a fully overlapping consensus.

To point out that Rawls's theory faces these difficulties is not to put forward a wholly immanent critique of that theory, because it is not to claim that that theory is inconsistent purely on its own terms. But it is to put forward a quasi-immanent critique of Rawls's theory, because it is to claim that his conception of justice is problematic on its *own* terms, if *Hegel's* account of the requirements of freedom is true.

What I hope has become clear in this essay is that Hegel and Rawls present two different conceptions of the same kind of state: the rational modern state. Rawls conceives of the modern state as a constitutional democracy in which basic rights are understood to be instituted by the (hypothetical) *agreement* of citizens and in which priority is given to the political liberty to *choose* those who govern. Hegel, by contrast, conceives of the modern state as a *Rechtsstaat* in which basic rights are understood to be determined by the very idea of freedom itself and in which the political liberty to choose who is to govern is restricted by certain undemocratic *requirements* of freedom. These two conceptions of the modern state are incommensurable insofar as they are based on different conceptions of political philosophy—one practical, one theoretical. Yet, we are not faced simply with a groundless choice between the two. For, even if Rawls's conception of justice is acceptable to free and equal persons, Hegel's account of freedom may still be true; but if Hegel's account is true, then Rawlsian justice as fairness threatens to be unstable on its own terms. This, in my view, gives us one possible reason for preferring Hegel to Rawls. Whether it is a good reason depends, of course, on whether Hegel's account of freedom is indeed true or not; and that, some will say, remains to be established.

NOTES

I should like to thank Ken Alpern (Hiram College) and Andrew Williams (University of Warwick) for reading through this essay with great care and attention and making helpful suggestions for improvement. I should also like to thank Ken Alpern for encouraging and inspiring me to write the essay in the first place.

1. A. MacIntyre, *After Virtue: A Study in Moral Theory*, 2nd ed. (London: Duckworth, 1985), p. 250.

2. S. Schwarzenbach, "Rawls, Hegel, and Communitarianism," *Political Theory* 19, 4 (November 1991): 552, 558. On Rawls's recognition of the social character of human beings, see, for example, T. M. Scanlon, "Rawls' Theory of Justice," in *Reading Rawls: Critical Studies on Rawls' "A Theory of Justice,"* ed. N. Daniels (Stanford: Stanford University Press, 1989), p. 177, J. B. Hoy, "Hegel's Critique of Rawls," *Clio* 10, 4 (1981): 409–11, and C. Kukathas and P. Pettit, *Rawls. "A Theory of Justice" and its Critics* (Cambridge: Polity Press, 1990), pp. 122–23.

3. J. Rawls, *A Theory of Justice* (Oxford: Oxford University Press, 1972), p. 13, and *Political Liberalism*, 2nd ed. (New York: Columbia University Press, 1996), pp. 41, 136. MacIntyre claims, wrongly, that Rawls "envisages entry into social life as—at least ideally—the voluntary act of at least potentially rational individuals with prior interests" (*After Virtue*, p. 251). See G. W. F. Hegel, *Elements of the Philosophy of Right*, ed. A. Wood, tr. H. B. Nisbet (Cambridge: Cambridge University Press, 1991), pp. 105–6 [§75 and Addition]. For the German text, see G. W. F. Hegel, *Werke in zwanzig Bänden*, ed. E. Moldenhauer and K. M. Michel (Frankfurt am Main: Suhrkamp Verlag, 1969ff.), VII [*Grundlinien der Philosophie des Rechts*]: 157–59. See also G. W. F. Hegel, *Vorlesungen über Rechtsphilosophie, 1818–1831*, ed. K.-H. Ilting, 4 vols. (Stuttgart: Frommann-Holzboog, 1974), III: 266–67. Further references to *Elements of the Philosophy of Right* will take the form: Hegel, *PR*, pp. 105–6 [§75 and Addition]; *Werke*, VII: 157–59. Further references to *Vorlesungen über Rechtsphilosophie* will take the form: Hegel, *VRP*, III: 266–67.

4. See Rawls, *A Theory of Justice*, pp. 15, 18–19.

5. See Rawls, *A Theory of Justice*, p. 259, *Political Liberalism*, p. 269, and Hegel, *PR*, pp. 228–31 [§§190–195]; *Werke*, VII: 347–51. Rawls's insistence that the "primary subject of justice" is the "basic structure of society" (rather than the character or soul of the individual) is thus by no means accidental, but follows directly from his "Hegelian" recognition that human interests are largely determined by society's institutional structure. That is to say, it follows from his fundamental agreement with Hegel that the way to educate someone in ethical matters is to "make him the *citizen of a state with good laws.*" See Rawls, *A Theory of Justice*, p. 7, *Political Liberalism*, p. 258, and Hegel, *PR*, p. 196 [§153]; *Werke*, VII: 303.

6. See Rawls, *A Theory of Justice*, pp. 178–79, 441–42, *Political Liberalism*, pp. 318–19, 322–23, and Hegel, *PR*, pp. 271–72, 282, 296 [§§253, 260, 270 (Hegel's note)]; *Werke*, VII: 395–96, 406, 421. See also G. W. F. Hegel, *Philosophie des Rechts*, ed. D. Henrich (Frankfurt am Main: Suhrkamp Verlag, 1983), p. 167: "Each one is what he is only insofar as he is this in the representation of another. Only through this moment of recognition in the representation of another does the individual have his existence (*Dasein*)" (my translation). Further references to the Henrich edition of the *Philosophie des Rechts* will take the form: Hegel, *PRH*, p. 167.

7. Rawls, *A Theory of Justice*, p. 5, *Political Liberalism*, pp. 35, 108, and Hegel, *PR*, pp. 240, 291, 353 [§§209, 270, 317]; *Werke*, VII: 360, 415, 483–84.

8. Rawls, *A Theory of Justice*, p. 5, *Political Liberalism*, p. 252, and Hegel, *PR*, pp. 189–91, 287 [§§142–147, 265 and Addition]; *Werke*, VII: 292–96, 412. See also Hegel, *VRP*, IV: 638–39.

9. See Rawls, *Political Liberalism*, pp. 9–10, 138, 194, 201, 215, 248, 304. Rawls does accept, however, that, when a society is not well ordered, it is appropriate to argue for political justice on religious grounds (see *Political Liberalism*, pp. 249–51). For Hegel's views on the relation between religion and public political debate, see Hegel, *PR*, pp. 298–301, especially p. 299, ll. 34–39 [§270]; *Werke*, VII: 424–27, especially 425, ll. 31–36. The reason Hegel argues that public political debate should be based on rational laws and principles of justice, rather than religious belief, is not, as it is for Rawls, that no agreement could be reached on the basis of religion, but that any agreement that is reached (and any ensuing laws and policies) would be based on *faith* and *feeling*, instead of argument "in accordance with principles" (*PR*, p. 299 [§270]; *Werke*, VII: 424–25). Legislation and government would thus not be fully rational, and perhaps not even fully informed, and so would "expose the state . . . to instability, insecurity, and disruption" (*PR*, p. 293 [§270]; *Werke*, VII: 418). Furthermore, Hegel notes, the church as an institution should be not granted any political role, because by its nature it speaks with an authority—namely, "the voice of God"—that other participants in the political process do not enjoy and so unbalances the political debate (see *PRH*, p. 265). For these reasons, Hegel concludes, "religion as such should not hold the reins of government" (*PR*, p. 304 [§270 Addition]; *Werke*, VII: 431; *VRP*, III: 740).

10. See Rawls, *A Theory of Justice*, p. 385, and *Political Liberalism*, pp. 10, 134–35, 141, 150, 391–92. Rawls's position is thus not as far removed from that of a communitarian, such as MacIntyre, as it might seem. For, as he states in *Political Liberalism*, "even though a political conception of justice is freestanding, that does not mean that it cannot be embedded in various ways . . . into the different doctrines citizens affirm" (p. 387). See Hegel, *PR*, p. 299 [§270]; *Werke*, VII: 425 (where Hegel points out that the state needs "religious accreditation"), and *Hegel's Philosophy of Mind. Being Part Three of the Encyclopaedia of the Philosophical Sciences (1830)*, tr. W. Wallace and A. V. Miller (Oxford: Clarendon Press, 1971), p. 283 [§552]; *Werke*, X: 355 ("if religion . . . is the consciousness of *'absolute' truth*, then whatever is to rank as right and justice, as law and duty, i.e. as *true* in the world of the free will, can be so esteemed only as it is participant in that truth, as it is subsumed under it and is its sequel").

11. Rawls, *A Theory of Justice*, p. 212, *Political Liberalism*, pp. 154, 179–80, and Hegel, *PR*, pp. 92, 295 [§§62, 270]; *Werke*, VII: 133, 420.

12. See Hegel, *PR*, pp. 240, 295 [§§209, 270 (including Hegel's note)]; *Werke*, VII: 360, 420–21.

13. Hegel, *PR*, pp. 301–2 [§270]; *Werke*, VII: 428; *PRH*, p. 225.

14. Rawls, *Political Liberalism*, p. xxvi.

15. Hegel, *PR*, pp. 92, 223 [§§62, 185]; *Werke*, VII: 133, 342.

16. Hegel, *PR*, pp. 240, 295–96 [§§209, 270 (Hegel's note)]; *Werke*, VII: 360, 421.

17. Rawls, *Political Liberalism*, p. 170.

18. Rawls, *Political Liberalism*, pp. 39, 64 [note 19].

19. For basic liberties protected by Rawls's well-ordered society, see *A Theory of Justice*, p. 61; *Political Liberalism*, pp. 232, 298, 335–37, 340. For some of the basic freedoms protected by Hegel's state, see *PR*, pp. 75, 79, 88–89, 95–97, 121, 164, 244, 253–54, 257–58, 295, 300, 353–56 [§§44, 48, 59, 66 and Addition, 94 Addition, 137, 213, 222, 224, 228, 270, 317–319]; *Werke*, VII: 106, 111–12, 128, 141–44, 181, 255, 365, 375–76, 380–81, 420, 426, 483–88; *VRP*, III: 251–52, 296–98.

20. Rawls, *A Theory of Justice*, pp. 99, 270–78, and *Political Liberalism*, p. 364.

21. Rawls recognizes that "in a socialist regime planners' preferences or collective decisions often have a larger part in determining the direction of production." But he also states explicitly that "both private-property and socialist systems normally allow for the free choice of occupation and of one's place of work"; see *A Theory of Justice*, pp. 270–71.

22. Hegel, *PR*, pp. 237, 285–86 [§§206, 262]; *Werke*, VII: 358, 410.

23. Hegel, *PR*, pp. 149, 151, 260, 287 [§§121, 124, 230, 265 Addition]; *Werke*, VII: 229, 233, 382, 412; *VRP*, IV: 639. According to Rawls, "everyone is assured an equal liberty to pursue whatever plan of life he pleases as long as it does not violate what justice demands" (Rawls, *A Theory of Justice*, p. 94). People gain satisfaction and happiness when they carry out their chosen plans successfully. All, therefore, have the liberty to pursue satisfaction as they conceive it. But satisfaction *itself* is not a right, for Rawls, and cannot be secured by the state and its laws. This is partly because Rawls believes that a liberal state must leave individuals free (within the limits imposed by justice) to do what they think is necessary to attain their chosen goals, and so must leave them free to fail to achieve the satisfaction they desire. But it is also because what constitutes satisfaction, or the successful carrying out of one's life-plan, is, in Rawls's view, largely subjective anyway, so there is no common, *objective* measure available to the state which could enable it to determine whether or not satisfaction has been achieved (*A Theory of Justice*, p. 95). All society can guarantee to its citizens, therefore, is an equal (or fair) share of primary goods, which it is presumed everyone needs in order to pursue (or as constituents of) their own satisfaction (*A Theory of Justice*, pp. 62, 92). For these primary goods there *is* an objective measure: one can determine clearly whether everyone is accorded the same rights and whether wealth is equally (or fairly) distributed (even if what constitutes wealth, for example, is partly socially determined). Primary goods are means everyone is assumed to need to pursue satisfaction, but an index of such goods does *not* provide a measure for determining whether or not satisfaction itself has actually been achieved (Rawls, "A Kantian Conception of Equality," in *Readings in Social and Political Philosophy*, ed. R. M. Stewart, 2nd ed. [Oxford: Oxford University Press, 1996], p. 215). Accordingly, justice as fairness does not seek to maximize satisfaction as such, but only to provide everyone with an equal (or fair) share of the *means* to satisfaction. (This, of course, is one way in which justice as fairness differs from utilitarianism. See *A Theory of Justice*, p. 280.)

24. Hegel, *PR*, pp. 271–72 [§253]; *Werke*, VII: 395. A similar point about satisfaction—although without reference to the corporations—is made by Francis Fukuyama; see Fukuyama, *The End of History and the Last Man* (Harmondsworth: Penguin Books, 1992), p. xviii: "Hegel saw rights as ends in themselves, because what truly satisfies human beings is not so much material prosperity as recognition of their status and dignity."

25. Hegel, *PR*, pp. 271–72 [§§252, 254]; *Werke*, VII: 394–96; *PRH*, p. 203: "The association must have the right . . . to determine the number of its members (*die Zahl ihrer Mitglieder zu bestimmen*)" (my translation).

26. See Rawls, *A Theory of Justice*, p. 275. Sibyl Schwarzenbach points out that "Rawls's theory has no equivalent to Hegel's notion of the economic corporation—no intermediate form of community between individual and state" ("Rawls, Hegel, and Communitarianism," p. 562). Rawls's rejection of "monopolistic restrictions" on the freedom of choice of occupation should not be taken to imply that he would prevent professional associations from ever withholding licenses from people. As I understand it, however, the implication of Rawls's position is that licenses should only be withheld when individuals are not properly qualified for the profession concerned. Licenses should not be withheld by such associations as a way of controlling the numbers of people in a given profession and so of preventing a surplus. As far as I can recall, Rawls does not discuss the issue of licensing in *A Theory of Justice* or *Political Liberalism*, but the view I have set out in this note is, in my judgment, implied by his general position.

27. Rawls, *A Theory of Justice*, p. 221.

28. Rawls, *A Theory of Justice*, pp. 222–23 (my italics), and *Political Liberalism*, p. 227.

29. Rawls, *A Theory of Justice*, pp. 231–32.

30. Hegel, *PR*, p. 347 [§308]; *Werke*, VII: 477.

31. Hegel, *PR*, pp. 288–89, 346–50 [§§268, 308–311]; *Werke*, VII: 413, 476–81.

32. Hegel, *PR*, pp. 346–48 [§§308–309]; *Werke*, VII: 476–78; *PRH*, p. 206. See also G. Heiman, "The Sources and Significance of Hegel's Corporate Doctrine," in *Hegel's Political Philosophy: Problems and Perspectives*, ed. Z. A. Pelczynski (Cambridge: Cambridge University Press, 1971), p. 125, and G. W. F. Hegel, *Lectures on Natural Right and Political Science: The First Philosophy of Right. Heidelberg 1817–1818*, ed. Staff of the Hegel Archives, tr. J. M. Stewart and P. C. Hodgson (Berkeley: University of California Press, 1995), p. 219 [§121]: "The Greeks and Romans made the natural line of descent from a progenitor the basis of their divisions. The basis we use, resting on one's trade (*Gewerbe*), on a common, enduring, and present interest one has freely chosen, is a superior one. To be sure, the citizens of a city can also be divided . . . according to districts, but this is an external, purely spatial relationship—the basis here is the lifeless numerical one." For the German text, see G. W. F. Hegel, *Vorlesungen über Naturrecht und Staatswissenschaft. Heidelberg 1817/18*, ed. C. Becker et al. (Hamburg: Felix Meiner, 1983), p. 169. Further references to this text will take the form: Hegel, *LNRPS*, p. 219 [§121]; *VNS*, p. 169.

33. Hegel, *LNRPS*, p. 286 [§153]; *VNS*, p. 236.

34. Hegel, *PR*, p. 348 [§309 Addition] (my italics); *Werke*, VII: 478; *VRP*, IV: 718. See S. Houlgate, "Hegel's Critique of the Triumph of *Verstand* in Modernity," *Bulletin of the Hegel Society of Great Britain* 35 (Spring–Summer 1997): 66–67.

35. Rawls, *A Theory of Justice*, pp. 73, 299–300, and *Political Liberalism*, pp. 327, 357–58, 423.

36. Hegel, *PR*, p. 332 [§291]; *Werke*, VII: 460–61.

37. Hegel, *PR*, pp. 235–37, 345 [§§203–204 and Additions, 306]; *Werke*, VII: 355–57, 475; *VRP*, III: 625–30.

38. Hegel, *LNRPS*, p. 284 [§152]; *VNS*, p. 234. See also Houlgate, "Hegel's Critique of the Triumph of *Verstand* in Modernity," p. 63.

39. See Rawls, *A Theory of Justice*, p. 300, and Houlgate, "Hegel's Critique of the Triumph of *Verstand* in Modernity," p. 63.

40. Rawls, *A Theory of Justice*, p. 130, and *Political Liberalism*, p. 73 (my italics). In *A Theory of Justice* Rawls conceives of moral theory as a whole as "part of the theory of rational *choice*" (p. 172, my italics).

41. Rawls, *A Theory of Justice*, pp. 12, 251–55, 257, and *Political Liberalism*, p. 144.

42. Rawls, *A Theory of Justice*, pp. 12, 257, 547.

43. Rawls, *Political Liberalism*, pp. 23, 79, 273, 324.

44. Rawls, *A Theory of Justice*, p. 21, and *Political Liberalism*, p. 75.

45. See Rawls, *Political Liberalism*, p. 221 (note 8): "It is incorrect to say that liberalism focuses solely on the rights of individuals; rather, the rights it recognizes are to protect associations, smaller groups, and individuals, all from one another in an appropriate balance specified by its guiding principles of justice."

46. Rawls, *Political Liberalism*, pp. 19, 77, 202, and *A Theory of Justice*, p. 505.

47. Rawls, *Political Liberalism*, p. 334: "The equal political liberties and freedom of thought are to secure the free and informed application of the principles of justice, by means of the full and effective exercise of citizens' sense of justice, to the basic structure of society."

48. Of all the basic liberties, the equal *political* liberties are clearly the most important for Rawls. Indeed, they are the ones whose "fair value" has to be maintained above all (*Political Liberalism*, p. 327). This means that citizens should not only be equally entitled to participate in the political process, but that that entitlement should actually be *worth* the same (or approximately the same) to all citizens, whatever their social or economic position. In other words, everyone should have not just the right, but also the *fair opportunity*, to hold public office and to influence the outcome of political decisions. There are two reasons why Rawls believes that the political process in particular should be kept open to all in this way. First of all, the political process plays a distinctive role in determining the laws and policies that are to regulate the basic structure of society and so is the process on which all other liberties depend (*Political Liberalism*, pp. 309, 328–29, 361). Second, the political process will only lead to a *just* outcome in which those other liberties are actually protected, if those with greater property and wealth are prevented from controlling the electoral process to their

advantage, and if all citizens have the means to be informed about political issues, are in a position to assess how various proposals affect their well-being, and have a fair chance to add alternative proposals to the agenda for political discussion (*Political Liberalism*, pp. 360–61, and *A Theory of Justice*, p. 225). The specific measures Rawls advocates to maintain such equal worth include keeping political parties independent of large concentrations of economic and social power (and of government control) through the public financing of elections (*Political Liberalism*, pp. 328, 357, 407), and establishing "rules of order" that guarantee fair access for all citizens and political groupings to public facilities, such as television and radio (*Political Liberalism*, pp. 296, 336).

Rawls points out that "in a well-governed state only a small fraction of persons may devote much of their time to politics." He deems this quite appropriate, however, because he does not share the "civic humanist" ideal that everyone *should* participate fully in political life. What is essential, in his view, is that everyone be *able* to participate in politics, if they so wish, that is, that "the constitution should establish equal *rights* to engage in public affairs and that measures be taken to maintain the *fair value* of these liberties" (*A Theory of Justice*, p. 228 [my italics]; see also *Political Liberalism*, pp. 206, 420).

49. Rawls, *Political Liberalism*, pp. 310, 335, 420.

50. Rawls, *Political Liberalism*, p. 291, and *A Theory of Justice*, pp. 60, 250, 302. It should be noted, by the way, that, although basic rights and liberties are inalienable within a Rawlsian well-ordered constitutional democracy, they do not have *absolute* priority in such a state. For, as Rawls notes, the ability to take advantage of these rights and liberties itself presupposes that citizens' basic *needs* be met. A "social minimum" providing for citizens' basic needs is thus actually "lexically prior" to the equal basic liberties (*Political Liberalism*, pp. 7, 228–29). It is not possible to determine the level of this social minimum independently, in Rawls's view: to establish it, "one must look to the society in question." What is essential, therefore, is that people enjoy the minimum training, education, and health care (as well as food, clothing, and shelter) that is deemed necessary in a given society in order to be able to take part in political and social life (*Political Liberalism*, pp. 166, 407, and *A Theory of Justice*, p. 275). Such a social minimum does not ensure that all the basic liberties are *worth* the same to all citizens, because it does not ensure that all citizens enjoy the same overall social, economic, and political benefits which would enable them to take equal advantage of their rights. But it does ensure that all citizens can at least *to some degree* avail themselves of the rights and liberties to which they are all equally entitled.

In Rawls's view, it is only when this social minimum has been secured for all citizens that the basic liberties should be regarded as fundamentally inalienable and be given priority. Before that point is reached, basic liberties do not and cannot have such priority (*Political Liberalism*, p. 297, and *A Theory of Justice*, p. 542). It may not be permissible to deny equal basic liberties in order to promote social and economic *gain*, therefore, but it is permissible to deny such liberties, if this is necessary to ensure that citizens have the minimum material means needed to take advantage of their liberties at all (*A Theory of Justice*, pp. 152, 247).

Hegel's concern that basic needs be met is well documented (see *PR*, pp. 154–55, 260–73 [§§127, 231–255]; *Werke*, VII: 239–41, 382–96), but not everyone credits Rawls with the same concern. One important commentator who does do so is H. L. A. Hart (see Hart, "Rawls on Liberty and its Priority," in *Reading Rawls*, p. 249).

51. Rawls, *Political Liberalism*, pp. 281–84, and *A Theory of Justice*, p. 151.

52. Rawls, *Political Liberalism*, p. 291, and *A Theory of Justice*, pp. 60, 302. As Rawls notes, the difference principle does not require that every single pay rise within a company and every sale that benefits a producer or retailer be seen to help the least well-off in society. The principle simply requires that differences in income and power in the economic, social, and political system as a whole, as well as the government's regular taxation and economic policies, work to maximize and not to reduce the expectations of the least well-off (*Political Liberalism*, pp. 282–83). Citizens are judged to be worse off than others, by the way, not because they fail to attain the same degree of "satisfaction" or "happiness," but because they have fewer "primary goods," that is to say, less income, wealth, and power, and fewer opportunities to improve their standard of living and to take advantage of their equal basic rights (*A Theory of Justice*, pp. 92–94).

It should be noted that the difference principle goes beyond the requirement that citizens' basic needs have to be met. The difference principle requires that inequalities in society work to the maximal advantage of the least well-off, even when all citizens are guaranteed the social minimum, and that principle would still have to be obeyed in a society of millionaires (*Political Liberalism*, pp. 228–29).

53. Rawls, *A Theory of Justice*, p. 256, and *Political Liberalism*, pp. 45, 73. T. M. Scanlon refers (approvingly) to Rawls's "ideal of each person as a rational chooser of his own ends" ("Rawls' Theory of Justice," p. 178).

54. Hegel uses the phrase "principles of justice" (*Prinzipien der Gerechtigkeit*) in §317 of the *Philosophy of Right* (see *PR*, p. 353; *Werke*, VII: 483).

55. Hegel, *PR*, p. 192 [§148]; *Werke*, VII: 297. See also *PR*, p. 27 [§2]; *Werke*, VII: 31 ("in philosophical cognition . . . the chief concern is the *necessity* of a concept").

56. See S. Houlgate, *Freedom, Truth, and History: An Introduction to Hegel's Philosophy* (London: Routledge, 1991), pp. 77–125, "The Unity of Theoretical and Practical Spirit in Hegel's Concept of Freedom," *Review of Metaphysics* 48 (June 1995): 859–81, and "Hegel's Critique of the Triumph of *Verstand* in Modernity."

57. Hegel's constitutional arrangements cannot be justified, Rawls maintains, by arguing "that the whole of society including the least favored *benefit* from certain restrictions on equality of opportunity" (*A Theory of Justice*, pp. 300–301 [my italics]). This is because such an argument invokes the difference principle to justify restrictions on the fair equality of opportunity, when the right to fair equality of opportunity itself has priority over the difference principle, according to the second principle of justice (*A Theory of Justice*, pp. 302–3). The

kind of restrictions on fair opportunity that Hegel advocates could perhaps be justified by claiming that "in the long run" such restrictions actually guarantee more *opportunities* to the least advantaged than would the absence of those restrictions (*A Theory of Justice*, p. 301). But, presumably, such a claim could only be made in a transitional society that is on the way to being well-ordered: for in a well-ordered society itself everyone is to have a fair chance of holding *any* position of authority in society. Moreover, under the first principle of justice the rights to vote and to run for *political* office are equal and inalienable and must be worth the same for all (*Political Liberalism*, p. 330). In Rawls's view, therefore, a well-ordered society that denies the vote to those who are not members of corporations, or which reserves seats in the upper house for one group of citizens and thereby denies others the opportunity to run for those positions, would clearly violate equal basic political rights and the principle of fair opportunity. (It should be noted, by the way, that although political representation may be unequal in Hegel's rational state, all citizens have an equal chance of influencing the debates in the legislature through helping to form public opinion [see Hegel, *PR*, pp. 352–58 (§§315–319); *Werke*, VII: 482–89].)

58. Rawls, *Political Liberalism*, pp. 22, 91.

59. See Rawls, *Political Liberalism*, p. 224, and Hegel, *PR*, pp. 13–14, 191, 288–89 [Addition to Preface, §§147, 268]; *Werke*, VII: 16–17, 295, 413–14; *VRP*, III: 93, IV: 582; *PRH*, p. 260: "Moreover, it is a feature of modern times above all that what is true should . . . occur with the consent (*Einwilligung*) and insight of the individual" (my translation).

60. The strongest Hegelian criticism of Rawls might be thought to be derivable from his well-known critique of contract theories of the state which, he claims, conceive of the state as a voluntary association of individuals based on their "arbitrary will and opinions" (*PR*, pp. 105, 277, 324 [§§75, 258, 281]; *Werke* VII: 157, 400, 453). As I pointed out earlier, however, Rawls does not actually contend that the state is a voluntary association. He recognizes that we are born into a given society and claims only that the principles of justice governing society should be "voluntary" in the sense that they should be principles that would be *agreed* to in a hypothetical original position. Furthermore, the parties in that original position do not, and cannot, base their arguments in favor of particular principles of justice on their "arbitrary will and opinions," because they are placed behind a "veil of ignorance" so that their "arbitrary will and opinions" remain unknown to them (*Political Liberalism*, pp. 285–86). Hegel's critique of contract theory would thus appear to have no direct and easy bearing on Rawls. Moreover, Rawls's acknowledgment that we are born into given societies, and that our interests are "fashioned" by society, deflates any possible "Hegelian" criticism that Rawls ignores the social and historical nature of human beings.

61. On Hegel's method in the *Philosophy of Right*, see *PR*, pp. 10–11, 26–27, 59–63 [Preface, §§2, 30–32]; *Werke*, VII: 12–14, 30–32, 83–87; *VRP*, III: 166–70. Hegel does not deny that, if they are true, the ideas developed by philosophy will overlap with many traditional assumptions about political and social life. But he does not adjust his philosophical ideas to bring them into "reflective equilibrium" with our ordinary considered judgments, as does

Rawls. His method is first to discern "the *necessity* of a concept" and, second, "to look around for what corresponds to it in our ideas and language." Far from being "the measure and criterion of the concept which is necessary and true for itself," therefore, our ordinary "representation" (of freedom, justice, and political life) "must rather derive its truth from the concept, and recognize and correct itself with the help of the latter" (*PR*, p. 27 [§2]; *Werke*, VII: 31–32). Philosophy is thus given a much stronger *critical* role by Hegel than it is by Rawls. For Rawls's idea of "reflective equilibrium," see *A Theory of Justice*, pp. 20–21, 51.

62. Rawls, *A Theory of Justice*, p. 122, and *Political Liberalism*, pp. 259, 294, 305.

63. Rawls, *Political Liberalism*, pp. 300, 339. See R. D. Winfield, *The Just Economy* (London: Routledge, 1988), p. 37.

64. Hegel, *PR*, p. 11 [Preface]; *Werke*, VII: 14 ("free thinking . . . does not stop at what is *given*"). J. B. Hoy takes a different view of the relation between Hegel and Rawls. In her judgment, Hegel would criticize Rawls for not being social and historical enough: "despite Rawls's agreement with Hegel on the social-historical character of individuals, his persistent Kantianism prevents a successful formulation of a theory of justice in terms of this essential sociality" ("Hegel's Critique of Rawls," p. 408).

65. Rawls, *Political Liberalism*, p. 9. See also *A Theory of Justice*, p. 581: "the argument for the principles of justice should proceed from some consensus."

66. Rawls, *Political Liberalism*, pp. xxii, 10, 129, 134, 395.

67. Rawls, *Political Liberalism*, p. 150: "Since we assume each citizen to affirm some such view, we hope to make it possible for *all* to accept the political conception as true or reasonable from the standpoint of their own comprehensive view, whatever it may be" (my italics).

68. Rawls, *Political Liberalism*, pp. 39, 64 [note 19], 375.

69. Such measures may include, in certain circumstances, restricting the exercise of free speech; see Rawls, *Political Liberalism*, pp. 348–56.

AUTHOR BIOGRAPHIES

Joel Anderson is assistant professor of philosophy at Washington University in St. Louis. His work in social philosophy focuses on the effects of social fragmentation on prospects for gender equality and for individual autonomy. His work in ethics focuses on personal autonomy, discourse ethics, critiques of instrumentalism, and clinical decision making involving victims of brain damage. He has published articles in *Philosophy and Social Criticism, Constellations*, and the *Deutsche Zeitschrift für Philosophie*, and is the translator of Axel Honneth's *The Struggle for Recognition: The Moral Grammar of Social Conflicts* (MIT, 1996).

Andrew Buchwalter is associate professor and chair of the Department of Philosophy at the University of North Florida. In 1992–93 he was Fulbright Research Professor at the Hegel-Archiv, Ruhr-Universität Bochum. His books include *Culture and Democracy: Social and Ethical Issues in Public Support for the Arts and Humanities*. He is presently completing a book on the contemporary significance of Hegel's political philosophy.

Ardis B. Collins is associate professor of philosophy at Loyola University Chicago. She is editor of *The Owl of Minerva*, a biannual international journal published by the Hegel Society of America, has served as editorial consultant for the *History of Philosophy Quarterly*, and edited a collection of essays entitled *Hegel on the Modern World* (SUNY Press, 1995). She has published a book on medieval and Renaissance philosophy, and has presented papers and published articles on *Hegel's Phenomenology of Spirit* and *Philosophy of Right*. The Hegel papers address the following issues: Hegel's epistemology; the critique of Kantian morality; work, language, and the workplace; the irrationality of nature; and epistemology, nature, and religion. In 1990–92 she served as vice president of the Hegel Society of America, and has served as its treasurer since 1996.

David C. Durst is associate professor of philosophy at the American University in Bulgaria. Publications include a book in German on

275

Hegel and Schiller and articles on contemporary continental philosophy, including "Heidegger on the Problem of Metaphysics and Violence," in *Heidegger Studies*. He is a member of the American Philosophical Association.

Stephen Houlgate is professor of philosophy at the University of Warwick. He is the author of *Hegel, Nietzsche and the Criticism of Metaphysics* (1986) and *Freedom, Truth, and History: An Introduction to Hegel's Philosophy* (1991), as well as numerous articles on Hegel, Kant, and Nietzsche. He is also the editor of *The Hegel Reader* (1998) and *Hegel and the Philosophy of Nature* (1998). He was president of the Hegel Society of America from 1994 to 1996.

Dudley Knowles is a senior lecturer in the Department of Philosophy at the University of Glasgow. He has published articles on moral and political philosophy and has a particular interest in Hegel's ethical and political theory.

Angelica Nuzzo is assistant professor of philosophy at DePaul University (Chicago). Her books include *Representation and Concept in Hegel's Philosophy of Right* (in Italian) and *Logic and System: On Hegel's Idea of Philosophy* (in Italian). She is the author of numerous essays on Kant, German idealism, modern philosophy, and translation theory. She is a member of the Hegel Society of America and of the *Hegel-Vereinigung* and collaborates with *Hegel-Studien*.

Alan Patten is assistant professor of political science at McGill University. He is the author of *Hegel's Idea of Freedom*, published by Oxford University Press.

Lawrence S. Stepelevich, who retired from teaching in 1966, was, from 1966 to 1968, president of the Hegel Society of America. From 1977 to 1996 he edited the journal of that society, *The Owl of Minerva*. His articles and books express his particular interest in the development of Hegelianism which followed shortly after the death of Hegel. His *Young Hegelianism: An Anthology* (1983) has remained in print, and is considered the best English language source of the writings of that period, whose representatives included Max Stirner, Bruno Bauer, and Ludwig Feuerbach.

Kevin Thompson is assistant professor of philosophy at Southern Illinois University–Carbondale. He is co-editor (with Lester Embree) of *Phenomenology of the Political*, and author of articles on nineteenth-

and twentieth-century European philosophy. He is currently working on a monograph, "Authority and Autonomy: Civil Society and State in Hegel's Political Philosophy."

Mark Tunick is associate professor of political science in The Honors College at Florida Atlantic University. His books include *Hegel's Political Philosophy* (Princeton, 1992) and *Practices and Principles: Approaches to Ethical and Legal Judgment* (Princeton, 1998).

Robert R. Williams is professor of German and religious studies at the University of Illinois at Chicago. He is president of the Hegel Society of America, author of *Hegel's Ethics of Recognition, Recognition: Fichte and Hegel on the Other, Schleiermacher the Theologian: The Construction of the Doctrine of God*, and numerous essays on Hegel and classical German philosophy and religion. He is currently translating *Hegel's Lectures on the Philosophy of Subjective Spirit 1827–28.*

Richard Dien Winfield is professor of philosophy at the University of Georgia. He is the author of *Reason and Justice* (1988), *The Just Economy* (1988), *Overcoming Foundations Studies in Systematic Philosophy* (1989), *Freedom and Modernity* (1991), *Law in Civil Society* (1995), *Systematic Aesthetics* (1995), *Stylistics: Rethinking the Artforms After Hegel,* (1996) and *The Just Family* (1998).

INDEX

www.ingramcontent.com/pod-product-compliance
Lightning Source LLC
Chambersburg PA
CBHW020340270326
41926CB00007B/252